The Sixth Sense Reader

Sensory Formations
Series Editor: David Howes
ISSN: 1741–4725

- What is the world like to cultures that privilege touch or smell over sight or hearing?
- Do men's and women's sensory experiences differ?
- What lies beyond the aesthetic gaze?
- Who says money has no smell?
- How has the proliferation of "taste cultures" resulted in new forms of social discrimination?
- How is the sixth sense to be defined?
- What is the future of the senses in cyberspace?

From the Ancient Greeks to medieval mystics and eighteenth-century empiricists, Karl Marx to Marshall McLuhan, the senses have been the subject of dramatic proclamations. Senses are sources of pleasure and pain, knowledge and power. Sites of intense personal experience, they are also fields of extensive cultural elaboration. Yet surprisingly, it is only recently that scholars in the humanities and social sciences have turned their full attention to sensory experience and expression as a subject for inquiry.

This pathbreaking series aims to show how the "sensual revolution" has supplanted both the linguistic and the pictorial turns in the human sciences to generate a new field—*sensual culture,* where all manner of disciplines converge. Its objective is to enhance our understanding of the role of the senses in history, culture, and aesthetics, by redressing an imbalance: the hegemony of vision and privileging of discourse in contemporary theory and cultural studies must be overthrown in order to reveal the role all senses play in mediating cultural experience. The extraordinary richness and diversity of the social and material worlds, as constituted through touch, taste, smell, hearing, sight and, provocatively, the sixth sense, are addressed in the volumes of this series as follows:*

Empire of the Senses: The Sensual Culture Reader (Ed. David Howes) documents the sensual revolution in the humanities and social sciences, and reclaims sensation as a domain for cultural inquiry.

The Auditory Culture Reader (Eds. Michael Bull and Les Back) articulates a strategy of "deep listening"—a powerful new methodology for making sense of the social.

The Smell Culture Reader (Ed. Jim Drobnick) foregrounds the most marginalized, and potentially subversive, sense of modernity, in addition to sampling how diverse cultures scent the universe.

The Book of Touch (Ed. Constance Classen) maps the tactile contours of culture, exploring the powerful and often inarticulate world of touch, the most basic of our senses.

The Taste Culture Reader (Ed. Carolyn Korsmeyer) serves up a savory stew of cultural analysis, blending together the multiple senses of the term *taste.*

Visual Sense: A Cultural Reader (Eds. Elizabeth Edwards and Kaushik Bhaumik) explores and interrogates the multiplicity of scopic regimes within and without the Western tradition.

The Sixth Sense Reader (Ed. David Howes) asks: What lies beyond the bounds of sense? Is the sixth sense ESP, electromagnetic sensitivity, intuition, revelation, gut instinct, or simply unfathomable?

*Full publication details are available from the publishers, Berg, 1st Floor, Angel Court, 81 St Clements Street, Oxford OX4 1AW, UK; or consult http://www.bergpublishers.com

The Sixth Sense Reader

Edited by David Howes

Oxford • New York

First published in 2009 by
Berg
Editorial offices:
1st Floor, Angel Court, 81 St Clements Street, Oxford, OX4 1AW, UK
175 Fifth Avenue, New York, NY 10010, USA

Berg is the imprint of Oxford International Publishers Ltd.

Library of Congress Cataloguing-in-Publication Data

The sixth sense reader / edited by David Howes.
p. cm. — (Sensory formations)
Includes bibliographical references and index.
ISBN 978-1-84788-261-5 (pbk.)
1. Extrasensory perception.   I. Howes, David, 1957–
BF1321.S58 2009
133.8—dc22
2009034922

A catalogue record for this book is available from the Library of Congress.

British Library Cataloguing-in-Publication Data

A catalogue record for this book is available from the British Library.

ISBN 978 1 84788 262 2 (Cloth)
ISBN 978 1 84788 261 5 (Paper)

Typeset by Apex CoVantage, LLC, Madison, WI, USA
Printed in Great Britain by the MPG Books Group, Bodmin and King's Lynn

www.bergpublishers.com

Contents

Acknowledgments

I owe the idea for this book to Kathryn Earle, Managing Editor at Berg. When she invited me to edit the *Sensory Formations* series, and we were discussing its scope, she suggested that the series simply must include a book on the sixth sense. A growing awareness of how much valuable material on perception fell outside the customary fivefold division of the sensorium has brought me to realize the wisdom of that suggestion.

Many friends, colleagues, and former as well as present students have contributed substantially either to the conceptualization or technical production of this book. They include Lucien Castaing-Taylor, George Classen, Darlene Dubiel, Charles Gagnon, Jean-Guy Goulet, Angelica Higuera, Pierre-Louis Houle, Elizabeth Hsu, Tim Ingold, Andrew Irving, Carol Laderman, Medina Lasansky, Jim Moore, Richard Newhauser, George Paul Meiu, Katja Neves-Graca, Richard Newhauser, Nigel Rapport, Corine Schleif, Mark M. Smith, Charles Spence, Paul Stoller, David Sutton, Anthony Synnott, Jojada Verrips, Karli Whitmore, Owen Wiltshire, Boris Wiseman, Olga Zikrata, all of my fellow editors in the *Sensory Formations* series, and all of the members of the Concordia Sensoria Research Team (CONSERT).

I have tried out different parts of my introduction in talks I have been invited to give at Cornell University, Harvard University, University of Vienna, University of Oslo, Oxford University, and, most notably, the symposium titled "The Five Senses in the Middle Ages and the Renaissance: Pleasure and Danger in Perception" at Arizona State University (January 2009), and the "Beyond Text? Synaesthetic and Sensory Practices in Anthropology" conference at Manchester University (June 2007). I wish to thank the organizers and audiences at each of these talks for their many encouraging words and helpful criticism.

I am grateful for the past and present financial support for the Sensory Formations project provided by the senior administration of Concordia University: particularly Fred Lowy, President; Martin Singer, Provost, and his successor, David Graham; and Graham Carr, Associate Dean Graduate Studies and Research. The research funding of the Social Sciences and Humanities Research Council of Canada and the Quebec Fonds pour la Formation de Chercheurs et l'Aide à la Recherche has also been vital to the realization of this project. Thanks are also due to Hannah Shakespeare and Anna Wright at Berg, for helping me to bring this book to fruition, as well as the three anonymous reviewers commissioned by Berg to evaluate this manuscript.

I am profoundly mindful of my indebtedness to my parents and other family members. I am very grateful to Emilia, Olof, and particularly George for always lending support when needed. My deepest thanks go to Constance who has always tried to provide me with a sense of direction and to our children, Jonathan and Emma, whose good sense (and nonsense) have been a constant source of inspiration.

Lake Memphremagog, Quebec

Introduction
The Revolving Sensorium
David Howes

The previous five volumes in the *Sensory Formations* series dealt with the senses of vision, hearing, smell, taste, and touch. All these senses correspond to bodily organs: the eyes, the ears, the nose, the mouth, and the skin or flesh. This book is about the sense (or senses) *without* an organ—the so-called sixth sense.

There are few more slippery topics than this "sense" that is not one. Indeed, so many different powers have been proposed to fit the sixth sense category—from magnetism to movement and from memory to clairvoyance—that its status as a category seems suspect. Furthermore, if the doors of perception are opened to allow a sixth sense, then why not a seventh, an eighth, a ninth, and so on? Perhaps the term *sixth sense* should be declared a "floating signifier"—a term "devoid of meaning and thus susceptible of receiving any meaning at all"—like the Polynesian word *mana* (Lévi-Strauss 1987: 55, 64). That way discussion could be ended without any further perturbations to the conventional Western bounds of sense.

While such a linguistic solution to the puzzle of the sixth sense might seem attractive, this book takes a different approach. Instead of limiting our analysis of the sixth sense to its use as a figure of speech, we want to explore the experiential dimensions of this tantalizing notion from a combined anthropological-historical perspective.[1]

Sensorium

The approach advocated in this volume is resolutely grounded in sensory experience and expression—or sensugraphic, if you will. It begins by reintroducing the notion of the *sensorium*.[2] Used interchangeably with the words *brain* and *mind* in the early modern period, *sensorium* straddles the divide between mind and body, cognition and sensation. The early modern usage both echoed the ancient doctrine of "the common sense" and foreshadowed the attempt in the late modern period to overcome the classic Western split between mind and body through the forging of such concepts as "the mindful body" (Scheper-Hughes and Lock 1987) and "embodied mind" (Varela, Thompson, and Rosch 1992).

In addition to denoting the "percipient centre," or "seat of sensation in the brain of man and other animals," the concept of the sensorium extended to include the circumference of perception. In illustration of the latter point, the *OED* quotes one usage from 1714: "The noblest and most exalted Way of considering this infinite Space [referring to 'the Universe'] is that of Sir Isaac Newton, who calls it the *Sensorium* of the Godhead," and another from 1861: "Rome became the common sensorium of Europe, and through Rome all the several portions of Latin Europe sympathized and felt with each other."

The notion of the *sensorium* is thus a very capacious or *holistic* one. Thanks to its holism it can stand for "the five senses," which is one way of construing the totality of percipience, but nothing prevents it from being extended to other constructions, other models, such as "the two senses" or "the seven senses,"[3] and so forth. This is a major advantage from the cross-cultural standpoint advocated in this Reader. For example, the Hausa of Nigeria have one word for sight (*gani*) and another (*ji*) for "hearing, smelling, tasting and touching, understanding, and emotional feeling, as if all these functions formed part of a single whole" (Ritchie 1991: 194). The Javanese "have five senses (seeing, hearing, *talking,* smelling and feeling), which do not coincide exactly with our five" (Dundes 1980: 92). The Cashinahua of Peru hold that knowledge resides in the skin, the hands, the ears, the genitals, the liver, and the eyes, hence six "senses"—or better, "percipient centers." "Does [the] brain have knowledge?" an ethnographer asked the Cashinahua, supposing it to constitute some sort of central processing center or data-bank: "'*Hamaki* (it doesn't),' they responded" (Kensinger 1995: 239), "the whole body knows."

Among the Cashinahua, "skin knowledge" (*bichi una*) is the knowledge of the environment (including the behavior patterns of animals and other people) one acquires through one's skin—through the feel of the sun, the wind, the rain, and the forest. Skin knowledge is what enables one to find one's way through the jungle and to locate prey. "Hand knowledge" (*meken una*) is what enables one to shoot an animal with bow and arrow or chop down a tree in the case of a man, while in the case of a woman the hands are the conduits by which knowledge of weaving, pottery making, cooking, and other skills enter the body. The eyes are the locus of the "eye spirit," which enables one to see the spiritual insides or substance of persons, animals, and things as opposed to their surface (which is the domain of skin knowledge). "Social knowledge is gained through and resides in the ears and therefore is called *pabinki una,* ear knowledge" (Kensinger 1995: 241). This usage reflects the centrality of speech in Cashinahua social life. "It is in one's liver that one feels joy and sorrow, fear and hope, distrust and pleasure," whence the term "liver knowledge" (*taka una*) to refer to knowledge of emotions (Kensinger 1995: 243). Finally, knowledge of one's mortality and immortality, or "life force," has its seat in the genitals.

The Hausa, Javanese, and Cashinahua perceptual paradigms challenge the conventional Western model of "the five senses." We are not accustomed to thinking of speech as a sense as do the Javanese, unlike the Hausa we think of perception and emotion as separate functions, and we balk at the Cashinahua suggestion that the brain is not the seat of cognition (while the thought of the liver and genitals as sense organs seems completely foreign). If we were more conscious of the history of the senses in the West, however, we would not be so dismissive. It can be argued that we have been blinded to sensory diversity by an overexposure to the now-standard five-fold arrangement of the sensorium, which can be found everywhere from children's books on "The Five Senses" to the compartmentalization of the senses in and by the discipline of psychology.[4]

Just as it is necessary to bracket the assumptions of the psychology of perception to make any headway in the study of the sensorium across cultures, like the Cashinahua or Hausa, so an awareness of the cultural contingency of sensory categorizations is the indispensable starting point of any inquiry into the varieties of sensory (and extrasensory) experience in history. As Louise Vinge observes in "The Five Senses in Classical Science and Ethics" (Chapter 5 of this Reader): "Sight, hearing, smell, taste and touch: that the senses should be enumerated in this way is not self-evident. The number and order of the senses are fixed by custom and tradition, not by nature. The regular order being subject to occasional change proves its arbitrariness" (p. 107).

If, following Vinge's lead, we inquire into the *invention* of the five senses in the West, we discover, first, that there was little agreement as to the number or boundaries of the senses in Antiquity, and, second, that there is more agreement between some of the early Western taxonomies of the senses and the non-Western models we have been considering than with our own modern one. Constance Classen excavates some of the early diversity of opinion in the introductory chapter to *Worlds of Sense:*

> Plato, for example, apparently did not distinguish clearly between senses and feelings. In one enumeration of perceptions, he begins with sight, hearing and smell, leaves out taste, instead of touch mentions hot and cold, and adds sensations of pleasure, discomfort, desire and fear. Aristotle thought to put an end to argument among philosophers on this matter by declaring that the intrinsic relationship between the senses and the elements ... required that there be no more than five senses. (Classen 1993: 2)

Classen goes on to say that Aristotle's authority ensured that five became the established number of senses in Western culture, but there was significant divergence from the norm.

> In certain cases it would seem that it was more important to divide the senses into a certain desired number than to categorize them according to their nature. Aristotle ... wanted the senses to number five in order to correlate with the elements [earth, water, air, fire and the quintessence]. For this reason, he condensed different sensations of temperature, hardness, and wetness into one sense of touch. However, when Philo, a first-century interpreter of the Old Testament, needed the senses to number seven for his allegorical purposes, he added the genital organs and speech onto the standard five.
> The thought of speech as a sense seems odd to us moderns. This is partly because we conceive of the senses as passive recipients of data, whereas speech is an active externalization of data. It is also because we think of the senses as natural faculties and speech

as a learned acquirement. The ancients, however, had different ideas on the matter. They were apt to think of the senses more as media of communication than as passive recipients of data. The eyes, for example, were believed to perceive by issuing rays which touched and mingled with the objects to which they were directed. (Classen 1993: 2)

As is evident from this passage, elements of both Plato and Philo's constructions of the sensorium align with elements of the Cashinahua, Javanese, and Hausa sensory taxonomies. The alignment is not perfect, to be sure, because we are dealing with historically and culturally distinct sensory worlds. Nonetheless, what is explicit or manifest in one tradition evidently remains a latent possibility in the other traditions, and occasionally outs itself. Only by plotting these points of convergence and divergence across sensoria can we arrive at a composite understanding of the full range of human powers as understood across cultures.

One way to imagine the ever-shifting divisions and relations between the senses in different cultures and historical periods is by analogy to a kaleidoscope. With each twist of its shaft, the kaleidoscope reveals a different alignment of shapes and colors.[5] Another less visualist analogy for imagining the composition of the sensorium would be by reference to a fugue, such as J. S. Bach's *Well-Tempered Clavier.* The essence of a fugue consists in the simultaneity of voices:

[A] melody is always in the process of being repeated by one or another voice ... Any series of notes is thus capable of an infinite set of transformations, as the series (or melody or subject) is taken up first by one voice then by another, the voices always continuing to sound against, as well as with, all the others. (Said 1983: 47)

With this image of the revolving sensorium in mind, consider the case of speech. The idea of speech as the sixth sense—that is, as a natural faculty, akin to sight or touch—has surfaced repeatedly in the history of the Western sensorium. One of the first to champion it was Philo, as noted above. It reappears from time to time, explicitly or implicitly in the Middle Ages: for example, in the confessional manuals, which mapped the sins onto the senses, where there is the occasional reference to "the five senses and speech," as if they formed a set (Woolgar 2006: 11–12). One source in which there is no ambiguity as to the sixth-sense status of *affatus* (speech or voice) is the great Catalan philosopher Raymond Lull's *Liber sexti sensus* (Book on the Sixth Sense), written at the turn of the fourteenth century. This book appears not to have survived, but we can infer something of its content from a line in another of Lull's works, where he speaks explicitly of *affatus* as the sixth sense: "and thus the *affatus* is the sixth sense, which went unrecognized for a long time."[6]

The seventeenth-century play *Lingua, or the Combat of the Tongue and the Five Senses for Superiority* (Tomkis 1607) picked up on speech's struggle for recognition and turned this into comedy (see Mazzio 2004; Vinge 1975: 98–103). In the play, female Lingua (Speech) is painted as "an idle prating dame," ever "babbling" by male

Auditus (Hearing) and denounced for her presumption (wanting to be considered a sense): "We were never accounted more than five," Auditus asserts. Common Sense, who is called on to judge the dispute, rules that Speech is not a sense, except in the case of women: "[A]ll women for your sake shall have six senses—that is seeing, hearing, tasting, smelling, touching, and the last and feminine sense, the sense of speaking" (quoted and discussed in Classen 1998: 74–75). A sixth sense for the second sex.

In the late twentieth century, the notion of speech—or rather, "language"—being a natural faculty once again attracted a champion in the person of Noam Chomsky. He argued that the human capacity for language is innate. Chomsky's hypothesis of the existence of a "language organ" in the human brain is now widely accepted by linguists (Anderson and Lightfoot 2002), though they tend to see it as a cognitive faculty, not a sensory organ the way Lull did speech. Not all contemporary linguists view language in the rarefied, innatist way Chomsky does, however. For example, Dan Everett argues that language is sensuous action among the Pirahã, with their "immediacy-of-experience principle" (Colapinto 2007). Another contemporary observer of language (albeit a popular writer, not a linguist) in whose work the ancient notion of language as a sensory power resurfaces is Lynn Truss, author of *Eats, Shoots & Leaves: The Zero Tolerance Approach to Punctuation!* Here is how she describes the experience of being a stickler for proper punctuation:

> The world cares nothing for the little shocks endured by the sensitive stickler. While we look in horror at a badly punctuated sign, the world carries on around us, blind to our plight. We are like the little boy in *The Sixth Sense* who can see dead people, except that we can see dead punctuation. Whisper it in petrified little-boy tones: dead pronunciation is invisible to everyone else—yet we see it *all the time.* No one understands us seventh-sense people. (Truss 2003: 3–4)

It is ironic that Truss demotes the sense of grammar from the sixth to the seventh rung of the sensorium even as she championed it. This demotion is due to the general trend in contemporary society to see the sixth sense not as speech but as a more spectral sort of power, such as clairvoyance, or "seeing dead people." The latter notion was popularized by the 1999 Hollywood blockbuster film *The Sixth Sense,* referred to by Truss. The idea of "seeing dead people" as portrayed in that film was itself a recycling of the idea of "hearing dead people" (i.e. communicating, through a medium, with the spirits of the departed at a séance), which was central to the Spiritualist movement of the mid-nineteenth century. The Spiritualist craze provoked such conflicted reactions, because of its challenge to both religious and scientific authority (Griffin 1997), that it spawned the creation of learned societies in both England and the United States dedicated to the investigation of "psychic phenomena." The circumstances (and controversies) surrounding the formation of the British Society for Psychical Research in 1882, and the mediation of the transition from "hearing" to "seeing dead people," are explored in the twin contributions by Pamela Thurschwell to this Reader (Chapters 8 and 10).

Psychic Sense (ESP)

Since the late nineteenth century the most prominent candidate for the position of sixth sense in the West has been "psychic" perception of one form or another. Besides spirit mediumship, the standard list of psychic powers includes thought transference or "telepathy," premonitions or "precognition," clairvoyance or "remote-viewing," and levitation or "psychokinesis." Generally speaking, psychic powers are scientized versions of the occult powers known to the Spiritualists, with the main difference being that they are deemed to be mental rather than spiritual.

The scientization/despiritualization of the occult began with the establishment of the above-mentioned societies for psychical research in the United Kingdom and the United States in the late nineteenth century. In the twentieth century, psychic research spread to universities, and government research laboratories. The substitution of technical terms such as *precognition* for premonitions, and *psychokinesis* for levitation was an important component of the process of rationalizing the occult. It created the impression that all of these historically disparate phenomena had a common denominator, and so could be jointly analyzed in the present. For example, "Second Sight," a peculiarly Scottish phenomenon (Feibel 2000; Cohn 1999), was abstracted from its original context and became a generic term (Busst 1995), interchangeable with precognition and remote-viewing—the new common denominators.

The scientization of the occult came to a head in 1934. It was in that year that J. B. Rhine of Duke University published *Extra-Sensory Perception*—a book which, somewhat surprisingly for an academic treatise, was picked up on by millions of readers. In this book, Rhine reported the results of a wide (and often ingenious) array of experiments that tested the psychic abilities of his research subjects. The most famous of these tests involved a pack of 25 cards, known as Zener cards, with each card displaying one of five symbols. Subjects were asked to predict the order of all 25 cards when spread before them on a desk, face down. If a subject consistently guessed more than five cards correctly, thereby defying the law of averages, this was taken to be evidence of psychic ability. It could not be due to coincidence or chance because the results were "statistically significant" (i.e. better than chance), particularly when the experiment was repeated numerous times.

By taking the study of psychic abilities out of the darkened séance parlor and into the harsh light of the laboratory, by replacing anecdotal accounts with statistical tables, by controlling for trickery, and, by devising so many ingenious *repeatable* experimental procedures, Rhine managed to attract an aura of scientificity to the investigation of psychic powers. Plain dry statistics produced in a laboratory setting enabled the murky powers of the occult to be garbed in the robes of scientific fact.

But it was by coining the term *extra-sensory perception* for the title for his book that Rhine showed the greatest ingenuity, as the following account illustrates: "He told a friend that he wanted 'to make it sound as normal as may be.' Perception was an established subject of psychology by that time, and Rhine hoped psychologists would recognize ESP as a branch of perception, rather than as some otherworldly, nonprofessional pastime" (Kagan, Daniels, and Horan 1987: 54).

The strategy worked. The discipline of parapsychology (another of Rhine's neologisms) was born, and thanks to the lobbying efforts of a host of prominent intellectuals, including Margaret Mead, the American Association for the Advancement of Science was persuaded to admit the Parapsychological Association as an affiliate in 1969.

ESP, also known as "the psi faculty,"[7] thus became the *next* sixth sense (see, for example, Pearson 2003; Jütte 2005: ch. 16), the new umbrella term for a wide range of "inexplicable" mental powers and "paranormal" experiences, including all those listed above, and others that Rhine had no time for, such as "Out-of-Body Experiences" (OBE), "Near-Death-Experiences" (NDE), and reincarnation (or "retrocognition"), to name but a few. These further additions to the "additional faculty" of perception invented by Rhine reflect the inability of the discipline of parapsychology to control the destiny of its brainchild. Indeed, the founding and institutionalization of parapsychology played a decisive role in the emergence of what David Hess (1993) has called a new "paraculture," referring to the "arena of debate" that crystallized in the 1960s (and continues to escalate) in which New Agers, debunkers or Skeptics, and parapsychologists argue endlessly over the *meaning* of the paranormal.

Why did the postulation of ESP as an "additional faculty" of perception attract so much popular and scientific interest? Various factors may be hypothesized, such as:

- that it responded to a perennial sense of there being a gap in the human sensorium, as expressed in the following quotation from the *OED* that dates from 1687: "It has been thought that we want a sixth Natural sense, by which we might know many things more than we do";
- that it provided an antidote to the antimentalism of behaviorism, the reigning paradigm in psychology at the time of its invention;
- that its potential use for intelligence and thought control purposes played into the clandestine war between the governments of the United States and USSR—and their respective secret services, the CIA and KGB—for world domination;[8]
- that the decline of organized religion, or unchurching of the American population, created an experiential void that ESP helped fill (whence the oft-quoted statistic that 60% of Americans report having had a paranormal experience, where formerly such experiences would have been given a theological rationale);
- that it fed into a wider fascination with the exploration of altered states of consciousness stimulated by experimentation with hallucinogens, meditation,

alternative therapies, and so on, as the New Age has migrated from the margins to the mainstream of American and European culture;[9]

- that "psychic artists" like Inigo Swann (and a multitude of others) found creative inspiration in ESP and rendered it sensible through their art;[10]
- that Hollywood found that it made for sensational plotlines as well as box office returns;[11]
- that people lost patience and faith in the supposed ability of "science" to explain everything, and so "the unexplained" proliferated and became reified—a category unto itself, in place of a transitional category of *yet* to be explained phenomena.[12]

Paranormalacy

One of the most original intervenors in the debate over the meaning of the paranormal is the controversial British biologist Rupert Sheldrake. In Chapter 11, Sheldrake takes issue with the categorization of telepathy and precognition as "paranormal" or "psychic" experiences, and also disputes their being assimilated to the category of the sixth sense. Identifying such experiences as paranormal is wrong-headed, Sheldrake argues, because most people (not to mention most animals) have experienced them, which makes them common and, therefore, *normal.* They only seem paranormal from the standpoint of the prevailing "materialist theory of the mind," which treats mental states as an aspect of the activity of the brain. But the theory that minds are confined to the insides of heads cannot account for psychic phenomena (which point instead to minds being *interconnected*) nor can it explain the lived experience or *phenomenology* of perception ("The images we experience as we look around us are just where they seem to be"; i.e. out there and not in our heads), so the materialist theory must be supplemented by a new theory that recognizes that "our minds stretch out into the world beyond our bodies" (p. 250). This is, of course, Sheldrake's own theory of the *extended* mind, which he expresses in terms of "pseudopodia of attention and intention," "morphic fields," and other concepts.

Significantly, Sheldrake devotes one of the appendices of his book *The Sense of Being Stared At and Other Aspects of the Extended Mind* to an appreciation and recuperation of the extramission theory of vision. This theory holds that the eyes perceive by emitting rays that touch and mingle with the objects to which they are directed (see Sheldrake 2003: 326–31). From the viewpoint of contemporary psychology, this theory is utter heresy, but not from Sheldrake's standpoint as a (somewhat maverick) biologist, or from the revolving perspective on the sensorium advocated in this Reader. Perhaps the time has come for extramission theory, which originated in Antiquity and flourished in the Middle Ages, and is also implicit in the widespread folk belief in the evil eye (see Kemp 1990: 36–40; Dundes 1980: 93–133; Sheldrake 2003: 183–97), to be reconsidered.

I will leave it to Sheldrake to spell out his arguments in support of the extended mind hypothesis, and to readers to judge what they think. There are three points about his stance, however, worth noting here. First, Sheldrake's theory is fundamentally "teleological" in that everything is supposed to have a potential that may be actualized. A baby is potentially an adult, an acorn is potentially an oak tree. This is on account of what Sheldrake calls their "morphic field" or inherent form (not to be confused with or reduced to their DNA alone). The teleological character of Sheldrake's theory, and the way in which he treats the senses as fitted to the cosmos, recalls the work of Aristotle. Where Sheldrake departs from Aristotle is in his use of the language of "probabilities" and "fields of energy," rather than purposes and elements, to describe the organization of nature.

Second, Sheldrake's theory is both continuous with and a threat to established natural science. It is a threat both on account of the popular reception of his ideas and the way he plays on the preoccupations and uncertainties of established science. In this regard, there are significant parallels between Sheldrake and Franz Anton Mesmer. Mesmer rattled the scientific establishment of late eighteenth-century France by positing the existence of a universal *medium* or "fluid" that united all parts of nature and through which all events (past and future) reverberated, along with a *sense*— variously dubbed: "the sixth sense," "the inner sense," "animal magnetism"—that registered the movements of this fluid. The cultural politics surrounding the scientific and popular reaction to Mesmer's theory of animal magnetism are discussed in Jessica Riskin's contribution to Part II of this Reader (Chapter 6). It is with a strong sense of déjà vu that one reads *Sheldrake and His Critics: The Sense of Being Glared At,* a special edition of the *Journal of Consciousness Studies,* and observes how his theory of "morphic resonance" (like Mesmer's universal fluid) and "the sense of being stared at" (like Mesmer's sixth sense) has polarized debate in the sciences.

Third, Sheldrake's theory of mind is fundamentally sensual in character, and it therefore occupies a middle ground between the extreme mentalism of the parapsychological and the extreme materialism of the neurobiological approaches to the study of consciousness. (Perhaps, in view of its sensuous thrust, Sheldrake should have called his theory a theory of "the extended sensorium" rather than "the extended mind.") This brings us to the fourth point: Sheldrake's denial of sixth-sense status to phenomena such as telepathy and precognition. In Chapter 11, he allows that "sixth sense" is a better starting point for conceptualizing psychic powers than, for example, "ESP" or "the paranormal." Treating psychic perception "as a sense" means recognizing "it is rooted in time and place; it is biological, not supernatural" (p. 249). However, as he goes on to point out: "The sixth sense has already been claimed by biologists working on the electrical and magnetic senses of animals." Hence, a more appropriate term for telepathy and the like would be "seventh sense," he argues.

Sheldrake's point is well taken. Psychologists (including parapsychologists) should not have the final word on what counts as a faculty of perception. As Sheldrake's

fellow biologist Maurice Burton observes in *The Sixth Sense of Animals:* "The statement that there are five senses, touch, taste, smell, sight, and hearing was sufficient
until about the year 1940," when certain animals were discovered to possess supplementary sensory powers (Burton 1973: 2). A little history of how animal perception
has been construed in the Western tradition will help us appreciate the full force of
Burton's statement.

Animal Senses

In premodernity, a different animal was employed to represent each of the five senses
based on its presumed acuity in that sense and its corresponding social connotations.
For example, the spider served to symbolize the sense of touch both because it was
believed to be sensitive to the least twitching of its web and because it symbolized
the feminine tactile acts of spinning and homemaking, as well as of seduction. The
eagle stood for sight because it was believed to have excellent eyesight and because
it represented masculine social dominance—the power to "oversee" or rule the world
(Classen 1998: 75–8; see also Vinge 1975: 47–53). One of the finest artistic depic-
tions of such a sensory bestiary can be found in the medieval series of six tapestries
known as *The Lady and the Unicorn,* which hang in the Musée Cluny in Paris.[13]
    In the nineteenth century, when the senses of man still provided the measure of
and for the senses of animals, and the search for patterns (i.e. Nature's plan) had yet
to be supplanted by the tracing of origins (i.e. the Darwinian theory of evolution),
the German embryologist Lorenz Oken came up with his own master plan of human
and animal sensory powers. Oken expounded a fantastic taxonomy that "arranged
the entire animal kingdom in a rising cycle of five, reflecting the successive addition
(or perfection) of sensory organs" culminating in "the highest animal," or most complete specimen, "that is, ... Man" (Gould 1985: 203–4). Oken even went so far as to
discriminate the "five races of Man" based on his five-part sensory scales:

1. The skin-man is the black, African
2. The tongue-man is the brown, Australian-Malayan
3. The nose-man is the red, American
4. The ear-man is the yellow, Asiatic-Mongolian
5. The eye-man is the white, European (Gould 1985: 204–5)

The following chart reflects the unfolding of Oken's five-part sensory wheels
across the classes of all animals, all mammals, advanced mammals, and humans (see
Table 1).
    As was the case with the medieval sensory bestiary, Oken's taxonomy was fun-
damentally dependent on the typologies of the Western social imaginary rather
than on any actual traits of the humans and animals concerned. Stephen Jay Gould

Table 1. Oken's Path of Progress by Wheels of Five, or Addition of Sensory Organs.
"The animal kingdom is only a dismemberment of the highest animal, that is, of Man."
(Adapted from the diagram in Gould 1985: 206.)

ALL ANIMALS		ALL MAMMALS		ADVANCED MAMMALS		HUMANS	
						Sight	European
						Hearing	Asian
						Smell	American
						Taste	Australian
				Sight	humans	**Feeling**	African
				Hearing	apes		
				Smell	bears		
				Taste	seals		
		Sight	carnivores & primates	**Feeling**	cats & dogs		
		Hearing	whales & hoofed mammals				
		Smell	bats & insectivores				
		Taste	sloths & marsupials				
Sight	Mammals	**Feeling**	rodents				
Hearing	Birds						
Smell	Reptiles						
Taste	Fishes						
Feeling	Invertebrates						

(1985: 204) observes: "Recalcitrant, complex nature behaves very badly whenever we try to force such simple schemes upon her (consider, for example, the difficulty of [Oken] identifying mammals with sight, when the lower class of birds contains species with vision more acute than any mammal's)." Living as we do in a post-Darwinian universe, in which the law of natural selection rules, we can only look upon Oken's taxonomy by fives and smile. Contemporary natural science tells us that there is no preordained plan, no underlying numerological consistency, to the universe—only contingency. But we should not feel smug in this knowledge: Oken's vision represented a summit of knowledge in the (pre-Darwinian) tradition of natural history stretching back to Aristotle. As Gould cautions us:

> The excitement of new theories [such as Darwin's theory] lies in their power to change contexts, to render irrelevant what once seemed sensible. If we laugh at the past because we judge it anachronistically in the light of present theories, how can we understand these changes of context? And how can we retain proper humility toward our own favoured theories and the probability of their own future lapse into insignificance? Honest intellectual passions always merit respect. (Gould 1985: 202)

In the mid-twentieth century, to pick up on Burton's statement again, the senses of animals were increasingly studied on their own account and not simply viewed as counterparts to the senses of humans. This development was due to advances in scientific instrumentation and close observation of animal behavior. The results revealed that animals respond to ranges of stimuli that elude perception by humans. Examples of this include echolocation in bats, electroreception in eels, the internal compass and "celestial navigation" in birds, infrared vision in reptiles, and vibrational or seismic sensitivity in elephants.[14] By comparison with the astounding range of animal perceptual powers, the senses of humans came to seem sadly impoverished. Chapter 2 of this Reader, by the Anglo-Argentine naturalist W. H. Hudson, deals with one example of this: namely, the sense of direction. Hudson notes that while animals seem to have a very fine sense of direction, the same cannot be said of humans, who are generally lost without their maps and compasses. Hudson notes from his own experience, however, that not all humans have lost their sense of direction, those who live "in a state of nature" and remain attentive to the natural world, such as the Argentine Gaucho, may, like animals, also possess the uncanny ability to always find their way home.

Both naturalists and parapsychologists have theorized that a number of "hidden," "secret" or "vestigial" senses—such as the homing sense, the vomeronasal organ, and the pineal gland (or "third eye")—might once have been generally shared by humans and then either atrophied through lack of use, or been suppressed by civilization (see Baker 1981; Watson 1999; Rivlin and Gravelle 1984: 67–71, 206–8). "Perhaps," the parapsychologists say, "people with apparent psychic powers are merely tapping into once-used but long-forgotten abilities" (Kagan et al. 1987: 58; see also Schoch and Yonavjak 2008: 47–50). The quest for sensory gifts beyond the ordinary human allotment has led some determined individuals to modify their bodies, for example, by having magnets implanted in their fingertips, thereby "extending the sense of touch into a sense of magnetism," but the results have been disappointing (Norton 2006).

Though the evidence is largely anecdotal, animals (like humans) have been reported to possess a wide range of psychic powers. Dogs, for example, have often been said to be so "in tune" with their human companions that they sense when the latter are returning home after an outing and wait expectantly by the door. N'kisi, a parrot who has acquired an astounding command of English (thereby challenging Chomsky's supposition that language is a uniquely human faculty), also appears to have remarkable telepathic powers. In laboratory controlled experiments N'kisi repeatedly spoke about images his human trainer was independently viewing in another room. In response to such intriguing data one might speculate that, in lieu of language, animals—or certain species—have developed extrasensory modalities for staying in touch with each other.[15]

All of these "discoveries" of animal senses warrant consideration as belonging to the category of the sixth sense, even if this means that category is now expanding to unmanageable proportions.[16] At the same time, greater reflexivity is called for in the extrapolation of conclusions based on this evidence. Consider, for example, the flurry of discussion surrounding the reports of wild animals and tribal peoples escaping the destruction wreaked by the tsunami that swept the Asian coastline on the morning of December 26, 2004, and which tragically claimed the lives of so many other local people and tourists. As regards animals: there were tales of elephants running for the hills an hour before the tsunami bore down, of dogs refusing to go out for their morning run on the beach, and of birds vacating their low-lying nesting grounds. As regards the tribal peoples living on the Indian archipelago of Andaman and Nicobar Islands (i.e. the Ongee, Sentinelese, and three other groups), amazingly, almost all were accounted for when government officials toured the area in the days following the disaster. A photograph of a naked Sentinelese man defiantly shooting an arrow at a government helicopter made the front page of many newspapers around the world.

Was it because of some "mysterious" sixth sense possessed by animals and tribal peoples alike that they were forewarned and fled to higher ground (Donaldson-Evans 2005)? Before positing the operation of some "supersense," and before lumping indigenous peoples and animals together, we need to take stock of just how capacious the known senses are. One wildlife expert observed, rightly: "Earthquakes bring vibrational changes on land and in water while storms cause electromagnetic changes in the atmosphere. ... Some animals have acute sense of hearing and smell that allow them to determine something coming towards them long before humans might know that something is there" (quoted in Mott 2005).

A local environmentalist, who had some familiarity with the Ongee and Sentinelese, stated that: "They can smell the air. They can gauge the depth of the sea with the sound of their oars" (quoted in Misra 2005). Given the ethnographic evidence concerning the Ongee's acute attention to olfactory and other sensory phenomena (Pandya 1993),[17] the observer was probably on the right track when he suggested that they could smell the tsunami coming. However, when he added that the Andaman Islanders "have a sixth sense which we don't possess," he was making a customary projection from within the Western tradition, which has often viewed acute perceptual abilities as extrasensory powers.

This raises an important point that naturalists tend to overlook when they presume to comment on the sensory abilities of indigenous peoples, allegedly "frozen in the Paleolithic past" (as one report put it). The point is: *All cultures are equally distant from nature* in that the experience of nature is always mediated by a given culture's cosmology or "world view," and by the social organization of labor and the sensorium. Rather than relegating tribal peoples to the distant past, and assimilating them to nature, naturalists need to recognize them as their contemporaries, who are as fully "socialized" as they are (see Fabian 1983; Mason 1989). At the same time, naturalists would be well advised to inquire into the "ethnotheories" of animal behavior that have been elaborated by indigenous peoples. Such alternative *cultural* perspectives on animal nature could well yield insights into animal senses as yet unsuspected and uninvestigated by Western-trained naturalists (see Straight, Chapter 16).[18]

The Continuum of Perception

The foregoing material emphasizes how our understanding and employment of the senses is mediated by culture. It is this cultural dimension of perception that makes the combined anthropological-historical approach to the study of the sensorium advanced in this Reader so necessary. In order to appreciate how this approach differs from the prevailing psychological and neurobiological theories of perception enshrined in the textbooks (e.g. Goldstein 2002), let us posit a continuum with the idea of perception as a neurobiological process at one end and the notion of perception as a cultural process at the other. The psychological and phenomenological perspectives fall in between these two extremes.

Neurobiological——Psychological——Phenomenological——Cultural

The neurobiological perspective is aptly summed up in the following quotation from a work by Howard C. Hughes:

> The events that culminate in perception begin with specialized receptor cells that convert a particular form of physical energy into bioelectric currents. Different sensors are sensitive to different types of energy, so the properties of the receptor cells determine the modality of a sensory system. Ionic currents are the currency of neural information processing, and current flows that begin in the receptors are transmitted through complex networks of interconnected neurons and, in the end result in a pattern of brain activity we call perception. We can distinguish a red 1957 Chevy from a blue 1956 Ford because each car produces a different pattern of neural activity. (Hughes 2001: 7)

On this account, perception is a matter of "information processing." It begins at the edge of the CNS (central nervous system) and is conditioned exclusively by the properties of the receptor organs (Keeley 2002; see further Hollingham 2004 on perception being "all down to our DNA").

The historical-anthropological approach is nicely captured in the following quote from Karl Marx (1987: 109): "The *forming of the five senses* is a labour of the entire history of the world down to the present," which may be glossed as follows:

> The objects we perceive in our surroundings—cities, villages, fields, and woods—bear the mark of having been worked on by man. It is not only in clothing and appearance, in outward form and emotional make-up that men are the product of history. Even the way they see and hear is inseparable from the social life-process as it has evolved over the

millennia. The facts which our senses present to us are socially preformed in two ways: through the historical character of the object perceived and through the historical character of the perceiving organ. (Horkheimer quoted in Levin 1997: 63 n1)

On this account, the sensorium is an historical formation. Perception begins at the edge of the manmade environment and is conditioned by the "social preformation" of the senses. Where we depart from Marx is in terms of recognizing that there are *multiple* sensory histories—or better, trajectories—not just one for all humanity. The social sensorium *revolves* historically and across cultures as much as it evolves over the millennia.[19] Furthermore, whereas Marx attributed priority to changes in the means and organization of production, with respect to the determination of perception, we take our cue from McLuhan (1964), and attach equal importance to changes in the means of communication—that is, to *media,* broadly construed. Pamela Thurschwell's essay (Chapter 8) on telepathy in this Reader provides an illustration of the interconnection between sensory modality and mode of communication. Thurschwell links the birth of the concept of telepathy to the invention of telegraphy, which stimulated the public's interest in the possibilities for long-distance communication.

The cultural anthropologist (or historian) would have it that any account of perception must begin by examining the cultural organization of the sensorium (and the cosmos) and descend via the phenomenological to the psychological and finally the physiological level of brain organization. The neuroscientist would hold the reverse. How can these two accounts be integrated? Presumably, the bottom-up approach of the neuroscientists and the top-down approach of the anthropologist would meet in the middle—that is, in the domain of the psychological/phenomenological. The transcultural psychiatrist Laurence Kirmayer suggests as much in his discussion of the "hierarchical systems view of neural organization":

Contemporary cognitive neuroscience understands mind and experience as phenomena that emerge from neural networks at a certain level of complexity and organization. There is increasing recognition that this organization is not confined to the brain but also includes loops through the body and the environment, most crucially, through a social world that is culturally constructed. On this view, "mind" is located not in the brain but in the relationship of brain and body to the world. (Kirmayer, in press)

Ideally, Kirmayer states, "we want to be able to trace the causal links up and down this hierarchy in a seamless way."

While we agree in principle with Kirmayer's scheme, in practice any meeting of minds between neuroscientists and anthropologists still seems a long way off. Neuroscientists rarely, if ever, ascend the hierarchy beyond the level of the psychological, and when they do invoke the cultural it is in terms that anthropologists would generally regard as too simplistic.[20] Conversely, while a number of anthropologists have attempted to trace the links (and the loops) from the cultural (including the cosmological) on down to the physiological, their attempts generally fall on deaf ears beyond their own discipline due to the perception on the part of psychologists that such a holistic view is fundamentally unscientific.[21] The fact that psychology is itself a cultural construct is not readily appreciated by those who practice it. For all their talk of the "plasticity" of the brain, neuroscientists are remarkably insensitive to cultural influences.

Plainly, there is a need for more cross-talk among the disciplines, and, arguably, there is no more potentially fruitful site to stage such a conversation than that of the sensorium, for the senses mediate the relationship between self and environment, mind and body, idea and object: *"The senses are everywhere"* (Bull, Gilroy, Howes, and Kahn 2006: 5). The first stage in this dialogue is to seek to uncover how the senses came to be compartmentalized in the Western tradition and perception reduced to patterns of brain activity.

Common Sense

As will be recalled, the Cashinahua reject the idea that the brain has any role to play in cognition—or "consciousness" for that matter. According to them, "the whole body knows." Aristotle would have agreed with their estimation of the brain. He regarded the heart as the seat of percipience and intelligence on account of its natural heat or life force (the brain being too cold).[22] The modern idea of consciousness was similarly foreign to Aristotle and his contemporaries (see Heller-Roazen 2007: 38–9); he spoke instead in terms of sentience. According to Aristotle, all living beings (including plants) have a nutritive soul, animals and humans share a sensitive soul, and humans alone possess a rational soul. It is the powers of the sensuous soul that concern us in what follows.

Aristotle held that every affection of the soul (or, act of perception) involves the "alteration" of one or more of the five sense organs by some object through the medium that conjoins them. (The trinity of organ, object, medium is integral to Aristotle's account of perception.) The objects of perception are not things as such but *provinces* of sensation. The province or "proper object" of vision is color, that of hearing is sound, that of smell is odor, that of taste is flavor. (The complexities of touch made it less amenable to such schematization, however much Aristotle tried to treat it as a unity: see Vinge pp. 108–10.) Within each province—and *exclusively* within each province, it must be stressed—sensation takes the form of "a kind of mean" between the two extremes of the pair of contraries proper to that province: sight between white and black, hearing between shrill and dull, and so on (with the province of touch left somewhat vague due to its complexity). The implication is that we perceive by means of differences, without positive things.[23] Each province of sensation has its own spectrum or ratio of sensible differences, defined as that which cannot be perceived by any other sense.

We have seen how Aristotle contrived to make the five senses and their respective media correlate with the primordial elements of Greek cosmology. Vinge has much more to say concerning how he pronounced and also dithered on this score in Chapter 5. We move on to a consideration of how Aristotle managed to resolve the questions generated by the provinciality (or exclusivity) of his theory of the sensory functions of the soul. What of those objects, such as figure, number, motion, and so on, known as the "common sensibles," which are perceived by more than one sense (for example, figure is perceived by vision and by touch)? What of complex sensations, such as the experience of eating grapes, which are both red and sweet?[24] How is it that we perceive *that* we see and hear, if a sense cannot perceive itself? Aristotle reasoned that there must be yet another sense, a shared sense, responsible for unifying, distinguishing, and coordinating the five senses and their deliverances. This power of the sensuous soul he called "the common sense" (*koinē aisthēsis,* or *sensus communis* in Latin translation). For Aristotle, "this 'sense' constitutes a power of perception that is common to all the five senses yet reducible to none of them" (Heller-Roazen 2007: 35). Is this then our mysterious sixth sense? Apparently not, for:

> Strictly speaking, the common sense [on account of its commonality and irreducibility] is ... not a sixth sense, ... it is nothing other than the sense of the difference and unity of the five senses, as a whole: the perception of the simultaneous conjunction and disjunction of sensations in the common sensible, the complex sensation, and finally, the self-reflexive perception [or, sense of sensing]. (Heller-Roazen 2008: 35)

The idea of the common sense was pregnant with significance, which it took many thinkers over many centuries to spell out. All this thinking is lost on most of us today, though. For us, common sense means, simply, common sense,[25] and has nothing to do with sentience. Tracing the successive elaboration and gradual dismemberment of the *sensus communis* would take a whole book, and indeed has: Daniel Heller-Roazen's 2007 book, *The Inner Touch: Archaeology of a Sensation.* But even that monumental treatise has its lacuna. In essence, the common sense is—or, *was*—the relational sense *par excellence,* the ratio of ratios, the medium of media. The last modern thinker to understand this was Marshall McLuhan (an Aristotelian at heart).[26] Unfortunately, as McLuhan's writings are no less elliptical than Aristotle's, they do not provide much guidance, and we are forced to rely on our own wits to proceed, while depending heavily on Heller-Roazen and Vinge.

If we wished to visualize the relations between the common sense and the five senses, one possible image is that of the "Wheel of the Senses" in the wall-painting at Longthorpe Tower, Peterborough, which dates from the mid-fourteenth century (see illustration 6 in Woolgar 2006: 27; figure 2 in Vinge 1975: 52). The painting depicts a wheel with five beasts representing the five senses positioned at the end of each of its spokes: the cock stands for sight, the boar for hearing, the vulture for smell, the monkey for taste, and, a spider in its web for touch. A king is shown behind the wheel, with his hand resting on one of its spokes. The king, who is emblematic of the common sense, exercises his dominion (and judgment) over the beasts, the senses. In another image, put forward by the great Persian philosopher of the early eleventh century, Avicenna, the relation is expressed thusly: "This power which is called the common sense is the center from which the senses ramify, and to which the senses return, like rays; and it is in truth that which senses" (quoted in Heller-Roazen 2007: 42). It must be emphasized that both of these images are overstatements of Aristotle's notion of the common sense, as we shall see presently.

When modern thinkers criticize Aristotle for the dogmatism of his assertion that "There is no sixth sense in addition to the five enumerated—sight, hearing, smell, taste, touch," and for his hierarchical ranking of the senses with vision at the apex, they are forgetting that he was also the inventor of the common sense, and that he did not just privilege vision (unlike, for example, Plato). It is true that he dubbed sight "the superior sense" because "it brings tidings of multitudes of distinctive qualities of all sorts" (i.e. it is the most comprehensive of the senses), but a little further on he affirms that "it is hearing that [indirectly] contributes most to the growth of intelligence" (through rational discourse), and elsewhere he says "in respect of touch we far excel all other species in exactness of discrimination" (because our skin is soft, not hard like a lobster's) and: "That is why man is the most intelligent of all animals" (Aristotle 1931b: 437a and 1931a: 421a). One could say that he distributed (different) laurels to each of the senses, as any wise ruler would.[27]

It is only in retrospect that one can read anything of import to physiology, psychology, theology, or other disciplines into Aristotle's writings. At the same time, because his treatises enjoyed such authority for so many centuries they constituted the touchstone, the foundation, for the spiritualization, psychologization, anatomization and socialization of the senses. For example, Louise Vinge relates how the early Church Father Origen read the Bible in light of the Greek philosophy of *aisthēsis* (sense-perception) and invented the doctrine of the "spiritual senses." This doctrine underwent extensive elaboration in the Middle Ages (Rudy 2002; Classen 1998) and received its most complete expression in the writings of the eighteenth-century natural-philosopher-turned-Christian-visionary Emmanuel Swedenborg. Swedenborg's "celestial sensorium," or "spiritual anatomy of the senses" is the topic of Chapter 7 of this Reader, by Leigh Schmidt.

The psychologization of the common sense has a particularly convoluted history due to the liminality of its position at the interface of the five senses, and at the interface of the corporeal and the incorporeal, or sensual and rational soul. In origin, it was not the king of the senses, as in the medieval elaboration (the wall-painting at Longthorpe Tower) mentioned earlier, but rather *primus inter pares,* or "first among equals." It was also largely on a par with the other three functions of the sensuous soul identified by Aristotle: imagination, the cogitative function, and memory. Being situated on the boundary of the five senses, and the boundary of the sensuous and rational soul, the common sense was a two-faced faculty. But it did not remain in this liminal position for long due to a couple of incidental observations by its author, which inflected the whole subsequent history of its elaboration (and eventual dismemberment).

In its apparent multiplicity, the common sense could be seen as analogous to the sense of touch, which Aristotle at one point allowed might be "more than one sense." (This observation was motivated by the difficulty of determining its object.) Elsewhere, Aristotle characterized touch as the "inward sense." (This observation was motivated by the difficulty of identifying its medium.) Subsequent commentators, poring over Aristotle's writings, seized on these remarks and fused them to form the basis of the doctrine of the "inner senses." The first intimation of this doctrine is given in the following line, which is commonly attributed to the Stoics: "the common sense is kind of inner touching, by which we are able to grasp ourselves" (quoted in Heller-Roazen 2008: 37). It is doubtful whether Aristotle would have agreed with this line, anymore than he would have agreed to the transplant of the seat of the soul from the heart to the brain, which resulted from his writings being read in light of those of the great second-century physician, Galen. This (con)fusion was, however, fundamental to the doctrine of the inner senses as Simon Kemp points out in *Medieval Psychology:*

> The inner senses or inward wits were psychological faculties that, throughout the Middle Ages, were assumed to be located in the ventricles of the brain. These ventricles were supposed to be sense organs performing functions such as remembering or imagining in the same way that the eye was responsible for seeing or the ear for hearing. The theory was created by assigning the various perceptual and cognitive facilities [*sic?*] identified by Aristotle in his *De Anima* to the spirit-filled cerebral ventricles described by Galen in his discussion of the anatomy of the brain. (Kemp 1990: 53)

According to Kemp,[28] the doctrine of the inner senses received its most complete expression in the works of Avicenna. Avicenna apportioned the common sense and imaginative faculty to the front and rear respectively of the front ventricle, the cogitative faculty and estimative faculty (or instinct) to the front and rear of the middle ventricle, and the memory to the rear ventricle of the brain. Two further observations of note: in earlier iterations, the common sense is sometimes included among the inner senses, and sometimes left out (see Ryan 1951; Heller-Roazen 2007). This history of flitting in and out of focus may be attributed to the common sense being neither "external" nor "internal" but rather *relational,* the boundary sense, in Aristotle's *own* writings. It was given an internal slant by some of Aristotle's commentators (most notably the Stoics), not Aristotle himself. Second, Avicenna, by characterizing the common sense as the "central power" (see above) basically inverted Aristotle's conception of it as shared—that is, as parted, not centered (see Heller-Roazen 2008: 40–5).

Kemp goes on to observe that the doctrine of the inner senses, thanks to its *linear* arrangement of the ventricles, anticipated the "information-processing" model of modern psychology: "incoming sensory information is transformed or processed in stages, and the output of each stage or level of processing becomes the input for the next" (1990: 60). But this was purely by chance, Kemp (1990: 58) says, since, if the truth be known: "Not only is the doctrine completely false in its physiological aspects—the ventricles of the brain fulfil no psychological functions at all—but also the adoption of the doctrine meant that the rational soul had many of its psychological [read: cognitive] functions stripped from it."

Stripped? Not from an Aristotelian perspective. It was rather the sensuous soul that was stripped of its faculties by the development of modern psychology, for the five external senses and the five internal senses (including imagination and memory) were all *sensory* powers, not cognitive powers, in the periods of which we speak. The amount of mental, or, as we moderns say, "cognitive" space that sensing, as opposed to thinking (the function of the rational soul), occupied in medieval psychology is indeed astounding. *Sentio ergo sum* was the watchword of the medieval conscience. (It is appropriate to speak of "conscience" here since the potential for using the senses immoderately was always very much on the classical mind, while the potential for using them sinfully weighed just as heavily on the medieval mind.) The birth of "consciousness" or cognition as we know it would have to await Descartes, who famously "call[ed] away all [his] senses" to discover the truth of his own existence: *cogito ergo sum,* "I think therefore I am" (quoted and discussed in Synnott 1991: 70). It helped that the anatomical basis of the doctrine of the inner senses was discredited by advances in physiology.

Even so, aspects of the Aristotelian account of sentience survived the Cartesian censure of the senses, and were (re)affirmed with a vengeance during the Age of Reason, which was also, it should be remembered, the Age of Sensibility. One of those aspects was the common sense, *sensorium commune,* which was transmuted into a generalized notion of sensibility (Barker-Benfield 1992; Vila 1998; Jütte 2005: 126–41). Jessica Riskin describes the reinvention of the common sense in eighteenth-century French philosophical and scientific circles in Chapter 6 of this Reader. Of particular note is her account of how Mesmer redefined this power as "the sixth sense," "the inner sense," "the basis of all sensation"—in short, animal magnetism; and, of how Mesmer's sixth sense got discredited and the power of imagination came unhinged from the other senses in the report of the royal commission charged with the scientific investigation of Mesmer's claims. In the opinion of the commissioners, those who "felt" Mesmer's sixth sense had overactive imaginations.[29]

The Multiplication of the Senses

The eighteenth century was something of a watershed in the history of the senses in view of the number of new senses that were put forward for discussion during this period—common sense being just one of them. James Moore, a specialist in the Scottish Enlightenment, provides a helpful sketch of the proliferation of senses in the philosophy of the day, especially as concerns the work of Francis Hutcheson (1694–1746):

> In *An Inquiry into the Original of our Ideas of Beauty and Virtue* (1725) Francis Hutcheson argued for the existence in human nature of a sixth sense, an internal sense that would complement the five external senses. He called it a moral sense which brings to mind an idea of virtue whenever one perceives a character or an action prompted by benevolence, kind affection or public spirit. He considered the moral sense analogous to the sense of beauty, a seventh sense, which brings before the mind an idea of beauty when it perceives uniformity in variety in compositions, landscapes, works of art and the order of the world.
>
> In another work, in *An Essay on the Nature and Conduct of the Passions and Affections, with Illustrations on the Moral Sense* (1728), he added an eighth sense, a public sense or a determination to be pleased with the happiness of others and uneasy at their misery, and a ninth sense, a sense of honour, which prompts us to be pleased by the approval of others and uneasy when our actions provoke condemnation by others.
>
> Hutcheson was much indebted to the notion of a *sensus communis* or sense of the community or public good in the writings of the third Earl of Shaftesbury. He also admired the work of the Cambridge Platonist, Henry More, who thought it the opinion of Aristotle that in the final determination of right conduct we should be guided by an "inward Sense." (James Moore, personal communication, 25 January 2009)

Moore goes on to say that Hutcheson's theory of the moral sense was taken up by other philosophers in Scotland:

> David Hume agreed that virtues and vices are determined by a moral sense; but Hume resolved the moral sense into sympathy with others, with qualities of character that are useful and agreeable to self and to others. Hume's scepticism with regard to the moral sense was repudiated by Henry Home who offered his own theory of the moral sense as a sense of remorse and dread of merited punishment. Adam Smith followed Hume in making sympathy, not the moral sense, the source of moral distinctions; but Smith considered utility to be merely one of the considerations that prompt us to sympathize with others. Adam Ferguson disagreed with his friends Hume and Smith; he agreed rather with Hutcheson in locating the origin of moral distinctions in a moral sense; he thought that the quality most esteemed by the moral sense was active intelligence, particularly when intelligence is exercised in the service of the public. Other Scottish philosophers— Thomas Reid, Dugald Stewart and Sir William Hamilton—replaced the moral sense by a more general theory of common sense. This was not a sixth sense or a special faculty of perception; it referred rather to the human capacity to apprehend reality unmediated by ideas; it was the precondition of perception, memory and the exercise of all the intellectual and active powers. (James Moore, personal communication, 25 January 2009)[30]

Without trying to follow the intricacies of these "internal senses" (as they may be called to distinguish them from the "inner senses" of the Middle Ages), a few general observations may be made. First, the inwardness of these senses points to a deepening sense of the interiority of consciousness, of the self. Second, they are all forms of "feeling" rather than thinking or reason, which is consistent with the "sentimental empiricism" of the period (see Riskin 2002) in contrast to the rational empiricism of today. Third, they are all very sociable rather than physical, particularly the moral sense, and that of the public good. The eighteenth-century understanding of the *sociability* of the senses (and perception) did not, however, endure for long, and it is the Scottish thinkers who are responsible for this. Whereas the moral *valuation* and moral *use* of the senses was intrinsic to classical and medieval sensory practice (Vinge, Chapter 5), the Scottish philosophers divorced the moral sense from the other senses. This opened the way for the amoralization of perception—that is, the reduction of sensation to "information-processing," or, simply, patterns of neural activity.

Beneath the Five Senses

Besides the world "beyond the five senses" (the supernatural, the paranormal), there is a world "beneath the five senses" (the visceral, the molecular)[31] to which modern science has increasingly sensitized us. Here is how Howard C. Hughes describes that world:

> There is also the world inside our bodies, and there are sensory organs that provide information crucial to internal bodily states. Our senses of balance, of body motion, and of posture, depend on sensory organs in the inner ear, in our joints, and in muscles. There are even organs that monitor such things as the levels of carbon dioxide in the blood, blood pressure, and blood glucose levels. These organs provide the brain with information essential to life, but they do not produce conscious sensory experiences (otherwise, people would be aware of the onset of hypertension, and it would less frequently go undetected). (Hughes 2001: 5)

An account of how this inner world was produced—that is, of the scientific practices that generated the physiological discoveries that gave definition to the "interoceptive" (as distinct from "inner" or "internal") senses of balance, body motion, and so on—is provided in Nicholas Wade's essay, "The Search for a Sixth Sense" (Chapter 1). These discoveries were inevitable, for we saw earlier how Aristotle blurred certain distinctions in his account of the sense of touch, and already by the eleventh century there were suspicions (voiced by Avicenna) concerning the oneness of the haptic sense (Kemp 1990: 46). Forced unions are bound to dissolve in time—especially when the cosmology that made them sensible or necessary no longer holds: Aristotle's four elements have become the 118 elements of Mendeleev's Periodic Table of the Elements (see Atkins 1997 and Illich 2000 on the significance of this switch).

While there are a number of earlier intimations of the interoceptive powers (see Heller-Roazen 2007: 163–78, 237–51), it appears to have been the eighteenth century's intense focus on *feelings* that brought the matter to a head, and precipitated the physiological discoveries of the nineteenth century. Take the case of kinaesthesia:

> Kinaesthesia, the sense of bodily movement, had been studied before the nineteenth century under a variety of other names, including "inner sense" and "organic" or "visceral" sensibility—all referring to those unclassifiable sensations that could not be traced accurately to one of the five known sense organs, but seemed to originate from the undifferentiated mass of the viscera. It was not until the early nineteenth century, however, that "muscle sense" was officially declared a "sixth sense" in its own right. The credit for this "discovery" is usually given to two physiologists: Charles Bell (1774–1842) and François Magendie (1783–1855). Working in England and France respectively in the mid-1820s, each independently discovered that the two sets of nerves carrying sensory impulses and motor impulses were attached to different parts of the spinal cord. Their findings suggested that if muscles were capable of receiving sensations as well as carrying out movements, they might have a sentience comparable to that of the eye or the ear. (Çelik 2006: 159)

The dissolution of the sense of touch into a panoply of senses—pressure, temperature, pain, as well as kinaesthesia, proprioception, balance, and so on—was only to be expected. Not so expected, perhaps, is the way vision has come to be dismembered by contemporary scientists into separate senses for light and color (and arguably, separate senses for red, green, and blue); or the way taste has fragmented into separate receptor organs for sweet, salt, sour, bitter (and for the fifth flavor, umami); or, the way, smell has been broken down into multiple receptors (see Jones 2006: 45 n26). "The more we study the structure of our sense organs, the more senses we appear to have" (Durie 2005: 35). A conservative estimate would put the number of senses at 10, but it is generally accepted that our senses number 21, and radical estimates put the number as high as 33 (see Table 2).

These figures confirm Vinge's point: "The number and order of the senses are fixed by custom and tradition, not by nature" (p. 107). But the question arises: Should the neurobiologists necessarily have the last word on what counts as a faculty of perception? Why prefer their account to that of the eighteenth-century Scottish philosophers, or the medieval philosophers, or, for that matter, the Cashinahua? Might not each of these "alternative" perceptual paradigms have something to teach us about the sensorium? Stephen Jay Gould's caution about understanding "changes of context" bears repeating. Where we differ from Gould is in suggesting that the history of the senses can profitably be read backward as well as forward (his chosen direction), and across different cultures or traditions (not just within our own tradition). Indeed, only in this way can we arrive at a composite understanding of the changing *contexts of perception*—that is, of all the "loops" through the environment, including "the social world that is culturally constructed" (Kirmayer, in press), that give the senses their

Table 2. A Measure of the Senses.
"There are many opinions about how many senses we have."
(Adapted from the table in Durie 2005: 36.)

SENSORY MODALITY	Conservative	Accepted	Radical	SENSORY MODALITY	Conservative	Accepted	Radical
Vision	■	□	□	Muscle stretch—Golgi tendon organs	□	□	■
Light	□	■	■	Muscle stretch—muscle spindles	□	□	■
Color	□	■	□	**Temperature**	■	□	□
Red	□	□	■	Heat	□	■	■
Green	□	□	■	Cold	□	■	■
Blue	□	□	■	**Interocepters**			
Hearing	■	■	■	Blood pressure	■	■	□
Smell	■	■	□	Arterial blood pressure	□	□	■
2,000 or more receptor types	□	□	■	Central venous blood pressure	□	□	■
Taste	■	□	□	Head blood temperature	□	□	■
Sweet	□	■	■	Blood oxygen content	□	■	■
Salt	□	■	■	Cerebrospinal fluid pH	□	■	■
Sour	□	■	■	Plasma osmotic pressure (thirst?)	□	■	■
Bitter	□	■	■	Artery-vein blood glucose difference (hunger?)	□	■	■
Umami	□	□	■	Lung inflation	□	■	■
Touch	■	■	□	Bladder stretch	□	□	■
Light touch	□	□	■	Full stomach	□	□	■
Pressure	□	□	■				
Pain	■	■	□				
Cutaneous	□	□	■				
Somatic	□	□	■				
Visceral	□	□	■				
Mechanoreception	■	□	□				
Balance	■	■	□				
Rotational acceleration	□	□	■				
Linear acceleration	□	□	■				
Proprioception—joint position	□	■	■				
Kinaesthesis	□	■	□				
TOTAL					10	21	33

meaning. In point of fact, as we shall see next, it is not the number of the senses but how we use them that counts.[32]

Crossing Sensory Borders

When exploring the uses and meanings of the senses across cultures the first impression one receives is often one of dramatic difference. For example, the divisions of the Cashinahua sensorium—skin, hands, ears, liver, eyes, genitals—seem to have little in common with the categorization of the senses in Western culture or science. For one thing, the Cashinahua appear to assimilate visual perception to "skin knowledge" (a feel for the world), while the eye functions like a spiritual X-ray machine (discerning the inner life of things). For another, their idea of hand knowledge (or, manual intelligence) as a special sense seems spurious from a Western perspective that holds that all of the nerves in the hand can be traced ultimately to the brain. Furthermore, the Cashinahua notion of the sensory powers of the liver does not square with any popular notions of perception in the West nor with the functions of any of the interoceptive organs as determined by scientists (see Table 2). Most perplexing, they do not even seem to regard the senses as receptors, but rather as *sensorimotor complexes.*

Cultural differences concerning the nature of the senses can be profound. However, one often finds, on the borders of the Western sensory model, suggestions of the alternative sensory capacities that one finds fully developed in certain non-Western cultures (and vice versa).

We have already seen, for example, how some elements of the Cashinahua sensory model would not have been alien to certain philosophers of antiquity. It is also possible to find similar alignments today. Thus, one can read within the work of contemporary Western scientists (psychologists and physiologists) that "the use of the hand shapes the brain" (Wilson 1998), that the liver or stomach is "the second brain" (Gershon 1998), that the skin has eyes (referring to the phenomenon of paroptic vision) and the eyes can register the invisible (Rensink 2000, 2004), and, that the senses should be considered as "perceptual systems" (Gibson 1966) or "simulated action" (Bagot, Ehm, Casati, Dokic, and Pacherie 1998: 22),[33] not passive receptors. It should be added that the Cashinahua consider their most precious knowledge to come from dreams and the ingestion of hallucinogens, which induce synaesthetic perceptions (e.g. seeing sounds, hearing colors) (Kensinger 1995: 217, 219–23; Keifenheim 1999).[34] The value the Cashinahua attach to synaesthetic perceptions would seem to be echoed in the following statement by no less a figure than V. S. Ramachandran, the doyen of neuropsychology:

> [F]ar from being a mere curiosity, synaesthesia deserves to be brought into mainstream neuroscience and cognitive psychology. Indeed, [precisely because the neural basis of synaesthesia is beginning to be understood] it may provide a crucial insight into some

of the most elusive questions about the mind, such as the neural substrate (and evolution) of metaphor, language and thought itself. (Ramachandran, Hubbard, and Butcher 2004: 881)

Other cross-cultural resonances can be found with regard to other sensory modalities. For example, W. H. Hudson at one point in his writings muses on the possible existence of an "atmospheric sense," a "wind sense" (Hudson 1923: 36–48). But his thoughts are inchoate, and quickly devolve into a discussion of "phantasms" (crisis apparitions) and telepathy. This is because he lacked a cultural model in terms of which to think about the experience of wind. By contrast, the Navajo have a highly elaborate philosophy of wind. According to the Navajo, wind is omnipresent, omniscient, and omnipotent. It is the ultimate source of all animation and knowledge because it is "the only substance or entity in the Navajo world with the inherent capacity to move and bear knowledge" (Witherspoon 1977: 53). An "instanding-wind soul" is dispatched to the body at birth and becomes its source of life and breath, thought and action—just as life ends when it departs. The capacity to speak a language also derives from the "instanding-wind soul." Speech, which the Navajo conceive of as "highly refined and patterned air in motion," is the outer form of thought, and it is borne from one being to another by the wind.

> All animate beings [plants and animals, gods and humans] depend on [wind]—live by it, move by it, think by it, and speak by it. Because it is the means of thought and speech, it knows all thought and actions. It can carry messages to the inner forms of all things. Because it is the source of all life and motion, it is the ultimate source of *hózhó* [the positive or ideal natural order]. To control air and to speak and sing the order, harmony, and beauty of *hózhó* is to make contact with the ultimate source of life and restore it to the ideal condition of *hózhó*. After a person has projected *hózhó* into the air through ritual form [e.g. through chanting the song cycle called Beautyway], he then, at the conclusion of the ritual, breathes that *hózhó* back into himself and makes himself a part of the order, harmony, and beauty he has projected onto the world through the ritual mediums of speech and song. (Witherspoon 1977: 61; see further 153–4)

The Navajo could have provided Hudson with a cultural model for making sense of his breezy intuitions. If Hudson's travels had taken him to a Buddhist temple in Thailand, on the other hand, he might have learned how to focus his breathing and summon those "phantasms" he experienced on a windswept street through practices of meditation. Thai Buddhists cultivate "mindfulness of in- and out-breathing" (*ānāpānasati*) through the technique of focusing on the tactile sensation of the breath in the nostrils, for example. Once they have attained the desired degree of concentration, they transfer their "mindfulness" to some meditation object. In one form of Buddhist contemplation, the object is a decomposing corpse (Collins 1997).[35] Meditators impress the physical sight of the corpse on their minds by staring at it, noting all the gruesome details; they then attempt to "reconstruct the image of the corpse within their 'inner seeing' (hen pai nai) or 'inner looking' (muang pai nai)" where it takes on an extraordinary vividness; the final stage involves visualizing their *own* bodies as corpses, as "assemblages," as mere "heaps" (Klima 2002: 178–9, 200–1; Collins 1997: 192–94). This stage is called "touring the charnel house within."

The objective of this meditative technique is to accede to "a realization of *anicca,* 'impermanence,' and *anatta,* 'no-self': [i.e.] in the body there never was anything present that could permanently keep it together, and nothing there that can ever be held to as 'Self'" (Klima 2002: 210).[36] The attainment of this realization of 'no-self' is further assisted by the way in which the mind is understood to be on a par with the senses, and indeed to be a sense, the sixth sense:

In Thai Buddhism, what is referred to in English as the "mind's eye" would fall within the rubric of the mind as the sixth differentiated sense organ, in addition to the Euro-American five. In this conception, the mind as a sense organ has as its objects the appearance of any phenomena that do not have material contact as a condition of their immediate possibility: in other words, inner picturing, monologue, intentions, thoughts. The advantage in Thai meditation of this six-sense perceptual model is that it does not privilege the mind as a separate receptor of the five senses, but treats it as a sense like any other. (Klima 2002: 201)

The difficulty in finding commonalities between Hudson's sensory musings and the perceptual practices of Thai Buddhists or between V. S. Ramachandran's scientific speculations and the sensory philosophy of the Cashinahua is, as every social anthropologist would know, a function of the particularity of culture. Not only ideas about the senses but perceptual experiences themselves are shaped by cultural models to such an extent that it is highly problematic to extract any one idea or experience from its own cultural context and try to position it within the sensory model of another culture. While culture plays such a large role in shaping sensory experience, however, it is largely ignored by the psychologists and biologists who study the senses. Thus while Ramachandran is interested in how synaesthesia may provide insights into how the senses—and the mind, and language—function he only wishes to study synaesthesia as a naturally occurring phenomenon (Ramachandran et al. 2004: 867–68; Baron-Cohen and Harrison 1997), not as a culturally informed practice. However, limiting synaesthesia to those with a genetic predisposition to experience cross-modal stimulation would be "like restricting music to those with perfect pitch" (Steven Feld, personal communication, 3 April 2000). The fact is that synaesthesia is the stuff of cultural expression, not just a rare neurological disposition (Classen 1990, 1998; Duplisea 1997; Campen 2007; Howes 2006a,b; Klima 2002: 215).

Even parapsychologists, whom one might expect would have a broader perspective on perception, are rarely concerned with the role of culture. With few exceptions (e.g. Braude 2007) parapsychologists only feel comfortable in the laboratory, not the field; they are only interested in "spontaneous" expressions of psychic powers, not ritualized ones; and, they privilege measurement (or "statistical significance") over meaning. Most critically, because of the extreme mentalism of their position, they seek to *eliminate* sensory cues, rather than investigate their role in the production of other states of consciousness. In the estimation of parapsychologists, the ideal test conditions for the demonstration of psychic abilities is the ganzfeld, or "total field." This procedure involves the erasure of any form of patterned sensory stimulation that might compete or interfere with the "internal attention state" that is the focus of the parapsychological investigation. The idea is to immerse the test subject or "percipient" in as homogeneous an environment as possible. Halved ping-pong balls are placed over the eyes while the room is bathed in a red light; "white noise" is pumped in, or headphones are placed over the ears, the temperature of the room is neither cold nor hot. Meanwhile, a "sender" in a separate room concentrates on some image and, ideally, there is a transfer of this image between the mind of the sender and the mind of the percipient.

As should be apparent, the parapsychology lab is a bastion of Cartesianism. The whole set-up is sense-blind. "Extrasensory perception" is a misnomer; "extrasensory cogitation" would be more accurate. What is missing from the ganzfeld procedure is any notion of "emplacement" (Howes 2003: 238 n1 and 2004: 7–8), of *contexts of perception.*

One useful way of transcending the limitations of the scientific study of the senses and investigating perception in cross-cultural contexts is to concentrate on the practices or "techniques" people employ to relate to the world through their senses in meaningful ways. Behind this use of the term *technique* is both Eliade's (1964) classic treatise in comparative religion, *Shamanism: Archaic Techniques of Ecstasy,* and Marcel Mauss's classic essay, "Techniques of the Body." Mauss famously wrote that: "The body is man's first and most natural instrument. Or more accurately, not to speak of instruments, man's first and most natural technical object, and at the same time technical means, is his body ... Before instrumental techniques there is the ensemble of techniques of the body" (Mauss 2007: 56).

Mauss's point concerning techniques of the body applies equally to the senses (Howes 1990), and can encompass both the breathing techniques of Thai Buddhists, and the hallucinogenic techniques of the Cashinahua. Under the guidance of a shaman, hallucinogenic visions enable the Cashinahua to attain a realization of the essential unity of the senses. The practitioner of Thai Buddhism, by contrast, employs the heightened concentration engendered by meditating on the breath to observe "that phenomena change from seeing, hearing, touching, and thinking, back and forth in a most fragmentary and startling way" (Klima 2002: 214). This observation in turn opens into the realization that perception—along with the notion of the self—is essentially fragmented.[37] "Consider this analogy," Alan Klima (2002: 213) suggests: "The four blades of an electric fan (read: multiple senses), run at high speed, appear to be one continuous, whole, circle of matter, but when you slow them down, it may no longer look like one continuous entity." Most people suffer from blurred attention, which is why they hold to the illusion of a self, but not so the Buddhist practitioner. The practitioner's concentration is so fine that he or she can perceive everything as if in slow motion, the same way he can control his breath.

The electric fan analogy gives a new twist to the image of the revolving sensorium we have been meditating on in this book. It seems to bring the "Wheel of the Senses" at Longthorpe Tower, Oken's five-part wheels of sensory progression, and even our own motif of the kaleidoscope of the sensorium, to a standstill. At a deeper level, however, it points to how even the sense of self—or of selflessness—may be fashioned by a particular set of sensory techniques.

The Experiential Turn

In order to explore the uses and meanings of the senses across cultures it is essential to be able to see things "from the native's point of view" (Geertz 1983: ch. 3), and to develop the capacity to "be of two sensoria"—one's own and that of the people under study (Howes 2003: 12). This is the particular challenge of the sense-minded anthropologist undertaking fieldwork. In "The Embodiment of Symbols and the Acculturation of the Anthropologist" (Chapter 15), Carol Laderman writes: "Anthropologists use their own bodies and minds as primary tools for the investigation of cultures. They participate as deeply as possible in the lives of those they study, at the same time maintaining sufficient distance to observe the workings of culture" (p. 319). She goes on to relate how, during her fieldwork in the Malay peninsula, she experienced aspects of the Malay self—such as *semangat,* "the breath of life" and *angin,* the archetypal "inner winds" (or personality types, temperaments)—as components of *her* self through participating in numerous healing ceremonies as a member of the presiding shaman's entourage.

In the great theatrical and therapeutic Malay shamanistic performance known as the *Main Peteri,* the first phase involves the shaman diagnosing the patient's *angin,* which has become blocked, causing the patient to fall ill. In the second phase: "The band strikes up appropriate music as the shaman retells the story of the *angin*'s archetype. When the correct musical or literary cue is reached, the patient achieves trance, aided as well by the percussive sounds of music and the rhythmic beating of the shaman's hands on the floor near the patient's body" (p. 319).

In the third phase, the patient is encouraged to act out his or her *angin,* and thus achieve release from the sickness through the restoration of balance. On one occasion, a shaman, who was like a father to her, induced a trance in Laderman herself (see Chapter 15 for her account of this profoundly transformative experience, and of a subsequent relapse into her Malay self when she was back home in New York).

Trance takes its place among the many practices and experiences that fall within the mysterious and marginal domain of the sixth sense in the West but are considered a standard perceptual practice in many non-Western cultures. Indeed, according to

Erika Bourguignon (1973), trance is part of religious practice in 90 percent of the world's societies. Trance is, therefore, a normal propensity of humanity, given the right context of perception, or proper ritual. It is mainly only in mainstream Western society, where there is no model to structure such "dissociated states," that it is diagnosed as a form of multiple personality disorder, or some other delusion.[38] In some societies, trance is understood to involve the presence of a spirit or power inside a person that changes or displaces that person's soul or personality. These sorts of altered states are known in the literature as possession trances. Other types of trances may involve the journey of a person's soul (shamanic flight), experiencing visions, or transmitting messages from spirits. The achievement of trance by the shaman is frequently accompanied by the accomplishment of paranormal feats, such as levitation and fire-walking (Eliade, Chapter 13).

The techniques for inducing trance vary widely. Some involve sensory and social deprivation (e.g. fasting, reclusive meditation), others involve sensory saturation (e.g. the Malay *Main Peteri,* a veritable orchestration of the senses under the direction of the shaman), while still others involve sensory exhaustion (e.g. running, dancing). The use of hallucinogens, such as peyote among the Huichol (Myerhoff, Chapter 14) or *ayahuasca* among the Cashinahua (Kensinger 1995), constitute another widespread technique for the production of extraordinary perception.

One of the earliest and finest general theories of all these techniques of ecstasy is Mircea Eliade's essay on "Sense Experience and Mystical Experience among Primitives," originally published in 1954, and reprinted here as the first chapter in Part IV. It is unfortunate that this gem of an essay is not better known since, even with all its faults,[39] it would have provided a much surer foundation for research on "shamanic consciousness," "mysticism," and "the paranormal" than much that has been published subsequently.

One of the latest attempts to bring a sensory anthropological perspective to bear on the vast terrain of "extraordinary experience" (Young and Goulet 1994; Goulet and Miller 2006; Straight 2007) is Lynne Hume's *Portals: Opening Doorways to Other Realities through the Senses.* Hume brings out well how "other realities" are accessed through the medium of the senses, either singly or, more commonly, in combination. *Portals* is a fitting companion to Eliade's essay, and the present volume.

One anthropologist whose work was inspired in part by Eliade is Barbara Myerhoff, who carried out research on the peyote hunt among the Huichol Indians of Mexico (Chapter 14). Myerhoff's ethnography is a classic example of the anthropology of extraordinary experience, or ecstasy. In the last few decades, there has been a paradigm shift from ecstasy as an object of study to ecstasy as a means of inquiry. The archetypal *patterns* of Eliade's comparative approach to the study of "the sacred" have been exchanged for the transformative *experience* of apprenticeship as a sorcerer or witchdoctor (Stoller and Olkes 1987; Turner 1994, 1996), of dreaming and sharing dreams with one's informants (Tedlock 1987, 1991; Young and Goulet 1994), and of experiencing trance firsthand (Desjarlais 1992; Laderman, Chapter 15).[40]

The experiential turn in anthropological theory and practice is intimately linked to the sensorial revolution in anthropology and other social science disciplines (Howes 2006a): Many of the leading "experiential anthropologists" have also figured in the vanguard of the emergent field of sensory anthropology. For example, it was Johannes Fabian's "critique of Western visualism" in *Time and the Other* that both inspired and opened the door to the exploration of other (non-Western) sensory orders in their own right (e.g. Stoller 1989), and it is Johannes Fabian who figures again as the principal theorist of ecstasis as the foundation of anthropological knowledge. He writes:

> much of our ethnographic research is carried out best when we are "out of our minds," that is, while we relax inner controls, forget our purposes, let ourselves go. In short, there is an ecstatic side to fieldwork which should be counted among the conditions of knowledge production, hence objectivity. (Fabian 2001: 31)
>
> [T]he triumph of logic and rationality, the clever architecture of theoretical artifices, and the cunning methods devised for novice researchers do not make science ... What they do promote is ascetic withdrawal from the world as we experience it with our senses.
>
> In the end, science conceived, taught and institutionalized in such a manner is senseless. (Fabian 2000: xii)

Fabian here suggests that the conventional anthropological method of "participant *observation*," should be replaced by "radical participation" or "participant *sensation*." Retaining the status of an observer is inimical to becoming a sensor. Becoming a sensor involves experimenting with one's senses, learning to be "of two sensoria" (Howes 2003), and opening oneself to the genius loci of a particular environment (Malnar and Vodvarka 2004), discovering all the ways that "as place is sensed, senses are placed; as places make sense, senses make place" (Feld 2004: 179).

The ecstatic side of fieldwork comes through clearly in Bilinda Straight's contribution to this Reader (Chapter 16), with its sensuous evocation of the Kenyan landscape and its profound meditation on death and resurrection among the Samburu. Straight describes certain cases in which individuals related to her had returned to life after death, and the numerous reports of such cases that circulate among the Samburu. Were her informants actually describing cases of Out of Body Experience (OBE) or Near Death Experience (NDE) familiar to us from the vast literature in parapsychology on this subject (Griffin 1997; Cardeña, Lynn, and Krippner 2000)?[41] Rather than employing such Western paradigms to make sense of her informants' experiences, Straight situates them within customary Samburu beliefs and practices concerning death. As we saw with trance, what is considered "paranormal" within one culture may simply be "normal" within another.

This anthropological approach to the study of sensory and extrasensory perception is valuable not only within non-Western contexts, but also for delving into the perceptual paradigms of the West. The ethnographer Ruth Barcan explores the New Age's version of the sixth sense—namely, intuition—and its relation to reason in

Chapter 9 of this volume. The emphasis in her essay is on the relations *between* intuition and reason, and on the ways in which practitioners and patients of "medical clairvoyance" (as well as their detractors) make sense of their experience. By starting with her informants' own categories and narratives, rather than with a "clever architecture of theoretical artifices" (Fabian), she shows that clairvoyance is not all "in the mind" (as parapsychologists would have it), but rather part of a consensual reality. Consensus—meaning "with the senses," or "sensing along with"—turns out to be the foundation of sociality, and of society itself, as well as of the self.

Michael Taussig also turns the anthropological lens back on Western society. In "Tactility and Distraction" (Chapter 12), he asks "What sort of sense is constitutive of ... everydayness" in a place like New York, for example? Drawing on the work of Walter Benjamin, he suggests that one's sense of a city is grounded in "peripheral vision," in "proprioception," or "a certain tactility" (what the Cashinahua would call "skin knowledge") rather than ocularity: it is sensational rather than ideational, a product of distraction rather than contemplation. Taussig goes on to sketch a theory of the "sensuous materiality" of "that art form known as 'magic,'" once again taking his cue from Benjamin on "the mimetic faculty." Taussig's theory applies equally to the "traditional magic" of the Malay shaman and the "new magic" ("the new real," "capitalist mimetics") of the Madison Avenue dream merchant, ever in search of ways to augment the sense appeal of commodities. Advertising is the most sensuous embodiment of "the arts" in the era of technologically mediated perception.[42]

How Many Senses Are There?

How many senses are there? While the reader can consult the ABCDERIUM of Extra/Sensory Powers that accompanies this book to gain a notion of the breadth of this question, there can be no definitive answer. There simply is no Archimedean point—independent of culture and history—from which to observe the operation of the senses. The one thing that can be said is that it is essential to guard against essentialism. This means recognizing that the compartmentalization of the senses in and by the discipline of psychology is but one categorization among others. It means recognizing that there can be no "natural history of the senses" (contra Ackerman 1990), only cultural histories. Above all, it means recognizing that it is not how we number the senses but how we *use* them that counts.

When we start to inquire into the uses of the senses, we are immediately brought to the issue of their emplacement and elaboration in a *particular* cultural context. Approached from this standpoint, even the familiar senses, the "known" senses, may stop seeming so familiar. Consider the case of *rasa,* "taste" in the Hindu sensorium: the Sanskrit gustatory vocabulary consists of six terms (not just four); Ayurvedic medical theory recognizes a range of "post-digestive tastes" (which are not the same as aftertastes); flavors have medicinal virtue; emotional states are classified as tastes (rather than what English-speakers call "feelings"); theatrical performances are savored and digested (rather than "seen"); dietary differences determine an individual's rank in the caste system (with its progressive vegetarianism); and, the order of the universe is held to depend on regular gustatory exchanges between humans and gods (see Pinard, 1991; Khare 2005; Schechner 2001; and also Mason 2006).

Numerous other examples could be cited of how uncommon the canonical five senses become in cultural practice, such as:

- the sense of temperature among the Tzotzil of Mexico, which provides the "structural support" (as Laderman [p. 311] would say) for the "thermal dynamics" of their conceptualization of the social and physical universe (Classen 2004b);
- the sense of balance among the Anlo-Ewe of Ghana, which "moors" (Laderman) their understanding of existence as an unending balancing act in which flexibility of mind and body are key (Geurts 2003);
- the sense of hearing among the Kalapalo of Brazil, with their "musical view of the universe" (Basso 1985);
- the ability of the Bushmen (ǀXam San) of South Africa to perceive things happening at a distance from the "tappings" they felt inside their bodies, which they likened to "whitemen's letters" (Bleek and Lloyd 1911: ch. 3);
- the sense of breathing among Thai Buddhists, which they cross with seeing to produce the concentration necessary to perceive the "impermanence" of the universe, and of the self (Klima 2002);
- the sense of color among the Desana of Colombia, which, informed by their hallucinatory visions, leads them to conceptualize the universe as a "field of color energies" (Classen 2004b).

Each of these elaborations and crossings of the senses gives a new twist to the kaleidoscope of the sensorium, and reveals the world in a different light. All of the volumes in the *Sensory Formations* series attest to this fundamental point concerning the cultural life of the senses.

It could be said that sensory anthropology leaves no sense unturned in its quest to chart the varieties of sensory experience across cultures (Howes 1991). Contemporary sensory psychology, by contrast, only turns inward, chasing neural impulses from receptor organ to brain. Physical sensation only interests the psychologist insofar as it provides the "information" or "data" to be converted into mental representation. Perception is a one-way street.

As will be recalled, the Ancients understood the senses differently: "They were apt to think of the senses more as media of communication than as passive recipients of data" (Classen 1993: 2). Perception was a two-way street for them, hence the extramission theory of vision flourished alongside the intromission theory, despite the seeming contradiction, and only came to be extinguished in the era of

Locke and Descartes. A similar understanding may be seen to underlie the anomalous (to us moderns) notion of speech being counted a sense: the passive ear had to have an active counterpart—the tongue; hearing was both complemented and completed by speaking. One can also find an elaboration of the double nature of sensation in the case of smell, which refers both to scents emitted and scents received. (As Doctor Johnson once joked to a lady who told him he smelled: "Madame, you smell, I stink.") And, of course, the same applies to touch: there is active touch and passive touch (Hsu 2000, 2005)—or rather, every act of touching involves the reciprocal fact of being touched by something or someone. Conceiving of the senses as channels of communication means that they can act outwardly, not just inwardly. (This is the key point insisted on by both Sheldrake and Taussig in their chapters in Part III.)[43]

The premodern notion of the senses as media of communication resurfaced in the mid-twentieth century in the work of Marshall McLuhan. In *Understanding Media: The Extensions of Man,* he proposed that media (broadly construed) be seen as both extensions and amputations (or detachments) of the sense organs: clothing as an extension of the skin, the telescope as an extension of the eye, the telephone of the ear, and so forth. McLuhan also saw in the electronic communications media of his day the potential for the coming to be of a "cosmic consciousness" as an effect of the multiple ways in which the mass media function as prolongations of the nervous system (McLuhan 1964: 81–4, 104–14; see further Jones 2006, Doidge 2007).[44] That potential has perhaps been realized, judging from David Chidester's "Zulu Dreamscapes," the last chapter in this volume. Chidester explores how media and the senses have become entwined in the globally interconnected phenomenon of tele-neo-shamanism. In this context, he analyzes how the mass mediation of the senses has allowed some South Africans, such as Zulu sangoma-turned-(neo)shaman Credo Mutwa, to "go global," and others, such as white South African expatriates, to "return home." There is even an extraterrestrial dimension to the sensorium as conceptualized by Credo Mutwa, whose alleged encounters with aliens have led him to aver that human beings possess a total of twelve senses.

Organization of the Chapters

The argument of this book is that one cannot know what the sixth sense entails in any of its contemporary manifestations unless one excavates its cultural roots, and attends to its context of expression. Like any other sense, the sixth sense has a history. Conversely, studying the sixth sense, which in the West has come to signify the sense of the outer limits of the knowable, throws the perimeters of perception into relief.

The selection of the essays in this volume was motivated by a desire to feature the work of authors who have made groundbreaking contributions to the history and/or anthropology of the senses, some *avant la lettre* (such as Vinge and Eliade), and the wish to foreground the work of select scholars in other disciplines, such as biology (Sheldrake) and psychology (Wade), who have valuable contributions to make to the sensorial revolution in the humanities and social sciences. With the advent of more cross-talk among the disciplines, the ranks of these other scholars are bound to swell; but such an outcome will depend on more scholars, particularly within the sciences, abjuring the reductionism that has so far impeded a multidisciplinary conversation centering on the sensorium from flourishing.[45]

The organization of the chapters in this volume is kaleidoscopic, constantly revolving, like the discussion in this introduction (with apologies to the reader who may, by this point, be feeling rather dizzy from all this talk of revolutions). Part I sets out various bearings on the sixth sense, commencing with the physiological: the discovery of the muscle, vestibular, and temperature senses (all of which would have been news to Aristotle, as Wade points out), and culminates in the mystical: the transcendence of the senses which, on Hollenback's account, shows a certain commonality across both history and cultures. In between these two extremes—the world beneath the five senses and the world beyond them—there are chapters on the sense of direction (Hudson) and perception at a distance (Bleek and Lloyd). The latter piece suggests that touch may not be the proximity sense it is commonly thought to be in the West, since it can act at a distance, too, according to the ǁxam San.

Part II, which is historical in orientation, opens with a chapter that delves into the "invention" of the five senses in the Western tradition (Vinge). This is followed by a chapter on the late eighteenth-century scientific investigation of mesmerism and the fateful discovery of the power of suggestion—fateful because it undermined the authority of the evidence of the senses (which the philosophers and scientists of that period took to be the foundation of all knowledge). This historical episode was a first in multiple ways (Riskin). The next chapter explores the eighteenth-century natural-philosopher-turned Christian-mystic Emmanuel Swedenborg's anatomy of the spiritual senses, and the reception of his revelations in mid-nineteenth-century America. This transplant gave birth to the first New Age movement in America (Schmidt). Subsequent chapters deal with the invention of telepathy and what this owed to telegraphy in the late nineteenth century (Thurschwell); the liberation of intuition and the repositioning of reason in the (second) New Age (Barcan); and, the mediation of the sixth sense in the phantom films of the late twentieth century (Thurschwell).

Part III, "Uncanny Sensations," consists of essays by a maverick biologist (Sheldrake) and a maverick anthropologist (Taussig) who, by virtue of their sense-minded approaches to the study of ESP and magic, respectively, reveal that these phenomena are perhaps not so uncanny as the title of this part implies. Their contributions mark a fundamental break with the conventional (psychologistic) understanding of perception in the West.

Part IV, which is cross-cultural in orientation, picks up where Part I left off. It begins with Eliade's sensory genealogy of mystical experience. Eliade's comparative and (to his mind) historical survey is followed by a series of case studies, rich in ethnographic detail, of the varieties of extraordinary perception: Myerhoff on how the doors of perception are opened through peyote use among the Huichol; Laderman on how the altered state of trance is modeled among the Malays; and Straight on how miraculous experience is possible among the Samburu. This part concludes with a chapter by Chidester on how the mass mediation of the senses has enabled shamanism to go global and also provided the medium for some to journey home.

The cultural history–anthropology of the sixth sense is replete with discontinuities, gaps, and restarts. In this respect it resembles the fugitive character of sense experience itself. It might be thought that all the different ideas of the sixth sense canvassed in this book are a testimony to the power of the human imagination, were it not that imagination is (or was, until the late eighteenth century) itself considered a sense, hence part of the perceptual kaleidoscope.

ABCDERIUM of Extra/Sensory Powers

The final section of this Reader consists of an ABCDERIUM of Extra/Sensory Powers. This feature is modeled after the "Abcderius" in *Sensorium: Embodied Experience, Technology, and Contemporary Art* (Jones 2006). An abcderium is "an Enlightenment-era format that uses the stochastic variable of the alphabet to generate categories for thinking. ... " (Jones 2006: 3). In *Sensorium,* the emphasis is on the generation of categories "for thinking the body through its technological mediations." Where this volume differs from *Sensorium* is in the attention it brings to bear on the "techniques of the senses" (Mauss 2007; Howes 2000), which exist before and alongside the technological mediation of perception.

Some readers, glancing over the ABCDERIUM, may see it as little more than "chaos with an index" (Glenn 2005), and to them some further specification is owed. A considered opinion would suggest that speech, proprioception (or kinaesthesia), and ESP all enjoy equal rights to the title of *the* sixth sense, at least in the Western tradition (and insofar as humans are concerned), while mind would be the prime candidate in the Buddhist tradition. The sense of beauty enjoys the strongest claim to the title of *the* seventh sense (though humor is rising). There is also the lesser distinction of being considered *a* sixth sense, *a* seventh sense, and so forth. It is less clear how this distinction should be distributed among the various candidates. Perhaps what we need is another Thomas Tomkis to write a play in which each and every one of the senses in the ABCDERIUM could play a role, and be judged (but by whom?). Ultimately, however, the real importance of the category of the sixth sense lies not in its promotion of this or that faculty, but in its power to open up the boundaries of conventional perceptual paradigms to new possibilities of perception.

Notes

1. Cognate approaches to the history of the social sensorium (or social history of the senses) include the work of Hoffer (2003), Jütte (2005), and Smith (2007). Cognate approaches to the anthropology of the senses include the work of Stoller (1997), Geurts (2003), and Hahn (2007). See generally Classen (1997, 2001, 2005), Howes (2004, 2008), Classen and Howes (2006), Bull and Back (2003), Korsmeyer (2005), Drobnick (2006), and Edwards and Bhaumik (2008).
2. A recent book in art history that explores the senses as media and the mediation of the senses has *Sensorium* for a title (Jones 2006). Perhaps, the term is making a comeback.
3. As an example of a seven sense model from within the Western tradition, consider the following entry from *Brewer's Dictionary of Phrase and Fable:*

   According to very ancient teaching, the soul of man, or his "inward holy body," is compounded of the seven properties which are under the influence of the seven planets. Fire animates, earth gives the sense of feeling, water gives speech, air gives taste, mist gives sight, flowers give hearing, the south wind gives smelling. Hence the seven senses are animation, feeling, speech, taste, sight, hearing, and smelling (*see* Ecclesiastes 17:5) (Room 1999: 1068).

   This is a good example of "divergence from the Aristotelian norm," as Classen would say.
4. We should think twice about disciplining our children's sensoria by subjecting them to such literature. It prevents them from developing a talent for synaesthesia (see Campen 2007).
5. Given enough twists, all of the possible combinations will have been manifested, in a seemingly limitless but finite series of variations. I owe the kaleidoscope analogy to McLuhan (1964) and the figure of a fugue of the five senses to Lévi-Strauss (1969: 147–64).
6. This quote is from Lull's *De virtute veniali et vitali et de peccatis venialibus et mortalibus* (On Venial and Life-Supporting Virtue and on Venial and Mortal Sins). In his *Ars brevis de inventione iuris* (Art for the Quick Discovery of Law) he again touches on the topic of speech as the sixth sense: "The common sense contains six particular powers coessential to it, but remains substantially undivided. These powers, each different in its organs, objects and figures are the following, namely: the powers of touch, taste, smell, sight, hearing and affatus (voice)" (Lull nd). The construction Lull places on the "particular powers" of "the common sense" is another good example of divergence from the Aristotelian norm. I am indebted to Richard Newhauser for bringing these references to my attention.

7. Where does the psi faculty come from? "The symbol ψ (psi) has long been used to represent the 'general psychical world' ... in contradistinction to the 'general physical world' represented by Φ [phi]" (Schoch and Yonavjak 2008: 9). Hence the term *psi faculty.* The extreme mentalism of parapsychology is otherwise reflected in the term *anomalous cognition,* which is the latest term for ESP.

8. On the psychic arms race see Buchanan 2003; Epstein 1989; Ebon 1986; Ostrander and Schroeder 1970.

9. "Blending with the neomysticism and antimaterialism of the 1960s and the self-realization movement of the 1970s, a pursuit of things psychic ... infiltrated the mainstream of twentieth-century culture [with the progressive normalization of the New Age]. ... New groups and movements arose to help psi enthusiasts escape the mundane world in ways ranging from simple meditation to astral voyaging and pagan rituals" (Kagan et al. 1987: 83–4). In this way a large segment of the American population became rechurched, just not in an organized form.

10. On psychic art see Kagan et al. 1987: 82–6; Durant and Marsching 2005; Fisher 2006.

11. On Hollywood's construction of the paranormal see Hess 1993: ch. 6; Edwards 2005; and Chapters 10 and 17 of this Reader.

12. The reification or hypostatization of "the unexplained" is reflected in such titles as *The X-Files™ Book of The Unexplained* (Goldman 2008) and *K.I.S.S. Guide to The Unexplained* (Levy 2002).

13. If the first five tapestries of *The Lady and the Unicorn* series are an allegory of the five senses, what of the sixth tapestry? It shows the maiden putting her jewelry away in a box and bears the inscription "A MON SEVL DESIR" on the blue pavilion in the background. It would appear that this tapestry expresses a "purely medieval conception" of the heart as the sixth sense. The heart differs from the other five senses by being "internal" instead of "external," and "spiritual" instead of "physical," but it is no less in need of mastery, if the soul is to be kept pure of sin (Boudet nd). If this interpretation is correct, then, rather than being a celebration of desire and courtly love, as used to be thought, perhaps *The Lady and the Unicorn* series is about the will and the renunciation of sensory pleasures, and we should therefore read the inscription as saying not "my only desire" but rather "according to my will only." Boudet (nd) actually suggests that we retain both interpretations.

14. On animal senses, besides Burton 1973, see Hudson 1923; Baker 1981; Uexküll 1982; Rivlin and Gravelle 1984: ch. 3; Hughes 2001; and O'Connell 2007.

15. The literature on the psychic powers of animals (or anpsi) is vast and at the center of it is Rupert Sheldrake. Regarding N'kisi see www.sheldrake.org.nkisi

16. The reader who is concerned by the apparent breach of scientific rationality perpetrated by postulating such a heterodox category might find it soothing to read

Needham (1975) on "polythetic classification." There is more than one way to constitute a category.

17. The Ongee have a calendar of scents; a fluid, wafting conception of space; and personal identity is also nose-centered. Theirs is an olfactory cosmology (see Pandya 2005; Classen 2004b: 153–57; Classen, Howes, and Synnott 1994). On the Ongee response to the tsunami see further Pandya 2005.

18. Ethnotheories of animal perception are all but ignored in the standard literature of ethology.

19. By way of example, Walter Ong (1982), who was a disciple of McLuhan, distinguishes four phases in the technologization of the word: "primary orality" (referring to the dominant form of communication in oral societies), "chirographic," "typographic" (referring to successive forms of literate society based on writing and the printing press respectively), and "secondary orality" (referring to the instantaneity and face-to-device-to-face quality of electronic communication in the wired society of today). See further Howes 1991: 170–75 and 2003: 113–21; Classen 2004b; Jütte 2005: ch. 9.

20. See, for example, Calvert, Spence, and Stein 2004 and for a critique Howes 2006b; Damasio 2000; and for a critique Geurts 2004. By contrast, neurologist Oliver Sacks is emphatic about how "culture tunes our neurons" (Sacks 2004), and psychiatrist Norman Doidge (2007) makes a valiant attempt to incorporate a cultural loop into his account of *The Brain That Changes Itself.*

21. See, for example, Laughlin (1994) on biogenetic structuralism.

22. Beare (1906: 327–29) makes it clear that Aristotle held that these functions reside in the heart. On the humoral theory underlying this categorization see Beare (1906: 328–29).

23. This phrase deliberately echoes the Saussurian notion that language consists of "differences without positive terms" (Saussure 1959), but I would be the last to suggest that we import a linguistic model into the study of how the senses function (see Howes 2003: ch. 1 and 2004: 1, 4).

24. The puzzle of complex sensations could be called the Humpty-Dumpty question, or how to put sensations together again. It receives a very different treatment now than it did in classical times (see Stevenson and Boakes 2004).

25. On common sense now see Heller-Roazen 2007 and Geertz 1983, ch. 4.

26. Actually, McLuhan was more a Thomist at heart, and he also had an ear for the writings of James Joyce. On the multiple sources of McLuhan's communications theory see Cavell 2002.

27. It is admittedly harder to see this in the case of smell, which Aristotle characterized as "the least perfect" of all the senses, though he also had much that was positive to say about how scents are "serviceable to health" (Aristotle 1931a: 434a and 1931b: 439a). As for taste, it remained in the shadow of touch because Aristotle only saw fit to characterize it as a "form of touch" (Aristotle 1931a: 434a and 1931b: 439a). Taste did not come into its own until the mid-eighteenth century, when it

was metaphorized into the aesthetic sense, the sense of discrimination (Howes and Lalonde 1991). Prior to that it was mainly associated with gluttony. The power of smell has a particularly conflicted history, being the most ethereal and the most animal of the senses at once (see Classen 1993: ch. 1 and 1998: ch. 2 as well as Classen, Howes, and Synnott 1994: passim).

28. In *Medieval Psychology,* Simon Kemp does a brilliant job of staging a conversation between medieval and modern psychology, though everything he has to say about medieval *psychology*—and particularly, *cognition*—is, strictly speaking, *avant la lettre.*

29. The afterlife of Mesmer's sixth sense is no less fascinating than its all too brief and highly contested existence. Mesmerism begat hypnosis, which in turn begat psychoanalysis, the science of "the unconscious" (see Tallis 2002; Hess 1993: 191 n1). If this genealogy of the unconscious is correct, that would make it a stand-in for Mesmer's sixth sense. This genealogy is not the only one. For example, Freud is "alleged to have said that if he could live his life over he would go into psychical research" (Kagan et al. 1987: 21, 26). One way or the other, the unconscious occupies the position of *a* sixth sense, if not the sixth sense.

30. This brief account condenses volumes of scholarship with inimitable grace and insight. To pursue this topic further see McCosh 1875; Broadie 2003; and Moore 2004 as well as Kivy 2003.

31. Regarding the revelation of the molecular world beneath the five senses see Locke (1975), whose thoughts on perception were very much influenced by advances in microscopy.

32. There is support for this notion of perception being a form of action (not representation) and the meaning of the senses being in their use in the work of Kevin O'Regan (see Phillips 2005).

33. "In affirming that 'perception is simulated action,' Alain Berthoz (*Le sens du mouvement,* 1997) insists on the fact that anticipation is an essential characteristic of the functioning of sensory systems, and that all perception should be studied as a function of the goal pursued by the organism" (Bagot et al. 1998: 22, my translation). The example is given of the way we adjust our step to mount a moving escalator, and are thoroughly perplexed if it is stopped.

34. Might synaesthesia be considered a *sui generis* mode of perception, a sixth sense? It has been suggested that the way in which some of the senses involuntarily fuse in the condition of synaesthesia "create[s] almost literally a sixth sense" (Mabrey 2002). See further Heller-Roazen (2007: 81, 240) on the original Greek meaning of this concept.

35. Klima claims that an autopsy photograph may be used in place of a corpse and serves equally well as a meditation object. His analysis would seem to be confined to cases involving this substitution, hence perhaps its overemphasis on visualization. At the same time, Klima (2002: 179) insists that: "The experience [of seeing the body in the body] is not simply visual but simultaneously

includes a feeling of actually, physically being that pile of bones, feeling as though one were truly a walking skeleton."

36. There are only perceptions, Buddhists say, instances of contact between a sense organ and a sense object. The trinity of organ, object, and contact is integral to the Buddhist account of perception, and cognition. Klima (2002: 214) explains:

> When visual contact happens, for instance, there is eye-viññaña (sight-presence). When auditory contact happens, viññaña is the there-ness of sound. ... When thinking happens (involving likewise a mind organ, mind object, and viññaña), viññaña is the presence of a mental event. Without viññaña, there can be no occurrence of phenomena, *that is, they are not there ...*

> The contacts appear to go on non-stop, but this is illusory. It is especially illusory to think there is an "I" apart from the perceptions doing the perceiving. This sense of "I-am-ness" is but an effect of the rapid alternation of sensory occurrences: there is only "thereness" (viññaña) in all six senses: "eye-seeing-thereness, ear-hearing-thereness, mind-knowing-thereness, and so on, occurring in rapid succession, too fast for an untrained attention to follow" (Klima 2002: 214).

37. There are only perceptions, Buddhists say. See above note 36. Compare Damasio 1999.

38. "Within the Western medical model," Elisabeth Targ et al. write, "reports of PREs [Psi-related experiences] are usually presumed to be linked to mental illness and emotional instability." They continue:

> The diagnostic criteria for several psychotic, personality, and dissociative disorders contain items that are similar to those endorsed by people reporting spontaneous PREs. ... Of the nine diagnostic criteria for schizotypal personality disorder specified in the fourth edition of the *Diagnostic and Statistical Manual of Mental Disorders* (*DSM–IV;* American Psychiatric Association, 1994), several resemble possible forms of PREs. These include ideas of reference (interpretation of causal events as having particular personal meaning), odd beliefs or magical thinking (e.g., "belief in clairvoyance, telepathy, or 'sixth sense'"; p. 645) and unusual perceptual experiences (e.g., hearing a voice). (Targ et al. 2000: 230)

> Similar things have long been said of the behavior of shamans by Western observers, but the pathological argument was already disputed and refuted by Eliade in 1954 (see Chapter 13). It is astonishing and perplexing that it should still retain any currency.

39. Eliade's faults include the "denial of coevalness" (Fabian 1983) as given in his notion of "the primitive" (or people "in the ethnographic stage"), and the projection of an essentially Christian framework onto the other religions of the world (see generally Znamenski 2007: ch 5).

40. There might be some naivety to the way anthropologists are using the term *experience*. Martin Jay (2006) provides a helpful corrective by enucleating the cultural history of this concept. The same could be said of the terms *ecstasy* and *imagination*. For a good cultural history of the latter concept see Kearney 1988.

41. Nor do the Samburu people who come back from the dead bear any resemblance to that other figment of the Western cine-magination—the zombie, as portrayed in the film *Night of the Living Dead,* for example. Rather, they tend to become prophets. At the same time, there are zombies in Africa, and their numbers are growing in the popular imagination. For a thorough analysis of the social circumstances responsible for this increasing "alien-nation" see Comaroff and Comaroff (1999).

42. See further *Mimesis and Alterity: A Particular History of the Senses* (Taussig 1993) and my chapter on "Hyperaesthesia, or, The Sensuous Logic of Late Capitalism" in *Empire of the Senses* (Howes 2004). The senses (including the sixth sense) are of passionate interest to advertisers, who have lately discovered that the management of sensation is the key to selling merchandise, particularly automobiles (see, for example, Lindstrom 2005 and Roberts 2005 on "the race to embrace the senses"). To cite but one example, here is an ad for the 2006 Hyundai Tucson:

    While the Hyundai Tucson is designed to excite all the senses, it also provides you with a "sixth sense" in the form of electronic stability control: a safety feature that anticipates trouble, then, automatically intervenes, reducing the likelihood of a rollover. The 2006 Hyundai Tucson: proof that, as senses go, you can never have too many.

43. Buddhists also recognize this thanks to the practice of "mindfulness of the in-breath and the out-breath." It is the same with temperature: the body feels temperature, but in states of intensive meditation it can also generate heat (see Eliade, Chapter 13).

44. The expression "cosmic consciousness" was coined by McLuhan's fellow Canadian, the psychiatrist R. M. Bucke (see Hollenback, Chapter 4).

45. A model example of abjuring reductionism and engaging a conversation across disciplinary boundaries and cultures is Laderman's discussion (in Chapter 15) of Western scientific theories of asthma, allergies, temperaments and so forth in connection with Malay conceptions of the inner winds: the two traditions are treated on a par, and there is no attempt to explicate the one in the terms of the other.

References

Ackerman, D. (1990), *A Natural History of the Senses,* New York: Random House.

Anderson, S. R. and Lightfoot, D. W. (2002), *The Language Organ: Linguistics as Cognitive Physiology,* Cambridge: Cambridge University Press.

Aristotle (1931a), *De Anima,* trans. J. A. Smith in W. D. Ross (ed.), *The Works of Aristotle,* vol. 3, Cambridge: Cambridge University Press, pp. 401a–435b.

Aristotle (1931b), *The Parva Naturalia,* trans. J. I. Beare and G. R. T. Ross in W. D. Ross (ed.), *The Works of Aristotle,* vol. 3, Cambridge: Cambridge University Press, pp. 436a–480b.

Atkins, P. W. (1997), *The Periodic Kingdom of the Elements,* New York: Basic Books.

Bagot, J.-D., Ehm, C., Casati, R., Dokic, J. and Pacherie, E. (1998), *L'ABCdaire des Cinq Sens,* Paris: Flammarion.

Baker, R. R. (1981), *Human Navigation and the Sixth Sense,* London: Hodder and Stoughton.

Barker-Benfield, G. J. (1992), *The Culture of Sensibility: Sex and Society in Eighteenth-Century Britain,* Chicago: University of Chicago Press.

Baron-Cohen, S. and Harrison, J. (eds) (1997), *Synaesthesia: Classic and Contemporary Readings,* Oxford: Blackwell.

Basso, E. (1985), *A Musical View of the Universe: Kalapalo Myth and Ritual Performance,* Philadelphia: University of Pennsylvania Press.

Beare, J. I. (1906), *Greek Theories of Elementary Cognition from Alcmaeon to Aristotle,* Oxford: Clarendon Press.

Bleek, W. H. I. and Lloyd, L. C. (1911), *Specimens of Bushmen Folklore,* London: George Allen & Co., Ltd.

Boudet, J.-P. (nd), *The Lady and the Unicorn,* Paris: Le Pérégrinateur Éditeur.

Bourguignon, E. (1973), "Introduction: A Framework for the Comparative Study of Altered States of Consciousness," in E. Bourguignon (ed.), *Religion, Altered States of Consciousness, and Social Change,* Columbus, OH: Ohio State University Press, pp. 3–35.

Braude, S. E. (2007), *The Gold Leaf Lady and Other Parapsychological Investigations,* Chicago: University of Chicago Press.

Broadie, A. (2003), *The Cambridge Companion to the Scottish Enlightenment,* Cambridge: Cambridge University Press.

Buchanan, L. (2003), *The Seventh Sense: The Secrets of Remote Viewing as Told by a "Psychic Spy" for the U.S. Military,* New York: Paraview Pocket Books.

Bull, M. and Back, L. (eds) (2003), *The Auditory Culture Reader,* Oxford: Berg.

Bull, M., Gilroy, P., Howes, D. and Kahn, D. (2006), "Introducing Sensory Studies," *The Senses and Society,* 1(1): 5–7.

Burton, M. (1973), *The Sixth Sense of Animals,* New York: Taplinger Publishing Co., Inc.

Busst, A. J. L. (1995), "Scottish Second Sight: The Rise and Fall of a European Myth," *European Romantic Review,* 5(2): 149–77.

Calvert, G., Spence, C. and Stein, B. (eds) (2004), *The Handbook of Multisensory Processes,* Cambridge, MA: The MIT Press.

Campen, C. van (2007), *The Hidden Sense: Synaesthesia in Art and Science,* Cambridge, MA: The MIT Press.

Cardeña, E., Lynn, S. J. and Krippner, S. (eds) (2000), *Varieties of Anomalous Experience: Examining the Scientific Evidence,* Washington, DC: American Psychological Association.

Cavell, R. (2002), *McLuhan in Space: A Cultural Geography,* Toronto: University of Toronto Press.

Çelik, Z. (2006), "Kinaesthesia," in C. A. Jones (ed.), *Sensorium: Embodied Experience, Technology and Contemporary Art,* Cambridge, MA: The MIT List Visual Arts Center and The MIT Press, pp. 159–62.

Classen, C. (1990), "Sweet Colors, Fragrant Songs: Sensory Models of the Andes and the Amazon," *American Ethnologist,* 17(4): 722–735.

Classen, C. (1993), *Worlds of Sense: Exploring the Senses in History and across Cultures,* London and New York: Routledge.

Classen, C. (1997), "Foundations for an Anthropology of the Senses," *International Social Science Journal,* 153: 401–412.

Classen, C. (1998), *The Color of Angels: Cosmology, Gender and the Aesthetic Imagination,* London and New York: Routledge.

Classen, C. (2001), "The Social History of the Senses," in *Encyclopedia of European Social History,* vol. IV, P. Stearns (ed.), New York: Charles Scribner's Sons, pp. 355–63.

Classen, C. (2004a), "The Witch's Senses: Sensory Ideologies and Transgressive Femininities," in D. Howes (ed.), *Empire of the Senses,* Oxford: Berg, pp. 70–84.

Classen, C. (2004b), "McLuhan in the Rainforest: The Sensory Worlds of Oral Cultures," in D. Howes (ed.), *Empire of the Senses,* Oxford: Berg, pp. 147–63.

Classen, C. (ed.) (2005), *The Book of Touch,* Oxford: Berg.

Classen, C. and Howes, D. (2006), "The Museum as Sensescape: Western Sensibilities and Indigenous Artifacts," in E. Edwards, C. Gosden and R. Phillips (eds), *Sensible Objects: Colonialism, Museums and Material Culture,* Oxford: Berg, pp. 199–222.

Classen, C., Howes, D. and Synnott, A. (1994), *Aroma: The Cultural History of Smell,* London and New York: Routledge.

Cohn, S. A. (1999), "A Historical Review of Second Sight: The Collectors, Their Accounts and Ideas," *Scottish Studies,* 33: 146–85.

Colapinto, J. (2007), "The Interpreter: Has a Remote Amazonian Tribe Upended Our Understanding of Language?" *The New Yorker,* 83(8), April 16, http://www.new yorker.com/reporting/2007/04/16/070416fa_fact_colapinto (accessed 15 January 2009).

Collins, S. (1997), "The Body in Theravada Buddhist Monasticism," in S. Coakley (ed.), *Religion and the Body,* Cambridge: Cambridge University Press, pp. 185–204.

Comaroff, J. and Comaroff, J. (1999), "Alien-Nation: Zombies, Immigrants, and Millennial Capitalism," *CODESRIA Bulletin* (3 & 4): 17–28.

Damasio, A. (2000), *The Feeling of What Happens: Body, Emotion and the Making of Consciousness,* London: Vintage.

Desjarlais, R. (1992), *Body and Emotion,* Philadelphia: University of Pennsylvania Press.

Doidge, N. (2007), *The Brain That Changes Itself: Stories of Personal Triumph from the Frontiers of Brain Science,* New York: Viking Penguin.

Donaldson-Evans, C. (2005), "Tsunami Animals: A Sixth Sense?" *Fox News* (January 9), http://www.foxnews.com/story/0,2933,143737,00.html (accessed 15 January 2009).

Drobnick, J. (ed.) (2006), *The Smell Culture Reader,* Oxford: Berg.

Dundes, A. (1980), *Interpreting Folklore,* Bloomington: Indiana University Press.

Duplisea, C. (1997), "Cross-Modal Synesthetic Sensory Metaphors: Communicating the Experience and Understanding of Power in a Maliseet Sweat Lodge Ceremony," in D. H. Pentland (ed.), *Papers of the Twenty-Eighth Algonquian Conference,* Winnipeg: University of Manitoba.

Durant, M. A. and Marsching, J. D. (2005), *Blur of the Otherworldly: Contemporary Art, Technology, and the Paranormal,* Baltimore: Center for Art and Visual Culture, University of Maryland, Baltimore County.

Durie, B. (2005), "Doors of Perception," *New Scientist* (29 January), 185 (no. 2484): 34–36.

Ebon, M. (1986), "KGB and ESP," *Midstream* (November): 28–32.

Edwards, E. and Bhaumik, K. (eds) (2008), *Visual Sense: A Cultural Reader,* Oxford: Berg.

Edwards, E. D. (2005), *Metaphysical Media: The Occult Experience in Popular Culture,* Carbondale: Southern Illinois University Press.

Eliade, M. (1964), *Shamanism: Archaic Techniques of Ecstasy,* trans. W. R. Trask, New York: Pantheon.

Epstein, E. J. (1989), *Deception: The Invisible War between the KGB and the CIA,* New York: Simon & Schuster.

Fabian, J. (1983), *Time and The Other: How Anthropology Makes Its Object,* New York: Columbia University Press.

Fabian, J. (2000), *Out of Our Minds: Reason and Madness in the Exploration of Central Africa,* Berkeley: University of California Press.

Fabian, J. (2001), *Anthropology with an Attitude: Critical Essays,* Stanford, CA: Stanford University Press.

Feibel, J. (2000), "Highland Histories: Jacobitism and Second Sight," *Clio,* 30(1): 51–77.

Feld, S. (2004), "Places Sensed, Senses Placed: Toward a Sensuous Epistemology of Environments," in D. Howes (ed.), *Empire of the Senses: The Sensual Culture Reader*, Oxford: Berg, pp. 179–91.

Fisher, J. (ed.) (2006), *Technologies of Intuition*, Toronto: YYZ Books.

Geertz, C. (1983), *Local Knowledge: Further Essays in Interpretive Anthropology*, New York: Basic Books.

Gershon, M. D. (1998), *The Second Brain: The Scientific Basis of Gut Instinct*, New York: HarperCollins Publishers.

Geurts, K. L. (2003), *Culture and the Senses: Bodily Ways of Knowing in an African Community*, Berkeley: University of California Press.

Geurts, K. L. (2004), "Consciousness as 'Feeling in the Body': A West African Theory of Embodiment, Emotion, and the Making of Mind," in D. Howes (ed.), *Empire of the Senses*, Oxford: Berg, pp. 164–78.

Gibson, J. J. (1966), *The Senses Considered as Perceptual Systems*, Boston, MA: Houghton-Mifflin.

Glenn, H. P. (2005), *Legal Traditions of the World*, Oxford: Oxford University Press.

Goldman, J. (2008), *The X-Files™ Book of The Unexplained*, vols. I and II, New York: HarperCollins.

Goldstein, E. B. (2002), *Sensation and Perception*, Pacific Grove, CA: Wadsworth.

Gould, S. J. (1985), "The Rule of Five," in *The Flamingo's Smile: Reflections in Natural History*, New York: W.W. Norton, pp. 199–211.

Goulet, J.-G. and Miller, B. G. (eds) (2006), *Extraordinary Anthropology: Transformations in the Field*, Lincoln: University of Nebraska Press.

Griffin, D. R. (1997), *Parapsychology, Philosophy, and Spirituality: A Postmodern Exploration*, Albany, NY: State University of New York Press.

Hahn, T. (2007), *Sensational Knowledge: Embodying Culture through Japanese Dance*, Middletown, CT: Wesleyan University Press.

Heller-Roazen, D. (2007), *The Inner Touch: Archaeology of a Sensation*, Cambridge, MA: Zone Books.

Heller-Roazen, D. (2008), "Common Sense: Greek, Arabic, Latin," in G. Nichols, A. Kablitz and A. Calhoun (eds), *Rethinking the Medieval Senses: Heritage, Fascinations, Frames*, Baltimore, MD: Johns Hopkins University Press, pp. 30–50.

Hess, D. J. (1993), *Science in the New Age: The Paranormal, Its Defenders and Debunkers, in American Culture*, Madison, WI: University of Wisconsin Press.

Hoffer, P. (2003), *Sensory Worlds in Early America*, Baltimore: Johns Hopkins University Press.

Hollingham, R. (2004), "In the Realm of Your Senses," *New Scientist* (31 January), 181 (no. 2432): 40–43.

Howes, D. (1990), "Les techniques des sens," *Anthropologie et Sociétés*, 14(2): 99–115.

Howes, D. (ed.) (1991), *The Varieties of Sensory Experience: A Sourcebook in the Anthropology of the Senses*, Toronto: University of Toronto Press.

Howes, D. (2003), *Sensual Relations: Engaging the Senses in Culture and Social Theory,* Ann Arbor: University of Michigan Press.

Howes, D. (ed.) (2004), *Empire of the Senses: The Sensual Culture Reader,* Oxford: Berg.

Howes, D. (2006a), "Charting the Sensorial Revolution," *The Senses and Society,* 1(1): 113–28.

Howes, D. (2006b), "Cross-Talk between the Senses," *The Senses and Society,* 1(3): 381–90.

Howes, D. (2008), "Can These Dry Bones Live? An Anthropological Approach to the History of the Senses," *Journal of American History,* 95(2): 119–28.

Howes, D. and Lalonde, M. (1991), "The History of Sensibilities: Of the Standard of Taste in Mid-Eighteenth Century England and the Circulation of Smells in Post-Revolutionary France," *Dialectical Anthropology,* 16: 125–35.

Hsu, E. (2000), "Towards a Science of Touch, Part 1," *Anthropology and Medicine,* 7(2): 251–68.

Hsu, E. (2005), "Tactility and the Body in Early Chinese Medicine," *Science in Context,* 18(1): 7–34.

Hudson, W. H. (1923), *A Hind in Richmond Park,* London: J. M. Dent and Sons, Ltd.

Hughes, H. C. (2001), *Sensory Exotica: A World beyond Human Experience,* Cambridge, MA: The MIT Press.

Illich, I. (2000), *H_2O and the Waters of Forgetfulness,* London: Marion Boyars Publishers.

Jay, M. (2006), *Songs of Experience: Modern American and European Variations on a Universal Theme,* Berkeley: University of California Press.

Jones, C. A. (2006), "The Mediated Sensorium," in C. A. Jones (ed.), *Sensorium: Embodied Experience, Technology, and Contemporary Art,* Cambridge, MA: The MIT List Visual Arts Center and The MIT Press, pp. 5–49.

Jutte, R. (2005), *A History of the Senses: From Antiquity to Cyberspace,* trans. J. Lynn, Cambridge: Polity Press.

Kagan, N. Daniels, P. and Horan, A. (eds) (1987), *Psychic Powers,* Alexandria, VA: Time-Life Books.

Kearney, R. (1988), *The Wake of Imagination: Toward A Postmodern Culture,* Minneapolis: University of Minnesota Press.

Keeley, B. (2002), "Making Sense of the Senses: Individuating Modalities in Humans and Other Animals," *Journal of Philosophy,* 99(1): 5–28.

Keifenheim, B. (1999), "Concepts of Perception, Visual Practice, and Pattern Art among the Cashinahua Indians (Peruvian Amazon Area)," *Visual Anthropology,* 12: 27–48.

Kemp, S. (1990), *Medieval Psychology,* New York: Greenwood Press.

Kensinger, K. (1995), *How Real People Ought to Live: The Cashinahua of Eastern Peru,* Prospect Heights, IL: Waveland Press.

Khare, R. S. (2005), "Food with Saints," in C. Korsmeyer (ed.), *The Taste Culture Reader: Experiencing Food and Drink,* Oxford: Berg, pp. 156–65.

Kirmayer, L. J. (in press), "On the Cultural Mediation of Pain," in S. Coakley and K. Shelemay (eds), *Pain and Its Transformations,* Cambridge, MA: Harvard University Press.

Kivy, P. (2003), *The Seventh Sense: Francis Hutcheson and Eighteenth-Century British Aesthetics,* Oxford: Clarendon Press.

Klima, A. (2002), *The Funeral Casino: Meditation, Massacre, and Exchange with the Dead in Thailand,* Princeton, NJ: Princeton University Press.

Korsmeyer, C. (ed.) (2005), *The Taste Culture Reader: Experiencing Food and Drink,* Oxford: Berg.

Laughlin, C. (1994), "Psychic Energy and Transpersonal Experience: A Biogenetic Structural Account of the Tibetan Dumo Yoga Practice," in D. E. Young and J.-G. Goulet (eds), *Being Changed by Cross-Cultural Encounters: The Anthropology of Extraordinary Experience,* Peterborough, ON: Broadview Press, pp. 99–134.

Lévi-Strauss, C. (1969), *The Raw and the Cooked: Introduction to a Science of Mythology,* vol. 1, trans. J. Weightman and D. Weightman, New York: Harper and Row.

Lévi-Strauss, C. (1987), *Introduction to Marcel Mauss,* London: Routledge.

Levin, D. M. (1997), "Introduction," in D. M. Levin (ed.), *Sites of Vision: The Discursive Construction of Sight in the History of Philosophy,* Cambridge, MA: The MIT Press, pp. 1–67.

Levy, J. (2002), *K.I.S.S. Guide to the Unexplained,* New York: DK Publishing, Inc.

Lindstrom, M. (2005), *BRAND Sense: Build Powerful Brands through Touch, Taste, Smell, Sight and Sound,* New York: Free Press.

Locke, J. (1975), *An Essay Concerning Human Understanding,* Oxford: Clarendon Press.

Lull, R. (nd), *Ars brevis de inventione iuris* (Art for the Quick Discovery of Law), trans. Y. Dambergs, http://lullianarts.net/infusa/5powers.htm (accessed 15 January 2009).

Mabrey, V. (2002), "A Sixth Sense," *CBSnews.com* (15 August), http://www.cbsnews.com/stories/2002/01/08/60II/main323596.shtml (accessed 15 January 2009).

Malnar, J. and Vodvarka, F. (2004), *Sensory Design,* Minneapolis: University of Minnesota Press.

Marx, K. (1987), *Economic and Philosophic Manuscripts of 1844,* trans. M. Milligan, Buffalo, NY: Prometheus Books.

Mason, D. (2006), "*Rasa,* 'Rasaesthetics' and Dramatic Theory as Performance Packaging," *Theatre Research International,* 31(1): 69–83.

Mason, M. M. (1989), "The Cultivation of the Senses for Creative Nostalgia in the Essays of W.H. Hudson," *Ariel,* 20(1): 23–37.

Mauss, M. (2007), "Techniques of the Body," in M. Lock and J. Farquhar (eds), *Beyond the Body Proper,* Durham, NC: Duke University Press, pp. 50–68.

Mazzio, C. (2004), "The Senses Divided: Organs, Objects and Media in Early Modern England," in D. Howes (ed.), *Empire of the Senses,* Oxford: Berg, pp. 85–105.

McCosh, J. (1875), *The Scottish Philosophy: Biographical, Expository, Critical, from Hutcheson to Hamilton,* London.

McLuhan, M. (1964), *Understanding Media: The Extensions of Man,* New York: Signet Books.

Misra, N. (2005), "Sixth Sense? Primitive Tribes Fled Beaches Long before Tsunami Struck," *Signs* (January 5), http://www.nativeamericanchurch.com/Signs/Sixth SenseTsunami.html (accessed 15 January 2009).

Moore, J. (2004), "Francis Hutcheson (1694–1746)," in *Oxford Dictionary of National Biography,* Oxford: Oxford University Press.

Mott, M. (2005), "Did Animals Sense Tsunami Was Coming?" *National Geographic News* (January 4), http://news.nationalgeographic.com/news/2005/01/ 0104_050104_tsunami_animals_2.html (accessed 15 January 2009).

Needham, R. (1975), "Polythetic Classification: Convergence and Consequences," *Man* (new series), 10: 349–69.

Norton, Q. (2006), "A Sixth Sense for a Wired World," *Wired* (7 June), http://www. wired.com/gadgets/mods/news/2006/06/71087 (accessed 15 January 2009).

O'Connell, C. (2007), *The Elephant's Secret Sense,* Chicago: University of Chicago Press.

Ong, W. J. (1982), *Orality and Literacy: The Technologizing of the Word,* London: Methuen.

Ostrander, S. and Schroeder, L. (1970), *Psychic Discoveries behind the Iron Curtain,* Englewood Cliffs, NJ: Prentice-Hall.

Pandya, V. (1993), *Above the Forest: A Study of Andamanese Ethnoanemology, Cosmology, and the Power of Ritual,* Delhi: Oxford University Press.

Pandya, V. (2005), "'When Land Became Water': Tsunami and the Ongees of Little Andaman Island," *American Anthropological Association Newsletter* (March), http://www.aaanet.org/press/an/0503pandya.htm (accessed 15 January 2009).

Pearson, T. (2003), *All about the Sixth Sense: Exploring the Extrasensory World,* Hod Hasharon, Israel: Astrolog Publishing House.

Phillips, H. (2005), "The Feeling of Colour," *New Scientist* (29 January), 185 (no. 2484): 40–3.

Pinard, S. (1991), "A Taste of India: On the Role of Gustation in the Hindu Sensorium," in D. Howes (ed.), *The Varieties of Sensory Experience,* Toronto: University of Toronto Press.

Ramachandran, V. S., Hubbard, E. M. and Butcher, P. A. (2004), "Synesthsia, Cross-Activation, and the Foundations of Neuroepistemology," in G. Calvert, C. Spence and B. E. Stein (eds), *The Handbook of Multisensory Processes,* Cambridge, MA: The MIT Press, pp. 867–83.

Rensink, R. (2000), "Seeing, Sensing, and Scrutinizing," *Vision Research,* 40(1): 1469–87.

Rensink, R. (2004), "Visual Sensing without Seeing," *Psychological Science,* 15(1): 27–32.

Riskin, J. (2002), *Science in the Age of Sensibility: The Sentimental Empiricists of the French Enlightenment,* Chicago: University of Chicago Press.

Ritchie, I. (1991), "Fusion of the Faculties: A Study of the Language of the Senses in Hausaland," in D. Howes (ed.), *The Varieties of Sensory Experience,* Toronto: University of Toronto Press, pp. 192–202.

Rivlin, R. and Gravelle, K. (1984), *Deciphering the Senses: The Expanding World of Human Perception,* New York: Simon & Schuster.

Roberts, K. (2005), *Lovemarks: The Future beyond Brands,* New York: PowerHouse Books.

Room, A. (1999), *Brewer's Dictionary of Phrase and Fable,* 16th edn, New York: HarperCollins.

Rudy, G. (2002), *Mystical Language of Sensation in the Later Middle Ages,* London: Routledge.

Ryan, E. J. (1951), *The Role of the "Sensus Communis" in the Psychology of St. Thomas Aquinas,* Carthagena, OH: The Messenger Press.

Sacks, O. (2004), "The Mind's Eye: What the Blind See," in D. Howes (ed.), *Empire of the Senses,* Oxford: Berg, pp. 25–42.

Said, E. (1983), "The Music Itself: Glenn Gould's Contrapuntal Vision," in J. McGreevy (ed.), *Glenn Gould Variations,* Toronto: Macmillan, pp. 45–56.

Saussure, F. de (1959), *Course in General Linguistics,* trans. W. Baskin, New York: McGraw-Hill.

Schechner, R. (2001), "Rasaesthetics," *The Drama Review,* 45(3): 27–50.

Scheper-Hughes, N. and Lock, M. (1987), "The Mindful Body: A Prolegomenon to Future Work in Medical Anthropology," *Medical Anthropology Quarterly* (new series), 1: 6–41.

Schoch, R. M. and Yonavjak, L. (eds) (2008), *The Parapsychology Revolution: A Concise Anthology of Paranormal and Psychical Research,* New York: Penguin.

Sheldrake, R. (2003), *The Sense of Being Stared At and Other Aspects of the Extended Mind,* New York and London: Random House.

Smith, M. M. (2007), *Sensing the Past: Seeing, Hearing, Smelling, Touching, and Tasting in History,* Berkeley: University of California Press.

Stevenson, R. J. and Boakes, R. (2004), "Sweet and Sour Smells: Learned Synesthesia between the Senses of Taste and Smell," in G. Calvert, C. Spence and B. E. Stein (eds), *The Handbook of Multisensory Processes,* Cambridge, MA: The MIT Press, pp. 69–84.

Stoller, P. (1989), *The Taste of Ethnographic Things: The Senses in Anthropology,* Philadelphia: University of Pennsylvania Press.

Stoller, P. (1997), *Sensuous Scholarship,* Philadelphia: University of Pennsylvania Press.

Stoller, P. and Olkes, C. (1987), *In Sorcery's Shadow: A Memoir of Apprenticeship among the Songhay of Niger,* Chicago: University of Chicago Press.

Straight, B. (2007), *Miracles and Extraordinary Experience in Northern Kenya,* Philadelphia: University of Pennsylvania Press.

Synnott, A. (1991), "Puzzling over the Senses: From Plato to Marx," in D. Howes (ed.), *The Varieties of Sensory Experience,* Toronto: University of Toronto Press, pp. 61–76.

Tallis, F. (2002), *Hidden Minds: A History of the Unconscious,* New York: Arcade Publishing.

Targ, E., Schlitz, M. and Irwin, H. J. (2000), "Psi-Related Experiences," in E. Cardeña, S. J. Lynn and S. Krippner (eds), *Varieties of Anomalous Experience: Examining the Scientific Evidence,* Washington, DC: American Psychological Association, pp. 219–52.

Taussig, M. (1993), *Mimesis and Alterity: A Particular History of the Senses,* New York: Routledge.

Tedlock, B. (ed.) (1987), *Dreaming: Anthropological and Psychological Interpretations,* Cambridge: Cambridge University Press.

Tedlock, B. (1991), "The New Anthropology of Dreaming," *Dreaming,* 1(2): 161–78.

Tomkis, T. (1607), *Lingua, or the Combat of the Tongue and the Five Senses for Superiority.*

Truss, L. (2003), *Eats, Shoots & Leaves: The Zero Tolerance Approach to Punctuation!* New York: Gotham Books/Penguin.

Turner, E. (1994), "A Visible Spirit Form in Zambia," in D. E. Young and J.-G. Goulet (eds), *Being Changed by Cross-Cultural Encounters: The Anthropology of Extraordinary Experience,* Peterborough, ON: Broadview Press, pp. 71–95.

Turner, E. (1996), *The Hands Feel It: Healing and Spirit Presence among a Northern Alaska People,* De Kalb: Northern Illinois University Press.

Uexküll, J. von (1982), "The Theory of Meaning," *Semiotica,* 42(1): 25–82.

Varela, F. J., Thompson, E. and Rosch, E. (1992), *The Embodied Mind: Cognitive Science and Human Experience,* Cambridge, MA: The MIT Press.

Vila, A. (1998), *Enlightenment and Pathology: Sensibility in the Literature and Medicine of Eighteenth-Century France,* Baltimore, MD: Johns Hopkins University Press.

Vinge, L. (1975), *The Five Senses: Studies in a Literary Tradition,* Lund: The Royal Society of the Humanities at Lund.

Watson, L. (1999), *Jacobson's Organ and the Remarkable Nature of Smell,* London: Penguin.

Wilson, F. R. (1998), *The Hand: How Its Use Shapes the Brain, Language, and Human Culture,* New York: Vintage.

Witherspoon, G. (1977), *Language and Art in the Navajo Universe,* Ann Arbor, MI: University of Michigan Press.

Woolgar, C. M. (2006), *The Senses in Late Medieval England,* New Haven, CT: Yale University Press.

Young, D. E. and Goulet, J.-G. (eds) (1994), *Being Changed by Cross-Cultural Encounters: The Anthropology of Extraordinary Experience,* Peterborough, ON: Broadview Press.

Znamenski, A. A. (2007), *The Beauty of the Primitive: Shamanism and the Western Imagination,* Oxford: Oxford University Press.

Part I
Bearings

The Search for a Sixth Sense
The Cases for Vestibular, Muscle, and Temperature Senses
Nicholas J. Wade

There is no sixth sense in addition to the five enumerated—sight, hearing, smell, taste, touch.

(Aristotle [Ross 1931: 424b])

The essential attribute of a new sense is, not the perception of external objects or influences which ordinarily do not act upon the senses, but that external causes should excite in it a new and peculiar kind of sensation different from all the sensations of our five senses.

(Müller [1843] 2003: 1087)

Introduction

The origins of neuroscience stretch back to antiquity, but particularly large strides were made in the nineteenth century (see Finger 1994). The gross anatomy of the brain was clarified, and its microanatomy was subjected to achromatic scrutiny; the cell and neuron doctrines were advanced; function was related to structure, initially fancifully (and phrenologically) and later with surgical precision; and a wide range of cognitive dysfunctions were linked with abnormalities in brain structures. Neuroscience emerged from the biological sciences because conceptual building blocks were isolated and the ways in which they can be arranged were explored. The two foundations on which the structure could be securely built were the cell and neuron doctrines. Many of those whose concepts built these blocks, like Bell, Purkinje, and Müller, also studied the senses.

The senses have always been at the heart of the neurosciences. Indeed, for Aristotle (ca. 384–322 B.C.), sensation was housed in the heart. At the beginning of the nineteenth century, with the growing knowledge of nerve function, the relation of the senses to the brain was explored in greater detail, and one question was repeatedly addressed: how many senses are there? The five senses of sight, hearing, smell, taste, and touch are rooted in our culture. No matter what neuroscience might divine, they are so defined in the popular imagination. The prominence of eyes, ears, nose, and tongue on the head, and the specific experiences associated with them, have acted in the past, as well as in the present, to fix these four senses. Touch presents more problems because its sensitivity is not localized to a particular sense organ, and the experiences derived from the skin are many and varied. Aristotle confronted these aspects of anatomy and experience and reached similar conclusions:

> In dealing with each of the senses we shall have first to speak of the objects which are perceptible by each ... I call by the name of special object of this or that sense that which cannot be perceived by any other sense than that one and in respect of which no error is possible; in this sense colour is the special object of sight, sound of hearing, flavour of taste. Touch, indeed, discriminates more than one set of different qualities. Each sense has one kind of object which it discerns, and never errs in reporting that what is before it is colour or sound (though it may err as to what it is that is coloured or where that is, or what is sounding or where that is). Such objects are what we propose to call special objects of this or that sense. "Common sensibles" are movement, rest, number, figure, magnitude; these are not peculiar to any one sense, but are common to all. (Ross 1931: 418b)

Later in *De anima* Aristotle distinguished between experience and organ:

> By a "sense" is meant what has the power of receiving into itself the sensible forms of things without the matter ... By "an organ of sense" is meant that in which ultimately such a power is seated. (Ross 1931: 424a)

This, again, provided problems for the experience of touch, because there was no specific organ associated with it. Once more, the issue was voiced by Aristotle:

> If touch is not a single sense but a group of senses, there must be several kinds of what is tangible. It is a problem whether touch is a single sense or a group of senses. It is also a problem, what is the organ of touch. (Ross 1931: 422b)

Touch, requiring contact in order to experience it, was often taken as the most important sense, and the one relative to which others could be related: "The primary form of sense is touch, which belongs to all animals" (Ross 1931: 413b). It is perhaps for this reason that Aristotle maintained that touch is a single sense, that the number of senses is restricted to five, and that: "there cannot be a special sense-organ for the common sensibles either" (Ross 1931: 425a). Boring's conclusion about this dogma was clear: "It was certainly Aristotle who so long delayed the recognition of a sixth sense by his doctrine that there are but five senses" (1942: 525). For Boring, as for most other historians of the senses, the additional one that emerged in the early nineteenth century was the muscle sense.

The analysis of experiences deriving from stimulation of the senses has often been placed in a philosophical context. However, the anatomy of the senses and the phenomena associated with them has guided the ways in which they can be classified. In what follows, the anatomical and phenomenological aspects of the senses will be emphasized. It will be argued that the separation of a muscle sense from touch was given empirical support in the late eighteenth century, as was the evidence for a movement or vestibular sense. The multiple dimensions of touch (like temperature and pressure) were voiced on phenomenological grounds in the same century, but received experimental support in the eighteenth and nineteenth centuries first from behavioral and galvanic studies, then later from anatomy.

Classical Considerations of the Senses

Aristotle's survey of the senses was more extensive than those of his predecessors (see Beare 1906). Most of the knowledge we have of the earlier Greek commentators derives from the writing of his pupil, Theophrastus (ca. 370–286 B.C.). Without his work "On the Senses" our understanding of early theories of the senses would be even more meager. Theophrastus categorized writers on the senses into two groups: those who considered that the senses were stimulated by similarities or by opposites. Thus, taste and touch could be treated as similar, since both involve contact. The means of sensing by sight, hearing, smell, and taste was speculated upon by most writers, but less was said about touch. For example, with regard to Alcmaeon (fl. 500 B.C.), Theophrastus wrote: "All the senses are connected in some way with the brain; consequently they are incapable of action if [the brain] is disturbed or shifts its position, for [this organ] stops up the passages through which the senses act. Of touch he tells us neither the manner nor the means of its operation" (Stratton 1917: 89–91).

Alcmaeon located the center of sensation in the brain, although Aristotle did not adopt this view, referring the processes of perception to the heart (see Beare 1906). In the context of touch, Anaxagoras (ca. 500–438 B.C.) discussed sensing warmth and cold, and Democritus (ca. 460–370 B.C.) contrasted heavy with light, and hard with soft. Plato (427–347 B.C.) wrote that touch distinguished between hot and cold, hard and soft, heavy and light, as well as rough and smooth. Theophrastus himself said relatively little about touch. His theory of the senses in general involved some intermediary between the object and the sense organ; for vision, hearing, and smell this could be more readily maintained than for touch.

Theophrastus did, however, discuss vertigo or dizziness (as when looking down from a great height) and the visual motion that accompanies it. According to the Roman commentator, Diogenes Laertius (fl. 3rd C), Theophrastus wrote a book on vertigo but it has not survived. Aristotle referred to the visual vertigo that follows drinking too much wine, and later Lucretius (ca. 98–55 B.C.) gave a graphic description of vertigo following rotation of the body: "The room seems to children to be turning round and the columns revolving when they themselves have ceased to turn, so much so that they can hardly believe all the building is not threatening to fall in upon them" (Lucretius 1975: 307–9). Ptolemy (ca. 85–165) was able to induce vertigo by visual means alone (see Smith 1996).

The approach by Galen (ca. 130–200) to the senses displayed the advantages of anatomical dissection. He berated Aristotle for denying that all the senses do not have connections with the brain: "Hence all the instruments of the senses—if we are to believe our eyes that see and our hands that touch them—communicate with the encephalon" (May 1968: 391). Galen's theory of the senses was physiological, and it was based on the concept of pneuma advocated by Empedocles (ca. 493–433 B.C.): "Unless the alteration in each sense instrument comes from the encephalon and returns to it, the animal will still remain without sense perception" (May 1968: 403). Galen restricted his discussion to the "four sense instruments in the head, namely, the eyes, ears, nose, and tongue, all of which take the source of their sensation from the encephalon" (May 1968: 400). He did refer to vertigo caused by observing whirling patterns as well as by body rotation. These were described in the context of diseases which lead to dizziness:

> All these affections start obviously in the head and especially the affection which is called *skotoma* (vertigo), the name of which indicates its nature. People who are subject to this ailment are affected by *skotoma* of their vision on account of the smallest causes, so that they often fall, especially when they turn round. Then, what happens to other people only after having turned round a great many times, that will overcome these people after one single turn. They can even be affected by vertigo, when they see another person or a wheel turning or anything else which whirls, even when their head had been overheated for any other reason. ... There is general agreement upon the fact that such frequent turning movements provoke an unequal, tumultuous and disorderly flow of humors and pneuma. Therefore it is only natural that people subject to skotoma are on guard against any motion of this kind. (Siegel 1970: 138)

Galen was probably describing a disorder that is now called Ménière's disease, after it was linked to disease of the vestibular system by Prosper Ménière (1799–1867) (Ménière 1861).

The situation remained relatively unchanged through the medieval period: "Aristotle's account of sensation and perception was held in great esteem in the Middle Ages, and his systematic approach and many of his specific doctrines were widely copied" (Kemp 1990: 35). Attention was directed principally at interpretations of vision, with much less heed paid to the other senses. Developments did occur in fusing Aristotle's account of the senses with Galen's pneumatic physiology, and the medical tradition of describing diseases of the senses became more refined. Conditions like visual vertigo were related to the movements of the animal spirit in the head. For example, Paulus Ægineta (fl. 680) noted that:

> Vertigo is occasioned by a cold and viscid humour seizing upon the brain, whence the patients are ready to fall down from a very slight cause, such as sometimes from looking

at any external object which turns round, as a wheel or top, or when they themselves are whirled round, or when their head has been heated, by which means the humours or spirit in it are set in motion. (Ægineta 1844: 374)

Generating visual vertigo, even in healthy individuals, by rotating the body and then stopping, was a source of regular reflection by medieval medical and optical writers (see Wade 2000a).

Vertigo accompanies many diseases and has been described frequently over the centuries in medical texts. It will be argued that the experimental study of vertigo in the eighteenth century heralded the appreciation of a sixth sense before experimental evidence for a muscle sense or the fractionation of touch was available.

Criteria for Classifying the Senses

The sources of evidence available to Aristotle (and to those who followed him over the next two thousand years) for distinguishing between the senses were phenomenology and gross anatomy. They could report on their experiences when stimulated, and they could relate them to their body parts. For example, sight ceased when the eyes were closed. Additional inferences could be drawn from disease or injury. Blindness and deafness would have been commonplace. Recourse was made to philosophy, usually linking the senses to the elements—fire, earth, water, and air—which permeated perception (see Beare 1906). The classical accounts of the senses drew principally upon psychological (or behavioral) evidence for their independence. In contrast, developments in the last few centuries have relied increasingly on anatomical and physiological indications of separate senses, and the behavioral dimension has been given less prominence.

While emphasizing the veridicality of sensing in general, Aristotle did entertain the possibility of errors (illusions) entering into a particular sense. The examples he mentioned in the first quotation in the Introduction were those of color or sound confusion and errors in spatial localization of colors or sounds. Illusions are often considered to be a modern preoccupation, based on specific theories of perception, but their origins are ancient and illusions can be investigated with little in the way of theory (see Wade 1990, 1998). If there is an assumption of object permanence, then an illusion occurs when the same object appears to have different properties (of color, position, size, shape, motion, etc.) under different circumstances. Aristotle's description of the motion aftereffect (in *De somniis*) was presumably considered worthy of note because the stones at the side of the river appeared stationary prior to peering at the flowing water but not afterward (see Wade and Verstraten 1998). Thus, the existence of an illusion might provide evidence of a sensory system. For example, we normally feel stable and still when we stand upright; however, an illusion of body motion can occur when we are standing upright—if we have previously rotated the body rapidly.

The situation regarding the senses was radically revised in the nineteenth century, with developments in physics, anatomy, and physiology. Sources of stimulation could be specified and controlled more precisely. This had already occurred in the context of color, with Isaac Newton's (1642–1727) methods of spectral separation of white light and mixing components of it (Newton 1704). Thomas Young (1773–1829) applied the method and found that all colors could be produced by appropriately compounding three primaries; he suggested that the eye was selectively sensitive to each (Young 1802). Young ([1807] 2002) also introduced the term *energy* in the context of weight, and this concept was related by others to different dimensions of sensitivity, like light and sound.

The link between energy and sense organs was forged soon thereafter. Charles Bell (1774–1842) is noted for discovering that the anterior spinal nerve roots carry motor nerves (see Cranefield 1974). His principal concern, however, was in specifying the senses and their nerve pathways to the brain. His experiments were described in a privately published pamphlet which also related stimulation to specific senses:

> In this inquiry it is most essential to observe, that while each organ of sense is provided with a capacity for receiving certain changes to be played upon it, as it were, yet each is utterly incapable of receiving the impression destined for another organ of sensation. It is also very remarkable that an impression made on two different nerves of sense, though with the same instrument, will produce two distinct sensations; and the ideas resulting will only have relation to the organ affected. (Bell [1811] 2000: 8–9).

In the context of vision, the demonstration of this fact had been known to Alcmaeon: pressure to the eye, even in darkness, produced the experience of light (see Grüsser and Hagner 1990). Bell was able to bolster this observation with the application of electricity to the eye:

> If light, pressure, galvanism, or electricity produce vision, we must conclude that the idea in the mind is the result of an action excited in the eye or in the brain, not any thing received, though caused by an impression from without. The operations of the mind are confined not by the limited nature of things created, but by the limited number of our organs of sense. ([1811] 2000: 12)

A similar sentiment, voiced with primary reference to the nerves and their pathways, was written a few decades earlier by John Hunter (1728–1793):

> For it is more than probable, that what may be called organs of sense, have particular nerves, whose mode of action is different from that of nerves producing common sensation; and also different from one another; and that the nerves on which the particular functions of each of the organs of sense depend, are not supplied from different parts of the brain ... it is more probable, that every nerve so affected as to communicate sensation, in whatever part of the nerve the impression is made, always gives the same

sensation as if affected at the common seat of the sensation of that particular nerve. (1786: 215–16)

Examples Hunter gave to support this contention were referred sensations arising after damage or amputation (of the penis). The seeds of this idea can be found in antiquity, although it was based on philosophical rather than physiological speculation. The doctrine of specific nerve energies, as it became called, was given further support by Johannes Müller (1801–1858), in a monograph on comparative physiology and on eye movements (Müller 1826) and it was amplified in his influential handbook of human physiology (Müller 1838, 1843, 2003). Although the doctrine was framed in terms of differences between the senses, it was used increasingly to determine qualitative distinctions within them (see Finger and Wade 2002).

Anatomy

Cells were described soon after the first microscopes were focused on animal matter. Robert Hooke (1635–1703) gave them their name and identified plant cells (Hooke 1665). A variety of animal cells, including nerve fibers, was described by Antonius van Leeuwenhoek (1632–1723) (van Leeuwenhoek 1675). The microscopic world remained rather blurred throughout the eighteenth century, due to the simple optical magnifiers employed. It was transformed by the introduction of powerful achromatic instruments in the 1830s, and rapid advances were made thereafter. Cell doctrine was most clearly articulated at the end of that decade by Theodor Schwann (1810–1882) (Schwann 1839). In 1832 Jan Evangelista Purkinje (1787–1869) obtained a powerful achromatic microscope and, together with his students, examined a wide range of structures (see Wade and Brožek 2001). The cerebellum was one of the structures he examined. Purkinje described the microscopic characteristics of the large cells in the "yellow" (white) matter to a meeting of natural scientists held at Prague in 1837: they are now called Purkinje cells.

Among the other cells that were isolated and described were specialized cells, called receptors; they could be related to the stimuli that excited them. Those located in well-defined sense organs were named on the basis of their morphology (rods, cones, hair cells, etc.), whereas the receptors in or beneath the skin were generally named after those who first described them (e.g., Golgi tendon organs, Krause end bulbs, Meissner corpuscles, Merkel discs, Pacinian corpuscles, and Ruffini cylinders). The isolation of receptors that were specialized to respond to specific forms of environmental energy was adopted as a criterion for defining the senses (Neff 1960).

Bell tried to stimulate his medical colleagues to abandon the notion "that the whole brain is a common sensorium" and to encourage isolation of nerve pathways:

It is not more presumptuous to follow the tracts of nervous matter in the brain, and to attempt to discover the course of sensation, than it is to trace the rays of light through the humours of the eye, and to say, that the retina is the seat of vision. Why are we to close the investigation with the discovery of the external organ? ... That the external organs of the senses have the matter of the nerves adapted to receive certain impressions, while the corresponding organs of the brain are put to activity by the external excitement: That the idea or perception is according to the part of the brain to which the nerve is attached, and that each organ has a certain limited number of changes to be wrought upon it by the external impression: That the nerves of sense, the nerves of motion, and the vital nerves, are distinct through their whole course, though they seem sometimes united in one bundle; and that they depend for their attributes on the organs of the brain to which they are attached. ([1811] 2000: 3 and 5–6)

The pathways from the receptors to more central sites, and to areas of the brain, took rather longer to trace. Even in the case of vision, where the optic nerve, chiasm, and tract had been described by Galen, the precise paths pursued remained hotly debated until the late nineteenth century. Cortical representation is now taken as one of the criteria for specifying a sensory system (Neff 1960).

Physiology

The manner in which the nerves themselves worked was hinted at by Luigi Galvani (1737–1798) when he made a case for "animal electricity" (Galvani 1791). He applied a discharge from a Leyden jar to the exposed crural nerve or muscle of an isolated frog's leg and it twitched. Galvani suggested that this was due to a special type of electrical fluid that accumulates in the muscles of animals (see Bresadola 1998; Piccolino 1997). Alessandro Volta (1745–1827) maintained that animal tissue was not necessary for a current to pass, and that Galvani's experiments were flawed. Volta had interests in the effects of electrical discharges on the senses; he carried out studies of galvanic light figures in the 1790s, and also found that intermittent stimulation produced longer lasting effects than constant stimulation. In his letter describing the pile or battery, Volta (1800) described how he applied electrical stimulation to the eyes, ears, nose, and tongue. He connected the wires from a battery between the mouth and conjunctiva of the eye, which resulted in the experience of light, even in a dark room. Moreover, he noted that the visual sensation was associated with the onset and offset of the current, and a continuous impression of light could be produced by rapid alternation of polarity (see Piccolino 2000). When he applied a current to the two ears he reported: "At the moment the circuit was completed I felt a shaking in the head" (Volta 1800: 427). This shaking did not last long; when the current was continued he experienced sound and then noise. The sensations were so disagreeable that he thought them potentially dangerous, and he did not wish to repeat them.

A few years earlier, Volta had applied a current to his tongue and noted an acidic taste (Piccolino 1997). Volta's pile did much to hasten experimental studies of the senses. Electricity was a common stimulus that could be applied to different sensory organs, inducing different sensations. Johannes Müller used the effects to support his doctrine: "The stimulus of electricity may serve as a second example, of a uniform cause giving rise in different nerves of sense to different sensations" ([1843] 2003: 1063). The first example was mechanical stimulation.

The action of nerves on muscles led first Carlo Matteucci (1811–1862) and later Emil du Bois Reymond (1818–1896) to propose the ways in which nerves propagate impulses (Brazier 1959, 1988). Experimental evidence of action potentials was to await technological advances in recording and amplifying small electrical signals; this was provided by Adrian (1928) who was able to record action potentials (Finger 2000). When recordings of nerve impulses could be made from individual cells in the visual pathway their adequate stimuli could be determined. Adrian coined the term *receptive field* to refer to this, and it was applied to other senses, too.

Thus, the criteria that have been applied to separating the senses are the quality of the experience, the nature of the stimulus, the gross and microanatomy of the receptor system, and the pathways to and representation on the cortex. The psychological dimension is the oldest of these, and yet less attention has been paid to behavioral evidence for distinguishing and adding to the senses than to that derived from anatomy and physiology. It is in this context that a claim can be made that the systematic consequences of vestibular stimulation preceded those for the muscle and skin senses.

Muscle Sense

Boring (1942) credited Bell with establishing the concept of the muscle sense, although Bell's claim had been rejected by William Hamilton (1788–1856) in his brief but scholarly history of the muscular sense (Hamilton 1846). The term *Muskelsinn* had been used by German writers in the eighteenth century, and it was suggested that the idea was described even earlier. For example, Julius Cæsar Scaliger (1484–1558) distinguished between active and passive dimensions of touch:

> And indeed this seems to be the case, for heaviness and lightness are perceived by touching, and everybody thinks that they recognise heaviness and lightness by handling. However, I am not convinced. I accept that motion is perceived by touch, but I deny that heaviness is. The most powerful argument is as follows. Heaviness is the object of motive power, which certainly consists in *action*. But touch only occurs by being *acted upon*. Therefore heaviness is perceived by a motive power, not by touch. For since there are two organs (I mean the nerves and the spirits), for sensing and for being moved, which are distinct from each other, it will be a mistake if we confuse the object of a motive force, with the object of a moved force. For touch is moved, and does not act. But a motive force moves a heavy body, but is not moved by it. This is obvious in the case of paralysis: heat is sensed, but the heaviness of the motive force is not sensed, because the

organs have suffered.—But is heaviness *sensed?* It is indeed sensed by the motive force, and judged by it; just as when something difficult is expressed through the power of the intellect itself, this power is active, not passive, when it expresses it. For it is common to all things in our world, which depend on matter, that they cannot act without also being acted upon. An objection could be raised about compression. ... There are two further reasons: because we sometimes sense heaviness even without touch, and because we do not sense by touch. The former is the case when someone's hand is placed on a heavy body, but they do not sense its heaviness. But the motive power senses without touching. A lead weight attached to a string is sensed as heavy, even though the hand does not touch the lead. Then in the latter case, when one's arm drops under its own weight, it is sensed as heavy. But it touches nothing. (Scaliger 1557 quoted in Hamilton 1846: 867)

Appeals to muscular sensitivity have been commonplace in philosophy, particularly among the empiricists. It proved central to the later common sense philosophers, too. For example, Thomas Brown (1778–1820) suggested it was a separate sense, and asked:

To what organ, then, are we to ascribe the external influences, which give occasion to these feelings of resistance and extension? It is not touch, as I conceive, that either of these be traced. Our feeling of resistance, in all its varieties of hardness, softness, roughness, smoothness, solidity, liquidity, &c. I consider as the result of organic affections, not tactual, but muscular; our muscular frame being truly an organ of sense, that is affected in various ways, by various modifications of external resistance to the effort of contraction. (1820: 78–79)

This statement appeared in Brown's book *Philosophy of the Mind,* although there was little philosophy in it. It was the physiological dimension of Bell's paper that led Boring to nominate him as the founder of this new sense. Bell (1826) argued that the anterior spinal nerve roots, which are involved in muscular contraction, also carry sensory signals. Moreover, a nerve circuit was proposed, which passes from the voluntary muscles to the brain. Muscle spindles were not isolated until four decades later (Kühne 1863). In fact, Bell had provided behavioral evidence for the muscular sense three years earlier, in the context of determining the visual direction of afterimages:

There is an inseparable connection between the exercise of the sense of vision and the exercise of the voluntary muscles of the eye. When an object is seen, we enjoy two senses; there is an impression upon the retina; but we receive also the idea of position or relation which it is not the office of the retina to give. It is by the consciousness of the degree of effort put upon the voluntary muscles, that we know the relative position of an object to ourselves. ... If we move the eye by the voluntary muscles, while the impression [of an afterimage] continues on the retina, we shall have the notion of place or relation raised in the mind; but if the motion of the eye-ball be produced by any other cause, by the involuntary muscles, or by pressure from without, we shall have no corresponding change of sensation. (1823: 178 and 179)

That is, the visual direction of an object is not determined by visual stimulation alone, but also involves information about the position of the eyes—otherwise objects would appear to move with every movement of the eyes. Helmholtz (1867) made a distinction between what have become called outflow and inflow theories. The former refers to deriving the eye movement information from efferent (centrally generated) impulses to the eye muscles, whereas the latter reflects use of afferent (sensory) signals from the eye muscles themselves.

It is surprising that Bell did not refer to the earlier experiments by William Charles Wells (1757–1817) on this topic, because Wells's (1792) monograph was referred to by Bell (1803) in the context of vertigo. Wells had performed the same experiment and reached a similar conclusion:

When we have looked steadily for some time at the flame of a candle, or any other luminous body, a coloured spot [afterimage] will appear upon every object, to which we shortly after direct our eyes, accompanying them in all their motions, and exactly covering the point, which we desire to see the most accurately. ... The apparent situation of the spot being ... at the same time affected by the *voluntary* motions of the eye, it must, I think, be necessarily owing to the *action* of the muscles by which these motions are performed ... the apparent direction of an object, which sends its picture to any given point of the retina, depends upon the state of action existing at the same time in the muscles of the eye, and consequently that it cannot be altered, except by a change in the state of that action. (1792: 65 and 70-71)

Bell also followed Wells (again without acknowledgment) in suggesting that the muscle sense is involved in the maintenance of balance: "Let us consider how minute and delicate the sense of muscular motion is by which we balance the body, and by which we judge of the position of the limbs, whether during activity or rest" (Bell 1823: 181). Both Wells (1792) and Bell (1823) provided evidence for a muscle sense based on perceptual experiments, but these were not considered to carry the same weight as Bell's (1826) anatomical dissections and physiological speculations:

The muscles have no connection with each other, they are combined by the nerves; but these nerves, instead of passing betwixt the muscles, interchange their fibres before their distribution to them, and by this means combine the muscles into classes. The question therefore may thus be stated: why are nerves, whose office is to convey sensation, profusely given to muscles in addition to those motor nerves which are given to excite their motions? and why do both classes of muscular nerves form plexus? To solve this question, we must determine whether muscles have any other purpose to serve than merely to contract under the impulse of the motor nerves. ... That we have a sense of the condition of the muscles, appears from this: that we feel the effects of over exertion and weariness, and are excruciated by spasms, and feel the irksomeness of continued position. We possess a power of weighing in the hand:—what is this but estimating the muscular force? We are sensible of the most minute changes of muscular exertion, by which we know the position of the body and limbs, when there is no other means of knowledge open to us. (1826: 166–167)

Bell provided phenomenological support for his physiological hypothesis. In addition, he drew attention to the ability to discriminate between small differences in weight when they are handled. This technique of comparing lifted weights was at the heart of Ernst Heinrich Weber's (1795–1878) psychophysics (see Ross and Murray 1978). In his first monograph devoted to the sense of touch, Weber (1834) distinguished between judging weights by touch alone or by the additional action of the muscle sense:

> The weight of an object is perceived in two ways: first by the touch-sense in the skin, and then by the special sense of the voluntary muscles. The latter sense tells us the degree of tension of the muscle when lifting weights and other objects. These two methods of discovering the weights of objects are very different: the former method depends upon the objective sense of touch, while the latter depends on the subjective sense of muscular kinaesthesis. This assumes, of course, that we call a sense "objective" when we use it to perceive objects that have a certain pressure on our organs and produces some effect; and that we call it "subjective" when we seem to perceive only the effect of the objects and not the objects themselves. (Ross and Murray 1978: 55)

In making this distinction between objective and subjective, Weber is displaying his reliance on the philosophy of Aristotle, rather than contemporary physiology (Ross 1999). Müller's doctrine of specific nerve energies was based on all sensation being subjective, that is, not in perfect accord with the stimulus giving rise to it.

The combination of Bell's tentative hypothesis of a nervous circle, the specific nerve energies doctrine, and psychophysical studies of lifted weights confirmed for many the force of the muscle sense as the sixth sense. By the end of the century, Charles Sherrington (1857–1952) was able to devote a chapter of a textbook to the muscular sense; he defined it as including "all reactions of sense rising in motor organs and their accessories" (1900: 1002). Six years later, he introduced a novel classification of the senses into extero-ceptors, proprio-ceptors, and intero-ceptors:

> The excitation of the receptors of the *proprio-ceptive* field in contradistinction from those of the *extero-ceptive* is related only secondarily to the agencies of the environment. The proprio-ceptive receive their stimulation by some action, *e.g.* a muscular contraction, which was itself a primary reaction to excitation of a surface receptor by the environment. (Sherrington [1906] 2000: 130).

In conclusion, the contention that the muscle sense is the sixth sense was reasonably well supported by phenomenology, physiology, and psychophysics in the nineteenth century.

Temperature Sense

Classical divisions of touch into independent qualities were often repeated up to the nineteenth century, when they were given some experimental support (see Finger 1994). For example, Thomas Reid (1710–1796) noted that: "by touch we perceive not one quality only, but many, and those of different kinds. The chief of them are heat and cold, hardness and softness, roughness and smoothness, figure, solidity, motion, and extension" (1764: 99).

Some experimental support for the distinction between the touch and temperature senses was provided by Erasmus Darwin (1731–1802) on the basis of an observation made by his son, Robert:

> The following is an extract from a letter of Dr. R. W. Darwin, of Shrewsbury, when he was a student at Edinburgh. "I made an experiment yesterday in our hospital, which much favours your opinion, that the sensation of heat and touch depend on different sets of nerves. A man who had lately recovered from a fever, and was still weak, was seized with violent cramps in his legs and feet; which were removed by opiates, except that one of his feet remained insensible. Mr. Ewart pricked him with a pin in five or six places, and the patient declared he did not feel it in the least, nor was he sensible of a very smart pinch. I then held a red-hot poker at some distance, and brought it gradually nearer till it came within three inches, when he asserted that he felt it quite distinctly. I suppose some violent irritation of the nerves of touch had caused the cramps, and had left them paralytic; while the nerves of heat, having suffered no increased stimulus, retained their irritability." ... The organ of touch is properly the sense of pressure, but the muscular fibres themselves constitute the organ of sense, that feels extension. Hence the whole muscular system may be considered as one organ of sense, and the various attitudes of the body, as ideas belonging to this organ, of many of which we are hourly conscious, while many others, like the irritative ideas of the other senses, are performed without our attention. (Darwin 1794: 122–23)

Erasmus Darwin was distinguishing not only between touch and temperature sensitivity, but also according the muscle sense its independence. A few years later, Bell stated:

> By the sense of touch we perceive several qualities, and of very different kinds: hardness, softness, figure, solidity, motion, extension, and heat and cold. Now, although heat be a quality, and cold be the privation of that quality, yet in relation to the body, heat and cold are distinct sensations. But in a more precise acceptance of the term, the sense of touch is said to be the change arising in the mind from external bodies applied to the skin. ([1803] 2000: 472)

Two years earlier, further experimental support for warmth and cold as sensory qualities had been obtained by Johann Wilhelm Ritter (1776–1810) using galvanic stimulation of the tongue. Ritter was an ardent student of galvanism and its general application. His interpretations of galvanic phenomena in the context of German Romantic philosophy has led to some neglect of his experimental work, but he did follow Volta in applying electrical discharges to the areas around his sense organs. Ritter's first reports regarding warm and cold were in 1801: "Another contrast in sensation is that between warm and cold ... if one brings into contact a zinc pole on the tongue and silver on the gums, that on the tongue feels very clearly warm, but it feels cold with silver in the same arrangement" (Ritter 1801: 458). Thus, stimulation by the positive pole produced the sensation of warmth, whereas the negative pole resulted in experiencing cold. Slightly earlier in the same year, Pfaff (1801) had described the sensation of coldness when he applied a current to his finger. Ritter (1805) extended the studies on temperature sensitivity on the tongue as well as the finger; he found that the sensation could vary according to the intensity and duration of the current. His general conclusion was that: "one must consider the sense of temperature (for warmth and cold) as essentially different from the common sense, and as a special sense" (Ritter 1805: 10). Galvanic stimulation resulted in a short shock as well as the particular sensation. In the case of temperature sensitivity, Ritter reported that the shock remained constant even when the sensation changed from warm to cold. Rather than merely speculating that warmth and cold are separate sensory qualities, Ritter afforded experimental evidence for this via his studies of galvanic stimulation.

Ernst Weber (1846) also followed Volta's lead in applying electric currents to the sense organs, although he was disparaging of Ritter's work. He added little to what was known at that time about galvanic stimulation, but he did conduct experiments that supported the existence of a temperature sense: "The sensations of warmth and cold are not like the sensations of brightness and darkness, for the former are positive and negative quantities between which lies a null point determined by the source of heat within us" (Ross and Murray 1978: 210). Weber's great contribution was the introduction of experimental methods, like determining two-point thresholds, which enabled quantification of sensitivity over the skin surface (Weber 1834). These could then be applied to establish acuity differences over the skin surface, and interpreted in terms of regions of receptiveness (Weber 1846). In addition, his experiments on discriminating lifted weights led to the relationship now known as Weber's law. Furthermore, Weber suggested that the sensory circles could be related to the underlying nerve supply:

> But no matter how the elementary nerves do extend to cover the skin, the suggestion may be put forward that the skin is divided into small *sensory circles,* i.e., into small subdivisions each of which owes its sensitivity to a single elementary nerve-fibre. Now my investigations have shown that two stimulations of similar kind applied to separate sites within a single sensory circle on the skin are felt as if they were made at one and the same site; and moreover, that the sensory circles of the skin are smaller in regions

provided with an accurate touch-sense and larger in areas provided with a less accurate touch-sense. (Ross and Murray 1978: 187)

Cutaneous sensory "spots" specifically responsive to touch (pressure) and pain, as well as warmth and cold, were isolated later in the century, using more sensitive and specific apparatus (see Norrsell, Finger, and Lajonchere 1999). A division of the skin senses into three separate systems (one to register temperature, a second for pressure, and a third for touch) was proposed by Ludwig Natanson (1822–1871). He supported the contention of peripheral independence by describing how these systems succumb in sequence when a limb "falls asleep" (Natanson 1844). Three sets of independent studies were reported in the 1880s by Magnus Blix (1849–1904), Alfred Goldscheider (1858–1935), and Henry Donaldson (1857–1938), and they are jointly credited with the discovery. All were principally concerned with establishing cold and warm spots. Blix (1884) continued in the tradition of applying low-intensity electric currents to the skin; he found separate warm and cold spots. Goldscheider (1884) stimulated the skin with a range of devices, like needles, heated brass cylinders, cooled capillary tubes, and brushes coated with ether to isolate the cutaneous spots. Donaldson (1885) discovered the warm and cold sensory spots independently in the course of moving metal points slowly over the skin.

The sensory spots could be mapped and attempts were made to match them to receptors revealed by histological sections of excised skin. Toward the end of the century Max von Frey (1852–1932) advanced the theory that the sensations of warmth, cold, pressure, and pain are subserved by specific end organs in the skin (von Frey 1895). His theory was based on meager evidence, and was soon under attack on empirical as well as theoretical grounds (see Sinclair 1967).

Ritter's observations faded into oblivion with the discovery of specific receptors in the skin. This provided the platform for Blix and others to relate structure to function. Perhaps it was the equation of cutaneous sensations with the underlying nerves that has given authority to Blix; he stated, "The different sensations of cold and warmth are produced by stimulation of separate specific nerve end-organs in the skin" (Blix 1882, translated in Zotterman 1959: 431). In the context of sensory physiology Blix had clearly defined a path that would be followed by others. For example, Zotterman (1959) opened his survey of thermal sensations thus: "Since the discovery by Blix of cold and warm spots from which adequate or electrical stimuli elicited cold and warm sensations, respectively, numerous authors have described the distribution of cold and warm spots in the skin" (431).

The phenomenological distinctions between the dimensions of touch, voiced since antiquity, were given some empirical support from the late eighteenth century and integrated with cutaneous anatomy and physiology in the late nineteenth century.

Movement Sense

What became known as the movement sense is mediated by the vestibular and muscle systems. The behavioral consequences of vestibular stimulation have long been appreciated, but they were not integrated with the anatomy and physiology of the semicircular canals until the late nineteenth century. Thus, the earlier claims for a movement sense were based almost entirely on behavioral evidence relating to apparent visual or body movement. That is, the vestibular system had been examined indirectly through studies of vertigo, which have a long history, as is evident from the quotations from Aristotle and Lucretius given in the initial section of this chapter.

Felix Platter (1536–1614) and Thomas Willis (1621–1675) heralded the early modern era of research on this sense by suggesting a mechanistic interpretation for vertigo in terms of motion of the animal spirit in the brain. Platter observed that:

> An intense, uniform, and extended movement of the head transfers itself in a similar way to the spiritus. Despite holding the head still afterwards, it appears to continue moving for a while, before it eventually feels still. This is the basis for dizziness, if one rotates the head and body in a circle for a long time. (Koelbing 1967: 89)

Willis defined vertigo as "an affection in which visible objects appear to rotate" (1672: 353), and devoted a chapter of his book to describing its pathology and the conditions that can induce it, including body rotation in healthy individuals. Platter and Willis interpreted vertigo in Galenic terms: motion of the animal spirit in the head produced the apparent motion during rotation, rather like smoke in a flask lagging behind that of the rotating vessel. Moreover, Willis described the visual motion that continues after body rotation ceases, and this was attributed to the continued motions of the animal spirit relative to the stationary head. Willis gave a graphic description of it in his Oxford lectures:

> Vertigo arises from the circular motion of the spirits, and, as it were, their rotations in the brain and its medullary part. It takes place just as smoke and vapour contained in a glass or phial are sent into similar motion if you spin the vessel round. This motion lasts longer in the smoke or vapour than in the vessel. Thus we find people whose spirits are very thin, and therefore flexible and weak, pass into vertigo as soon as the body or head is rotated and this sensation persists after the body has ceased its turning motion. (Dewhurst 1980: 113–14)

So little was then known about the functions of the brain that this interpretation was long held. Even when the attraction of the animal spirit was waning, the logic of the explanation was retained. In his medical text on vertigo, Herz (1786) modified the interpretation slightly by referring to movement of nervous humors in the brain rather than animal spirits, but how these humors moved remained mysterious.

In the eighteenth century, François Boissier de Sauvage (1706–1767) discussed vertigo in his classification of diseases, and described it as: "an hallucination which takes place when stationary objects appear to move and rotate around us. ... The cause of vertigo is nothing other than an impression on the retina which is equivalent to that excited by objects that paint their images successively on different parts of that membrane" (1772: 50).

He drew parallels between vertigo and visual persistence with rapidly moving lights, and suggested that the sensitivity of the retina was changed by the retrograde movements of blood in the vessels supplying it. He did discuss the effects of body rotation, and the possibility of unconscious eye movements was entertained.

An alternative to speculating on processes in the retina or brain was to study the phenomenon of vertigo itself. Eighteenth-century interest in vertigo was principally medical, and most observations on it were made in that context. For example, Robert Whytt (1714–1766) included giddiness among the symptoms for nervous diseases:

> Many people of a delicate, nervous, and vascular system, after stooping and suddenly rais-ing their head, are apt to be seized with a *vertigo*, which is sometimes accompanied by faintness. In this case, the vessels of the brain being too weak, seem to yield more than usual to the weight of the blood, when the head is inclined; and afterwards, when it is suddenly raised, and the blood at once descends towards the heart, those vessels do not contract fast enough, so as to accommodate themselves to the quantity of blood remaining in them: At the same time the brain, on account of its too great sensibility, is more affected than usual, by any sudden change in the motion of the fluids through its vessels. (1765: 309)

Diseases of the inner ear were discussed by Bell ([1803] 2000), but their as-sociation with vertigo was not explicitly entertained. While he mentioned that "Of the diseases of the labyrinth, there is little on record" (Bell [1803] 2000: 451), he did observe that inflammation around the auditory nerve was accompanied by an increased sensitivity to slight head movements and to vertigo.

The paradox of these investigations is that the gross anatomy of the labyrinthine organs was reasonably well known at that time. Albrecht von Haller (1708–1777) gave the following description of its structure:

> Two other passages lead from the tympanum to the *labyrinth*, or innermost chamber of the ear. ... There is a nervous pulp in the vestibulum distinguished from the parietal bone by the vapour surrounding it. Into this open the five mouths of the semicircular canals, the foramen ovale, and the passages of the nerves and the arteries. ... The larger posterior and lower of these circles is perpendicular; also the middle and upper one is placed towards the perpendicular; but the outermost and least is horizontal. (1786: 283–84)

No functions were assigned to the labyrinth, but its inclusion in the chapter on hearing conformed to the received view that the semicircular canals are implicated in auditory localization. The structures of the inner ear were represented with accuracy and clarity by Antonio Scarpa (1752–1832) toward the end of the eighteenth century (Scarpa 1789), and his "beautiful plates" were copied by Bell (1803).

At the beginning of the nineteenth century, galvanic stimulation was applied to the regions around the ears, and provided some indication that more than hearing was involved in the structures of the inner ear. As was noted above, Volta (1800) reported that his head seemed to be shaking when current was applied to his ears. Ritter (1801) described the dizziness generated by experiments on applying galvanic stimulation to the head. A similar account was given by Augustin: "If one surrounds the ears with wire ... one becomes dizzy and sees electrical lights" (1803: 129).

Purkinje (1820) carried out further studies on galvanic stimulation of the ear and the subsequent vertigo that it induced. He constructed a voltaic pile from twenty zinc and copper pairs and applied the current to the ear. The immediate sensations were of light flashes and a metallic taste, and then he reported feeling dizzy. It was like a motion from ear to ear, and its direction depended on the polarity of stimulation. He felt nauseous following ten minutes continuous stimulation, and experienced aftereffects for the following two hours. These effects could only be produced when the current was applied to the ears; similar application elsewhere on the head did not produce vertigo. Purkinje extended his observations in a later article:

> The direction of the rotary motion from vertigo goes from right to left if the copper pole is in the right ear, and the zinc pole is in the left, and in the opposite direction from left to right, if the copper pole is applied to the left and the zinc pole to the right ear. As often as the galvanic current is alternated, the vertigo is experienced in the opposite direction and lasts for a longer or shorter time according to the longer or shorter application. (1827: 297)

More systematic investigations were conducted by Eduard Hitzig (1838–1907). In examining the effects of vestibular stimulation, one year after co-discovering the motor cortex, Hitzig (1871) applied electrical currents between the mastoid bones and recorded not only the direction of apparent visual motion but of actual body and eye movements. When the head moved in one direction the eyes moved in the opposite direction. The actual and apparent movements of the body were in the same direction. Hitzig found that the effects of galvanic stimulation were more pronounced when they were applied with the head tilted, and that it was difficult to maintain balance under these conditions. Two blind subjects felt that their bodies were rotating when the current was applied, as did sighted subjects with their eyes closed.

Experiences associated with vestibular stimulation are unlike those of seeing or hearing because they are referred to other bodily organs. Thus, motion illusions based on body rotation relate to the feelings of body rotation, as well as of visual motion. It is these aspects that were investigated before galvanic studies were undertaken, and it is in this regard that the essential aspects of vestibular function had been outlined experimentally. The investigations were conducted initially by Wells (1792), although they were not related to the vestibular system itself (see Wade 1998, 2003), nor were they recognized by historians. The received opinion was clearly stated by Boring:

> The history of what has been called vestibular equilibration, the static sense, ampullar sensation, giddiness, vertigo, the sense of rotation, and the sensibility of the semicircular canals is voluminous and simple. It is voluminous because there has been so much written about it: in 1922 Griffith cited 1685 titles from 1820 on. It is simple because it can all be organized about Purkinje's description of dizziness (1820–1825), Flourens' discovery that lesions of the semicircular canals produce muscular incoordination in the plane of the affected canals (1824–1830), the Mach-Breuer-Brown experiments and their theory of the function of the canals (1873–1875), and the discovery of vertiginous habituation by the psychologists of the U.S. Army (1918), Griffith (1920) and Dodge (1923). (1942: 535)

The history is certainly voluminous, but it is not simple. Robert Bárány (1876–1936), who was awarded the Nobel Prize in 1914 for his vestibular researches, surveyed its history. He remarked that he had come across (but did not cite) over one hundred dissertations on vertigo from the sixteenth to the eighteenth centuries. These were, however, dismissed as adding little to what had been known to the ancients:

> The reality is that they all say much the same thing. In the Middle Ages one had become fully accustomed to the complete description. Whoever wrote a book studied the texts of his predecessors and wrote more or less the same thing with small variations. For example, regarding the interesting question of vertigo from rotation, many authors have speculated whether it is accompanied by unconscious eye movements. It did not occur to any of them to rotate themselves a few times and to feel if their eyes were moving, or to ask his good friend to rotate and observe his eyes. The often insightful considerations would only be carried out at the writing table. The first to make the observations that will be discussed here was *Purkinje* in 1825. (Bárány 1913: 396–7)

Both Bárány and Boring were correct in citing the physiological experiments of Pierre Flourens (1794–1867), and the hydrodynamic theory of Ernst Mach (1838–1916), Josef Breuer (1842–1925), and Alexander Crum Brown (1838–1922). However, Boring placed undue reliance on the historical accuracy of Griffith's (1922) monograph, as have others (see Kornhuber 1974; Wendt 1951). Perhaps all of them were in thrall of Mach's historical authority, which was amplified in his book on movement perception (Mach 1875; Young, Henn, and Scherberger 2001). Mach commenced:

> The work before you attempts, for the first time, to present a complete chapter of physiology, to which the incontestable Purkinje (Purkyne), Flourens and Goltz have laid the

foundations. ... The elder Darwin and Purkyne have studied the remarkable subjective sensations of rotation that take place if one rotates rapidly several times and then stops suddenly. (1875: iii and 1)

Brown (1878a) similarly surveyed the past in Purkinje's favor. With regard to the aftereffects of body rotation he wrote:

Purkinje studied the conditions under which this apparent rotation occurs, and arrived at the following conclusions, which have been confirmed by all succeeding observers:— 1. That the direction of apparent motion of surrounding objects depends upon the direction of the preceding real motion of our body, and is always opposite to it. 2. That the axis about which the apparent motion takes place is always that line in the head which was the axis of the preceding real rotation. (1878a: 634)

In a second article by Brown (1878b) mention is made of Erasmus Darwin's investigations of body rotation; post-rotational nystagmus is both described and illustrated, but again its initial observation is credited to Purkinje.

Erasmus Darwin was also mentioned by Griffith (1922), Boring (1942), and Cohen (1984), but they did not recount the reasons why he chose to carry out his studies. It was William Porterfield (ca. 1696–1771) whose speculations regarding the link between eye movements and post-rotational visual motion stimulated renewed interest in the visual dimension of vertigo in the late eighteenth century (see Wade 2000b, 2003). Motion was the last of the phenomena of vision described in the second volume of Porterfield's *Treatise on the Eye, the Manner and Phœnomena of Vision,* and his analysis of it was subtle. Vertigo was the final phenomenon discussed in the final section:

But, before I dismiss this Subject, I shall endeavour to explain another *Phœnomenon* of Motion, which, tho' very common, and well known, yet, so far as I know, has not as yet had any Solution given to it. If a Person turns swiftly round, without changing his Place, all Objects about will seem to move in a Circle to the contrary Way, and the Deception continues, not only when the Person himself moves round, but, which is more surprising, it also continues for some time after he stops moving, when the Eye, as well as the Objects, are at absolute Rest. (Porterfield 1759: 424–25)

The evidence that the eyes do not move following rotation was subjective. Porterfield was not conscious of any movements of his eyes and so he was convinced that they remained stationary following rotation. The situation was clarified by Wells (1792); he distrusted the recourse to subjective experience in deciding upon a matter of science, and he found that experiments with afterimages were preferable because of their increased objectivity. It was Wells's monograph that galvanized Erasmus Darwin to deliberate further on vertigo, and it was Wells who engaged in a public dispute with Darwin concerning the involvement of eye movements in visual vertigo following body rotation (see Wade 2003).

It is clear that all these commentators have ignored Wells's (1792) seminal studies on vertigo. He conducted sophisticated experiments on post-rotational vertigo and nystagmus long before Purkinje's studies. Wells's analysis of vertigo should be considered as heralding the first clear behavioral evidence for the vestibular sense. His experiments satisfied Müller's requirement, cited at the head of this chapter, "that external causes should excite in it a new and peculiar kind of sensation different from all the sensations of our five senses"; the external causes are linear and angular accelerations, and the sensation is one of rotation both of the body and the visual scene.

A common feature of many of Wells's experiments on vision was the use of afterimages to assess the manner in which the eyes moved. He used the term *spectra* to describe afterimages; they were so called by Robert Darwin (1766–1848), Erasmus's son and the father of Charles, in an article a few years earlier (Darwin 1786). Wells enlisted afterimages to determine how the eyes move during post-rotational vertigo, although his initial observation was accidental: "During a slight fit of giddiness I was accidentally seized with, a coloured spot [afterimage], occasioned by looking steadily at a luminous body, and upon which I happened at that moment to be making an experiment, was moved in a manner altogether independent of the positions I conceived my eyes to possess" (1792: 95).

Wells capitalized on this happy accident and provided experimental evidence to link the pattern of eye movements to the direction of visual vertigo. Wells proceeded to examine the effects systematically. He gave the first clear description of the fast and slow phases of post-rotational nystagmus, and its decreasing amplitude with time. Furthermore, he described how the direction of post-rotational afterimage motion was dependent on head position during rotation. Wells was not aware of feeling his eyes moving after rotation and so he asked another person to rotate and then stop "and I could plainly see, that, although he thought his eyes were fixed, they were in reality moving in their sockets, first toward one side, and then toward the other" (1792: 97). In the space of a few pages, Wells encapsulated the essential features of vestibular function as they are expressed through eye movements and post-rotational vertigo.

Robert Darwin's (1786) article was reprinted in full as the final chapter in the first volume of his father's book *Zoonomia,* which was published two years after Wells's *Essay upon Single Vision.* Darwin's *Zoonomia* was the culmination of many years of thought and writing, and so the chapter entitled "Vertigo" reflected ideas that had been nurtured prior to the appearance of Wells's *Essay.* He commenced by noting that "the disease called vertigo or dizziness has been little understood" (Darwin 1794: 231). Darwin listed the conditions which can induce vertigo and the symptoms accompanying it. The inducing conditions are visual, as in looking down from a tall tower or viewing a whirling wheel, or postural, as in seasickness or rotating the body. These were related to the importance of vision in maintaining postural equilibrium.

Darwin also described the vertigo and double vision that accompanies drunkenness. The example of post-rotational vertigo is described thus:

> When a child moves round quick upon one foot, the circumjacent objects become quite indistinct, as their distance increases their apparent motions; and this great velocity confounds both their forms, and their colors, as is seen in whirling round a many colored wheel; he then loses his usual method of balancing himself by vision, and begins to stagger, and attempts to recover himself by his muscular feelings. This staggering adds to the instability of the visible objects by giving a vibratory motion besides their rotatory one. The child then drops to the ground, and the neighbouring objects seem to continue for some seconds of time to circulate around him, and the earth under him appears to librate like a balance. In some seconds of time these sensations of a continuation of the motion of objects vanish; but if he continues turning somewhat longer, before he falls, sickness and vomiting are very liable to succeed. (Darwin 1794: 235)

The first volume of *Zoonomia,* containing Darwin's deliberation on vertigo, appeared in May or June of 1794 (see King-Hele 1999), two years after Wells's monograph. Wells must have read it with mounting indignation, as he wrote two rejoinders as letters to the September and October issues of *The Gentleman's Magazine* for the same year (Wells 1794a, 1794b). In the first, Wells demonstrated that visual vertigo occurs with rotation in darkness, contrary to the Darwins' speculation. It was concerned principally with the logic of Darwin's theory, although it did mention some experimental observations, too. In the second, Wells described experiments indicating that the eyes move following body rotation and provided more details about how they move.

One significant factor that emerged from Erasmus Darwin's deliberations on vertigo was the invention of the human centrifuge. This was described and illustrated in the third edition of *Zoonomia* (Darwin 1801); however, it was not initially enlisted to study vertigo, but employed as a device for treating the insane!

Purkinje unknowingly repeated many of Wells's experiments on body rotation, although he was able to add a mechanically rotating device to study vertigo. In one study he described the effects of being rotated for one hour in such a contrivance. Initially Purkinje examined the introspective aspects of post-rotational vertigo and made many experimental manipulations of it. Purkinje described rotary and post-rotational eye movements and suggested that "visual vertigo is a consequence of the conflict between unconscious involuntary muscular actions and voluntary conscious ones in the opposite direction" (1820: 95). Among the few sources of earlier research he cited were a translation into German of Erasmus Darwin's *Zoonomia* (Darwin, 1794) and Herz's (1786) medical text on dizziness and its treatment.

Purkinje deduced a general principle from his experiments: "that the midpoint of the head (considered as a sphere), around which the initial rotation was performed, invariably determined the direction of apparent motion regardless of the subsequent position of the head" (1820: 86). Kruta (1964) referred to this as "Purkinje's law of vertigo." There was no clear indication of how such motions in the head could be detected, and his initial interpretation was that motion of the brain itself lagged behind that of the head, with particular influence exerted by the cerebellum. Purkinje concluded his first article with a statement that was soon to be realized: "It remains for a future work to establish the possible movements in the brain which measure its structure and organization" (1820: 125). Purkinje later wrote several briefer articles on vertigo, but his interpretation of it did not change substantially (see Wade and Brožek 2001). The dimension that Purkinje added to Wells's studies was the application of galvanic stimulation to the ears.

The significance of the vestibular system to the maintenance of posture and balance slowly emerged after Flourens conducted his lesion studies, initially on the cerebellum and later on the semicircular canals (Flourens 1824, 1830, 1842). In the year that his first book was published he sectioned the semicircular canals of pigeons: "On 15 November 1824, I cut the two horizontal semicircular canals of a pigeon. This lesion was immediately followed by two habitual phenomena: the horizontal oscillation of the head, and the turning of the animal in the same direction" (Flourens 1842: 452).

In later experiments, he was able to demonstrate that sectioning a particular semicircular canal elicited nystagmus in the same plane, as well as disturbances of posture and equilibrium: the bodies of the experimental animals always turned in the direction of the severed canal. Similar results were obtained with rabbits.

Despite providing this experimental evidence, Flourens did not make the link between semicircular canal function and the movement sense. This was to wait another fifty years, when Mach, Breuer, and Brown independently formulated the hydrodynamic theory: during head rotation the endolymph in the canals displaces receptors in the ampulla, signalling angular accelerations and exerting control over posture and eye movements.

Mach (1873, 1875) constructed a rotating chair that was mounted in a frame that could also rotate, and he examined the perception of the visual vertical during static tilt and also visual aftereffects of body rotation. From experiments using this apparatus he concluded that it was not angular velocity that was sensed, but angular acceleration. Brown (1874) based his analysis on thresholds for detecting body rotation on a revolving stool; the thresholds were lowest when the head was positioned so that one of the semicircular canals was in the plane of rotation. Breuer (1874) made systematic lesions of the semicircular canals of pigeons and dogs; he also distinguished between the canal receptors and the otolith organs of the vestibular system, which detected orientation with respect to gravity.

Mach placed these observations in the context of Aristotle's strictures about the senses:

But at times some extremely artless animadversions are heard that almost nonplus us. "If a sixth sense existed it could not fail to have been discovered thousands of years ago."

Indeed, there was a time, then, when only seven planets could have existed! But I do not believe that any one will lay any weight on the philological question whether the set of phenomena which we have been considering should be called a sense. The phenomena will not disappear when the name disappears. It was further said to me that animals exist which have no labyrinth, but which can yet orientate themselves, and that consequently the labyrinth has nothing to do with orientation. We do not walk forsooth with our legs, because snakes can propel themselves without them! But if the promulgator of a new idea cannot hope for any great pleasure from its publication, yet the critical process which his views undergo is extremely helpful to the subject-matter of them. (1910: 297)

Mach, Breuer, and Brown continued to investigate the consequences of the hydrodynamic theory of semicircular canal function, but Brown, in 1878, made a particularly astute prediction: if deaf-mutes have defects in all the parts of the inner ear, then they will not be able to experience vertigo:

A great deal of valuable information might be obtained by carefully testing the delicacy and accuracy of the sense of rotation in deaf-mutes. Many deaf-mutes have not only the cochlea, but the whole internal ear, destroyed; if, then, the inmates of deaf and dumb establishments were systematically tested by means of such experiments as Mach and Brown made upon themselves, experiments which would, no doubt, greatly interest and amuse them, and if the condition of the internal ear were, in each case of *post-mortem* examination of a deaf-mute, accurately noted, we should soon obtain a mass of information which would do more to clear up the relation between the sense of rotation and the semicircular canals than any number of experiments on animals unable to describe to us their sensations. (Brown 1878b: 658)

William James (1842–1910) put this to the test with a specially constructed devise for rotating the body. Almost all normal observers experienced vertigo. However, of over 500 deaf-mutes tested, almost 200 experienced no dizziness (James 1882). The results were confirmed by Kreidl (1891), who found that over 80 percent of congenitally deaf individuals experienced no vertigo following rotation. Moreover, there were no nystagmic eye movements in those who did not experience vertigo. As Brown described in a lecture some years later: "Just as there are blind men and deaf men, so there are men who have lost or never had the sense of rotation. Such persons are always deaf-mutes" (1895: 27).

Mach extended his own research to examine visual orientation during body tilt, as well as visual motion following body rotation. He was able to use his rotating chair and to exclude the visibility of the surround. His research on orientation was stimulated by an experience of visual disorientation when traveling in a vehicle:

Thus my attention was drawn to this point by the sensation of falling and subsequently by another singular occurrence. I was rounding a sharp railway curve once when I suddenly saw all the trees, houses, and factory chimneys along the track swerve from the vertical and assume a strikingly inclined position. What had hitherto appeared to me perfectly natural, namely, the fact that we distinguish the vertical so perfectly and sharply from every other direction, now struck me as enigmatical. Why is it that the same direction can now appear vertical to me and now cannot? By what is the vertical distinguished for us? (Mach 1910: 286–87)

Mach appreciated that judgments of orientation are made with respect to frames of reference. Normally those available from the senses correspond with the cardinal directions defined by gravity, but occasionally this accord is disrupted. Mach did have recourse to the structures within the inner ear—the "secret reference"—that could "indicate these positions of the body", and he conducted experiments with his tilting chair to confirm it.

Wells (1792) was similarly searching for the sixth sense that occupied many scholars throughout the nineteenth century, and he also discussed the manner in which we can orient our bodies with respect to gravity, and how our judgments of visual orientation are influenced by changes in body posture. He was aware, on theoretical grounds, that there must be some system that registers the position of the body with respect to gravity: "In the estimates we make by sight of the situation of external objects, we have always some secret reference to the position of our own bodies, with respect to the plane of the horizon" (Wells 1792: 85). Although he asked "What is there within us, to indicate these positions of the body?" (Wells 1792: 86), he could not answer to his satisfaction, since he could only draw on the actions of the voluntary muscles. Thus, the orientational aspects of otolithic function were examined behaviorally, as well as the rotational consequences of semicircular canal stimulation.

The receptors that mediate vestibular sensitivity are closely linked to those for hearing. Hair cells in the cochlea were first observed in the 1850s, and they were later identified in the vestibular system (see Finger 1994). In the twentieth century, the fine detail of the hair cell receptors could be observed with electron microscopes and a cortical projection from the vestibular nuclei was demonstrated.

The vestibular sense is unusual in various respects. First, the sensory experiences following stimulation are not localized as they are with the other senses; we feel giddy or see the world spin rather than have a single sensation like sight or hearing. Second, the gross anatomy of the vestibular system was known long before its function was appreciated. Third, systematic evidence indicating the action of the semicircular canals (in vertigo) was available from the late eighteenth century. Nonetheless, behavioral studies which provided support for a new sense were not accorded the status given to isolating specific receptors or establishing projections to the brain. It was the behavioral dimension that encouraged Brown to state: "I am not sure whether in this account of the sense of rotation, of its organ, and of the use of it, I have carried all my hearers with me, and convinced you of the real existence and the real practical use of this sense" (1895: 28).

Conclusion

Aristotle restricted the number of senses to five for theoretical rather than empirical reasons, although the sense of touch or feeling remained an enigma. The subsequent search for a sixth sense fractionated feeling into movement (vestibular) and muscle senses and multiple dimensions of cutaneous sensitivity. Ancient phenomenological distinctions between the senses of feeling were given empirical support from the late eighteenth century. First, the dependence of visual vertigo (and eye movements) on the direction of head rotation provided evidence for a movement sense. Shortly afterward, the separation of touch from temperature sensitivity was demonstrated both behaviorally and by galvanic stimulation. The muscle sense was established by psychophysical experiments. The success of the search for a sixth sense reflected the advances made in anatomy, physiology, and psychophysics in the nineteenth century.

The criteria for distinguishing between the senses were extended from sensory quality and gross anatomy to include microanatomy (of receptors and sensory pathways), physiology (of nerve stimulation and extirpation), and psychophysics (stimulus manipulation and behavioral measurement). Evidence for the separation of the senses relied more on microanatomy and physiology than on psychophysics.

Studies of the movement sense provide a telling example of the manner in which our understanding of perception has been advanced by the specification of sense. The gross anatomy of the vestibular system was described before its function was appreciated; the visual consequences of vestibular stimulation were subjected to observation and experiment between these two events. Rotating the body to induce vertigo resulted in post-rotational nystagmus and apparent visual motion, the directions of which were dependent upon head orientation during rotation. Applying electric currents to the outer ears produced feelings of dizziness, as well as movements of the body and of the eyes. These responses to rotation and galvanic stimulation could be understood when the hydrodynamic theory of semicircular canal function was advanced in the 1870s. Moreover, the absence of these responses in many who were deaf and dumb added to the evidence for a separate sense.

In an historical sense, it is difficult to imagine originating a classification of the senses that did not depend on anatomical and perceptual distinctions. Such a classification would have preceded others based on energy because the characteristics of perception were described long before there was an adequate understanding of energy sources in the environment. These categories were later reinforced by evidence from neuroanatomy and neurophysiology: specialized receptors respond to features of the stimulus and these are analyzed in discrete regions of the brain.

The number of senses has always been arbitrary, depending on the criteria that are applied. Adding one or more senses to Aristotle's five reflected the advances that were taking place in nineteenth-century neuroscience.

Acknowledgments

The author wishes to thank Stanley Finger for astute comments on an earlier draft of this paper, an anonymous reviewer for constructive comments, and Helen Ross for translating the quotation from Scaliger.

References

Adrian, E. D. (1928), *The Basis of Sensation,* London: Christophers.

Ægineta, P. (1844), *The Seven Books of Paulus Ægineta,* vol. 1, trans. F. Adams, London: The Sydenham Society.

Augustin, F. L. (1803), *Versuch einer vollständigen systematischen Geschichte der galvanischen Elektricität und ihre medizinischen Anwendung,* Berlin: Felisch.

Bárány, R. (1913), "Der Schwindel und seine Beziehungen zum Bogengangapparat des inneren Ohres. Bogengangapparat und Kleinhirn, (Historische Darstellung. Eigene Untersuchungen)," *Naturwiss,* 1: 396–401.

Beare, J. I. (1906), *Greek Theories of Elementary Cognition from Alcmaeon to Aristotle,* Oxford: Clarendon.

Bell, C. ([1803] 2000), *The Anatomy of the Human Body. Vol. III. Containing the Nervous System,* in N. J. Wade (ed.), *The Emergence of Neuroscience in the Nineteenth Century,* vol. 1, London: Routledge/Thoemmes.

Bell, C. ([1811] 2000), *Idea of a New Anatomy of the Brain; Submitted for the Observations of His Friends,* in N. J. Wade (ed.), *The Emergence of Neuroscience in the Nineteenth Century,* vol. 1, London: Routledge/Thoemmes.

Bell, C. (1823), "On the Motions of the Eye, in Illustration of the Uses of the Muscles and of the Orbit," *Phil Trans Royal Soc,* 113: 166–86.

Bell, C. (1826), "On the Nervous Circle which Connects the Voluntary Muscles with the Brain," *Phil Trans Royal Soc,* 116: 163–73.

Blix, M. (1884), "Experimentelle Beiträge zur Lösung der Frage über die specifische Energie der Hautnerven," *Z Biol,* 20: 141–56.

Boissier de Sauvage, F. (1772), *Nosologie Méthodique, ou distribution des maladies en classes, en genres et en espèces, suivant l'esprit de Sydenham, & la méthode des botanistes,* vol. 4, Lyon: Bruyset.

Boring, E. G. (1942), *Sensation and Perception in the History of Experimental Psychology,* New York: Appleton-Century.

Brazier, M. A. B. (1959), "The Historical Development of Neurophysiology," in J. Field, H. W. Magoun, and V. E. Hall (eds), *Handbook of Physiology. Neurophysiology,* vol. 1, Washington, DC: American Physiological Society, pp. 1–58.

Brazier, M. A. B. (1988), *A History of Neurophysiology in the 19th Century,* New York: Raven.

Bresadola, M. (1998), "Medicine and Science in the Life of Luigi Galvani (1737–1798)," *Brain Res Bull,* 46: 367–80.

Breuer, J. (1874), "Über die Funktion der Bogengänge des Ohrlabyrinthes," *Wiener med Jahrb,* 4: 72–124.

Breuer, J. (1875), "Beiträge zur Lehre vom statischen Sinne," *Wiener med Jahrb,* 5: 87–156.

Brown, A. C. (1874), "Preliminary Note on the Sense of Rotation and the Function of the Semicircular Canals of the Internal Ear," *Proc Roy Soc Edin,* 8: 255–7.

Brown, A. C. (1875), "On the Sense of Rotation and the Anatomy and Physiology of the Semicircular Canals of the Internal Ear," *J Anat Physiol,* 8: 327–31.

Brown, A. C. (1878a), "Cyon's Researches on the Ear, I," *Nature,* 18: 633–5.

Brown, A. C. (1878b), "Cyon's Researches on the Ear, II," *Nature,* 18: 657–9.

Brown, A. C. (1895), *The Relation between the Movements of the Eyes and the Movements of the Head,* London: Frowde.

Brown, T. (1820), *Sketch of a System of the Philosophy of the Human Mind,* Edinburgh: Bell, Bradfute, Manners & Miller, and Waugh & Innes.

Cohen, B. (1984), "Erasmus Darwin's Observations on Rotation and Vertigo," *Hum Neurobiol,* 3: 121–8.

Cranefield, P. F. (1974), *The Way In and the Way Out: François Magendie, Charles Bell and the Roots of the Spinal Nerves,* Mount Kisco, NY: Futura.

Darwin, E. (1794), *Zoonomia; or, the Laws of Organic Life,* vol. 1, London: Johnson.

Darwin, E. (1801), *Zoonomia; or, the Laws of Organic Life,* vol. 4, 4th edn, London: Johnson.

Darwin, R. W. (1786), "New Experiments on the Ocular Spectra of Light and Colours," *Phil Trans Roy Soc,* 76: 313–48.

Dewhurst, K. (1980), *Thomas Willis's Oxford Lectures,* Oxford: Sandford.

Donaldson, H. H. (1885), "On the Temperature-Sense," *Mind,* 10: 399–416.

Finger, S. (1994), *Origins of Neuroscience. A History of Explorations into Brain Function,* New York: Oxford University Press.

Finger, S. (2000), *Minds behind the Brain,* New York: Oxford University Press.

Finger, S. and Wade, N. J. (2002), "The Neuroscience of Helmholtz and the Theories of Johannes Müller. Part 2. Sensation and Perception," *J Hist Neurosci,* 11: 234–54.

Flourens, P. (1824), *Recherches Expérimentales sur les Propriétés et les Fonctions du Système Nerveux dans les Animaux Vertébrés,* Paris: Baillière.

Flourens, P. (1830), "Expériences sur les canaux semi-circulaires de l'oreille," *Mém Acad Roy des Sci,* 9: 455–66.

Flourens, P. (1842), *Recherches Expérimentales sur les Propriétés et les Fonctions du Système Nerveux dans les Animaux Vertébrés,* 2nd edn, Paris: Baillière.

Frey, M. von (1895), "Beiträge zur Sinnesphysiologie der Haut," *Sächs Akad Wiss Leipzig,* 47: 166–84.

Galvani, L. (1791), "De viribus electricitatis in motu musculari," *De Bononiensi Scientiarum et Artium Instituto atque Academia Commentarii,* 7: 363–418.

Goldscheider, A. (1884), "Die specifische Energie der Temperaturenerven," *Monatsschr prak Dermatol,* 3: 198–208.

Griffith, C. R. (1922), *An Historical Survey of Vestibular Equilibration,* Urbana: University of Illinois Press.

Grüsser, O.-J. and Hagner, M. (1990), "On the History of Deformation Phosphenes and the Idea of Internal Light Generated in the Eye for the Purpose of Vision," *Doc Ophthalmol,* 74: 57–85.

Haller, A. (1786), *First Lines of Physiology,* trans. M. Cullen, Edinburgh: Elliot.

Hamilton, W. (1846), *The Works of Thomas Reid, D. D.,* Edinburgh: MacLachlan, Stewart.

Helmholtz, H. (1867), "Handbuch der physiologischen Optik," in G. Karsten (ed.), *Allgemeine Encyklopädie der Physik,* vol. 9, Leipzig: Voss.

Herz, M. (1786), *Versuch über den Schwindel,* Berlin: Voss.

Hitzig, E. (1871), "Ueber die bei Galvanisiren des Kopfes entstehenden Störungen des Muskelinnervation und der Vorstellungen vom Verhalten im Raume," *Arch Anat Physiol wiss Med,* 716–70.

Hooke, R. (1665), *Micrographia: or Some Physiological Descriptions of Minute Bodies Made by Magnifying Glasses with Observations and Inquiries Thereupon,* London: Martyn and Allestry.

Hunter, J. (1786), *Observations on Certain Parts of the Animal Œconomy,* London.

James, W. (1882), "The Sense of Dizziness in Deaf-mutes," *Am J Otol,* 4: 239–54.

Kemp, S. (1990), *Medieval Psychology,* New York: Greenwood Press.

King-Hele, D. (1999), *Erasmus Darwin. A Life of Unequalled Achievement,* London: De La Mare.

Koelbing, H. M. (1967), *Renaissance der Augenheilkunde. 1540–1630,* Bern: Huber.

Kornhuber, H. H. (1974), "Introduction," in H. H. Kornhuber (ed.), *Handbook of Sensory Physiology. Volume VI/1. Vestibular System. Part 1: Basic Mechanisms,* New York: Springer, pp. 3–14.

Kreidl, A. (1891), "Beiträge zur Physiologie des Ohrenlabyrinthes auf Grund von Versuchen an Taubstummen," *Arch gesamt Physiol,* 51: 119–50.

Kruta, V. (1964), *M.-J.-P. Flourens, J.-E. Purkyne et les Débuts de la Physiologie de la Posture et de l'Équilibre,* Paris: Alençonnaise.

Kühne, W. (1863), "Die Muskelspindeln," *Arch path Anat Physiol klin Med,* 28: 528–38.

Leeuwenhoek, A. van (1675), "Microscopical Observations from Mr. Leeuwenhoeck, Concerning the Optick Nerve," *Phil Trans Roy Soc,* 9: 378–80.

Lucretius (1975), *De Rerum Natura,* trans. W. H. D. Rouse, Cambridge, MA: Harvard University Press.

Mach, E. (1873), "Physiologische Versuche über den Gleichgewichtssinn des Menschen," *Sitzungsb Wiener Akad Wiss,* 68: 124–40.

Mach, E. (1875), *Grundlinien der Lehre von den Bewegungsempfindungen,* Leipzig: Engelmann.

Mach, E. (1910), *Popular Scientific Lectures,* 4th edn, trans. T. J. McCormack, Chicago: Open Court.

May, M. T. (1968), *Galen. On the Usefulness of the Parts of the Body,* Ithaca, NY: Cornell University Press.

Ménière, P. (1861), "Mémoire sur des lésions de l'oreille interne donnant lieu à des symptoms de congestion cérébrale apoplectiforme," *Gaz méd Par,* 16: 597–601.

Müller, J. (1826), *Zur vergleichenden Physiologie des Gesichtssinnes des Menschen und der Thiere, nebst einem Versuch über die Bewegung der Augen und über den menschlichen Blick,* Leipzig: Cnobloch.

Müller, J. (1838), *Handbuch der Physiologie des Menschen für Vorlesungen,* vol. 2, Bonn: Hölscher.

Müller, J. (1843), *Elements of Physiology,* 2nd edn, trans. W. Baly, London: Taylor and Walton.

Müller, J. (2003), *Müller's Elements of Physiology,* Bristol: Thoemmes.

Natanson, L. N. (1844), "Analyse der Functionen des Nervensystems," *Arch Physiol Heilk,* 3: 515–35.

Neff, W. D. (1960), "Sensory Discrimination," in J. Field, H. W. Magoun, and V. E. Hall (eds), *Handbook of Physiology. Neurophysiology,* vol. 3, Washington, DC: American Physiological Society, pp. 1447–70.

Newton, I. (1704), *Opticks: or, a Treatise of the Reflections, Refractions, Inflections and Colours of Light,* London: Smith and Walford.

Norrsell, U., Finger, S. and Lajonchere, C. (1999), "Cutaneous Sensory Spots and the 'Law of Specific Nerve Energies': History and Development of Ideas," *Brain Res Bull,* 48: 457–65.

Pfaff, C. W. (1801), "Vorläufige Nachricht von seinen galvanischen Versuchen mit Voltaischen Batterie," *Ann Phys,* 7: 247–54.

Piccolino, M. (1997), "Luigi Galvani and Animal Electricity: Two Centuries after the Foundation of Electrophysiology," *Trends Neurosci,* 20: 443–8.

Piccolino, M. (2000), "The Bicentennial of the Voltaic Battery (1800–2000): The Artificial Electric Organ," *Trends Neurosci,* 23: 147–51.

Porterfield, W. (1759), *A Treatise on the Eye, the Manner and Phænomena of Vision,* vol. 2, Edinburgh: Hamilton and Balfour.

Purkinje, J. (1820), "Beyträge zur näheren Kenntniss des Schwindels aus heautognostischen Daten," *Med Jahrb des kais-könig österreich Staates,* 6: 79–125.

Purkinje, J. (1827), "Ueber die physiologische Bedeutung des Schwindels und die Beziehung desselben zu den neuesten Versuchen über die Hirnfunctionen," *Mag ges Heilk,* 23: 284–310.

Reid, T. (1764), *An Inquiry into the Human Mind, on the Principles of Common Sense,* Edinburgh: Millar, Kincaid & Bell.

Ritter, J. W. (1801), "Versuche und Bemerkungen über den Galvanismus der Voltaischen Batterie," *Ann Phys,* 7: 431–84.

Ritter, J. W. (1805), "Neue Versuche und Bemerkungen über den Galvanismus," *Ann Phys,* 19: 1–44.

Ross, H. E. (1999), "The Prehistory of Weight Perception," in P. R. Killeen and W. R. Uttal (eds), *Fechner Day '99: The End of 20th Century Psychophysics,* Tempe, AZ: The International Society for Psychophysics, pp. 31–6.

Ross, H. E. and Murray, D. J. (1978), *E. H. Weber: The Sense of Touch,* London: Academic Press.

Ross, W. D. (ed.) (1931), *The Works of Aristotle,* vol. 3, Oxford: Clarendon.

Scaliger, J. C. (1557), *Exotericarum Exercitationum Liber Quintus Decimus, De Subtilitate, ad Hieronymum Cardanum,* Paris: Vascosani.

Scarpa, A. (1789), *Anatomicae Disquisitiones de Auditu et Olfactu,* Pavia: Galeati.

Schwann, T. (1839), *Mikroskopische Untersuchungen über die Übereinstimmung in der Struktur und dem Wachsthum der Tiere und Pflanzen,* Berlin: Reimer.

Sherrington, C. S. (1900), "The Muscular Sense," in A. E. Schäfer (ed.), *Text-book of Physiology,* vol. 2, Edinburgh: Pentland, pp. 1002–25.

Sherrington, C. S. ([1906] 2000), *The Integrative Action of the Nervous System,* New York: Scribner. Reprinted in N. J. Wade (ed.), *The Emergence of Neuroscience in the Nineteenth Century,* vol. 8, London: Routledge/Thoemmes.

Siegel, R. E. (1970), *Galen on Sense Perception,* Basel: Karger.

Sinclair, D. (1967), *Cutaneous Sensation,* London: Oxford University Press.

Smith, A. M. (1996), *Ptolemy's Theory of Visual Perception: An English Translation of the Optics with Introduction and Commentary,* Philadelphia: The American Philosophical Society.

Stratton, G. M. (1917), *Theophrastus and the Greek Physiological Psychology before Aristotle,* New York: Macmillan.

Volta, A. (1800), "On the Electricity Excited by the Mere Contact of Conducting Substances of Different Species," *Phil Trans Roy Soc,* 90: 403–31.

Wade, N. J. (1990), *Visual Allusions: Pictures of Perception,* Hove, East Sussex: Lawrence Erlbaum Associates.

Wade, N. J. (1998), *A Natural History of Vision,* Cambridge, MA: MIT Press.

Wade, N. J. (2000a), "William Charles Wells (1757–1817) and Vestibular Research before Purkinje and Flourens," *J Vestib Res,* 10: 127–37.

Wade, N. J. (2000b), "Porterfield and Wells on the Motions of Our Eyes," *Perception,* 29: 221–39.

Wade, N. J. (2003), *Destined for Distinguished Oblivion: The Scientific Vision of William Charles Wells (1757–1817),* New York: Kluwer/Plenum.

Wade, N. J. and Brožek, J. (2001), *Purkinje's Vision. The Dawning of Neuroscience,* Mahwah, NJ: Lawrence Erlbaum Associates.

Wade, N. J. and Verstraten, F. A. J. (1998), "Introduction and Historical Overview," in G. Mather, F. Verstraten, and S. Anstis (eds), *The Motion After-Effect: A Modern Perspective,* Cambridge, MA: MIT Press, pp. 1–23.

Weber, E. H. (1834), *De Pulsu, Resorptione, Auditu et Tactu,* Leipzig: Koehler.

Weber, E. H. (1846), "Der Tastsinn und das Gemeingefühl," in R. Wagner (ed.), *Handwörterbuch der Physiologie,* vol. 3, Braunschweig: Vieweg, pp. 481–588.

Wells, W. C. ([1792] 2003), *An Essay upon Single Vision with Two Eyes: Together with Experiments and Observations on Several Other Subjects in Optics,* London: Cadell. Reprinted in N. J. Wade, *Destined for Distinguished Oblivion: The Scientific Vision of William Charles Wells (1757–1817),* New York: Kluwer/Plenum.

Wells, W. C. ([1794a] 2003), "Reply to Dr. Darwin on Vision," *Gent Mag,* 64: 794-7. Reprinted in N.J. Wade, *Destined for Distinguished Oblivion: The Scientific Vision of William Charles Wells (1757–1817),* New York: Kluwer/Plenum.

Wells, W. C. ([1794b] 2003), "Reply to Dr. Darwin on Vision," *Gent Mag,* 64: 905-7. Reprinted in N.J. Wade, *Destined for Distinguished Oblivion: The Scientific Vision of William Charles Wells (1757–1817),* New York: Kluwer/Plenum.

Wendt, G. R. (1951), "Vestibular Functions," in S. S. Stevens (ed.), *Handbook of Experimental Psychology,* New York: Wiley, pp. 1191–223.

Whytt, R. (1765), *Observations on the Nature, Causes, and Cure of Those Disorders Which Have Commonly Been Called Nervous Hypochondriac, or Hysteric,* Edinburgh: Becket, Du Hondt, and Balfour.

Willis, T. (1672), *De Anima Brutorum,* London: Wells & Scott.

Young, L. R., Henn, V. and Scherberger, H. (2001), *Fundamentals of the Theory of Movement Perception by Dr. Ernst Mach,* New York: Kluwer/Plenum.

Young, T. (1802), "On the Theory of Lights and Colours," *Phil Trans Roy Soc,* 92: 12–48.

Young, T. ([1807] 2002), *A Course of Lectures on Natural Philosophy and the Mechanical Arts,* London: Johnson. Reprinted by Thoemmes Press, Bristol.

Zotterman, Y. (1959), "Thermal Sensations," in J. Field, H. W. Magoun, and V. E. Hall (eds), *Handbook of Physiology. Neurophysiology,* vol. 1, Washington, DC: American Physiological Society, pp. 431–58.

–2–

Sense of Direction
W. H. Hudson

Judging from myself (a very bad case I dare say), the sense of direction is a dwindling one in our civilised state, and in many of us appears to be wholly gone. Yet to man living in a state of nature it is of vital importance, as it is to all animals endowed with locomotive organs—wings, fins, legs and, in the ophidians, ribs and scales. The snake does not, as Tautus taught us, move by means of its fiery spirit. And we know that snakes, with practically no horizon at all and so short-sighted that they can have no landmarks, do yet possess the sense of direction in a remarkable degree. Thus, there are authentic cases on record of tame snakes travelling long distances back to the home from which they had been removed—incidents similar to those we are accustomed to hear every day with regard to our domestic animals and pets. Apart from such cases, we see from observation of their habits that the snake could not do very well without such a sense.

As to insects, a little observation of wasps, bees, ants and others, both social and solitary, that cannot carry on the business of life without constantly returning to one point, is enough to show that they could not exist without such a sense. It is perhaps most easily seen in the ants. Take your seat on the turf on a chalk down and look at the ground, and you will see a minute black ant hurrying about on his business. You don't know how long he has been abroad, but the chances are you will get tired of watching him before he returns to his home. For a home he has, a minute hole somewhere under the grass leading into his subterranean galleries, where he spends part of his time; and as his sense-organs are specialised in two directions, he will then move about as freely in the dark, and know just what to do and how to do it, as well as out in the brilliant sunlight. Night and day, and above ground and underground, are all one to him. If, when watching him, you try the experiment of putting a finger close to him he is overwhelmed with astonishment; at first struck motionless, and then, recovering his faculties, he rushes wildly away. The near approach of your finger to him was like a tremendous tornado charged with every violent animal smell in the world bursting suddenly upon a horse, let us say. But soon he recovers from his panic and goes on with his everlasting quest, and you are obliged to go after him on your hands and knees to keep him in sight. He is probably now leagues away from his home, still hurriedly pushing his way through the endless forest. For to him the grasses are like trees and their stems like trunks, and they stand up and lean and lie about in all positions. He goes round this one, crawls under the next, and climbs over a third, and cannot see a distance of half an inch before him. Tired of watching him you get up and go away, and he goes on and on and will continue to go on until he finds what he is looking for, and then will set out on his return, working his way through that interminable forest, that boundless contiguity of shading grasses, straight to his home.

And as with serpents and insects, and fishes and batrachians, so it is with birds and mammals, all of which when out and away from home on their various quests are, as the poet says of the migrating bird, "lone wanderers, but not lost." There is not a village or hamlet in the kingdom, nor, I imagine, anywhere in the world, where you will not be told strange yet familiar stories of a domestic or pet animal returning from long distances to its old home over ground unknown to it where it could never have memorised the landmarks. Such instances are so common that anyone who thought it worth his while could collect a volume full of them in a few weeks. In my early home on the Argentine pampas we thought less about cats and dogs in this connection than horses; for it was in a region where, as the gauchos say, the horse is the legs that carry you. It was a common thing to hear a gaucho say, when his horses, or some of them, had been stolen, that he counted on the recovery of such a one, seeing that however far they took him from his home and district, however long they kept him hobbled or collared to another horse, he would, on the first opportunity that offered, make his escape and find his way back.

It remains to speak of the sense of direction in man. He is dependent on the same senses and faculties as any other rapacious mammal in his quest for food. No doubt the higher we go in the organic scale the less dependent the animal is on instinct pure and simple: in other words, the more does intelligence enter into the instinctive act. Thus, we will find an instinct common to mammals and birds less intelligent and more perfect in the latter. In birds, we may say, the sense of direction is more nearly infallible than in mammals. Thus, you will see a basketful of homing pigeons released at the Marble Arch, the birds all flying off in various directions to their homes in different parts of the country, from twenty or thirty to a couple of a hundred miles distant; and the chances are that not one out of twenty-five or thirty will fail to turn up at its destination. As the pigeon has existed in a domestic state for thousands of generations, it may be assumed that its homing faculty is not as perfect as in the wild bird. The bird has this faculty in greater perfection than the mammal because he needs it owing to his wings, which give him an immensely wider range and swifter motion. The mammal, moving on the ground, has more need of intelligence in every act of its life, in every step it takes, and no doubt memorises more. Yet I would say that the mammal, including man in a state of nature, is no more able to do without that sense than the small ant, that "lone wanderer, but not lost," on the grassy down.

I would say, then, that as mentality enters more into the actions of man, even in his most primitive state, than in other mammals, the sense of direction is less perfect in him than in them. Also that in highly civilised man, especially in urban districts, the sense is so weak as almost to be regarded as obsolescent. Like the sense of smell it is not needed, and in that condition its decay is inevitable. Nevertheless, when the need comes it revives, and when one is among savages or semi-civilised men much given to roaming, one meets with instances of the sense as acute and efficient as in the lower animals. I heard a good deal said on this subject early in life; as a boy it interested me because when I took to long solitary rambles, on foot or horseback, I made the discovery that I had a rather poor sense of direction, and when I got lost, which happened from time to time in a fog or at night and even in broad daylight when I was out of sight of all known landmarks, it had an extremely distressing effect on me and appeared to be a danger. Later, when I had grown up, I had some discussion on the subject with a young gaucho friend. One day in company he told us of a day spent in a search after lost horses at a long distance from the ranch where he had his temporary home. He had a companion with him, and when they were from nine to ten leagues from home night came very suddenly on them, with a black cloud covering the whole sky and rain in torrents. His companion cried out that there was nothing to do but dismount and spend the night sitting on their saddles and trying to keep themselves dry by wrapping their skin horse-rugs and ponchos round them. My friend laughed at such a proposal and said that they would go back and would be at home in about four hours or so, and would then be able to dry their clothes and get something to eat. The other was incredulous; it was all a flat plain with no road and not a star to show them the way. Nevertheless, they set out and arrived before midnight at the hovel which was their destination, and only when they dismounted and pushed the door open could he convince his companion that no road or light of star was needed to find your way back; nothing, in fact, was wanting but one's own sense.

It was just that sense, I told him, that I was without, and I knew that many others were in the same condition, otherwise we would not hear of people getting lost. That he possessed this sense in such perfection seemed almost incredible.

He replied that to him it seemed incredible that any sane person complete in his senses should be without it. He had to believe there were such men, just as there were others blind or deaf or idiots from birth. It made him laugh. For how could any-one, no matter how far he might go in a strange district, or how many turns he might take, fail to know just where he was and the exact direction of the place he wished to return to? You could take him blindfolded fifty leagues off into any place unknown to him, and lead him now in this direction, now in that, then take off the bandage in a dark night and set him free, and he would not be lost. Naturally he would know the right direction to take. How could he help knowing it?

I was surprised at hearing all this, as up till then I had looked on this young gaucho friend who did not know a letter of the alphabet as a good-natured half-fool. He was a big fellow, so dark, with such thick lips and such broad nostrils, that one supposed he had negro blood in him, and, negro-like, he was much given to laughter. But he had coarse lank black hair which was not negro-like. As he had been so much on horseback he waddled on the ground, and was like a big clumsy animal walking with difficulty on his hind legs. Then there were his garments: a waistcoat or blouse as a rule, new and of some crude, glaring colour, yellow or scarlet or blue, and all the others old and frayed and the colour of clay. As a rule he was without boots, being a poor devil, with his big iron spurs buckled on his bare feet. But now I conceived a great respect for him, and envied him the possession of something which I lacked and greatly missed.

This is perhaps an extreme case; nevertheless, men of that kind, who were never lost and never at a loss, were not uncommon on our Argentine frontiers. A man of that kind who had a bold and adventurous spirit as well was called a *Rastreador,* and was employed to go out into the desert and spy on the Indians.

It is probable that even in our ultra-civilised state there are individuals among us who possess the sense in a high degree although they may not know it themselves, just as there are those who have a sense of smell acute as that of any pure savage. This would not be strange: more wonderful is the fact that on some rare occasion the faculty should revive and burn in its pristine power in an individual in whom it had appeared to be non-existent. Here is a case in point.

Years ago, when following a discussion on a sense of direction in man in one of the weekly journals, I read of an instance of this reversion of the brain to a past state—a recovery of a lost sense. It occurred to a man, a dweller in a town, who went with a friend for an autumn holiday in a forest district in North America. They camped on the borders of a forest at a distance from any settlement, and the narrator, taking his gun, went off alone into the woods to look for something to shoot. He spent long hours in the forest, and at last when he was deep in it, surrounded on all sides by trees, and remembered that he had taken many turns, it suddenly came on him with a shock that he was lost, miles distant probably from his starting-point, and had not the faintest idea in which direction it was. He was terribly distressed, for the day was drawing to a close and he feared that to whichsoever side he directed his steps it would perhaps only take him further away. He fired several shots in the hope that some hunter or someone looking for him would hear them and come to his rescue. But no one came, and no answering shot or shout broke the silence. Then, when his distress was greatest, when he was in despair, all at once a light came to him, a sudden sense of relief, a feeling and a conviction that he knew exactly which direction to take. So convinced was he, that he set out not only confidently but gladly. And his instinct proved right: he came out of the wood and found the camp before him.

This narrative interested me deeply, simply because it so closely resembled an experience I once had—the one and only time when I have known the full meaning of such a sense—its certitude and its value to the lower animals and to man living in a state of nature, as he has existed for (let us say) a million years. My case was this. I was in a forest, and in the middle of a thick wood covering an area of several miles, with dense thickets and bogs and streams on its borders. I had been in it for several hours watching some woodland birds I was interested in, and, absorbed in my occupation, night surprised me and a sudden darkness caused by a cloud overspreading the sky; I realised that I was lost, since I did not know in which part of the wood I was, or which direction to take, and could not see on which side the sun had gone down. I feared, too, that if I tried to get out I should most probably get among the bogs and streams and dense thickets. And it was getting cold, as I was in the thinnest summer clothes and had been perspiring profusely. And suddenly, while standing there peering into the thick blackness all round me and feeling keenly distressed, relief came, and it was as if I had been captive and was unexpectedly set free. I did not know where I was and where the feared bogs were, but I knew in which direction to go. There was no hesitation, no shadow of a doubt. Off I went rejoicing where my supernatural faculty, as it then almost seemed to be, commanded, and after walking for half an hour came upon a blacker blackness where the undergrowth was so dense that it was extremely difficult to force my way through it. Again and again I came to places like that, yet dared not attempt to get round these thickets, fearing that if I varied the least bit from the bee-line I was making I might lose the sense of direction that guided me. I must, I felt, keep the line. Eventually I got free of the wood, and coming into an open space I dimly discerned a dwarf tree with a stout malformed trunk which I recognised as one of my landmarks on the borders of the wood, and there saw that I was actually making a bee-line for my destination. Now I knew where I was, and remembered that another smaller wood lay before me; then a mile or so of open grassland to the lonely farmhouse I was making for.

The feeling I had experienced on that one occasion, from the moment it came to me in the depths of that dark wood that I knew my way, was one of intense elation: it affected me like the recovery of something infinitely precious, so long lost that I had been without hope of ever finding it again; and it was like the recovery of sight to a blind man; or like that "vision of Paradise" which a temporary recovery of the sense of smell had seemed to Wordsworth as he sat in a garden full of flowers; or like the recovery of memory in one who had lost that faculty. And this elation lasted until I recognised the landmark, the deformed tree, and began to memorise the wood that yet remained to be got through and the open ground beyond it. Memory and thinking took the place of something which had been like an inspiration, an intuition, and had a sobering effect. I had to rely on my memory and reasoning faculties now.

It was a strange experience—perhaps the strangest I have ever had, when I remember the many occasions on which I have lost myself and have had long anxious hours of wandering in some unfamiliar place with no faintest intimation of any such helpful sense in me. For if this sense is so feeble in or so lost to us, how came it to revive and function so perfectly on this one occasion? The psychologist cannot help me, seeing that he takes no account of such a faculty; nor the physiologist, since there is no corresponding organ known to his science. But there is, there must be, an organ, albeit unrecognisable, a specialised nerve in the brain, I suppose, which keeps a record of all our turns and windings about, and ever, like the magnetic needle, swings faithfully round to point infallibly in the direction to which we desire in the end to return. This, at all events, is how it must be in the lower animal, and in savage men. Admitting so much, how came it to revive and function so perfectly in an individual who had appeared to be without it? I can only suppose that it is not actually obsolete in us, that it still exists and continues to function feebly—so feebly, indeed, that we rarely or never become conscious of it. If this be so, I take it that on this one occasion the nerve was highly excited by my mental agitation, the sense of being lost in that dark wood, and that in that state it recovered its function and the record of all the changes of direction I had taken in my roamings about, and eventually produced that conscious feeling of confidence and elation.

Bushman Presentiments

Wilhelm H. I. Bleek and *Lucy C. Lloyd*

Bushman Presentiments.—They feel in their bodies that certain events are going to happen. There is a kind of beating of the flesh, which tells them things. Those who are stupid, do not understand these teachings; they disobey them, and get into trouble,—such as being killed by a lion, etc.—The beatings tell those who understand them, which way they are not to go, and which arrow they had better not use, and also warn them, when many people are coming to the house on a wagon. They inform people where they can find the person of whom they are in search, i.e., which way they must go to seek him successfully.

[*Editor's note.* The following text was recorded, translated and annotated by Wilhelm Bleek and Lucy Lloyd, who made it their life's work to preserve the language and folklore of a "disappearing race"—the Bushmen of South Africa. The narrator ǁkábbo was an elder of the ǀxam San people (and something of a sorcerer), who had been arrested and transported to prison in Cape Town for allegedly stealing livestock. Bleek arranged for ǁkábbo to be released into his custody and stay in his family's home, where the two along with Lloyd engaged in intense collaborative work on the ǀxam San language over a period of many months in 1873–74. ǁkábbo overstayed his prison sentence, but eventually left to rejoin his wife and fellows.

The interest of this text lies in the way it gives expression to a theory of touch (one of the so-called proximity senses) acting at a distance. According to ǁkábbo some things which cannot be seen can nevertheless be felt, because people can empathize (i.e. "feel along") with other people and animals in their environment—providing they can keep still enough to heed the "tappings" at different points on or in their bodies. ǁkábbo gives a very graphic description of this unique form of tactile communication, which transcends species boundaries and turns the conventional Western understanding of touch inside-out. At the same time, some of what ǁkábbo has to say resonates with popular Western notions of premonitions.

In the original, the following English text appears next to the ǀxam San text, and the parentheses and other annotations represent an effort to fill in and/or mark the gaps between the two languages.]

[The following text was given in February and March, 1873 by ǁkábbo:]

The Bushmen's letters[1] are in their bodies. They (the letters) speak, they move, they make their (the Bushmen's) bodies move. They (the Bushmen) order the others to be silent; a man is altogether still, when he feels that ( ) his body is tapping (inside). A dream speaks falsely, it is (a thing) which deceives. The presentiment is that which speaks the truth; it is that by means of which the Bushman gets (or perceives) meat, when it has tapped. The Bushmen perceive people coming by means of it. ( ) The Bushmen feel a tapping (when) other people are[2] coming.

With regard to an old wound, a Bushman feels a tapping at the wound's place, while the tapping feels that the man (who has the old wound) walks, moving his body. The one man feels ( ) the other man who comes; he says to the children: "Look ye around, for grandfather, for grandfather seems to be coming; this is why I feel the place of his body's old wound." The children look around; the children perceive the man coming. They ( ) say to their father: "A man is coming yonder." Their father says to them: "Grandfather (his own father) comes yonder; he would come to me; he was the one whose coming I felt at the place of his old wound. I ( ) wanted you to see that he is really coming. For ye contradict my presentiment, which speaks truly."

He feels a tapping (at) his ribs; he says to the children: ( ) "The springbok seem to be coming, for I feel the black hair (on the sides of the springbok). Climb ye the Brinkkop standing yonder, that ye may look around at all the places. For I feel the springbok sensation." The other man agrees with him: "I think (that) the children (should) do so; for ( ) the springbok come in the sun; for the Brinkkop standing yonder is high; they shall look down upon the ground. And then they can see the whole ground. They can therefore (?) look inside ( ) the trees; for the springbok are wont to go hidden inside the trees. For the trees are numerous. The little river beds are also there. They are those to which the springbok are wont to come (in order) to eat in them. For, ( ) the little river beds have become green.[3] For I am wont to feel thus, I feel a sensation in the calves of my legs when the springbok's blood is going to run down them. For I always feel blood, when I am about to kill springbok. For I sit ( ) feeling a sensation behind my back, which the blood is wont to run down, when I am carrying a springbok. The springbok hair lies behind my back." The other agrees with him (saying): "Yes, my brother."

***

"Therefore, we are wont ( ) to wait (quietly); when the sensation is like this, when we are feeling the things come, while the things come near the house. We have a sensation in our feet, as we feel the rustling of the feet of the springbok with which the ( ) springbok come, making the bushes rustle. We feel in this manner, we have a sensation in our heads, when we are about to chop the springbok's horns. We have a sensation in our face, on account of the blackness of the stripe on the face of the springbok;[4] we feel a sensation in our ( ) eyes, on account of the black marks on the eyes of the springbok. The ostrich is one, for whom we feel the sensation of a louse;[5] as it walks, scratching the louse; when it is spring,[6] when the sun feels thus, it is warm.

"Then it is that ( ) the things go from us. They go along, passing opposite to the hut. Therefore, we early cross the things' spoor, when we early go to hunt. For, the things which ( ) are numerous are used to come first, when we are lying in the shade of the hut; because they think that we are probably lying asleep in the noonday's sleep. For we really ( ) lie down to sleep the noonday's sleep. But we do not lie sleeping at noon, when we feel this sensation. For we are used to feel like this when the things are walking; when ( ) we have felt the things coming, as they walk, moving their legs. We feel a sensation in the hollows under our knees, upon which blood drops, as we go along, carrying (the game). ( ) Therefore, we feel this sensation there.

"Therefore, the little boys do not lie in the shade inside the hut; they lie in the shade above yonder, so that they may beckon to us, when they have perceived the things, ( ) when the things walk at that place. They will beckon, making us see; for we are wont, sitting at a distance, to watch them, as they sit above yonder. Therefore, we say to each ( ) other, that the children appear to have seen things. For, they beckon. They point to that place, while they point to the place towards (?) which the things are walking, where the Brinkkop mountains lie thus spread out (?). So we may quickly chase the things at the hill which lies across, to which the things are walking. The things walk, putting themselves in front of it;[7] we will quickly pass behind it, while it still lies away (from the springbok). We will stand nicely (ready) for ( ) the things, that we may not steal up abreast,[8] of the things, (but) that we may steal up in front of the things, at the place[9] to which the leader goes."

Notes

1. The word *!gwē* was used by the Bushmen to denote both letters and books. ||kábbo explained that the beatings in their bodies, here described, are the Bushman's "letters," and resemble the letters which take a message or an account of what happens in another place.
2. The Bushman, when an ostrich is coming and is scratching the back of its neck with its foot, feels the tapping in the lower part of the back of his own neck; at the same place where the ostrich is scratching.
   The springbok, when coming, scratches itself with its horns, and with its foot; then the Bushman feels the tapping.
   When a woman who had gone away is returning to the house, the man who is sitting there, feels on his shoulders the thong with which the woman's child is slung over her shoulders; he feels the sensation there.
3. That is, the grass and the little bushes of the river bed.

4. A black stripe that comes down in the centre of the forehead, and terminates at the end of the nose.

5. An insect which bites the ostrich, a black insect; an "ostrich louse" as the Bushmen describe it.

6. ǁkábbo explains that ǁgū means "de bloem tijd".

7. That is, putting their faces towards the mountain.

8. That is, not at the side of the game as it goes along, but right in front of its path.

9. The Bushmen are at the back of the hill, waiting for the springbok to cross it, coming to the place where they (the Bushmen) are.

—4—

Anatomy of Mysticism
Jess Byron Hollenback

From time to time in history, one encounters singularly gifted men and women called mystics, individuals who have often played pivotal roles as innovators, revitalizers, and reactionary conservators of their respective religious traditions. A quick glance at the more prominent names from among their ranks provides convincing proof of their historical and religious significance. Muhammad, Paul, Jesus of Nazareth, Gautama Buddha, Moses, Augustine of Hippo, Plotinus, the prophet Ezekiel, Ibn al-'Arabi, al-Ghazzali, Black Elk, and Milarepa make up the list of famous mystics who have made their mark in the history of their respective religious traditions. What particular gift distinguishes mystics from ordinary men and women? The answer is their susceptibility to certain unusual states of consciousness by means of which they come into direct contact with a domain of experience that almost always remains inaccessible to the human mind in its ordinary waking state. While conscious or in a trance-state, mystics enter into another world, a realm of "spiritual" things, beings, and powers. Although these spiritual phenomena usually remain imperceptible to the five physical senses in their normal mode of operation, this mystical state of consciousness often brings these spiritual entities into the mystic's field of aware-ness with a compelling vividness and concreteness equaling or even surpassing that of ordinary sense objects.

The religious, cultural, and social importance of mystics does not, of course, derive solely from their unusual experiences. Their importance also derives from their remarkable ability to endow any kind of symbolism, mythology, or metaphysic (including even nineteenth-century European materialism)[1] with a hitherto unsus-pected dimension of significance and meaning, as well as their peculiar penchant for having spiritual experiences that seem to empirically confirm for them and their co-religionists that the nature of reality is actually congruent with the description provided by their respective scriptures and myths. With respect to the first point, Paul's and Muhammad's reinterpretations of events and personages in the Old Testa-ment serve as examples of how mystics can play a major role in endowing the myths and symbols of their particular religious traditions with a new meaning. With respect to the second point, as important as mystics' contributions have been to the develop-ment of new hermeneutic frameworks and symbolisms within religious traditions, it is equally important that a mystic's religious community also exerts a powerful influence on both the content of his peculiar experiences and the distinctive manner in which he responds to them. In short, the relationship between the mystic and his community is one of reciprocal interdependence, a fact that no study of mysticism can afford to ignore. It is a serious error to regard the mystical experience as though it were simply the consequence of some purely intrapsychic process that exists in total isolation from the mystic's historical and cultural milieu.

What features distinguish "mystical" experience from other types of experience? In an attempt to answer this question, I display four classic examples of this phenom-enon, one after another, so as to bring the distinctive features of mystical experience into the sharpest possible relief. However, the reader should bear in mind that because the existential coloration of each mystic's particular experience, as well as that expe-rience's distinctive imagery and symbolism, remain indissolubly determined by the mystic's cultural and religious environment, mystical experiences necessarily exhibit a remarkable degree of diversity. For this reason, no matter which four examples one chooses to illustrate the essential features of this mode of experience, one must recog-nize that these choices can only give the reader a partial insight into the range of varia-tion that occurs within the phenomenon. This means that some of the characteristics I isolate as common to each of these classic episodes will manifest themselves weakly, if at all, in other mystics' experiences.

Four Examples of Mystical Experience

An Eskimo Shaman's Enlightenment

In the following narrative, Aua, an Iglulik Eskimo from the northwestern coast of Hudson Bay, describes the unusual experience that came to him the moment he first realized that he had become a shaman. He had sought instruction from many famous shamans, but their teaching had apparently not yet given him any significant results. Aua withdrew into solitude (a traditional shamanic practice among the Eskimo) where, for a time, he seems to have undergone a period of great mental distress and instability. After he had withdrawn, he related to Rasmussen:

> I soon became very melancholy. I would sometimes fall to weeping, and feel unhappy with-out knowing why. Then, for no reason, all would suddenly be changed and I felt a great, inexplicable joy, a joy so powerful that I could not restrain it, but had to break into a song, a mighty song, with room only for the one word: joy, joy! ... And then in the midst of such a fit of mysterious and overwhelming delight I became a shaman, not knowing myself how it came about. But I was a shaman. I could see and hear in a totally different way. I had gained my *quamaneq,* my enlightenment, the shaman-light of brain and body, and this in such a manner that it was not only I who could see through the darkness of life, but the same light also shone out from me, imperceptible to human beings, but visible to all the spirits of the earth and sky and sea, and these now came to me and became my helping spirits.

My first helping spirit was my namesake, a little aua [a female shore-spirit somewhat akin to a small elf]. When it came to me, it was as if the passage and the roof of the house were lifted up, and I felt such a power of vision, that I could see right through the earth and up into the sky; it was the little aua that brought me all this inward light, hovering over me as long as I was singing. Then it placed itself in a corner of the passage, invisible to others, but always ready if I should call it. (Quoted in Rasmussen 1929: 118–19)

A Modern Hindu Awakens Kundalini

My second example of a mystical experience recounts the story of how Gopi Krishna, a contemporary practitioner of yoga, first aroused that peculiar vital energy that hatha yoga treatises call *kundalini*. This strange, subtle, spirit-like energy resides in a latent unmanifest state within the lowest of those subtle energy centers or *chakras* that supposedly line the backbone but that are invisible to ordinary visual or anatomical inspection. The practitioners of hatha yoga maintain that when an individual becomes adept at certain techniques of mental concentration, he begins to excite this normally dormant energy into a state of activity. Once this happens, kundalini begins to move like a luminous fluid up the spinal cord, its movements upward being accompanied by a dramatic transformation in the yogin's mode of consciousness.

Gopi Krishna's dramatic arousal of kundalini culminated seventeen years of meditational practice in which he had finally learned how to sit undistractedly in yoga postures for hours, breathing slowly and rhythmically while he simultaneously centered his entire attention on a luminous lotus that he imagined as glowing at the very top of his head. Gopi Krishna had therefore already attained considerable success in *pranayama,* the technique of mental concentration through "visualization" and breath control that constitutes one of the cornerstones of yoga.

One day, while Gopi Krishna was totally absorbed in contemplating the imaginary lotus, he suddenly felt a peculiar sensation at the base of his spine. However, as soon as he began to pay attention to this strange sensation (and thus divert his previously focused attention from its exclusive concentration on the glowing lotus), he noted that the feeling began to dissipate. On the other hand, if he kept his attention tightly centered on the lotus despite this strange feeling at the base of his spine, the sensation reappeared. He repeated this procedure several times, holding his attention fixedly on the glowing lotus despite the steadily intensifying strength of the spinal sensation. Then something snapped.

Suddenly, with a roar like that of a waterfall, I felt a stream of liquid light entering my brain through the spinal cord.

Entirely unprepared for such a development, I was completely taken by surprise; but regaining self-control instantaneously, I remained sitting in the same posture, keeping my mind on the point of concentration. The illumination grew brighter and brighter, the roaring louder. I experienced a rocking sensation and then felt myself slipping outside of my body, entirely enveloped in a halo of light. It is impossible to describe the experience accurately. I felt the point of consciousness that was myself growing wider, spreading outward while the body, normally the immediate object of its perception, appeared to have receded into the distance until I became entirely unconscious of it. I was now all consciousness, without any outline, without any idea of a corporeal appendage, without any feeling or sensation coming from the senses, immersed in a sea of light simultaneously conscious and aware of every point, spread out, as it were, without any barrier or material obstruction. I was no longer myself, or to be more accurate, no longer as I knew myself to be, a small point of awareness confined in a body, but instead was a vast circle of consciousness in which the body was but a point, bathed in light and in a state of exaltation and happiness impossible to describe. (Krishna 1971: 12–13)

Saint Augustine's Vision of the Infinite Light

The next account of a classic mystical experience comes from Saint Augustine's famous autobiography, *The Confessions*. It describes an illumination experience that came to Augustine during a time when he had immersed himself in the study of Neoplatonism shortly before his final conversion to Christianity. In this passage Augustine writes as though he were talking to God. He related that, one day, with the help of God,

I entered into my inmost being. This I could do, for you became my helper. I entered there, and by my soul's eye, such as it was, I saw above that same eye of my soul, above my mind, an unchangeable light. It was not this common light plain to all flesh, nor a greater light, as it were, of the same kind, as though that light would shine many, many times more bright, and by its greater power fill the whole universe. Not such was that light, but different, far different from all other lights. Nor was it above my mind, as oil is above water, or sky above earth. It was above my mind because it made me, and I was beneath it, because I was made by it. He who knows the truth, knows that light, and he who knows it, knows eternity. (Augustine 1960, VII, ch. 10: 170–71)

Richard Maurice Bucke's Experience of Cosmic Consciousness

That experience of so-called cosmic consciousness that overwhelmed Richard Bucke one evening furnishes us with one of the most perfect examples of how mystical experiences often give their recipients a compelling sensation that they have not only contacted ultimate reality itself but also comprehended its nature. Bucke relates that as he was driving home from a poetry-reading session in a warm mood of "quiet, almost passive enjoyment," he suddenly discovered that he was

wrapped around as it were by a flame-colored cloud. For an instant he thought of fire, some sudden conflagration in the great city; next, he knew that the light was within himself. Directly afterwards came upon him a sense of exultation, of immense joy-ousness accompanied or immediately followed by an intellectual illumination quite impossible to describe. Into his brain streamed one momentary lightning-flash of the Brahmic Splendor which has ever since lightened his life; upon his heart fell one drop of Brahmic Bliss, leaving thenceforward for always an aftertaste of heaven. Among other things he did not come to believe, he saw and knew that the Cosmos is not dead matter but a living Presence, that the soul of man is immortal, that the universe is so built and ordered that without any peradventure all things work together for the good of each and all, that the foundation principle of the world is what we call love. (Bucke 1969: 9–10)

This description clearly demonstrates that Bucke did far more than just perceive something unusual. His vision was more than just a perception of something, it was also, as he put it, a blissful "intellectual illumination," a type of experience that conveyed to him what he regarded as an unshakeable insight about the foundational principles of the cosmos.[2]

From these four examples, it is easy to see that the mystical experience is a mode of awareness that differs sharply from both the dream-state and ordinary waking consciousness.

Distinctive Features of the Mystical Experience

Seven Common Characteristics

Most mystical experiences exhibit seven distinctive attributes that, when taken together, distinguish them from other modes of human experience.

1. The mystical experience is a radical, trans-sensory metamorphosis of the subject's mode of consciousness that takes place while he or she is awake.
2. It is a mode of consciousness that gives the subject both privileged access to and knowledge of those things that his or her particular culture and religious tradition regards as ultimately real. In other words, it is no mere "perception" of another domain of experience—it is a revelation that concerns those things that are of supreme ontological significance for that individual's particular cultural and religious community.[3]
3. It is an experience that gives the subject privileged knowledge about those matters that his or her religious tradition considers to have the utmost importance for human salvation. In other words, it gives mystics knowledge about matters that are of ultimate soteriological concern to their communities.[4] This is yet another sense in which the mystical experience is not mere "perception" but rather something that compels a response to it with all of one's being.
4. It is heavily laden with affect.
5. It is an illumination that is both literal and metaphorical.

6. It is fundamentally amorphous and its content historically conditioned. The mystical experience is amorphous insofar as it has no predetermined form. The particular images, insights, emotional states, and volitions that it generates derive most of their specific character and intensity from religious and philosophical assumptions that the mystics bring with them into the experience prior to its onset. Moreover, the content of each mystic's experience validates the mythology or metaphysic that he or she takes for granted as being self-evidently true. In other words, there is not only an essential contextuality to the mystical experience but also a reciprocal interdependency between the presuppositions that underlie a mystic's interpretation of his or her experience and the content of that experience. For this reason, it is inappropriate to speak of either the experience or its interpretation as though one were epistemologically prior to the other.

7. It is a mode of experience that usually has its genesis in the recollective act.

Notes

1. The Spiritualist mediums of nineteenth-century Europe and America, with their exhibitions of poltergeist phenomena and ectoplasmic manifestations, show that some nineteenth-century mystics attempted a novel reconciliation of materialistic science and the Christian dogma of the reality and immortality of the human soul. Their experiences of those phenomena seemed to prove to them that religion could be saved from the criticisms of scientific materialists because they claimed that their capacity to produce ectoplasms and poltergeists indicated that the soul had a material aspect and was, therefore, like the matter of Newtonian physics, eternally subsistent.

2. Not surprisingly, Bucke's ontological and metaphysical concerns were those that preoccupied many of his philosophically inclined contemporaries. Like them, he, too, was concerned with the following questions: What is the nature of the relationship between "matter" and "spirit"? Which of these two entities has greater ontological dignity; that is, which of the two is more "real" than the other? Is spirit autonomous from matter? If so, what evidence supports this conclusion? Bucke thought that his experience of cosmic consciousness helped him to resolve these metaphysical questions by giving him empirical evidence for the ontological priority of spirit over matter. After all, this vision showed him that "the cosmos is not dead matter but a living Presence." Bucke also thought that he had saved Christianity from vulgar philosophical materialism because his vision had proved to his own satisfaction, at least, that "the soul of man is immortal" and that the universe is not cold and indifferent to human beings but, in some peculiarly sensed and empirically demonstrable way, loving and concerned about their welfare. He and his secularized contemporaries could now once again live confidently in a reenchanted universe that was alive, loving, and endowed with personality. His vision had directly demonstrated that

the dreary, impersonal, and inanimate cosmos of the philosophical materialists and positivists was a fallacy. Furthermore, this vision had convinced Bucke that the Christ of the New Testament was none other than the experience of cosmic consciousness itself. (Bucke [1969: 6] explicitly identified Jesus Christ with the phenomenon of cosmic consciousness. "The saviour of man is Cosmic Consciousness—in Paul's language—the Christ.") When one acknowledged this admittedly unusual interpretation of Christ as an experience rather than as a man, there was no problem bringing the Bible into harmony with science since one could now accept an interpretation of Christ that was free of all the mythological baggage that had made Christianity and science so incompatible in the past.

3. Ontology is that branch of philosophy that deals with the ultimate nature of being, of that which exists. Hence, the term *ontological* means simply that which pertains to what is ultimately real.

4. The word *soteriological* means of or pertaining to the process which leads to salvation. Soteriological knowledge is therefore something quite distinct from ontological knowledge.

References

Augustine of Hippo (1960), *The Confessions of St. Augustine,* trans. John K. Ryan, Garden City, NY: Image Books.

Bucke, R. M. (1969), *Cosmic Consciousness: A Study in the Evolution of the Human Mind*, New York: E.P. Dutton.

Krishna, G. (1971), *Kundalini: The Evolutionary Energy in Man,* Berkeley, CA: Shambala.

Rasmussen, K. (1929), *Intellectual Culture of the Iglulik Eskimos. Report of the Fifth Thule Expedition, 1921–24*, Copenhagen, Denmark: Glydendalske Boghandel.

Part II
Historical Investigations

The Five Senses in Classical Science and Ethics

Louise Vinge

Sight, hearing, smell, taste and touch: that the senses should be enumerated in this way is not self-evident. The number and order of the senses are fixed by custom and tradition, not by nature. The regular order being subject to occasional change proves its arbitrariness. Therefore, we can describe the enumeration of the five senses as an artificial series of natural elements.

"The five senses" is one of several concepts consisting of categories with a defined number of elements, all somehow covering life or the universe: "the four seasons," "the four elements," "the four temperaments," "the seven arts," "the seven deadly sins," "the seven ages of man," "the twelve months," etc.[1]

Aristotle on the Senses and Their Functions

It is not quite true, as is sometimes said, that Aristotle introduced the partition of perception into five separate senses.[2] This division in itself had been accepted long before and was even subjected to criticism. But naturally it later gained a position that was almost unshakeable simply because it was authorized by Aristotle. His discussion of the senses and their perceptions was new in another way. He studied them in a wide context, that is, as part of his inquiry into the soul, and this inquiry was conducted by new methods (see Düring 1966: 571).

Aristotle's two most important works on psychology and the senses are usually called *De Anima* and *De Sensu et Sensibilibus*.[3] The latter is one of the so-called *Parva Naturalia*. Aristotle sees the soul and its different capacities as intimately connected with and dependent on the body. He stresses this in both works. In the introduction to the *De Sensu* he enumerates many of these functions: sensation, memory, reason, desire to satisfy hunger and thirst, feelings of pleasure and pain; further sleep and waking, youth and age, respiration and expiration, life and death. He continues: "That all the phenomena we have mentioned are common to soul and body is clear; for all of them either are accompanied by sensation or result from it ... and that sensation is produced in the soul by way of the body can be proved, and is indeed clear without proof" (*De Sensu*, ch. 1, 436 b 1). "The animate differs from the inanimate by possessing life" Aristotle says in a passage of the *De Anima* (II: 2, 413 a 20 ff.); anything which has one of the qualities reason, sense-perception, local movement and rest, nutrition, decay and growth has life, he continues. Things that merely grow and decay are thought to have life. But "being an *animal* depends on having the faculty of perception; even things that cannot move, but have sense-perception, we describe as animals and not merely as living things" (413 b 1 ff.). In this way Aristotle brings together the conceptions of soul, life and perception. The primary perception common to all is touch. And "where there is perception, there are pain and pleasure, and where these are, there is appetite" (414 a 20 ff.). Touch is necessary to the other senses, as it is necessary for nutrition (414 a 29 ff.; 414 b 32 ff.). In the *De Anima,* Aristotle has a general discussion of the importance of nutrition to life followed by a review of man's different senses. His first principle is, that "perception consists in being affected; it is an alteration." He repeats in several places that perception in itself is passive (e.g., III: 2, 426 a 2).

The objects of sense-perceptions are of two kinds: those which are specific to the various senses, such as color, sound and smell, and those which are common to all of them, such as movement and rest, number, size and form, etc.

Two interdependent problems are of importance to Aristotle when he is studying the functions of the sense-organs from a more technical point of view. One is the relation between the senses and the four elements, the other is how sensation is transmitted from the object to the sense-organ, which "media" serve the various kinds of objects and organs. Aristotle took over the problem of the elements from his predecessors (Düring 1966: 562). He treats it both in the *De Sensu* (ch. 2) and in the *De Anima.* In the former work he is more absorbed by it, in the latter he approaches it with less interest. In the *De Sensu* he says that scholars have tried to combine the sense-organs and the elements, but as there are only four elements, the fifth sense presents a difficulty. All of them have made the organ of sight consist of fire. But, Aristotle objects, why then can we not see in darkness? The eye contains water, which can absorb light; water, then, is the element of sight. The element of hearing is air, that of smell is fire, that of touch is earth. Taste is a form of touch, he adds, and so the sum comes out even.

In the *De Anima* (III: 1, 425 a 3) this model is much less rigid: "Now the only elements of which sense-organs are composed are air and water (the pupil of the eye being composed of water, the organ of hearing of air, the organ of smelling of either air or water), while fire is either the organ of no sense or common to all (since nothing that can perceive is wholly devoid of heat), and earth is either the material of no sense-organ or in a special degree present in that of touch; so that there cannot be any sense-organ other than those composed of water or air." In this work, Aristotle is much more interested in the question of how sensations are transported to the sense-organs from the objects, that is, of the "media" of the organs. To sight, this is "the transparent," something, air for instance, that is moved by color and brings it to the eye. This is demonstrated by the fact that if an object is placed immediately on the eye, it cannot be seen (*De Anima,* II: 7, 419 a 6 ff.). It is the same with hearing and smell:

nothing that touches the sense-organ brings about perception, but it is necessary that sound and smell first affect a medium. The medium of sound is air, and that of smell has no name (*De Anima* II: 7, 419 a 30 ff.). For taste and touch there must be a corresponding medium: the "flesh" and the tongue are to the organ of touch (taste being a kind of touch) what air and water are to sight, hearing and smell. If the sense-organ were to touch its object, no sensation would occur, just as we do not see an object laid directly on the eye. The organ of touch, then, must be inside us (*De Anima* II: 11, 423 b; cf. II: 7, 419 a 22 ff.).

Aristotle discusses the number and order of the senses without changing established ideas, but possibly, it seems, refuting one or more predecessors such as Democritus, who thought that there were more than five senses (Aristotle 1961: 268). Man's senses number five, and there cannot be more, for one thing because of their relations to the elements, he says (*De Anima* III: 1, 425 a 3 ff.) (Beare 1906: 246). The order of the senses is, as a matter of course, that sight comes first (*De Anima* III: 3, 428 b 30 f.), hearing next, smell in the middle: "There is an odd number of senses, and an odd number has a middle; the sense of smell comes midway between the tactile senses (touch and taste) and those that operate through a medium (sight and hearing)" (*De Sensu* chap. 5, 445 a 4 ff.). Also, it is the order sight, hearing, smell, taste and touch that decides the composition of the *De Anima* (in the *De Sensu,* only sight, smell and taste are taken up).

There is an enumeration of various perceptions in Plato (*Theaetetus* 156 b) beginning with sight, hearing and smell; it leaves out taste and instead of touch mentions "perceptions of becoming cold and of burning heat." Plato adds to the series perceptions of pleasure and discomfort and desire and fear, and speaks of the existence of many other perceptions, with and without name. "The senses," then, are not for Plato distinguished from "the feelings." But Plato arranges the senses mentioned in the same order as Aristotle was to give them.[4]

At the beginning of the *De Sensu,* Aristotle discusses which sense is the most important and valuable one: "Sight is in its own nature more valuable with a view to the necessities of life, but hearing is incidentally more conducive to knowledge." The reason is of course that it is by hearing that speech is perceived (*De Sensu,* ch. 1, 437 a 3 ff.). But in several places touch is called "the first sense"; it is the one most necessary for the maintenance of life.

When treating the separate senses Aristotle first analyses what their special object is. The object of sight is color; light, too, is necessary in order for sense-perception to come about (*De Anima* III: 7, 418 a 26 ff.). "The transparent" is made transparent by fire; light is the color it takes. Aristotle does not deal with the construction of the eye— classical scientists did not know much about this (Beare 1906: 5–9) but as was mentioned above, refutes the theory that its inner parts consist of fire (Beare 1906: 82). He cannot accept, then, the older theory that rays issuing from the eye reach the object. Nor does he find satisfactory the so-called theory of emanation, which maintains that particles are sent out from the object, but left the problem without a final solution.

Sound as the object of hearing is the next point Aristotle takes up in the *De Anima*. He discusses in detail how sound is produced, analysing it as potential and actual sound (*De Anima* II: 8). Those things have sound, that can move air, which in its turn can reach the air in the ears (Boring 1942: 321). The voice is a kind of sound, and therefore it is included under the same heading; its dependence on the organ of breathing is emphasized.

The sense of smell is more difficult to treat, says Aristotle in the *De Anima*, because the nature of smell is less clear than that of sound or color. And our sense of smell is less acute than it is in many animals. The sense of taste, on the other hand, is more exact, because it is a form of touch, and this sense is better in man than in any other animal. The well-developed sense of touch is the condition of man's intelligence (*De Anima* II: 9, 421 a 7 ff.). The scanty discussion of the sense of smell at this point is compensated by a long exposition in the *De Sensu* (ch. 5), where pleasant and unpleasant smells are treated. The healthy effect of pleasant smells is heavily underlined.

The sense of taste, according to Aristotle, is a form of touch. But it is dependent on moisture: a substance must be fluid in order to give a sensation of taste, and the tongue must be wetted (*De Anima* II: 10, 422 a 8 ff.). Touch in itself poses many problems, among them this one: is it one sense or several? When analysing the other senses, Aristotle has found that they each work within its pair of contraries: sight between white and black, hearing between shrill and dull, taste between bitter and sweet. But for touch, there are several such pairs of contraries: hot and cold, solid and liquid, hard and soft, etc. He solves the problem by showing that the other senses also have several pairs of contraries (II: 11, 422 b 17 ff.). The question of the medium of touch, the discussion of "flesh," accounted for above, takes up most of the space. At the end of the *De Anima*, Aristotle widens the importance of touch among the senses: it is the only sense that an animal cannot live without. Touch is the sense that living beings have just for the sake of being—the others we have for the sake of well-being (III: 13, 435 a 11 ff.; the idea is repeated in the *De Sensu*, ch. 1). On closer analysis, all the sense-organs are found to perceive by touch, but through a medium (*De Anima* III: 13, 435 a 11 ff.). This is contradicted, though, by the *De Sensu*: "Democritus and most of those who write about sensation do a very absurd thing in making all sensible things objects of touch. For if this be so, each of the other senses must be a form of touch; which is impossible" (ch. 4, 442 a 29 ff.).

Through his discussion of general qualities, perceived by several or all senses, such as number, movement and rest, form, and of special qualities mutually connected, such as the fact that a white thing seen is also a certain man, Aristotle is led to suppose the existence of what he in some places calls *koinē aisthēsis*, "communis sensus," the common sense (Beare 1906: 250–336, on Aristotle from p. 276; Düring 1968: 578). In his introduction to the *De Anima*, Ross emphasizes the fact that this is not to be understood as something above, higher than the separate senses, but as their common nature (Aristotle 1961: 33). To the functions of the common sense besides the perception of general and special qualities, belongs the perception of sensation itself (this is, as Ross says, one of the first places where the problem of conscience is taken up at all). The distinction between the sensations of different senses, too, is made by the common sense. Finally, the coordination of the sense-organs' rest, which takes place during sleep, results from the suspension of the common sense.

Another conception denoting a general function of the soul, introduced by Aristotle in his analysis of the senses and their general qualities is *(ωαντασία)*, something that receives and retains the sense-perceptions before they are turned into conceptions, knowledge, memories or opinions. But recollection depends on its function, and it is intimately connected with reason, the intellect. It does not, of course, receive sight-impressions only, but perceptions of all the senses, as is shown by the fact that we can remember sounds, smells, tastes and touch-perceptions (Beare 1906: 290).

Aristotle's psychological theories did not have any immediate significance, as little as his other works. Only in Late Antiquity and the Middle Ages were his works made accessible, arranged and commented on. Views, problems and formulas from the *De Anima* then influenced everything written on the five senses and on the structure and functions of the soul. After Aristotle were then repeated the questions of the objects and media of the senses, of their relations to the elements, their number (Boring 1942: 525) and importance, of the unity of touch and so on, and the concepts of *sensus communis* and *fantasia (imaginatio)* became common in psychology.

The Five Senses in Ethical Precepts and Spiritual Experience

Xenophon

The senses give knowledge about the outside world—but they can also give pleasure. Each sense enjoys its special objects. Pleasure, though, may be a temptation, and therefore the senses and their functions also have a moral aspect. A passage that in the course of time influenced the way in which the five senses were described and treated in literature and art occurs in the well-known fable of Hercules at the cross-roads, as Xenophon tells it in his *Memorabilia*. His source is, as he states, Prodicus the sophist, in whose work *The Horae* it had been told. The female being who tempts Hercules to choose the pleasant way of life seizes upon the pleasures of the five senses.

> You shall taste all the sweets of life; and hardship you shall never know. First, of wars and worries you shall not think, but shall ever be considering what choice food or drink you can find, what sight or sound will delight you, what touch or perfume; what tender love can give you most joy, what bed the softest slumbers; and how to come by all these pleasures with least trouble. (Xenophon [1923] 1965: 97)

In this passage, the rhetorical elegance is considerable, with its anaphores and forms of verbs with similar endings in parallel phrases. The effort to bring about stylistical symmetry, though, has forced the author to violate the logic of the content. The pleasures are arranged in three pairs. But "food and drink" are objects of the same sense, taste, whereas next come appeals to sight and hearing, smell and touch, arranged in two pairs. Still it is apparent that the various sense-organs and their fields decide the pattern. The pleasure that Eudaimonia-Kakia promises shall involve all five senses. One observes that Xenophon has taste come first, sight and hearing, smell and touch following. Whether Xenophon wants the climax of the allurements to be understood as homosexual intercourse, as the passage is sometimes interpreted,[5] seems to be a moot point: the verb may mean "to enjoy oneself" without erotic implications. But there is a possibility of seeing sexual pleasure as the natural end of the series of the allurements of the senses, particularly as mention is also made of "what bed gives the softest slumbers."

Philo

In his discussion of the importance of the Xenophon passage for the development of a topos called "the banquet of sense," Frank Kermode (1971) says that this way of treating pleasures in a series where each sense is represented with its particular object seems to have been neglected by the older imitators of Xenophon, such as Silius Italicus, who applies the fable of Hercules at the cross-roads to Scipio in his *Punica*. Kermode supposes that the use of the series of the senses in connection with the Hercules theme was not revived until the Renaissance. There is, however, an important imitation of the Xenophon passage which has been disregarded in this context.[6] This passage demonstrates that even during the classical period the allurements of Eudaimonia-Kakia were quite clearly arranged to fit the five senses; seductive pleasure was described as a way from the experiences of sight to those of touch.

It is in Philo Judaeus that we find this imitation of the conversation of Pleasure and Virtue from the Hercules fable in Xenophon.[7] Hercules at the cross-roads is exchanged for a man with two wives, hating each other and filling the house with their quarreling. The apparition of Pleasure is described in great detail. Philo tells of her elaborate coiffure, her flower-patterned dress, the golden jewellery she wears and the perfume of her breath. Whereas the Pleasure of Xenophon came alone, she is here followed by eleven allegorical figures: Recklessness, Faithlessness, Adulation, Falseness, Impiety, etc. She offers her gifts and does not let slip the opportunity to emphasize how each sense will be given its joys:

> With me you will find freedom from the sense of restraint, from the fear of punishment, from the stress of business, from the discipline of labour; you will find colours all and sundry, sweet modulations of melodious sound, costly kinds of food and drink, abundant varieties of delicious perfumes, amours without ceasing, frolics unregulated, chamberings unrestricted, language unrepressed, deeds uncensored, life without care, sleep soft and sweet, satiety ever unfilled.

And she repeats:

> I will join you in considering what food and drink would charm your palate, what sight would please your eyes, what sound your ears, what perfume your nostrils. (Philo 1929, II: 111)

The retinue of Virtue is much larger, and when revealing all the vices that Pleasure induces in those who love her, she is very detailed: more than one hundred and fifty words for various bad qualities are enumerated in a long catalogue.

That Philo has imitated Xenophon is beyond doubt (see 1929, II: 489; Cohn 1919: 222). At the beginning of his fable, he has tried to give it a new frame, the marriage with the two wives, but very soon he has left this idea, returning to the allegory of the cross-roads. The similarities in details are numerous, too; not least the series of senses in Pleasure's speech. There are also significant changes: in the first variation, the order is changed so that the pleasures of the eye come first, then those of the ear, then taste, smell and touch. In the second variation he follows Xenophon more closely, starting with "food and drink" and continuing with sight and hearing. But above all we note that he states straight out that the pleasure of touch is sexual intercourse.

Commentators suppose that the characterization of Pleasure is to be understood as a polemic with the Epicureans, of whom Philo has the common misconception that they care only for the sensual pleasure of the body. There are passages in the speech of Virtue, too, which allude directly to the Epicurean opinion of the soul's dependence on the body and the senses (Cohn 1919: 225).

But this is far from being the only passage where Philo occupies himself with the five senses. On the contrary, it could be maintained that he chose Xenophon's tale for his model simply because it contained the passage on the pleasures of the senses. A German scholar, Ernst von Dobschütz, has observed that Philo speaks "auffallend häufig" [with striking frequency] about the five senses; he states: "Er verwendet die Fünfzahl allegorisch, wo immer es geht" [He uses the number five allegorically whenever possible—Ed.] (Dobschütz 1929: 380). Dobschütz has a good collection of examples of how Philo applies his allegorical method in order to find the five senses in the tales of the Old Testament. Time and again, Philo returns to their value and moral aspects in his expositions of the Bible; their relation to body and soul seems to be one of his central problems. He uses several graphic images to emphasize his doctrine.

In his explication of *Genesis* Adam is seen as Mind, Eve as the senses. The senses are exposed to the enslaving allurement of the objects: beauty enslaves sight, good food and sweets enslave taste, the harp and the flute hearing, etc. But reason can govern them, for "Mind is superior to Sense-perception" (Philo 1929, I: 452). Philo compares Mind to a charioteer who either controls his horses, directing them at his will, or loses his command of them, so that they leave the road, governed by their instincts, and end in the ditch. (Obviously, this image is modeled on the famous passage in Plato's *Phaedrus,* although we do not deal here with transcendence.⁸) Philo also compares Mind to the helmsman of a ship, or to the governor of a city. If the senses are given power, he explains, the same confusion will arise in man as in a house where the slaves take power. "The mind is set on fire and all is ablaze, and that fire is kindled by the objects of sense which sense-perception supplies" (§ 224). On the other hand, they can also be the guards of the body, helping the soul to triumph and keep to the straight path. If they are hurt by violence or malady, the soul falls into misery (Philo 1929, I: 20).

Abraham's life, too, Philo explicates as an account of the relation between body, senses and soul; among other things a most speculative interpretation of numbers helps him to support his explication (IV: 240–53). In his interpretation of the tale of the destruction of the land of the Sodomites, the Pentapolis, Philo has another exposition on the senses. The five cities are the five senses, "the instruments of the pleasures."

> For we get pleasure either by seeing varieties of colors and shapes in objects (whether possessed of physical life or not), or by hearing very melodious sounds or through taste in matters of food and drink, or through smell in fragrant perfumes or through touch in soft and warm and also in smooth substances. Now of the five, the three most animal and servile are taste, smell, and touch, which cause particular excitation in the cattle and wild beasts. ... The other two have a link with philosophy and hold the leading place—hearing and sight. (VI: 74–85)

But the ears are in a moral sense below sight, hearing being more passive. The eyes turn to their objects and affect them. Sight has the highest place, exalted by God to be the Queen of the other senses. Philo takes up the image of sight being established "as it were in a citadel" (§ 150), an image probably derived from Plato's *Timaeus* (70 A) and here for the first time introduced into biblical exegesis. The eye, too, it is which exposes the feelings and moods of the soul, which shows the images of dreams, and above all bestows on us the benefit of showing us light, and observing and judging the world and its pleasures. Because of this, Philo says, it was right that one of the five cities was allowed to exist after the destruction, for sight is not confined to mortal things but strives upwards, to the immortal things and rejoices in contemplating them.

In other places, too, Philo praises the sense of sight as the highest one, most eloquently in his treatise on the laws. In a passage there he praises sight and hearing as the senses that give a good life, while smell and taste are purely for the maintenance of life; an Aristotelian idea, which is here given an accentuated form (Philo 1929, VII: 296). Still more enthusiastic is a digression to the prescriptions on how he who has deprived another man of an eye is to be punished. Sight is the source of knowledge and wisdom, through sight we get to know the universe, and reason can draw conclusions about it. Sight is next to mind, and therefore it is placed highest among the senses, even literally. And the eye reveals all feelings and moods of the soul, as a proof of their relationship. Because of this, anyone who has injured another man's eye must lose one of his own (III: 590).

Philo is usually said to be an advocate of asceticism and an outspoken enemy of the senses and their world. This is not quite justified. He warns us for the pleasures, as enemies of the senses, because by surfeit the power of the senses to discern is impaired or destroyed (III: 374). His hostility to the world is far from being total. He can praise the senses, and above all, in the spirit of Plato, the eye, most eloquently, only because they show us light and other necessary conditions of life and transmit knowledge to be adapted by the mind. It is not hostility to the senses one finds in Philo, but a philosophy of strict moderation.

Philo often enumerates the senses as a series in the accepted order: sight, hearing, taste, smell (or smell, taste), and touch (Dobschütz 1929: 380). In some contexts he adds to this series speech and the genital organs in order to reach the number of seven;[9] sometimes he just mentions speech as an additional sense (Philo 1929, XXII: 334). But the rule is that the number is five, and the order from sight to touch.

Origen

Even though the texts of the Old Testament and particularly the *Song of Songs* often speak about sense-impressions and pleasures of the senses, the enumeration of the five senses in a fixed series does not belong to Jewish literature (Dobschütz 1929: 383). Philo, as we saw, had to arrange and interpret his biblical texts according to his allegorical methods in order to impose the pattern of five senses upon them.

When Origen uses the series of the five senses in an interpretation of the Bible, he proceeds in a similar way. Apparently he takes the series as an existing and useful rhetorical pattern, bringing together passages from different works in the Bible to fill it out. This happens in his *Contra Celsum* (written about AD 248), in a discussion of how visions and other experiences of things divine perceived by the senses are to be explained (Origen 1967, I: 48). He does not really want to believe that Heaven actually, literally, has opened up for the prophets or Jesus. The experience has probably, he says, met a spiritual, divine sense-organ, rather as a dream vision arises without external influence. He refers to Solomon by quoting the *Book of Proverbs* (2: 5): "Thou will ... find a divine sense."[10] And this sense has different forms:

> the sight that can see things of a higher nature than bodies, such as cherubim and sera-phim, the hearing that hears things not formed in air, the taste that knows the living bread that descended from Heaven giving life to the world, and the smell that perceives the perfumes about which St. Paul is speaking when he says that he is "the good smell of Christ to God", the touch through which St. John says that he touched the Word of Life with his hands. (Origen 1967, I: 202–3)

Origen thus thinks that some people are blessed with a set of "spiritual senses" having the power to perceive transcendental phenomena. He brings forward examples of objects of these senses taken from various passages in the doctrines of faith, giving a new sense to metaphorical expressions.

> In this way they [the holy prophets] saw what they profess to have seen and heard what they claim to have heard, in this way they received impressions of the same kind when, as they said, they swallowed a volume given to them. Further it was in this way that Isaac "smelled the smell" of his son's "holy dress". (Origen 1967, I: 206–7)

And even for touch Origen has found a passage from the Bible to quote: Jesus "touched" the leper to cure him both of his actual leprosy with his touch, and of another leprosy with his really divine touch.

In this way Origen explains all the extraordinary visions, sounds perceived and other statements as to sense-impressions that the critical reader of the Bible might want to question or take as figurative: they are experienced with the aid of a special set of spiritual sense-organs.

Notes

1. "The five senses" being regarded as belonging to this kind of concept is evident from many facts, for instance the fourteenth century wall-paintings of Longthorpe Tower, near Peterborough in England, where the twelve months, the seven ages of man and the five senses appear together in the same room as various cyclic representations of the life of man. In a sermon by Hugh of St. Victor, one part devoted to the five senses is inserted between a section on the Holy Trinity and another on the six works of mercy, followed by one on the seven virtues.

2. This happens in, among other works, older editions of the *Encyclopedia Britannica* s.v. "Psychology, History of," and in Edwin G. Boring, *Sensation and Perception in the History of Experimental Psychology* (1942: 5, 8 and passim), earlier editions of which were one of the sources of the article of the *Encyclopedia.*

   Even before Aristotle, Greek philosophers had treated perception and the functions of the sense-organs. Their various views have been collected and criticized both in the works of Aristotle and, more systematically, in a work on the senses by Theophrastus, Aristotle's friend and pupil (Stratton 1917). But Aristotle's own works on the senses are by far the most important to be written on the subject during the classical period. His approach to the problems as well as his analyses are original, and their influence on medieval psychology is paramount. Because of this, it is reasonable to introduce Aristotle's discussion in some detail, and for older Greek theory on the senses refer the reader to works such as those by Beare (1906) and Stratton (1917).

3. The works will be quoted from *De Anima* (1961) edited, with Introduction and Commentary, by Sir David Ross, and *Parva Naturalia* (1955), a Revised Text, with Introduction and Commentary by Sir David Ross. On the relation between the two see Düring 1966: 558, 562.

4. It appears from Theophrastus' work that there was no consensus among his predecessors as to the order of the senses. Theophrastus' own order is the same as Aristotle's: sight, hearing, smell, taste and touch. This order he applies when a philosopher did not himself deal with the senses in a series but his theories had to be collected from various places in his work. Such was the case with Plato. Anaxagora's opinions, on the other hand, are given in the reversed order, from touch to vision. Alcmaeon's views are dealt with in the order hearing, smelling, taste, vision; and those of Diogenes are gone through twice beginning with smell and continuing with hearing through sight to taste. I take this to mean that these philosophers used the orders in which Theophrastus accounts for their ideas. This again implies that the order of the senses was not self-evident to the Greeks before Aristotle. On the other hand, the order of Anaxagoras and Clidemus from touch to vision or the reverse may be genuine, i.e. not arranged by Theophrastus, and so let us understand that this order was not invented by Aristotle but taken up and rationalized by him. See Düring 1968, col. 255, and, more detailed, Beare 1906: 11–92.

5. So in the translation by Dakyns quoted by J.F. Kermode 1971: 86.

6. Panofsky has noticed the description of Voluptus in Philo, without observing, however, that it is a variation of the Hercules fable (see Panofsky 1930: 110 n)

7. The tale is part of the *De Sacrificiis Abelis et Cain,* § 20 ff. In some editions the tale is also found in the *De Specialibus Legibus,* I: 280 ff. It has also been printed separately, under the title of *De merce de meretriciis non accipienda.* I use the Colson–Whittaker text and translation (Philo 1929).

8. In the first part of his article "The Uncontrollable Steed" (1972), Sander L. Gilman discusses, rather arbitrarily, classical and Old Testament instances, among them the *Phaedrus* passage. Philo's use of the image is left unnoticed.

9. *Quod Deterius Potiori Insidiari Soleat,* ch. 46, § 168, Philo 1929, II: 132f. Dobschütz remarks: "Dies ermöglicht es, auch an Stellen, wo die Siebenzahl vorkommt, die Lehre von den fiinf Sinnen anzubringen" [This makes it possible, even in places where the number seven appears, to bring in the teaching of the five senses—Ed.]; he adduces other examples (Dobschütz 1929: 382).

10. Karl Rahner (1932: 116) has demonstrated that Origen here uses another expression, *aesthesis theia,* than the Septuagint or the *Vulgate.* The latter texts have *epignosis theou* and *scientiam Dei,* i.e. "the knowledge of God."

References

Aristotle (1955), *Parva Naturalia,* a Revised Text, with Introduction and Commentary by Sir David Ross, Oxford: Clarendon Press.

Aristotle (1961), *De Anima,* edited with Introduction and Commentary by Sir David Ross, Oxford: Clarendon Press.

Beare, J. (1906), *Greek Theories of Elementary Cognition from Alcmaeon to Aristotle,* Oxford: Clarendon Press.

Boring, E. G. (1942), *Sensation and Perception in the History of Experimental Psychology,* New York: D. Appleton-Century Co.

Cohn, L. (1919), *Die Werke Philos von Alexandria in deutscher Uberretzung,* Breslau.

Dobschütz, E. (1929), "Die fünf Sinne im neuen Testament," *Journal of Biblical Literature, 48.*

Düring, I. (1966), *Aristoteles. Darstellung und Interpretation seines Denkens,* Heidelberg: Carl Winter.

Düring, I. (1968), "Aristoteles," *Paulys Real-Enzyklopädie der classischen Altertumswissenschaft,* Suppl.-band 11, Stuttgart.

Gilman, S. L. (1972), "The Uncontrollable Steed: A Study of the Metamorphosis of a Literary Image," *Euphorion, 66.*

Kermode, J. F. (1971), "The Banquet of Sense," in *Shakespeare, Spenser, Donne,* London: Routledge & Kegan Paul.

Origen (1967), *Contre Celse,* trans. M. Borret, Paris: Cerf.

Panofsky, E. (1930), *Hercules am Scheidewege und andere antike Bildstoffe in der neueren Kunst,* Berlin: B. G. Teubner.

Philo (1929–53), *Philo,* trans. F. H. Colson and G. H. Whittaker, 10 vols. and suppl., London: Loeb.

Rahner, K. (1932), "Le Début d'une doctrine des cinq sens spirituels chez Origène," *Revue d'Ascétique et de Mystique, 13.*

Stratton, G. M. (1917), *Theophrastus and the Greek Physiological Psychology before Aristotle,* London: Allen & Unwin.

Xenophon ([1923] 1965), *Memorabilia and Oeconomicus,* trans. E. C. Marchant, London and Cambridge, MA: Loeb.

6

The Mesmerism Investigation and the Crisis of Sensationist Science

Jessica Riskin

Happy the systematic philosopher to whom nature has given ... a strong imagination.

—D. Diderot (sarcastically), *De L'interpretation
de la nature* (1753)

When imagination speaks to the multitude, the multitude no longer knows either dangers
or obstacles ... . Nations follow sovereigns, and armies their Generals.

—J.S. Bailly, Exposé des expériences qui ont été faites pour
L'examen du magnétisme animal (1784)

Men united are no longer subject to their senses.

—B. Franklin et al., Rapport des commissaires chargés par le
Roi de L'examen du magnétisme animal (1784)

In the spring of 1784 Paris was the scene of an official investigation of great notoriety concerning a man's alleged ability to channel a weightless fluid using a pointed rod. The affair was that of Franz Anton Mesmer, who for five years had entertained, titillated, and ostensibly cured a growing segment of Parisian society, channeling their animal magnetic fluids by means of his wand, conductive bathtubs, magnetic eyes, and healing touch. His inquisitors were the members of two royal commissions appointed to investigate his practice.

The royal investigation of mesmerism was a landmark event in several respects. It involved the first formal, psychological tests using what would come to be called a placebo sham. The investigators devised a method for, in their terms, isolating the action of Mesmer's hypothetical animal magnetic fluid from the action of the patient's imagination. In addition to being the first recorded instance of the use of a placebo and of, in modern terms, a method of blind assessment, the mesmerism investigation was the first known formal investigation of scientific fraud.[1] It was therefore a crucial episode in the history of psychology, medical testing, experimental practice, and state authority to police scientific conduct. In each domain the mesmerism investigation represented an institutional recognition of the deeply problematic nature of sensory evidence: sensations would no longer be considered direct inscriptions of an outside world upon the mind of the observer.

My primary interest here, however, is not in the importance of the mesmerism investigation to subsequent developments in psychology, medicine, experimental practice, or the relations between science and the state, but instead in its relations to what came before. I will be locating it at the height of the Age of Sensibility. Mesmerism itself, its popularity, the appointment of the royal investigating commissions, and the content of their radical conclusions—all reflected the prior elevation of feeling as the basis of both natural knowledge and social union.

The mesmerism investigation has received surprisingly little attention from historians not because it has seemed unimportant, but because it has seemed unproblematic. The tendency has been to assume that the commissioners simply recognized a charlatan for what he was.[2] But here I am interested precisely in why the commissioners decided that Mesmer's application of sentimental empiricism was illegitimate. I understand the mesmerism investigation as a crisis, a seismic event along the fault lines in sensibilist natural science, triggered by its friction against popular culture on one side and political authority on the other.[3]

The argument I develop here has two parts. First, mesmerism posed a problem for established natural science not by departing from it, nor by violating its rules, but, on the contrary, by too literally applying its central credo, the credo of sensibility. Mesmerism was a kind of caricature of natural science in the sentimental-empiricist idiom. Like any caricature, it worked by exposing and magnifying the vulnerabilities of its subject—in this case, the sentimental-empiricist elevation of feeling as the ultimate arbiter of truth. An argument from feeling cannot be refuted except by undermining the principle on which it rests: if people felt a thing, either it existed or feeling was not the measure of truth. Writhing and groaning, Mesmer's patients dramatized the process of feeling. Moreover, what they felt, according to Mesmer, was the etherial medium of sensation itself, which permeated the cosmos. They thereby demonstrated—in sentimental-empiricist terms—the real existence of this imponderable fluid of sensibility. To deny it was to undermine the authority of sensation.

Second, I suggest that the commissioners charged with investigating mesmerism, confronted by its wild popularity, composed an explanation of mesmeric effects that challenged the central axiom of sentimental empiricism, the axiom that feelings were responses to a world outside the mind and were therefore the bedrock of natural knowledge. Mesmerism drove the commissioners to develop a theory of how one could have feelings that were not responsive to the outside world. Philosophical consensus recognized a mental faculty responsible for *in*sensibility, detachment from the outside world and its proper action upon the five senses. This was the faculty of imagination.[4]

Rejecting mesmerism, the commissioners turned toward this faculty of the imagination and conjured it into a formidable power. In the mesmerism commission reports, imagination became sensibility's nemesis. Imagination could overwhelm the sensible body so literally as to throw it into fits of convulsions. And while sensibility was the basis not only of knowledge but of moral sentiment and sociability—as shown elsewhere (Riskin 2002: ch. 3, 4)—imagination now became the root of social pathology. Imagination, the commissioners would ultimately warn, could release the audiences of popular science displays from the tenuous grip of their senses and turn them into a revolutionary mob.[5]

Mesmerism as a Caricature of Sentimental Empiricism

Imagine for a moment, wrote A.J.M. Servan, legal philosopher and mesmerist member of the Parlement of Bordeaux, that

> from the depths of America, an almost unknown land, a man even more unknown than his country, stood up to cry: "men listen to me! I have the power to draw thunder from the sky, and I can often force it to fall upon any point on earth it pleases me to choose": what mockery from one pole to the other! ... Franklin ... you would have been condemned to eat crow, and to abandon right then and there your physics and your genius. (Servan 1784: 88)

Benjamin Franklin had been spared this fate, Servan suggested, despite the obvious implausibility of his claim, because its truth had been empirically confirmed. Consider, then, he urged, the no less plausible, and equally empirically supported, claims of Mesmer.

Historians debating whether Mesmer was a charlatan have sometimes defended him by arguing that he sincerely believed in his doctrine (see e.g., Zweig 1932: 12–14; Vinchon 1971: 11; Lopez 1966: 169). But it would be difficult to deny that Mesmer, whether or not deliberately deceitful, had certain characteristics of the charlatan. A charlatan's manipulation lies not merely in presenting a false theory as true, but in making the false theory plausible. A successful quack exploits the preoccupations and uncertainties of established science, turning its own foibles against it. Mesmer's theory is not so much a departure from credible philosophy as an exaggeration of it. Even Lavoisier, Mesmer's chief inquisitor, remarked upon the "skill and confidence with which animal magnetism is presented." Mesmer's admixture of "truths of fact and observation" with "pretended results of a purely hypothetical principle" comprised a body of doctrine that, Lavoisier conceded, "inspires awe, even among enlightened doctors" (Lavoisier [1784] 1862–1893, III: 508). In other words, Mesmer was a master, perhaps unconsciously, in the art of quackish parody.

To see mesmerism as a parody of contemporary empiricist science can explain an apparent contradiction revealed in Robert Darnton's 1968 study of the meaning of mesmerism for the political culture of the late Enlightenment. Darnton argues that mesmerism marked no clear departure from established science in the climate of the 1780s, a decade that he says had almost succeeded, with its succession of philosophical crazes, in erasing the line "dividing science from pseudoscience." At the same time, however, he presents mesmerism as a subversive affront to academic science.

Darnton attributes the "anti-establishment" cast of mesmerism, despite its continuities with established science, to two related factors. The first was its popularity: mesmerism was rejected by the academies but raised enormous popular interest. However, as his account reveals, the academies' rejections of mesmerism were ambivalent and internally disputed. The second subversive quality Darnton identifies in mesmerism was its style, which was "mystical" and "romantic," a reaction against the "cold rationalism of midcentury." Yet as suggested elsewhere (Riskin 2002: ch. 2, 4)—and Darnton's own discussion affirms—that established French natural science during the second half of the eighteenth century was itself shaped by a general reaction against what its practitioners considered the cold rationalism of an earlier generation.

In other words, mesmerism was both in keeping with *and* a threat to established natural science (see Darnton 1968: 11–16, 29, 37–38, 42–45, 165, 60n.).[6] Ultimately, Darnton suggests, the alliance between mesmerists and political radicals was one of expedience. Chronicling the emergence of a partnership between academic science and government in late eighteenth-century France, Charles Gillispie has characterized their relations as purely instrumental, an opportunistic exchange of "weapons, techniques, information" for funding, institutions, and authority, with no involvement of philosophy or principle (Gillispie 1980: 549). Darnton tells a complementary story, describing a marriage of convenience between "radical" natural philosophy, in the form of mesmerism, and radical politics in the form of Revolutionary Rousseauism. Prominent Revolutionaries, including Brissot de Warville, Jean-Paul Marat, and Jean-Louis Carra, had been denied official sanction for their endeavors in natural science, leaving them bitter toward the academies, and embraced mesmerism as a "vehicle" for their political programs. Marat's "desire to avenge himself against the Academy of Sciences," Darnton claims, "provided the main thrust behind his ... revolutionary career," as well as the occasion for his interest in mesmerism (see Darnton 1968: vii, 3–5, 90–100, 161, 163–64, 110–11).

While academic science and government bureaucrats established the pragmatic alliance that provided the moral to Gillispie's story, a "curious" allegiance between "scientific and political extremism" animates Darnton's. Both engagements are essentially institutional rather than philosophical, and perhaps this explains why neither Gillispie in his study of the scientific and political establishments, nor Darnton in his analysis of the scientific and political anti-establishments, devoted much attention to the royal investigation of mesmerism in the summer of 1784. The important thing in both discussions is the simple fact that the investigation took place, drawing a distinct line between science and pseudoscience. For Gillispie, there was "no point in recounting" the commissions' procedures, for they merely demonstrated the obvious truth that "susceptibility to magnetism was a function of suggestibility, poverty and ignorance" (Gillispie 1980: 281).

But how was the line between science and pseudoscience drawn? If Mesmer's theory seems largely continuous with those of the most established natural philosophers, what ultimately made it quackery to most (though not all) of the commissioners? And if Marat, Carra, and Brissot were attracted to mesmerism because of their bitterness toward the scientific establishment, why were half the members of the Parlement of Paris and a defecting contingent from the Faculty of Medicine (see La Harpe cited in Darnton 1968: 87) similarly seduced? What made mesmerism both absurd and plausible? How did it appeal to subversives and establishmentarians alike? From a contemporary rather than historical perspective, these were the very questions that motivated the royal commissions' 1784 investigation of mesmerism, and their proceedings contain an implicit answer: mesmerism was related to established natural science neither by being antithetical to it, nor quite by being continuous with it, but by taking its central tenets, the tenets of sentimental empiricism, so very literally as to produce what amounted to a caricature of them.[7]

Sensationists said that the natural world physically inscribed knowledge and sentiment upon the soul through the five senses. Mesmer offered them the medium by which this inscription took place: a universal, imponderable fluid of sensibility. As a leading mesmerist pointed out, invoking the chemists' phlogiston, there was nothing new about hypothesizing a universal fluid. Another remarked that people "incessantly say that all is linked in nature; ... they never stop talking of the great chain of being." Here was a physical basis for the great chain, a single fluid uniting all the parts of nature. After all, what could this general unity mean without a material foundation? The conformity of Mesmer's theory with this idea "adopted by all the centuries and all the enlightened men" made it, his supporters argued, "extremely plausible" (Deslon 1784: 2–3; Servan 1784: 74–5, 81).

Franklin himself might easily have allowed the plausibility of Mesmer's claim that a "universal fluid exists in nature, a fluid which penetrates all animate or inanimate bodies" (Mesmer 1784: 33). In the midst of his summer spent investigating mesmerism, Franklin wrote out some "loose thoughts" on his own "universal fluid," a proper quantity of which, he said, constituted health in human bodies. Franklin credited his universal fluid with comprising light, heat, and the "greatest Part" of combustible bodies; with causing growth in animals and vegetables; with separating the particles of fluids and airs; and with maintaining smokes and vapors in their ethereal state (Franklin 1907, IX: 227–30). Though he left unspecified the relation of his universal fluid to electrical and magnetic phenomena, he shared Mesmer's belief in the celestial origins of magnetism. Franklin speculated that the magnetic fluid existed "in all space; so that there is a magnetical North and South of the universe." He concluded fancifully that were it "possible for a man to fly from star to star, he might govern his course by the compass" (Franklin 1907, VIII: 599–600).

Many academic philosophers, including Franklin, also found credible the clinical exploitation of imponderable fluids. From the earliest days of the Leyden jar, electricians, among them Nollet, had tested its efficacy in treating paralysis and reported some success. Nollet had ultimately judged dubious the evidence of good effects from electrical shocks but had suggested another medicinal application of electricity: using electrification to quicken circulation and to hasten the "evaporation" of disease from the body (Torlais 1954: 68; Heilbron 1979: 353–4).[8] In the early 1750s, in response to European trials of the medicinal effects of electricity, Franklin employed two very large Leyden jars to dispense powerful shocks, three times daily, to the paralyzed limbs of several patients. He reported having observed beneficial effects, but only limited and never permanent. Nevertheless, he remained modestly optimistic that, "under the direction of a skilled physician," electrical treatments could effect full and permanent cures. Franklin's faith in the medicinal potential of electricity was not shaken by his findings against mesmerism. The year following the investigation, he recommended electrical shocks as a possible treatment for insanity (see Franklin 1907, III: 425–27; IX: 308–9; X: 85; IX: 309).

Thus Mesmer did not depart from the standard wisdom by relating health to the regulation of imponderable fluids in the body; he merely stated a commonly held belief among natural philosophers. He was acquainted with such beliefs as a result of his training, having received his medical degree in 1766 from the University of Vienna for a (possibly plagiarized) thesis on the influence of the motions of the planets upon the human body. Mesmer then hesitated to take up a medical career.[9] For six years he depleted his fortune (or, rather, his wife's) by hosting sumptuous musical soirées at their luxurious estate and by passing his time restlessly reading in and among the several branches of natural science. From these explorations, Mesmer must have derived his intuitive grasp of contemporary natural philosophy's overarching preoccupation: the origin of knowledge in sensibility and of error in system-building. He adopted, for example, the fashionable position regarding the misleading artificiality of words.

In his autobiographical sketch, he reported having once, in order to eradicate linguistic contamination from his ideas, formed a "bizarre plan" that, thanks to a strenuous "effort" had proved successful: "I thought for three months without language" (Mesmer 1781: 102).

Mesmer began his memoir on animal magnetism with a series of avowals of sensationist orthodoxy: "Man is by nature an Observer"; the child's first task is to learn to employ his sensory organs; the "primary source of all human knowledge" is "experience." He also drew the commonplace connection between rationalism and arrogance, condemning the "ambition for knowledge" that led philosophers to replace observations with abstract systems (Mesmer 1799: 44–45, 96). Mesmer and his followers made much of his avoidance of medical systems. Doctors, one wrote, "believe more what they imagine than what they see: systems are always infinitely dearer to them than experiments" (Servan 1784: 89). Claiming to have discovered the power by which nature herself effected cures, Mesmer said his function was merely to help and hasten the natural reestablishment of harmony. His fondest wish was to "preserve my fellow-man ... [from] the incalculable hazards of drugs and their application" (Mesmer 1799: 130, 46–48; see also Servan 1784: 96, 116; Bonnefoy 1784: 39, 72, 86–87). This was a selling point even with Mesmer's critics, including Franklin, who perceived a hidden advantage in the mesmeric craze if those who were given to fancying themselves ill might be persuaded "to forbear their drugs in expectation of being cured by only the physician's finger or an iron rod pointing at them" (Franklin 1907, IX: 182–83).

When Mesmer first turned to the practice of medicine, he adopted a technique of the ex-Jesuit astronomer Pater Hell (who moonlighted in medicine), applying magnets to the ailing parts of his patients. Mesmer soon elaborated this practice, adding a theory from his doctoral thesis, which hypothesized a fluid from the stars that flowed into a northern pole in the human head and out of a southern one at the feet, a "tide [that] takes place in the human body" (Mesmer 1766: 15). He also added more magnets, to channel the ebb and flow of the astral current, before dispensing with magnets altogether, leaving the doctor's bare hands and magnetic personality as the principal therapeutic instruments. Illness, Mesmer surmised, resulted from bodily obstructions of the universal fluid, which he claimed to remedy by touching his patients' bodies at their magnetic poles. The cures, paralleling the Leyden commotion during the restoration of equilibrium, involved violent "crises," or fits of writhing and fainting. These contributed to the notoriety of Mesmer's methods. In 1778, following a succession of public and bitter disputes over the authorship, the efficacy, and the moral rectitude of his science, Mesmer fled his native city. He left his last two patients in the care of his estranged wife. Having exhausted her tolerance—and Vienna's credulity—he headed for Paris (see Vinchon 1971: 26–27, 24, 46–47).

There he encountered a public already primed for his performances. Parisians, like Londoners and other cosmopolitan Europeans, had been attending popular science courses since the turn of the century, and in rapidly increasing numbers since the 1740s.[10] In these courses, they had witnessed the extraordinary powers of the physicists' imponderable fluids, particularly electricity. Nollet taught one of the most fashionable popular science courses in the capital and filled it with electrical displays. Audiences for philosophical amusements had also learned the dogma of sentimental empiricism. They had been taught that knowledge resided in sensory experience and responsive feeling—in sensibility. Public lecturers continually announced their purpose to educate their pupils by striking their senses. Nollet promised in his course never to "pass beyond a sensible physics"; and Priestley, who gave popular lectures in London, wrote that "the curiosity and surprize of young persons should be excited as soon as possible; nor should it be much regarded whether they properly understand what they see, or not. ... We are, at all ages, but too much in haste to *understand* ... the appearances that present themselves to us" (Nollet 1754–1765, I: 237; Priestley 1779–1786, I: x). By the 1770s the audience for popular science had learned to cultivate not so much a rational understanding of natural phenomena, as a sensitivity to them. They were ready for Mesmer.

Arriving in Paris in February 1778, Mesmer established a clinic that became an overnight success. Soon mesmeric salons had sprung up throughout the city. Inside, their atmosphere was murky and suggestive, with drawn curtains, thick carpets, and astrological wall decorations. Mesmer himself dressed impressively in a lilac taffeta gown. Patients gathered, joined by ropes, around *baquets,* tubs filled with miscellaneous bits of glass, metal, and water, from which flexible iron rods protruded. They pressed these rods to their left hypochondria (upper abdomens) and joined their thumbs to increase the communication of the magnetic fluid. Alternatively, they opposed their own magnetic poles to those of the magnetizer by placing their knees between his. He then pressed and prodded their bodies with a mesmeric wand or, more often, his fingers. By means of these titillating practices, he provoked the notorious mesmeric crises. For especially violent crises, mesmeric salons included separate rooms lined with mattresses (Darnton 1968: 6–10). Unable to attend to all the ailing Parisians who arrived in droves on his doorstep, Mesmer was forced to designate a surrogate: he "magnetized" a tree near the porte Saint-Martin to accommodate the overflow.

His quest for official sponsorship met with more mixed results. Mesmer applied in succession to all of the relevant learned bodies—first the Academy of Sciences, next the Society of Medicine, and, finally, the Faculty of Medicine. Like the ebb and flow of the astral tide, the philosophes were attracted and repelled by Mesmer's doctrine. Le Roy, the Franklinist electrician, then director of the Academy of Sciences, invited Mesmer to present his theory at a meeting of the Academy and hosted a demonstration of it in his own laboratory. This first display of Mesmer's science in Paris was met not just with skepticism but with outright laughter. Afterward, Le Roy would have nothing to do with Mesmer, despite Mesmer's repeated applications for his attention (see Mesmer 1781: 106–7; Lopez 1966: 170; Vinchon 1971: 54–55). Félix Vicq-d'Azyr, then perpetual secretary of the Society of Medicine, rapidly developed the same attitude, as did the delegation of twelve members of the Faculty of Medicine who agreed to witness a series of Mesmer's treatments (see Vinchon 1971: 49–60, 69–72, 80; Gillispie 1980: 266–70).

But the chemist Claude-Louis Berthollet joined the mesmeric Society of Harmony and persevered for a fortnight before storming out in midsession, proclaiming that he had been duped (Lavoisier [1784] 1862–1893, III: 505–6; Vinchon 1971: 125–26; Darnton 1968: 52). The mathematician, naturalist, and explorer Charles-Marie de La Condamine was intrigued by mesmerism and wrote to Franklin on the eve of the investigation for information, hoping to discover a new means to "comfort the poor inhabitants of the countryside" (La Condamine to Franklin, 8 March 1784 (Benjamin Franklin Papers Archives, Yale University; hereafter FPA)). And the botanist and doctor Antoine-Laurent de Jussieu, having served on the Royal Society of Medicine commission to investigate Mesmer, dissented from its negative final report. He judged the commissions' own explanation—attributing mesmeric crises to the power of imagination—insufficient to explain the dramatic effects. Jussieu sought a more material cause in the "principle of heat," permeating the air, constantly active, and "insinuating itself into bodies." He proposed the Franklinist-sounding hypothesis that this principle, inhabiting all bodies in their normal state, was induced by rubbing to form "atmospheres" around them. These, he said, were the "physical influence of man upon man" (Jussieu 1784: 188–89; see Vinchon 1971: 135; Darnton 1968: 107; Zweig 1932: 70–1; Duveen and Klickstein 1955: 297). Meanwhile, on the Faculty of Medicine, as mentioned above, a significant contingent was converted to mesmerism, including Charles Deslon, physician to the comte d'Artois. "Never," the Academy mesmerism commission would ultimately tell their colleagues, "has a more extraordinary question divided the minds of an enlightened Nation" (Bailly 1784: 4).

Deslon became for a time Mesmer's leading disciple. When he branched off to form his own mesmeric practice, two other patients/students took over the role. They were Nicolas Bergasse, a lawyer from Lyon, and Guillaume Kornmann, a banker from Strasbourg. Bergasse and Kornmann, with Mesmer, started the Society of Harmony, and within two years they had earned almost 350,000 livres and spawned three provincial societies. Since only those who could afford the fee of a hundred louis appeared on their roster, they were mostly from the ranks of the nobility or wealthy entrepreneurs, bankers, lawyers, and doctors (see Darnton 1968: 51–52; Vinchon 1971: 108–20, 139–40).

Mesmerists claimed that their doctrine was empirical, despite the fact that the animal magnetic fluid could not itself be directly sensed by the regular five senses. Some attempted unsuccessfully to render the mesmeric fluid perceptible, but for the most part, with Deslon, they allowed that it was "neither visible nor palpable" and could only be known by its effects (Deslon 1784: 4). They argued, not unreasonably, that other imponderables were similarly known only through their effects. One could see neither mineral magnetism, nor the imponderable cause of heat, nor the force of gravity (see Bonnefoy 1784: 34–35; Deslon 1784: 3–5; Bergasse 1785: 22). The same was true for the action of the will upon the body. One mesmerist argued that since the commissioners admitted this influence without being able to see it other than by its effects, why should they deny the same courtesy to animal magnetism (Anon. 1784: 24)?

Also, Mesmer defined animal magnetism as a "sixth sense" and, invoking a standard sentimental-empiricist axiom, cited its sensory nature to explain why he could neither describe nor define it. Senses were prior to ideas and could only be "experienced" (Mesmer 1781: 103). The marquis de Puységur, a loyal disciple who invented the technique of hypnotism and was therefore probably the most influential mesmerist with regard to the later history of psychology,[11] adopted this line of argument. As a sixth sense, animal magnetism had to be felt to be understood. "To *feel*" he wrote, "one needs neither *intellect* nor *science,* and [the science] of M. Mesmer is felt better than it can be expressed" (Puységur 1786: 73–74, 147). Both Mesmer and Puységur invoked the Enlightenment's favorite epistemological metaphor, suggesting that it was as useless to try to explain the magnetic "sense" as it would be "the theory of colors to someone blind from birth" (Mesmer 1781: 135; Puységur 1786: 74–75). They thus effectively exploited a vulnerability of sentimental empiricism: to make feeling the ultimate test of truth was to render unanswerable all claims founded in feeling. If people felt animal magnetism, then according to sensibilist logic, it must be real.

Not only was animal magnetism a sixth sense, but it was the basis of the other five and of sensibility itself. Puységur announced that it was "concerning our *sensations* that [Mesmer] has come to enlighten us," and, therefore, "his doctrine tends to lend support to all the truths that, until now, spoke only to the *mind*" (Puységur 1786: 147–48). Bergasse concurred; until Mesmer, the "theory of our sensations" had been "still unknown, despite the efforts of the Leibnitzs, the Lockes, and the Condillacs" (Bergasse 1785: 50). Mesmer claimed that the animal magnetic fluid provided a material foundation for sensation, as "an agent acting on the inmost substances of the nerves of the animal body" (Mesmer 1799: 89, 93, 127).

Here was a direct extrapolation from contemporary sensory physiology, from the nervous ether common to post-Newtonian theories of sensation. As shown elsewhere (Riskin 2002: ch. 2), physiologists widely subscribed to an impression theory of sensation, according to which sensations were the motions of a nervous fluid propagated inward from the senses through the nerves. They arrived ultimately at the *sensorium commune,* a junction of nerves in the brain, where they met and combined, impressing themselves upon the brain's matter.[12] In keeping with these principles, Buffon called the brain itself an "internal, general and common sense" (Buffon 1753: 323), and Mesmer similarly hypothesized that his sixth sense was an "internal sense" located at the nexus where sensory impressions met after traveling inward along the nerves, a "union and interlacing" of the external senses.

Mesmer's inner sense, the basis of all sensation, revealed things that common sensory experience withheld. The internal sense was "related to the whole universe" and could perceive distant past and future events (Mesmer 1799: III). This idea, too, was arguably in keeping with contemporary physiological theory, which made sensation the interface between the motions of etherial fluids inside and outside of the brain. While any one sense conveyed only a specific sort of impression, the *sensorium commune* received whole impressions of the world outside. Its role in sensationist physiology and psychology was to embody the mind's openness to the world (see Riskin 2002: ch. 2). Accordingly, Mesmer's sixth sense was an organ that registered the movements of the universal fluid through which all events reverberated. Why should these reverberations not reflect the past, foretell the future, and even receive the imprint of human thoughts or "wills" (Riskin 2002: 121)?

Puységur claimed his hypnotized subjects, or "somnambulists," perceived hidden facts about their own and others' states of health by means of a "true sensation." And they were able furthermore to "pre-sense" their future sufferings and the dates of their cures. Puységur quoted one of his somnambulists as having said, "It is that I feel in advance ... the ill that will befall me" (Mesmer 1781: 135; Puységur 1786: 74–75). By means of the internal sense, Mesmer reasoned, people were "in *rapport*" with all of history and with the wills of others. The internal sense was the instinct by means of which people were "able to understand either the 'harmony' or the 'dissonance' which substances exert upon our structure." Like Diderot, Mesmer judged sensitive instinct to be truer than reason (Mesmer 1799: 120–21).[13]

The sixth sense, the basis of the other five—sensation itself in its purest form— was also capable of functioning independently. Mesmer proposed that for the internal sense to function at its peak, the other senses must in fact be silent. According to his theory of somnambulism, sleep was the interruption of the link between the *sensorium commune* and the external senses. During sleep the internal sense became the "sole organ of sensation; its impressions turn out to be independent of the external senses." The impressions of the internal sense were revealed to the sleeper, at last left undistracted by common sensation. Somnambulism resulted when sleepers attempted to express or act upon their internal sensations as though they were external. Mesmer also understood madness in terms of the internal sense as "gradations of imperfect sleep." Madness was a sensory disorder whose cure took the form of "perfecting the sensations" (Mesmer 1799: 122–25, 126, 127).

But madness and dreaming were both also forms of truth telling, since the internal sense reflected the most basic and universal truths. Mesmer and most of his disciples claimed that the magnetic fluid could only be sensed by a conscious subject in a state of disharmony or ill health. "The nature of our sensations," Mesmer explained, "is that they are nothing else but the perception of differences in proportions," thus the magnetic fluid—like Franklin's electrical fluid—must be in a state of imbalance to be felt. Bergasse thought that "sick beings are the only subjects suited" to reveal the reality of universal magnetism. And Puységur confirmed that once his somnambulists were cured, they "admit that they no longer *feel* anything." Illness and madness, weakening the grip of the external five sensations, magnified the internal sixth. Mesmer compared animal magnetism to the microscope, lending philosophers a view of the invisible, and madmen and sleepwalkers were also like scientific instruments: "These subjects can, in a sense, be compared to a telescope," for they magnified the effects of the stars through their fluid medium (see Mesmer 1781: 135–36; Mesmer 1799: 124; Puységur 1786: 75; Deslon 1784: 17; Bergasse 1784b: 108–11).

Unconsciousness was sensibility, and madness lucidity. These apparent contradictions were familiar from the writings of sentimental empiricists, as in *D'Alembert's Dream*, in which Diderot's fictional d'Alembert, talking in a feverish sleep, realizes a truth to which his waking self is blind, that sensibility permeates the material world (Diderot 1767). His own sensibility, connecting him with the feeling world around him, speaks clearly only when his rational mind is silenced. Mesmer merely carried the logic of sentimental empiricism to its extreme with his animal magnetic fluid and the sixth sense upon which it acted: bypassing the familiar, weak, and imperfect five senses, they connected the individual mind directly to the universe as a whole. Through the reverberations of the animal magnetic fluid—the medium of sensibility—one could sense the past and future, the motions of the cosmos, the action of the wills of others. Mesmer also took the sentimental empiricists at their word by giving them a cosmic ether of sensibility that could be known only and utterly by feeling its effects. To refute mesmerism, established natural philosophy had to undermine two axioms of its own most cherished doctrine: the immediate and absolute sensory connection between mind and world, and the ultimate authority of feeling.

The Investigation and Its Result: The Imagination

In March and April 1784, the baron de Breteuil, minister of the Department of Paris, appointed two commissions to investigate mesmerism. The first, from the Academy of Sciences and the Faculty of Medicine, included Le Roy, the astronomer Jean-Sylvain Bailly, the chemist Jean Darcet, and the doctor Joseph-Ignace Guillotin, and was chaired by Antoine Lavoisier and Benjamin Franklin; the second, from the Royal Society of Medicine, included Jussieu and was chaired by Pierre-Isaac Poissonier. Deslon was better placed than Mesmer to negotiate with government ministers and maneuvered himself into the position of primary subject of the examination. It was he who collaborated with the two commissions, despite Mesmer's and Bergasse's angry protests to Franklin (see Vinchon 1971: 134; Duveen and Klickstein 1955: 291; Schaffer 1983b: 84).

From the beginning of their investigation, the commissioners operated on the hypothesis that mesmeric effects were due to no fluid of sensation, but instead to the faculty of imagination. This had been Berthollet's pronouncement when he angrily abandoned the Society of Harmony (see Lavoisier [1784] 1862–1893, III: 505–6). He had blamed a most controversial faculty. The imagination was the subject of profound ambivalence on the part of sentimental empiricists. Lorraine Daston and Jan Goldstein have each called attention to the eighteenth-century preoccupation with the imagination. Goldstein argues that the prevailing sensationalist psychology made the imagination, "situated at the point of intersection between mind and body," newly suspect (Goldstein 1998: 30). And Daston observes that the "errors that most terrified Enlightenment savants ... were errors of construction, of a world not reflected in sensation but made up by the imagination" (Daston 1998: 76).[14]

According to the scheme set forth in d'Alembert's "Discours préliminaire" to the *Encyclopédie,* imagination was one of three branches of the human mind, along with memory and reason, and was responsible for a corresponding third of human knowledge, the fine arts.[15] Diderot defined imagination as the "faculty of painting for oneself objects that are absent, as though they were present" (Diderot

1784: 250). Closely allied to memory,[16] the imagination was the more sensitive, passionate faculty. While memory was cool and calm, recalling only the "signs" and "words" associated with sensible objects, imagination was warm and vivid (Diderot 1761: 45; Condillac 1746, part I: 44–45);[17] it recalled the objects themselves, by "resuscitat[ing]" the very sensations originally provoked (Diderot 1784: 250).[18] These features of the imaginative faculty made it crucial to the mind's impressionability and therefore to its functioning. La Mettrie reckoned that "all the parts of the soul can justly be reduced to imagination." Condillac credited the imagination with "all the fecundity ... of which [the mind] is capable" (La Mettrie 1748: 112; Condillac 1749: 238). Diderot made imagination responsible for the mind's capacity to grasp the entirety of an object. Without its ability to make extrapolative leaps from parts to whole, he reckoned, one would see only a muddle of details (Diderot 1784: 226). He accordingly extolled the imagination as that "quality without which one is neither a poet, nor a philosopher, nor an *homme d'esprit,* nor a reasonable being, nor a man" (Diderot 1758: 218).

On the other hand, the visceral images called forth by the imagination represented "as many occasions to go astray" (Diderot 1784: 250).[19] Differing from madness "only by more and less" (Condillac 1746, part I: 22), the imagination was easily bamboozled. "There is a great difference," Diderot's protagonist in the *Entretien sur le fils naturel* (1757) observes, "between painting something in my imagination, and putting it in action before my eyes. One can make my imagination adopt any notion one likes. ... It is not the same with my senses" (Diderot 1758: 157). Here, indeed, was a central area of ambiguity, the relation of the imagination to the senses. On the one hand, imagination and sensation worked collaboratively. The imagination drew upon sensory experience, making use "of the eye in showing objects where they are not; of taste, of touch, of the ear." It was "the internal eye," and those lacking imagination were "hard" and "blind in the soul, as blind people are in the body" (Diderot 1784: 252, 250, 254). On the other hand, the imagination and the senses were in perpetual conflict. The senses had always to be "on guard against our imagination" and to "ceaselessly warn us of the absence of objects that we want to imagine" (Condillac 1754, part I: 39–40). Worse, the imagination was the more powerful element in this struggle, since it, unlike the senses, was "without limits" (Condillac 1746, part I: 27). Ultimately, the imagination was untrustworthy, "a faculty which exaggerates and misleads," and that "sees all that pleases it, and sees nothing more" (Diderot 1784: 255; Condillac 1749: 222). Imagining could therefore be most "dangerous," Condillac counseled; "if we do not make ourselves master of this operation, it will inevitably mislead us" (Condillac 1746, part I: 115, 118, 113).

Thus, sentimental empiricists were suspicious of the imagination for much the same reason that they distrusted the rational faculty. Both imagination and reason, sensibilists feared, could lead the mind deep into itself, away from the sensory channels that opened it to its surroundings. "The man of imagination strolls through his [own] head like a visitor to a palace," Diderot wrote, " ... He goes here and there, he

does not come out" (Diderot 1784: 250; see also *Réfutation d'Helvétius* 1774: 309).[20]
La Mettrie similarly warned that the imagination, if "too much abandoned to itself"
and allowed merely to "look at itself in the mirror," would quickly lose its purchase
on the world. "See that bird on the branch, it always seems ready to fly away," he
cautioned, and "the imagination is the same" (La Mettrie 1748: 117).

Along with solipsism, sentimental empiricists suspected the overly imaginative—
like the excessively rational—of arrogance. Imagination allowed philosophers to
believe that nothing lay "beyond the range of their mind," and that they could "know
everything." It led them therefore to construct all-encompassing, "bold," and "extraordinary" systems (Condillac 1746: 67, 16). Together, imagination and reason,
seducing the mind into the intricacies of its own recesses, constituted the antithesis of sensibility: the spirit of system. Descartes, sentimental empiricists' favorite
exemplar of the misguided system-builder, had a "vivid" and "fertile" imagination
(Condillac 1746, part II: 280–81). D'Alembert wrote that the taste for systems was
"suited to flatter the imagination," and Diderot sarcastically proclaimed, "Happy the
systematic philosopher, to whom nature has given ... a strong imagination" (Diderot
and d'Alembert 1751, I: 116; Diderot 1753: 192). Condillac advised that those in
whom "imagination dominates" were "accustomed to seeing badly" and ill suited to
philosophical research, yet their imaginings "dazzle" (Condillac 1749: 239, 237)[21]
the mind. These "men of imagination," he lamented, "do not fail to get their systems
adopted" (Condillac 1749: 138).

The imagination's suspect relations to the operations of the five senses offered the
mesmerism investigators an opportunity to resolve a problem that had been force-
fully raised by Mesmer's results. Sentimental empiricists had often contrasted the
outward focus of sensation, the body's response to the outside world, with the inward
tendency of reason, which, Diderot wrote, "tends to live within itself" (see Diderot
1753: 185).[22] But mesmerism challenged this easy contrast by making manifest the
very internal nature of sensations: they take place, after all, utterly and only inside
the person experiencing them. Only a mesmeric patient could say whether he or she
felt the presence of the animal magnetic fluid. In an effort to recover the correlation
between sensory impressions and the world outside the mind, the commissioners from
the Society of Medicine argued that what Mesmer had revealed was not the basis of
sensation, but the extent to which the mind—through its imaginative faculty—could
hijack the senses, reversing them in their tracks. His "inner sense" was nothing but
the turning of the senses inward. The commissioners therefore introduced their own
distinction between "internal" and "external" sensations in opposition to Mesmer's.
Accordingly, external senses remained the basis of all knowledge, while internal sensations were "equivocal, often illusory" impressions produced inside the mind by the
imaginative faculty (Poissonier 1784: 7–8).

The members of the Academy commission similarly sought to distinguish sensations produced from within, by the imagination, from sensations produced by
external sources. When they began their investigation, by undergoing their own

series of treatments at Deslon's clinic, they took a "necessary precaution" that would become highly controversial after the reports were published. They took care "not to be too attentive" to their own impressions. In response to Mesmer's argument for the reality of his animal magnetic fluid from the sensibilities of his patients, the commissioners adopted a policy of deliberate insensibility. They professed to avoid having too "fixed" an attention. Animal magnetism, if real, should forcibly "fix their attention" for them. To focus too intently upon one's own sensations was to risk producing imagined ones from within.[23] One historian has summarized the commissioners' efforts to ignore their internal sensations as the strenuous avoidance of "self-absorption."[24] Not only reason but sensation, they now realized, could, if misdirected by the imagination, have an inward focus.

The results of this deliberately inattentive self-experimentation amounted to little: one commissioner on a single occasion felt a pain in his belly that lasted all day and was accompanied by fatigue and malaise. But he attributed these symptoms to the "powerful pressure" that had been exerted on his chronically delicate stomach by a zealous magnetizer. Otherwise none of them felt a thing even when, in the interests of thoroughness, they subjected themselves to a marathon course of three consecutive days (see Franklin et al. 1784: 20–2; Poissonier et al. 1784: 5–6, 23).

The commissioners now turned from self-experimentation to experimentation on others. Here their procedure reflected their sense that the solipsism and self-absorption of the overly imaginative—and Mesmer's manipulation of his patients' imaginations—were urgently social problems. Once again, the moral and the epistemological were inseparable. Sentimental empiricists made sensibility the basis not only of natural knowledge but of moral feeling and community (see Riskin 2002: ch. 2 and 3). Imagination, appropriating the senses and turning them inward, was a potential source of social instability and fragmentation.[25] To operate, as the commissioners believed Mesmer did, on the imaginations of crowds of people presented a serious threat to the social order.

The investigators assumed that sensibility and imaginativeness varied by social class, and they divided their subjects accordingly.[26] They first brought seven sick members of the "*classe du peuple*" to Franklin's house at Passy. Four of these—an asthmatic widow, a woman with a tumor in her leg, and two children, one scrofulous and the other a convulsive—felt nothing. A couple showed some effects: a man with a tumor in his right eye had pain and watering in his left; and a woman who had been knocked over by a cow exhibited shoulder movements "similar to those of a person on whose face one sprinkles drops of cold water." Next, the commissioners invited to their private room at Deslon's establishment some "invalids from society" and also had Deslon magnetize Franklin and his entire household at Passy.[27] Only two of these "society" patients felt anything, both minor and otherwise explicable effects, a passing sensation of warmth in one case and alternate feelings of sleepiness and agitation in the other.

The results of these initial tests would seem inconclusive for both the popular and the patrician samples. Nevertheless, the commissioners decided that mesmeric treatments elicited a greater response from the popular classes than from enlightened society (or, for that matter, from the commissioners themselves, who were "armed," as they said, "with philosophical doubt"). The people, out of ignorance, a fervent desire to be cured, and an eagerness to please their betters, were rendered less able "to realize their sensations" than wealthier patients, and so more subject to their imaginations (Franklin et al. 1784: 23–32).

Bailly's supplementary report, "to be placed before the eyes of the King and reserved for His Majesty alone," presented a similar argument concerning the effects of mesmerism upon women. This top-secret document treated a subject so delicate that Bailly, having sent the original to Franklin to look over before the official signing, requested him to burn the covering letter (Bailly to Franklin, 8 September 1784, in FPA; Duveen and Klickstein 1955: 293). Noting that mesmeric patients were usually women and mesmerists always men, Bailly described a certain "convulsive state that has been confused with the other crises." This state resulted from a cause not detailed in the public reports, a cause that was "hidden ... but natural." It was the "dominion that nature gives to one sex over the other, to engage and arouse it." The intimacy of doctor and patient during mesmeric procedures, Bailly wrote, was especially hazardous when combined with the effects of the imagination, whose action rendered women unable to "realize what they are experiencing" (Bailly 1784: 43–44).[28]

That the imagination could have dramatic effects upon the body was by no means a new idea in 1784; it had been gaining currency over the course of the eighteenth century. Doctors and physiologists had catalogued many cases, for example, in which a pregnant woman's imagination influenced the shape of her fetus (see Rousseau 1969: 120–23; Rousseau 1971; Huet 1993; Goldstein 1998: 40, and n 24). In an affair of the 1720s and 1730s, of which mesmerism would later be reminiscent, the imagination was even charged with causing convulsions. The earlier episode involved a Jansenist cult that arose at the grave site of the deacon François de Paris. Its adherents trembled and moaned, and claimed to be cured of their physical ills, in much the same manner Mesmer's patients later would. The so-called convulsionaries of Saint-Médard said they were the recipients of God's will and the beneficiaries of divine miracles. Doctors who disbelieved these claims, like Mesmer's investigators, found that the dramatic effects were caused instead by the subjects' imaginations.[29]

When the mesmerism commissioners set out to measure the extent to which "the imagination can influence our sensations," they themselves noted that the great power exerted by the imagination over animal functions had already been well appreciated: "It revives with hope, it chills with terror. In a single night, it whitens the hair" (see Lavoisier [1784] 1862–1893, III: 510; Bailly et al. 1784: 15).[30] Indeed, the notion that the imagination could have physical effects made good sense in the context of the predominant physiological understanding of the imagination as a bodily function of nervous fluids and fibers. But the commissioners' explanation of mesmeric crises differed importantly from previous assessments of the corporeal effects of imagination. They claimed not just that the imagination could imprint itself upon the body, but that it could hijack the senses, redirecting them inward. Undermining the trustworthiness of sensation, the commissioners' power of imagination presented an urgent problem for sentimental-empiricist epistemology.

The problem at hand, that is, as the commissioners understood it, was epistemological rather than physiological. Midway through their investigation, Bailly reported, the commissioners "ceased to be *Physiciens* becoming nothing more than Philosophes." They abandoned fluids and took up epistemology. But they retained the sober methods of the *physicien.* "We operated, as one does in Chemistry," by means of decompositions and recompositions (Bailly 1784: 9–10). The second phase of their investigation, therefore, combined an epistemological subject—the influence of the imagination upon bodily experience—with a scientific method, to create the first deliberately psychological tests. These tests involved the first instance of blind assessment using a "placebo" (Kaptchuk 1998: 393–99).

The experimental protocol, drawn up by Lavoisier, centered upon two procedures. The first would isolate the fluid from the imagination, magnetizing subjects without their knowledge. The second would isolate the imagination from the fluid, persuading them that they were being magnetized when they were not. Lavoisier gave detailed directions for deceiving test subjects. He instructed the examiner, for example, to "appear from time to time to address M. Deslon in an undertone" in order to give a blindfolded subject the impression that Deslon was present. After thirty minutes of this pretense, a commissioner would announce that the trial was finished but would ask the patient, ostensibly no longer being magnetized, to retain the blindfold and report his or her sensations. Then Deslon would enter the room and begin a treatment in earnest (see Lavoisier [1784] 1862–1893, III: 509–10, 511–13, 519–20).

The primary instrument for separating the subject's imagination from the animal magnetic fluid was the blindfold. The commissioners included an exhaustive description of the device they invented:

This bandage was composed of two rubber caps, whose concavity was filled with eiderdown; the whole was enclosed and sewn into two round pieces of fabric. These two pieces were attached to one another; they had strings that tied in back. Placed upon the eyes, they left in their interval a space for the nose, and complete liberty for breathing, without one's being able to see anything, even the light of day, neither through, nor over, nor under the bandage. (Franklin et al. 1784: 37–38)

Acting in concert with the blindfold was a rule of silence that the commissioners imposed upon Deslon and all but one of themselves (who conducted the interrogations) to make it impossible for subjects to know who was in the room at any moment (Lavoisier [1784] 1862–1893, III: 509–10).

In a letter to Franklin several years later, Guillotin recalled their earlier collabo-
ration in the "very important though highly ridiculous affair of animal magnetism"
(Guillotin to Franklin, 18 June 1787, in FPA). Consider the comedy they enacted
before a woman from the "*classe du peuple*" with ailing eyes. Having arranged her in
a room with the carefully constructed blindfold, they persuaded her that Deslon had
arrived to magnetize her. In fact, Deslon was in another room attempting to magnetize the gouty and kidney-stone-ridden yet healthily skeptical Franklin. A commissioner played the role of the magnetizer, entering the room "affecting the stride of
M. Deslon." His collaborators then "pretended to speak to M. Deslon, praying him
to begin; but we did not magnetize the woman." Instead, they "sat calmly" and, by
the power of suggestion alone, triggered violent convulsions that were loudly audible
to their colleagues in the next room. There another young woman suffering from a
"nervous affliction" had been told that the ubiquitous Deslon was magnetizing her
from behind a closed door; she had responded similarly.

Sigaud de la Fond, no doubt having heard about these experiments from his
colleagues on the Faculty of Medicine, joined in. In order to study the extent of
the imaginative influence, he began to advertise himself as a mesmerist and soon
acquired a reputation throughout the city. By means of his notoriety, he acted upon
the imaginations of passing Parisians. Once he cured the migraine of a young artist
he met on the Pont Royal. Another time a young lady in the rue Colombier asked
him if he was on his way to Mesmer's hotel. "Yes," he responded, "and I can magnetize you [right here]." Pointing his finger at her, he later told the commissioners,
he could have thrown her into convulsions had she not begged him to stop (Franklin
et al. 1784: 46–47, 39–41).

While isolating the imagination from the hypothetical fluid, the commissioners
complementarily isolated the fluid from the imagination. In one case they invited
a laundress reputed to be sensitive to magnetism into a room in Franklin's house
under the pretext of wanting some washing done. They maneuvered her into a
chair in front of a doorway from which they had previously removed the door and
replaced it with paper. While she was magnetized from behind the paper, she sat
"conversing gaily" for half an hour about her health and other topics. Meanwhile,
a commissioner sat at a desk taking surreptitious notes, pretending to write out a
catalog of books.

The commissioners magnetized (and pretended to magnetize) their subjects indirectly as well as directly, through objects such as a basin of water and a set of china
cups. Curiously, and almost without fail, the unmagnetized objects induced violent
crises while the magnetized ones had no effect. Franklin's grandson, Benny Bache,
an unimpressed fifteen-year-old, matter-of-factly recorded one such experiment in
his diary: "My grandpapa ... [and] the commissioners are assembled today with
Mr. Delon [*sic*]," he wrote, and "they are gone into the garden to magnetize some
trees." On this occasion the patient in question, a boy of twelve, collapsed at the
farthest tree from the magnetized one. Deslon reportedly explained that trees were

all naturally magnetic, to which the commissioners dryly responded that in that case "a person sensitive to Magnetism could never hazard to go into a garden without risking convulsions"(Lavoisier [1784] 1862–1893, III: 520–23; Bache, "Diary," 15 January 1784–15 January 1785, in FPA; Franklin et al. 1784: 44).[31]

But two could play that game. For example, the medical commission had suggested that mesmeric convulsions had perfectly ordinary causes, like the warmth, perspiration, and agitation of air occasioned by mesmeric massage. A mesmerist responded: "Eh! what will become of these unfortunates ... unable to take a step, execute the slightest movement, suffer the opening of a door, tolerate the approach of any being, without falling into convulsions?" (Bonnefoy 1784: 64).[32] And what about the imagination as the cause of mesmeric effects? A mesmerist responded, "Why do we not see crises multiplying at our tragic plays, at theaters?" (Anon. 1784: 17; see also Deslon 1784: 29). If the imagination had the power to effect such a response, Deslon wrote more seriously, then "there will no longer be anything certain, either in our ideas or in our sensations" (cited in Schaffer 1983b: 87).

Indeed, the commissioners' attribution of mesmeric effects to the imagination did call everything in doubt. According to the central axiom of sensationism, sensations were the material impressions upon the brain of an external world. Yet Mesmer's investigators claimed that his patients' sensations did not originate outside themselves, but instead had an internal source. Furthermore, both mesmerism commissions were at a loss to explain the material basis of this internal source of sensations. Contemporary sensationist physiology generally attributed imagination to something much like Mesmer's animal magnetic fluid: an etherial medium flowing through the fibers of the nerves. In sensation, this nervous fluid was set in motion by external ethers, in turn moving the nerve fibers through which it traveled; in the operations of imagination and memory, the same movements of nervous ether and nerve fibers were re-created by the brain itself (see, for example, Bonnet 1754: ch. 4, 5, 6; Bonnet 1764, part V: ch. 6; Bonnet 1769: 178–79).[33]

But the power of imagination that the mesmerism commissioners cited corresponded to no such material agent. The commissioners rejected Mesmer's claim that he could manipulate the fluid responsible for sensation; they therefore denied that mesmeric effects were due to the motions of a sensory ether. In addition to subverting the sensationist principle that sensations necessarily originated in the world outside the mind, the commissioners also undermined, in their reaction against Mesmer's blunt application of it, the materialism of sensationist psychology. They distinguished what they called "moral" from physical causes of physical feeling (Lavoisier [1784] 1862–1893, III: 510; Franklin et al. 1784: 23–32). Insisting that mesmeric patients were responding to no material medium, but instead to a "moral" force, their own imaginations, the commissioners opened themselves to an obvious question: What precisely was this faculty of "imagination"? It seemed a more mysterious and troubling cause than Mesmer's magnetic fluid. How could one account for its undeniable, material influence upon the body?

The commissioners cast about unsuccessfully for plausible explanations. They speculated that the "intimate *rapport* of the intestine[,] the stomach and the uterus with the diaphragm" bore upon the question. "There exists a certain sympathy," they hazarded, "a communication, a correspondence between all the parts of the body, an action and reaction," whereby sensations received at the center would radiate outward. The "affections of the soul," perhaps, made an impression upon the central nerve center, which weighed, in turn, upon the stomach. In the end the commissioners capitulated, attributing everything to the unspecified "power by which the imagination is able to act upon the organs and trouble their functioning" (Franklin et al. 1784: 61–63).

The problem of what the imagination might be, in material terms, so troubled the Society of Medicine commissioners that they hesitated to cite it as the essential cause of crises and ultimately assigned it only the secondary position of "accessory cause," giving priority to unproblematic, physical causes: the "extended application of hands, the heat produced by this application, the irritation excited by rubbing." In order to fit this conclusion to the facts, the medical commissioners were forced to consider only those facts that appeared "ordinary, constant." They deliberately set aside those that were "rare, unusual, marvelous"—the most striking effects of mesmerism—such as convulsions caused by "a finger or a conductor, [pointed] through the back of a well-padded seat ... sensations felt while approaching a tree, a basin, a body or area that has previously been magnetized" (Poissonier et al. 1784: 17, 24–25). Mesmerist supporters understandably objected to this policy of selective empiricism. "You have thus seen facts, facts that surprised you, extraordinary facts ... —[and] *You ignored them*" (Bonnefoy 1784: 53).

Mesmerists were also quick to point out that the Academy commissioners' faculty of imagination begged the question: If mesmeric effects were due to imagination, to what was imagination due? One mesmerist demanded how the "*imagination,* without any other intermediary agent," could cause such dramatic results. Surely it was impossible, another critic wrote, "that a body exercises an action upon another without an intermediary being." Some "medium or milieu" must transmit motions and modifications among bodies. "What is *imagination?*" Deslon demanded to know; for "Messieurs the Commissioners put it a great deal into play without defining it." He claimed a proper physicist could only understand the imagination as "a fluid that flows through us." Otherwise, what might it mean to "*strike,*" or to "*disturb,*" the imagination?[34]

If the imagination were a fluid, it might participate in producing or hindering mesmeric effects. Or perhaps the magnetic fluid moved the imaginative fluid. Servan proposed that the imagination and magnetism might be merely two different names for the same phenomenon. Could the magnetic fluid not be the source of all "intellectual functions"? Imagination was one branch of a tree whose trunk was sensation; the unknown sap flowing through the tree, the "minister of sensation," was the fluid to which the mesmerists referred. In that case the imagination would not be a "source from which to derive your proofs against Mesmer's fluid." On the contrary, the commission's experiments would have served to confirm the strength of Mesmer's force. The commissioners had done nothing more than "oppose Mesmer's agent to itself" and arrive at the same principle by a different route (Anon. 1784: 31, 17, 19–20; Bonnefoy 1784: 50, 65; and Servan 1784: 31, 52–59, 60–68, 100–2).[35]

While the commissioners treated the facts selectively and dispensed with material causes, critics of their reports responded like sober empiricists. They referred their detractors to solid "fact" and reminded them that "observations of the effects that nature operates ... are not the exclusive property of the *Philosophes;* universal interest has made almost all individuals into so many Observers" ("Dialogue" in Bergasse 1784a: 187; Mesmer in Bergasse 1784b: 8–9). James Hutton had written to Franklin the year before the investigation that it seemed to be a "fact" that Mesmer had cured Court de Gebelin. "Now you are philosopher enough, if a Fact really is, not to dispute the Fact, though the *quo modo* has all the appearance of Quackery" (Hutton to Franklin, 2 May 1783, in FPA). The facts did put the commissioners in an uncomfortable spot, for the observed effects of mesmerism, whatever their causes, were uncontested and the immaterial force of imagination seemed an implausible explanation. At the end of August, Franklin observed that the "report makes a great deal of talk. Everybody agrees that it is well written, but many wonder at the force of imagination described in it as occasioning convulsions" (quoted in Duveen and Klickstein 1955: 299).

In a sense, then, it was the mesmerism investigators, and not Mesmer or his followers, who acted as the true radicals. Mesmerism itself was a faithful extrapolation from sensationist doctrine, a theory of sensibility according to which the human body was an instrument vibrating in a universal, material medium, its feelings directly responsive to the cosmos as a whole. It was the commissioners who extracted from mesmerism a new and radical force, the power of imagination: an immaterial force capable of causing physical sensations. It was they who derived from mesmerism a conclusion that seriously undermined their own sensationist methods and principles. For if the imagination were capable of such feats, how (as mesmerists pointed out) could the senses ever be trusted? Moreover, the commissioners had nothing to offer in its place, no plausible explanation for their mysterious force of imagination.

They therefore presented their findings without explanation, as "facts for a science that is still new, that of the influence of the moral upon the physical." Mesmerism had been the first "great experiment concerning the power of the imagination." Sentimental empiricists, fusing the moral with the physical, sentiment with sensation, had argued that one could neither feel without perceiving nor perceive without feeling. But Mesmer, with his bald reduction of perception to feeling, drove the commissioners to distinguish the two afresh. In the wake of their investigation, the relations between knowledge and sensation were newly problematic. And while the root of the problem was epistemological, its domain was social. Bailly concluded, "What we have learned is that man can act upon man, at any moment and almost at will, by striking the imagination" (Bailly et al. 1784: 12, 16, 15).

To initiate their new moral-physical science—and once again reflecting their assumption of the importance of sensibility as a basis for social union—the commissioners concluded their reports on a political note. Bailly sketched a moral physics of two forces: imitation, by which man "forms, perfects himself," and imagination, by which he "acts, becomes powerful." Imitation was a conservative force, the source of habits, conventions, national character, prejudice, and patriotism. Imagination was a radical force, the "eminently active faculty, author of good and evil," the source of progress. Imitation grasped only what it saw; imagination saw the whole, the "future as well as the present, the worlds of the universe as well as the point where we are." Imitation was stable and imagination, volatile. Imitation held communities together; imagination destabilized them and set loose their collective powers: "When imagination speaks to the multitude, the multitude no longer knows either dangers or obstacles. ... Nations follow sovereigns, and armies their Generals." In opposing ways, both imitation and imagination had the potential to overwhelm the senses: while imagination focused the mind on its own fancies, imitation could make a person blindly follow others. As long as the two balanced one another, all was well. But when they worked together, they could produce fearsome results (Bailly et al. 1784: 12–15).

The commissioners had noticed that the effects of mesmerism were more pronounced in public sessions attended by crowds of patients than in private ones. Their discussion of this crowd phenomenon reflected a new preoccupation with crowds in the wake of such events as the bread riots of 1775–76. Read retrospectively, it also acquires extra resonance from its publication date, five years before the Revolution. The commissioners proposed that in crowds, the force of imitation combined with imagination to inspire a kind of collective "intoxication." The same phenomenon occurred at theatrical events and in armies on the day of battle. The "sound of the drums, the military music, the noise of cannons" accomplished what Mesmer's eerie harmonica music and impressive costumes did during seances; they "raised the imaginations to the same pitch." Meanwhile imitation instilled the emotions of each in the imaginations of all, overwhelming sensation, for "men united are no longer subject to their senses." Together, imagination and imitation defeated sensibility and erected in its place a "fanaticism" that, the commissioners judged, "presides at these assemblies." Imagination was the original source of "revolts" and "seditions." The imagination, Lavoisier concluded, although "obscure and hidden," was "an active and terrible power" (Bailly 1784: 12–16; Franklin et al. 1784: 64–67; Lavoisier [1784] 1862–1893, III: 524; see Rudé 1959: ch. 2 and Rudé 1964: ch. 1).

Mesmerists turned the commissioners' crowd psychology against them. Their "violent" reaction against mesmerism, Servan charged, had arisen from their own *esprit de corps,* for crowds always tended to regard extreme positions as heroic, and moderate ones as cowardly (Servan 1784: 95–96). Meanwhile, Galart de Montjoie—a mesmerist, novelist, and future anti-Jacobin writer—declared the commissioners were guilty of the spirit of system. In a letter addressed to Bailly just after the reports were published, Montjoie protested that "to always cry out against systems, as though there were a science without system," was itself a form of system-building and "a great abuse, Monsieur." One should rather accept imperfect systems, just as one must accept "governments, [though] there is perhaps none that does not offer some abuse." Men were "made in such a way, that there are principles which, bad in themselves, must yet be respected." Someone who did not realize this essential fact of humanity was indeed a "man of System, a very dangerous man" (Montjoie 1784: 57–59).

Thus, in the commission reports and the ensuing dialogue between commissioners and mesmerists, insensibility—the insensibility of crowds, of the popular classes, of royal commissions with their *esprit de corps* and *esprit de système*—became a real and dangerous political force. The commissioners had made mesmerism into the source of a new psychology, a nascent theory of the unconscious that credited the mind with startling powers over the body. This new psychology meant, too, that a person could render others insensible by manipulating their imaginations. Insensibility was no longer simply the detachment from one's proper sensations; it could now mean false sensations so powerful as to cause seizures. And insensibility could now have consequences even worse than system-building: it could bring about fanaticism and rioting. Where the imagination was unleashed, a dangerous insensibility threatened the land.

Notes

1. On the importance of the mesmerism investigation in the history of blind assessment and placebo controls, see Kaptchuk 1998. On the emergence in early modern medicine of a professional and state role in policing the boundaries of legitimate science see Bynum and Porter 1987, Porter 1989, and Lingo 1986.

2. Robert Darnton, in his classic *Mesmerism and the End of the Enlightenment in France* (1968), devotes only two pages (62–64) to the official investigation of mesmerism; Charles Gillispie similarly passes over the event in *Science and Polity in France at the End of the Old Regime* (1980: 281), as having successfully delineated pseudoscience from science.

3. In her study of mesmerism in Victorian Britain, Alison Winter characterizes mesmerism as a central instance of Victorians' preoccupation with "the influence they felt from each other" and the "sympathies that bound them." This preoccupation lay at the heart of Victorian worries about the relations between men and women, between doctors and patients, and among members of different social classes. Thus Winter uses mesmerism as a lens to study these areas of Victorian social life (see Winter 1998: 12). I propose that mesmerism was

similarly situated in late Enlightenment France at a most fraught intersection: that of sentimental empiricism with popular and academic science and state control.

4. On "distrust of the imagination in science" see Daston 1998. On distrust of the imagination in the French Enlightenment, see Jan Goldstein 1998. Goldstein argues that the imagination was uniquely suspect, "believed to be the principal entryway for error and disorder, and potential site for the capture of the will and loss of self-control." Fear of the imagination did not originate in the eighteenth century, Goldstein writes, but it did importantly transform at the hands of sensationist epistemology: "The dangers of the imagination had already been underscored by the Cartesian psychology of the seventeenth century. But the sensationalist psychology of the eighteenth century reiterated those dangers and, more important, gave them a new inflection," by making environment crucial to the control, or loss of control, of the imagination (Goldstein 1998: 30). In what follows, I suggest that one way in which sensationism inflected French Enlightenment fear of the imagination was by setting the imagination up as the antithesis of sensibility. While sensibility focused the mind outward through the senses, imagination drew the mind inward, away from its sensory interface with the outside world.

5. Goldstein describes the way French Enlightenment writers viewed the faculty of imagination as socially dangerous unless held in check by "the consensual force of the community." Therefore solitary activities such as "reading novels, masturbating, pursuing one's trade outside the supervision of a guild, and speculating on the stock market" were particularly hazardous. At the same time, crowds also "harbored danger because they encouraged imagination's potential for contagion." In both cases—in solitude and in an unruly crowd—the individual imagination was loosed from communal control (Goldstein 1998: 30). Here, drawing on Goldstein's observation, I take up the same worry from the opposite direction. While French sensationists warned that the absence of community could turn the imagination into a source of instability, as Goldstein points out, they simultaneously cautioned that the imagination undermined social cohesion. It did so by acting counter to that attribute that opened and connected the individual to the world around him or her and to its other inhabitants, sensibility.

6. On proto-romanticism in mid-century natural philosophy and its appeal to those excluded from academic science, see also Hahn 1971: 139–40.

7. In her study of sensibility in literature and medicine, Anne Vila characterizes mesmerism as "more than just pseudoscience or charlatanism; rather, it was a cunning recasting of mainstream Enlightenment medical ideas" (Vila 1998: 297). I suggest that mesmerism appropriated not only mainstream medical ideas, but, more generally, the central preoccupation of contemporary natural and moral science—the primacy of sensibility as the source of natural knowledge

and social union—and that Mesmer's recasting of this principle took the form of carrying it to its logical extreme.

8. On contemporary medical uses of electricity and magnetism, see Gillispie 1980: 270–72.

9. The following sketch of Mesmer's career draws upon accounts in Darnton 1968: 47–81; Vinchon 1971: 21–63; Gillispie 1980: 261–89; and Mesmer's own telling of the story in Mesmer 1781.

10. On the emergence of popular science courses in the late seventeenth and eighteenth centuries, see Sutton 1995; Stewart 1992; and Schaffer 1983. On the relations between mesmerism and popular science in Paris in the 1770 and 1780s, see Darnton 1968.

11. On the origins of modern psychology in mesmerism, see Crabtree 1993: ch. 5 and 17.

12. On the notions of a nervous ether and a *sensorium commune* in eighteenth-century sensory physiology, see Riskin 2002, ch. 2: 25–27.

13. On Diderot's preference of sensitive instinct to reason, see Riskin 2002: 98.

14. See *supra*, nn. 4, 5. Eighteenth-century ambivalence regarding the imagination can be seen in the fact that, as G.S. Rousseau has shown, "Enlightenment physiologists centered their attention on the diseased rather than the healthy imagination," producing "a preponderance of works concerned with madness and the malfunctioning imagination" (Rousseau 1969: 118, 123). On eighteenth-century suspicion of the imagination as the source of sexual fantasies, see Rousseau 1990: 41–42. On the feminine gendering of the imagination in Enlightenment natural philosophy, see Terrall 1999: 258–59.

15. History was the province of memory, meanwhile, and philosophy of reason (see d'Alembert in Diderot and d'Alembert 1751, I: xlvii–li).

16. "Imagination is the memory of forms and colors" (Diderot 1784: 367). "Imagination is the faculty of recalling images" (Diderot 1758: 61). On the relation between imagination and memory, see also Condillac 1746, part I, §2, ch. 2: "On Imagination, Contemplation and Memory." For an argument that Lockean sensationism reconfigured the relations between imagination and reason, see Tuveson 1960: ch. 4. Tuveson writes that "a certain passivity of the experiencing mind and an enhancement of the importance of extrarational mental activities" in sensationist epistemology transformed imagination from an active, creative faculty to one that merely received and preserved sensory impressions. This new imagination supplanted reason as the central mental faculty (Tuveson 1960: 88–91).

17. Imagination was "that vivid memory, that makes appear present what is absent" (Condillac 1754, part II: 221).

18. Condillac distinguished memory, which "recalls things only as past," from imagination, which "redraws them with such force, that they appear present" (Condillac 1754, part I: 37). And Helvétius wrote that the imagination sought

"to reclothe in sensible images the abstract ideas and principles of the sciences" (Helvétius 1758: 491).

19. "The imagination goes quickly when it goes astray, because nothing is as fertile as a false principle" (Condillac 1749: 53).

20. Enthusiasts of "gigantic imagination" could see only "the phantoms of their heads."

21. "By excess or by lack of imagination, the intelligence is ... very imperfect" (Condillac 1749: 240).

22. On the contrast between inward-looking reason and outward-looking sensibility, see Riskin 2002: ch. 2.

23. See Franklin 1784: 18–21. A critic of the commissioners' methods argued that in empirical research one must "dispose the human machine in the most favorable manner to receive the impression" (Servan 1784: 36–38).

24. *Self-absorption* is a term in Simon Schaffer's "Self Evidence" (see Schaffer 1983b: 80–85). Although Schaffer describes the commissioners as having worried about the pitfall of "self-absorption" in philosophical research, he interprets their primary concern to have been the opposite problem, the vulnerability of the researcher to the influence and manipulation of others. In the face of this vulnerability, Schaffer writes, the commissioners were concerned to preserve their self-possession. They understood mesmerists to have assumed control of their subjects' bodies as though they were puppets or automata. According to Schaffer, by demonstrating their immunity to mesmeric manipulation, the commissioners reaffirmed the sanctity of individual autonomy. However, because the commissioners maintained their immunity to mesmerism by scrupulously diverting their attention away from their internal sensations, it seems to me that avoidance of self-absorption, and not preservation of self-possession, was their dominant concern. Or, to put it differently, the commissioners feared losing their self-possession not simply to an outside manipulator, but to that manipulator's exploitation of their own tendency to become absorbed in themselves.

25. On the sensationalist correlation between the imagination and social fragmentation, see Goldstein 1998: 30 and *supra,* nn. 4, 5. In her discussion of the mesmerism debates, Lindsay Wilson has focused upon critics' perception of mesmerism as a social problem. She argues that mesmerism, used predominantly to treat the *maladies des femmes,* appeared as part of a more general phenomenon, an increased influence of women on late Enlightenment French culture. This cultural prominence of women, anti-mesmerists feared, undermined "traditional values of hierarchy, privilege and patriarchy." In making this argument, Wilson distinguishes the social from the epistemological dimension of the mesmerism debate, writing, for example, that the commissioners' strategy was "to avoid plunging into the problem of epistemological certainty at all cost. Instead [they] focused on public relations" (Wilson 1993: 123, 107).

However, I mean to suggest that just as sentimental empiricism was inseparable from a social theory that founded social unity in sensibility, so, reciprocally, anti-mesmerists' social worries about instability were inextricably tied to their epistemological worries about insensibility.

26. This taxonomic principle provoked little comment; one critic did object that the greater credence the commissioners gave to the testimony of subjects from the "*classe plus élevée*" than from the "*classe du peuple*" reflected "the most marked partiality" (Bonnefoy 1784: 48).

27. The Society of Harmony's lodges were necessarily attended almost exclusively by noble and wealthy bourgeois clients because of the admissions fee (See Darnton 1968: 48).

28. See Bailly 1784: 43–44. On eighteenth-century physiological theories regarding sensibility and the passions in women, particularly in relation to the work of Pierre Roussel, see Williams 1994: 54–56. On the commissioners' theory of female susceptibility to mesmerism, see Wilson 1993: ch. 5.

29. On the Saint-Médard convulsionaries and the power of imagination, see Goldstein 1998: 40–48; and Wilson 1993: ch. 1. On the mind/body problem in eighteenth-century physiology and medicine, see Staum 1980: ch. 2 and 3.

30. The sexual effects of the imagination provided another example of its manifest influence upon the body. See Rousseau 1990: 291–330, especially 318–20.

31. Deslon's own account of his explanation differs: he claims to have argued that the boy was feeling the delayed effects of an earlier mesmeric session (Deslon 1784: 22).

32. See Bonnefoy 1784: 64; Deslon likewise protested that the touch employed in mesmeric massage was "always soft and light" (Deslon 1784: 27).

33. For secondary discussions of the physiology of the imagination in the eighteenth century, see Rousseau 1969: 109–11; and Ilie 1995: 3, 209, 232–33, 301, 356. In an alternative to the etherial theories, La Mettrie proposed that the imagination was "a sort of medullary screen on which objects painted in the eye are projected as by a magic lantern" (La Mettrie 1748: 113).

34. See De Saint Paul to Franklin, 10 December 1784, in FPA; Anon., 1784: 15, 49; Bonnefoy 1784: 22; Bergasse 1785: 41; Deslon 1784: 29, 31; and Servan 1784: 65. On the imagination theory begging the question, see Miller 1995: 59.

35. Another mesmerist pointed out that the commissioners themselves had said that moral causes exerted a powerful and disruptive influence upon the physical body. In that case, why had they introduced moral causes so liberally into their own experiments? By toying with their subjects' imaginations, had they not rendered their own investigation invalid? Rather than choosing the most suggestible subjects possible, they should have sought the least sensitive. For example, they should have chosen men rather than women—or better yet, plants and vegetables (Bergasse 1784b: 122–29).

References

Anon. (1784), *Réflexions impartiales sur le magnétisme animal*, Geneva.

Bailly, J. -S. ([1784] 1957), "Rapport secret sur le Mesmérisme, ou Magnétisme animal," in D. I. Duveen and H.S. Klickstein, "Documentation," *Annals of Science*, 13(1): 42–46.

Bailly, J. -S., et al. (1784), *Exposé des expériences qui ont été faites pour l'examen du magnétisme animal*, Paris.

Bergasse, N. (1784a), *Considérations sur le magnétisme animal, ou sur la théorie du monde et des êtres organisés,* The Hague.

Bergasse, N. (1784b), *Receuil des pièces les plus intéressantes sur le magnétisme animal*, Paris.

Bergasse, N. (1785), *Observations de M. Bergasse sur un écrit du docteur Mesmer,* London.

Bonnefoy, J. B. (1784), *Analyse raisonnée des rapports des commissaires chargés par le Roi de l'examen du magnétisme animal*, Lyon.

Bonnet, C. ([1754] 1779–1783), "Essai de psychologie," vol. 8, in *Oeuvres d'histoire naturelle et de philosophie de Charles Bonnet,* 8 vols, Neuchâtel: S. Fauche.

Bonnet, C. ([1764] 1779–1783), "Contemplation de la nature," vol. 4, in *Oeuvres d'histoire naturelle et de philosophie de Charles Bonnet,* 8 vols, Neuchâtel: S. Fauche.

Bonnet, C. (1769), *La Palingenésie philosophique,* Geneva: Philibert et Chirol.

Buffon, G. ([1753] 1954), *Oeuvres philosophiques de Buffon,* ed. J. Piveteau, Paris.

Bynum, W. F. and Porter, R. (eds) (1987), *Medical Fringe and Medical Orthodoxy, 1750–1850,* London: Croom Helm.

Condillac, E. B. de (1746), *Essai sur l'origine des connaissances humaines,* Amsterdam: P. Mortier.

Condillac, E. B. de ([1749] 1991), *Traité des systèmes,* Paris: Fayard.

Condillac, E. B. de ([1754] 1788), *Traité des sensations,* London.

Crabtree, A. (1993), *From Mesmer to Freud: Magnetic Sleep and the Roots of Psychological Healing,* New Haven, CT: Yale University Press.

Darnton, R. (1968), *Mesmerism and the End of the Enlightenment in France,* Cambridge MA: Harvard University Press.

Daston, L. (1998), "Fear and Loathing of the Imagination in Science," *Daedalus,* 127(1): 73–95.

Deslon, C. (1784), *Observations sur les deux Rapports de MM. les Commissaires nommés par Sa Majesté pour L'Examen du Magnétisme animal*, Paris.

Diderot, D. ([1753] 1998), "De l'interpretation de la nature," in *Oeuvres philosophiques,* pp. 167–244, Paris: Garnier.

Diderot, D. ([1758] 1966), "De la poésie dramatique," in P. Vernière (ed.), *Oeuvres estéthiques,* pp. 179–287, Paris: Garnier.

Diderot, D. ([1761] 1998), "Eloge de Richardson," in P. Vernière (ed.), *Oeuvres philosophiques,* pp. 23–48, Paris: Garnier.

Diderot, D. ([1767] 1998), "Le Rêve d'Alembert," in P. Vernière (ed.), *Oeuvres philosophiques,* pp. 285–371, Paris: Garnier.

Diderot, D. ([1774] 1875–1877), "Réfutation suivie de l'ouvrage d'Helvétius intitulé *L'Homme,*" vol. 2, pp. 275–346 in J. Assezat and M. Toyrneux (eds), *Oeuvres complètes,* 20 vols, Paris: Garnier.

Diderot, D. ([1784] 1964), *Elements de physiologie,* ed. J. Mayer, Paris: Didier.

Diderot, D. and d'Alembert, J. (eds) (1751–1772), *Encyclopédie, ou, Dictionnaire raisonné des sciences, des arts et des métiers,* Paris.

Duveen, D. and Klickstein, H. (1955), "Joint Investigations," *Annals of Science,* 2: 271–302.

Franklin, B. (1907), *The Writings of Benjamin Franklin,* ed. A. H. Smyth, 10 vols, New York: Macmillan.

Franklin, B., Lavoisier, A., et al. (1784), *Rapport des commissaires chargés par le Roi de l'examen du magnétisme animal,* Paris.

Gillispie, C. (1980), *Science and Polity in France at the End of the Old Regime,* Princeton, NJ: Princeton University Press.

Goldstein, J. (1998), "Enthusiasm or Imagination? Eighteenth-Century Smear Words in Comparative National Context," *Huntington Library Quarterly,* 60(1 & 2): 29–49.

Hahn, R. (1971), *The Anatomy of a Scientific Institution: The Paris Academy of Sciences, 1666–1803,* Berkeley, CA: University of California Press.

Heilbron, J.L. (1979), *The History of Electricity in the 17th and 18th Centuries,* Berkeley, CA: University of California Press.

Helvétius, C. -A. (1758), *De l'esprit,* Paris: Durand.

Huet, M. H. (1993), *Monstrous Imagination,* Cambridge, MA: Harvard University Press.

Ilie, P. (1995), *The Age of Minerva, Vol. 2: Cognitive Discontinuities in Eighteenth Century Thought, From Body to Mind in Physiology and the Arts,* Philadelphia: University of Pennsylvania Press.

Jussieu, B. de ([1784] 1826), "Rapport de l'un des commissaires chargés par le Roi de l'examen du magnétisme animal," in A. Bertrand, *Du magnétisme animal en France, et des jugements qu'en portés les sociétés savants,* Paris.

Kaptchuk, T. J. (1998), "Intentional Ignorance: A History of Blind Assessment and Placebo Controls in Medicine," *Bulletin of the History of Medicine,* 72(3): 389–433.

La Mettrie, J. O. de ([1748] 1981), *L'Homme-machine,* ed. P. -L. Assoun, Paris: Denoël/Gonthier.

Lavoisier, A. L. ([1784] 1862–1893), *Oeuvres de Lavoisier,* 6 vols, J. B. Dumas (vols 1–4) and E. Grimaux (vols 5–6) (eds), Paris: Imprimerie Impériale.

Lingo, A. K. (1986), "Empirics and Charlatans in Early Modern France: The Genesis of Classification of the 'Other' in Medical Practice," *Journal of Social History,* 19: 583–604.

Lopez, C. ([1966] 1990), *Mon Cher Papa: Franklin and the Ladies of Paris,* New Haven, CT: Yale University Press.

Mesmer, F. A. ([1766] 1980), "Physical-Medical Treatise on the Influence of the Planets," in *Mesmerism, A Translation of the Original Scientific Writings of F. A. Mesmer,* trans. G. Bloch, Los Altos, CA: William Kaufman, pp. 3–20.

Mesmer, F. A. (1781), "Précis historique des faits relatives au magnétisme animal jusqu'en avril 1781," in A. Pattie and J. Vinchon (notes and commentary), *Le Magnétisme Animal. Oeuvres publiés par Robert Amadou,* Paris: Payot, pp. 93–194.

Mesmer, F. A. ([1784] 1980), "Discourse by Mesmer on Magnetism," *Mesmerism, A Translation of the Original Scientific Writings of F. A. Mesmer,* trans. G. Bloch, Los Altos, CA: William Kaufman, pp. 23–38.

Mesmer, F. A. ([1799] 1980), "Dissertation by F. A. Mesmer, Doctor of Medicine, on His Discoveries," *Mesmerism, A Translation of the Original Scientific Writings of F. A. Mesmer,* trans. G. Bloch, Los Altos, CA: William Kaufman, pp. 89–130.

Mesmer, F. A. (1980), *Mesmerism, A Translation of the Original Scientific Writings of F. A. Mesmer,* trans. G. Bloch, Los Altos, CA: William Kaufman.

Miller, J. (1995), "Going Unconscious," *New York Review of Books,* (20 April): 56–65.

Montjoie, G. de (1784), *Lettre sur le magnétisme animal,* Paris.

Nollet, J. (1754–1765), *Leçons de physique expérimental,* 4th edn, 6 vols, Paris.

Poissonier, P. -I., et al. (1784), *Rapport des Commissaires de la Société Royale de Médecine, nommés par Le Roi pour faire l'examen du Magnétisme animal,* Paris.

Porter, R. (1989), *Health for Sale: Quackery in England, 1660–1850,* Manchester: Manchester University Press.

Priestley, J. ([1779–1786] 1977), *Experiments and Observations Relating to Various Branches of Natural Philosophy,* 3 vols, New York: Kraus.

Puységur, A. M. -J. ([1786] 1986), *Mémoires pour servir á l'histoire et á l'établissement du magnétisme animal,* G. Lapassade and P. Pédelahore (eds), Bordeaux: Editions Privat.

Riskin, J. (2002), *Science in the Age of Sensibility: The Sentimental Empiricists of the Eighteenth Century,* Chicago: University of Chicago Press.

Rousseau, G. (1969), "Science and the Discovery of the Imagination in Enlightened England," *Eighteenth-Century Studies,* 3: 108–35.

Rousseau, G. (1971), "Pineapples, Pregnancy, Pica, and the *Peregrine Pickle,*" in G. S. Rousseau and P. G. Boucé (eds), *Tobias Smollet: Bicentennial Essays,* New York: Oxford University Press.

Rousseau, G. (ed.) (1990), *The Languages of Psyche: Mind and Body in Enlightenment Thought,* Berkeley, CA: University of California Press.

Rudé, G. (1959), *The Crowd in the French Revolution,* Oxford: Oxford University Press.

Rudé, G. (1964), *The Crowd in History, 1730–1848,* New York: Wiley.

Schaffer, S. (1983a), "Natural Philosophy and Public Spectacle in the Eighteenth Century," *History of Science,* 21, part I, no. 51: 1–43.

Schaffer, S. (1983b), "Self Evidence," in J. Chandler, A. I. Davidson and H. D. Harootunian (eds), *Questions of Evidence*: *Proof, Practice, and Persuasion across the Disciplines,* Chicago, IL: University of Chicago Press, pp. 56–91.

Servan, A. (1784), *Doutes d'un Provincial, Proposés à M. M. Les Médecins— Commissaires, chargés par le Roi, de l'examen du Magnétisme animal,* Lyon.

Staum, M. S. (1980), *Cabanis: Enlightenment and Medical Philosophy in the French Revolution,* Princeton, NJ: Princeton University Press.

Stewart, L. R. (1992), *The Rise of Public Science: Rhetoric, Technology, and Natural Philosophy in Newtonian Britain, 1660–1750,* New York: Cambridge University Press.

Sutton, G. (1995), *Science for a Polite Society: Gender, Culture, and the Demonstration of Enlightenment,* Boulder, CO: Westview.

Terrall, M. (1999), "Methaphysics, Mathematics and the Gendering of Science in Eighteenth-Century France," in W. Clark, J. Golinski and S. Schaffer (eds), *The Sciences in Enlightened Europe,* Chicago, IL: University of Chicago Press, pp. 246–71.

Torlais, J. ([1954] 1987), *Un Physicien au siècle des lumières. L'Abbé Nollet. 1700–1770,* Paris: Jonas Editeur.

Tuveson, E. (1960), *The Imagination as a Means of Grace: Locke and the Aesthetics of Romanticism,* Berkeley, CA: University of California Press.

Vila, A. (1998), *Enlightenment and Pathology: Sensibility in the Literature and Medicine of Eighteenth-Century France,* Baltimore, MD: Johns Hopkins University Press.

Vinchon, J. (1971), *Mesmer et son secret: Textes choisis présentés par R. de Saussure,* Toulouse: Privat.

Williams, E. (1994), *The Physical and the Moral: Anthropology, Physiology, and Philosophical Medicine in France, 1750–1850,* Cambridge: Cambridge University Press.

Wilson, L. (1993), *Women and Medicine in the French Enlightenment: The Debate over Maladies des Femmes,* Baltimore, MD: Johns Hopkins University Press.

Winter, A. (1998), *Mesmerized: Powers of Mind in Victorian Britain,* Chicago: University of Chicago Press.

Zweig, S. ([1932] 1962), *Mental Healers: Frantz Anton Mesmer, Mary Baker Eddy, Sigmund Freud,* New York: Ungar.

7

Swedenborg's Celestial Sensorium
Angelic Authenticity, Religious Authority, and the American New Church Movement
Leigh Eric Schmidt

In 1696 John Aubrey, a fellow of the Royal Society, published in London a book entitled *Miscellanies, "a* collection of *Hermetick Philosophy." "Natural Philosophy* hath been exceedingly advanced within Fifty Years last past," he began, "but methinks, 'tis strange that *Hermetick Philosophy* hath lain so long untoucht. It is a Subject worthy of serious Consideration." There followed his observations on, among other things, astrology, omens, dreams, apparitions, visions, oracles, crystal gazing, and ecstasies. Aubrey also had a whole chapter on voices, ranging from Augustine's "Take, read," to a personal acquaintance of his own who had twice heard an ethereal command to translate Luther's *Tischreden* into English. Another section of Aubrey's compendium took up the knockings of spirits on bedsteads and walls— phenomena for which Puritan Richard Baxter's *Certainty of the Worlds of Spirits* (1691) was the leading source. (The extent of such lore is a reminder of the larger history behind the "audible realities" and "peculiar noises" of mid-nineteenth-century Spiritualism, all those portentous "knockings, rappings, jarrings, creakings, tickings" that aroused so much Victorian wonder.) A little later in the volume, Aubrey offered a chapter entitled "Converse with Angels and Spirits" in which one "Angelical Revelation" after another was recounted. The rubric was conventional— Heinrich Cornelius Agrippa's *Three Books of Occult Philosophy,* for example, had a section called "Of the Tongues of Angels, and of Their Speaking amongst Themselves, and with Us."[1]

Aubrey's umbrella for all these wonders was Hermetic philosophy, a designation derived from the ancient writings attributed to the Egyptian magus Hermes Trismegistus, whose wisdom was taken to be a primeval anticipation of the highest truths of Christian revelation and pagan philosophy. Through Renaissance rediscovery and reworking, the Hermetic tradition, evident in Aubrey's usage, had come to embrace a loose combination of Christian, Neoplatonist, biblical, and kabbalistic elements. Among its hybrid components was a desire to know the hidden speech of angels and spirits, to enter the sensorium of the celestial world. Aubrey's piety included an affirmation of an arcane acoustics in which celestial voices, angelic conversations, mystical words, and heavenly harmonies were avidly pursued.

Though Aubrey felt that Hermetic philosophy was falling out of favor with the ascent of the new natural philosophy, it would prove highly adaptable and almost endlessly renewable. In contrast to the Baconian and Lockean cultivation of the bodily senses as the experimental avenue for the advancement of knowledge, these esoteric currents regularly overflowed conventional sensory channels. Interested less in the management of the senses than in their transformation, these mixed Hermetic, Christian, and kabbalistic streams emphasized the supreme reality of the celestial world and the practices by which that realm was penetrated, its influences attracted, or its inhabitants invoked. These multilayered traditions flourished beside, within, through, and beyond the Enlightenment. Esoteric books of mystical illumination circulated widely on both sides of the Atlantic, and their influence was evident around almost every bend, from the alchemical, Pythagorean fascinations of Newton to the cosmological visions of Joseph Smith. Hermetic dreams hardly slumbered in the modern aftermath (fittingly a new edition of Aubrey's *Miscellanies* appeared in 1857 and another in 1890). The aural arcana of that harmonial world formed, as this chapter will show, a persistent counterpoint to the increasingly demystified acoustics of the new natural philosophy (see Schmidt 2000: ch. 4).[2]

Such inquiries, especially those into the speech of angels and into the spiritual senses beyond the body, were massively extended by one of the Enlightenment's own, the Swedish natural-philosopher-turned-Christian-mystic Emanuel Swedenborg (1688–1772). In a portentous move in the 1740s, Swedenborg shifted from the learned theaters of anatomy and mechanical invention to the heavenly spheres of angelic conversation and apocalyptic unfolding. Operating within the severe limits imposed by the Lutheran establishment, Swedenborg published all of his religious writings beyond Sweden's borders (especially in the freer climes of London and Amsterdam) and gathered almost no following in his homeland during his lifetime. Instead, a considerable audience for his memorable accounts arose in England and the United States, where his ideas steadily percolated in the 1780s and 1790s and became an especially strong brew in the first half of the nineteenth century. Spawning a vast publishing enterprise and an extended network of adepts and dabblers, Swedenborg became one of the era's consummate bearers of immediate revelation and an inspiration for several of America's homegrown revelators. Eventually, he even became for some an angelic spirit guide, a dead-yet-living contact for heavenly wisdom.[3]

He and his Anglo-American progeny, who crystallized into the Church of the New Jerusalem (or "New Church"), were particularly savvy synthesizers of natural philosophy and immediate revelation. More eclectic than most evangelicals, Swedenborgian seekers fused the empiricist exactitude of experimental philosophy to a dualistic spiritualizing of the scriptures, the body, the senses, animals, dreams, landscapes. Everything harbored hidden correspondences; all the world was a hieroglyph. To Swedenborg and those who followed his lead, the trick to reharmonizing the universe was not to ignore the materialistic, rationalistic, and experimental dimensions of the Enlightenment, but to transmute them into a spiritual inquiry every bit as thorough, substantial, and precise. Versed in Hermetic cosmologies and kabbalistic hermeneutics, Swedenborg sought to throw open the arcana of scripture and the mysteries of the heavenly world to rational understanding and empirical report. Resisting the deistic separation of reason and immediate revelation, he offered religious enlightenment by way of the Enlightenment.[4]

The opening up of the interior senses—for example, to speak inwardly with angels, as Swedenborg did—was, by the mid-nineteenth century, rarely sufficient. The voices from spirit-land that people desired were increasingly materialized and incarnated, though devoted leaders of the New Church mostly opposed this turn (as a betrayal of Swedenborg's authority, as well as his sharp dualism). For many, transcending the bodily senses was finally not as satisfying as having the physical evidence at hand. One avenue, with decidedly evangelical and eschatological valences, was the gift of speaking in tongues, which received a burst of attention from the 1830s into the 1850s. Could the Holy Spirit (or good spirits) descend upon people and make the human tongue the passive vehicle of heavenly communications? Spiritualist mediumship often edged into tongue-speaking, and there was a lively exchange in popular religion (Mormon, Shaker, Spiritualist, and evangelical) over the presences of these spectral voices long before the rise of Pentecostalism.

The restoration of this apostolic gift of speaking in unknown languages proved to be merely one repercussion among many in this "new age" of spirit presences and angelic conversations. (The "new age" was, by the way, an apocalyptic designation pushed especially by nineteenth-century Swedenborgians.)[5] Sometimes the spirits provided catchy choruses for singing in earthly circles; sometimes the angels dictated entire books through automatic writing; and sometimes heavenly voices were even mediated through speaking trumpets, as the acoustic recreations of the Enlightenment were dramatically reenchanted. Eventually, as spirits even took up the telephone, the acoustic technologies of modernity seemed to have been turned completely against the Enlightenment uses of Fontenelle and Brewster (see Schmidt 2000: 88–90, 130–31, 151), made part of a communications network in a wonderland of good vibrations.

Talking with Angels; Or, the End of Artifice

Swedenborg's religious experiences over the last three decades of his life are as richly documented and intriguingly complex as any figure of the eighteenth century. Through dreams, visions, and voices, through prayer, meditation, and eucharistic participation, through bodily denials and sexually charged spiritual unions, Swedenborg turned inward, seeking the Lord and his angels and warring with Satan and his sirens. It was a contemplative struggle on the grandest scale, worthy of a desert saint, a medieval recluse, or, more proximately, a pietist mystic like Jacob Boehme. Drawn, as was John Wesley, to the Moravians and their devotionalism, Swedenborg remained deeply marked by such pietistic strains within his native Lutheranism (he was the son of a wonder-guided Lutheran bishop). After 1743, though, he gradually moved beyond these more familiar forms of devotionalism through studied techniques of slowed breathing and through the progressive opening of his "spiritual sight." From the mid-1740s to the end of his life, he developed the ability to "converse with angels and spirits in the same manner as I speak with men," and a hallmark of his piety became a near endless stream of communications with angels. (The angels were understood to be the spirits of people who had once lived on earth and who were now arrayed in various habitations, kingdoms, and spheres in heaven.) Despite a considerable doctrinal and exegetical corpus, Swedenborg captured the attention of his British and American readers above all through these memorable relations of things heard and seen in the spiritual world.[6]

The attention these experiences garnered him was as much negative as positive. As early as Immanuel Kant's *Träume eines Geistersehers* (1766), Swedenborg's familiarity with angels met a gush of ridicule and made him a leading exhibit in medical psychology. One of Swedenborg's staunchest defenders in antebellum America, George Bush—a graduate of Princeton Seminary, a former tutor at the nearby college, and a professor at New York University—knew that vindicating Swedenborg meant defending both his motives and his sanity. The common view, Bush noted, was that the Swede's revelations were either "designed imposture" or "unconscious illusion," especially the latter. His spiritual travels were thus widely dismissed as "a strange medley of hallucinations," a product of "religious mania," "the fruit of a distempered brain." As critic Enoch Pond concluded summarily, "His mind was disordered; it had become unbalanced; and he was, to a degree, *insane.* There can be no reasonable doubt of it." No matter how wide open the religious world of the early republic seemed, talking with angels carried a steep price. Benjamin Rush, in his *Medical Inquiries and Observations upon the Diseases of the Mind,* specifically pathologized those who "see and converse with angels." Accordingly, Swedenborg was regularly read out of the ranks of the reasonable.[7]

By the 1830s and 1840s, these prominent Enlightenment ways of explaining Swedenborg's religious voices were as likely to surface in popular settings as learned ones. Hence, in 1842 in Indiana a New Church preacher found himself in a formal debate with a Presbyterian minister on the bumptious resolution that "Emanuel Swedenborg was an insane person, or a blasphemer and a knave."[8] John Wesley, in particular, had been crucial for blessing this interpretive course in evangelical circles, largely sidestepping the theological content of Swedenborg's visions by recycling suspect accounts of the mystic's fevered mind. Diagnoses of mental malady—calls for the "shutting up of Swedenborg in a madhouse"—weighed very heavily on New Church evangelism, on anyone who wanted to take these religious experiences seriously. So desperate were apologists to establish Swedenborg's rationality that they went to extreme lengths even to deny his basic pietism, publishing articles proclaiming "Swedenborg Not a Visionary" and "Swedenborg Not a Mystic." Hardly a testimonial came from the press that did not bespeak the necessity of confronting the charge of insanity, of denying that these revelatory encounters were "the effects of a disordered state of the brain, which the science of physiology professes to explain." The New Church battle with materialist explanations was not abstract but highly personal, deeply bound up with feelings of disrespect and insult.[9]

Swedenborg proved hard to confine, though, because of certain social advantages. An aristocratic cosmopolitan, he carried the respected standing of a natural philosopher, and these badges of genteel credibility helped his experimental reports of angelic conversations gain a hearing that they would have otherwise been denied. A scion of the Enlightenment and the right social circles, he was hard to dismiss as a vulgar enthusiast, one of the weak-minded and credulous. Certainly those Americans who "received" Swedenborg's teachings, as did the scholar George Bush, almost invariably made this point about his learning (and, implicitly, the social position that went with it). For example, Margaret Hiller, a New England convert at the turn of the nineteenth century, singled out Swedenborg's "extensive erudition," his uniting of philosophical learning with religious vision, as a principal attraction.[10] Emerson, both hagiographer and critic of this "colossal soul," was similarly drawn to Swedenborg's preparations "in shipyards and dissecting-rooms." "One is glad to learn that his books on mines and metals are held in the highest esteem by those who understand these matters," Emerson remarked dryly.[11] Because Swedenborg had first been a student of astronomy and anatomy, a Cartesian rationalist, a productive mathematician, an improver of mines and trade, a cognoscente of air-pumps and microscopes as well as of speaking trumpets and acoustic tubes, his admirers were able to accrue greater credit for him as a visionary. Because Swedenborg was clearly as committed as anyone to the advancement of knowledge, because he brought all of his energies for precise mapping and classification to his grand tours through heaven and hell, his followers were able to present this kabbalistic mystic and pietist pilgrim as, through it all and at bottom, a man of science.[12]

Beyond his conversations with angels and beyond his hybridity as natural philosopher and Christian visionary, Swedenborg offered other attractions. Among his biggest allures was as an inspired guide to scriptural interpretation, with much of his theological writing taking the form of extended commentaries on the hidden spiritual meanings of biblical texts, recondite correspondences beneath the literal words. "*He* will furnish you with a *key* to unlock the holy treasures of Divine Wisdom contained in the written Word of the Lord"—so claimed convert Elizabeth Jones in 1816 in a letter to her Presbyterian pastor in Newburgh, New York, on her reasons for switching to the New Church. Carrying this weapon into exegetical combat, Jones, an "unlearned female," was able to "forget my own inferiority" and stoutly defend

Swedenborg's views of scripture as well as his Christ-centered views on the Trinity. In a heavily Protestant culture, riven with strife over biblical subtleties, inspired commentaries like those of Swedenborg (or, later, Mary Baker Eddy) carried the hope of finding a solid foundation beneath all the disputes. Though new prophets necessarily only added to the scriptural melee, the hope was always one of interpretive healing. "The right of private judgment in the interpretation of Scriptures, which is the first principle of Protestantism, has introduced a perfect anarchy into the Christian world," despaired a Swedenborgian preacher in Boston in 1818. "Every year, every day, may give birth to new sectaries and new creeds. Where is the umpire? where is the judge?" The New Church, like those who later turned to Joseph Smith and the *Book of Mormon,* thought they had that final referee—a new key to the scriptures in the form of Emanuel Swedenborg's inspired glosses.[13]

Swedenborg was also well tailored for the American religious milieu in many of his liberal doctrinal emphases, which were easy to make part of a mounting anti-Calvinist polemic. (In one of his visions, Swedenborg actually encountered Calvin in the spirit world, and it turned out the reformer had been spending altogether too much time in an otherworldly brothel.)[14] On original sin, predestination, and the damnation of infants, Swedenborg adopted sharply anti-Calvinist views, in keeping with wider Enlightenment currents.[15] Much of his theological work was infused with liberal predilections—the hallowing of charity, free will, usefulness, marriage love, and progress through education (the angelic tutelage of children was a prominent activity of heaven). Sharing in wider universalistic currents, he opened salvation to all those, inside or outside the church, who sustained a regenerate life of active benevolence and loving affections toward their neighbors. His realized eschatology in which the Last Judgment had already been accomplished in the spiritual world in 1757 invited dreams of a new era of millennial progress in which the advancement of learning, technology, and civil liberty could be enfolded as evidence of the dawning of the New Jerusalem.[16] Likewise, his reinterpretation of the Trinity in terms of the oneness of Christ played to Enlightenment sentiments (the belief that such three-in-one mathematics would never add up), and so did his dismissal of tangible miracles as illusory. His American disciples became adroit at such maneuvers. "The age of *external* miracles has doubtless passed away," Margaret Hiller noted, but, at the same time, Swedenborg's experiences "exhibited a species of *internal,* or *spiritual miracle,* absolutely *new* and truly *astonishing.*" Swedenborg, often reduced now to a metaphysical bridge into Spiritualism, offered many attractions to his Anglo-American audiences.[17]

For all his liberal affinities, Swedenborg talked with angels, matched wits with evil spirits, dreamed extraordinary dreams, and pored over the Apocalypse. Whatever else gained him his considerable readership (by the 1820s, *Heaven and Hell* was already an American bestseller, rivaling the novels of James Fenimore Cooper and Walter Scott for sales), the leading impetus was surely the mystic's numerous points of connection with popular forms of supernaturalism.[18] Swedenborg was both symptom and spur of the oracular mode in the early republic. Mystical auditions and epiphanic dreams were Protestant commonplaces, part of a religious culture of divine intimacy cultivated through biblical immersion, prayer, meditation, and revival. *An Account of a Trance or Vision of Sarah Alley,* published in Poughkeepsie in 1798, was representative. Taken on an out-of-body tour of heaven and hell by an angel serving as guide, Alley even encountered Jesus himself. "Christ told me I could not enter there yet," she said—"that I must return to the world, and warn the people thereof to repent."[19] Swedenborg's encounters with everyone from Moses and Aristotle to the apostles and Luther, with angels and spirits of all kinds, were received within this culture of visions, dreams, and voices, a world in which it was not especially unusual for God "to make extraordinary discoveries and revelations to particular persons."[20] Many came to see Swedenborg as embodying a new epoch of "a more intimate fellowship with saints and angels," an imminent time of restoration when "angels shall converse with men as familiarly as they did with Adam before the fall."[21]

What precisely did people learn about the speech of angels through all of Swedenborg's interior discoveries? On the face of it, the auditory world of the angels sounded a lot like the earthly world. As Swedenborg related in *Heaven and Hell,* at the opening of his chapter on the speech of angels: "The Angels converse together, as we do on earth, and in like manner on various subjects, whether of a domestic, civil, moral, or spiritual nature. ... The speech of angels is equally divided into words with our's, and alike sonorous and audible, for they have mouths, tongues and ears, as we have." But these close correspondences between earthly and spiritual realms hid fundamental differences. To begin with, the speech of the angels was cosmopolitan and unified: "There is but one language used throughout heaven, so that all of every society, however distant, understand one another." It was also exceedingly condensed and precise, such that angels were "able to express more in one word than we can do in a thousand." Against the deistic suspicion of the artificiality of all human language and hence all revelation—that no words could ever match the purity, universality, or exactitude of nature's geometry—Swedenborg heard a celestial language of just such clarity and scope. In Baconian and Cartesian frameworks, mere words were impugned for their inconstancy, frailty, and vernacular provinciality, and whole new classificatory and experimental languages were dreamed to help deliver the learned out of such contingency into universal knowledge. From this "want of a universal language," Paine would draw the skeptical conclusion as crisply as anyone: "Human language, whether in speech or in print, cannot be the vehicle of the Word of God." In talking with angels, Swedenborg discerned a rejoinder to the absorption of revelation into the language of nature, to the very dismissal of the oracular power of words.[22]

Swedenborg embraced the philosophical ambition for a universal language, but he kept that dream within the frameworks of Christian eschatology and Adamic restoration. The exalted range of angelic speech stemmed not from such sources as abstracted mathematical formulas or cleverly designed ideographs, but instead from a knowledge of the secrets embedded in scripture. Those mysteries, including the esoteric significance of biblical numbers and the Hebrew alphabet, shaped angelic expression, infusing both its oral and written forms. Much of the potency of heavenly communications grew out of the access that the angels had to these divine encryptions, the copious meanings hidden in "the very flexures and curvatures" of the Hebrew letters, as well as "the sounding of them." Such angelic words, imbued with presence, transcended the philosophical suspicions that gnawed at the trustworthiness of ordinary words, those arbitrary signs that seemed ever harder in the eighteenth century to shore up with a divine origin. For the undisciplined mutability and estranging localism of human languages, Swedenborg offered a religious balm: angelic fluency, not pure mathematics or learned ingenuity, would reverse the consequences of Babel. The lexicons of natural philosophy, however important, ultimately paled before the condensed surpluses of heavenly wisdom.[23]

Among the most crucial ways that the speech of angels differed from human speech was in the fate of artifice. Swedenborg, one in a great company of early modern moralists who inveighed against hypocrisy and dissimulation, found in the spiritual world a realm where guile was consistently undone, where aristocratic masks and courtly intrigues fell away. Mutterers and whisperers, for example, fared poorly in heaven, and those spirits who remained inclined to conceal their real thoughts with a calculated softness of voice were exposed by the very nature of heavenly communication. "Such speech is heard at greater distances and more loudly than open speech," Swedenborg reported happily. Also, flatterers and wheedlers—all "those who speak differently from what they think"—were subject to unmaskings of various kinds. One hypocrite, for example, was presented as a spiritual dartboard in which arrows rained down upon his head until his pretense was punctured, thus revealing his "true character." In Swedenborg's heaven, the senses of the angels were exquisitely discerning, and their fine-tuned ears, in particular, permitted them to make a complete register of the inner lives of others through perceiving subtle "variegations in the voice." "The angels know the disposition and qualities of another from his speech, his affection from the sound of his voice," Swedenborg related. "I have heard the angels declare what life another person has led from only hearing him speak."[24]

At times, the capacity of the angels to penetrate the hearts and minds of others appeared sinister, even inquisitorial. In this Christian vision of total exposure, nothing remained hidden. The deceitful, the seducing, the backbiting, the cajoling, and the fraudulent were turned inside out; they were bared of all casuistic reserve and equivocation—"not the least room is left for evasion or denial." So thoroughgoing were the probings of the angels that Swedenborg, the dissecting anatomist, described their discriminating powers as a kind of autopsy of the spiritual body: "When all that a man had done here in his natural body is made manifest to him after death, then the examining angels inspect his face, and commence their inquest, which begins at the fingers of each hand, and is from thence continued throughout the whole body."

Putting an end to artifice and deceit would not be accomplished without merciless invasions of body and spirit. A heaven of such relentless honesty—where every tone of the voice, where every look of the face, automatically opened the recesses of the soul to inspection—was not without its terror. Was it any wonder that those hypocrites who tried forlornly to persist in their disguises began, Swedenborg reported, to feel "anguish and pain, to change countenance, and to be struck in a manner lifeless"? With an Augustinian or Kantian absolutism, Swedenborg's heavenly kingdom tolerated no secrets and no lies, and few pains were spared in rooting them out. His angelic societies, endlessly purifying themselves of artifice, had a dystopic underside.[25]

The heart of Swedenborg's mystic listening centered on the speech of the spiritual and celestial angels. The universal language of the angels was not "learnt" but "natural"; it flowed "spontaneously from their affections"—indeed, the very sound of their voices corresponded completely with their affections, so that their language "may be called a sounding affection, and a speaking thought." There were no gaps, no slippages, no broken signs, no arbitrary conventions, "it being impossible for them to utter any thing which does not correspond with their affection." In an evocative turn of phrase, Swedenborg described the speech of one angel as so harmonious and delightful that it was "as if Love itself had spoken with a tongue."[26] At another point, caught up in the sheer purity of angelic speech, he experienced these words in incarnational form as "a virgin who was dressed beautifully in a robe of white neatly gathered at the breast, and who was graceful in the movements of her body" (in the same vision, the speech of evil spirits was represented to him as "the hind-quarters of a horse").[27] For the subsequent imagining of a Romantic self—one absorbed with spontaneous expression and pure sincerity—Swedenborg's celestial angels would provide an exalted model. "These angels are without any garment or covering, for nakedness corresponds to Innocence," the seer related. Their childlike simplicity and artlessness, embodied in their Edenic nudity, put an end to the artifices of social life and imagined the ultimately transparent self.[28]

Swedenborg's most empyrean conversations with the angels performed important cultural work in the here and now. American followers took his lessons about angelic speech to heart and dreamed new kinds of intimacies and interiors through them. As New Churchman Richard DeCharms explained in 1856, "the external man is now too generally a hypocrite, and speaks a language which the soul does not feel"; and again, "the internal man is now so hid under feigned and false appearances, which we are taught from infancy to assume, that the expressions of the external man are no longer the natural language of the soul." In the world of the angels, DeCharms explained, "thoughts themselves would speak ... communicated by undulations of the heavenly aura, as sounds are in our own air." American adepts took special delight in Swedenborg's rendering of angelic speech, in all those pure spirits who were incapable of thinking one thing and speaking another: "They do not know what hypocrisy is, and what fraudulent disguise is, and deceit." With their complete restoration of the unity of feelings and words, interiors and exteriors, Swedenborg's angels offered an idealized remaking of the self—pure and genuine, plainly expressive of loving affections, wholly open in character. These angels, tearing away all the masks of polite society, proved very easy to transpose into American middle-class saints of authenticity.[29]

Bodies, Spirits, Senses: The Penetrating Eye, the Obedient Ear, and the Tasteless Angel

Swedenborg's proficiency in talking with angels and in describing their speech was enmeshed in a highly complicated sensorium. No other Christian visionary paid such close, dissecting attention to the bodily and spiritual senses, and this intensive inquiry flowed out of Swedenborg's natural philosophy, especially his work as an anatomist. The seer had studied the five senses at length, composing a whole disquisition upon them as well as writing separate essays on the ear and the eye. Synthesizing the experiments of others and pursuing his own probings of the body, he was bent on an ambitious Cartesian project of arriving at "knowledge of the soul" through "anatomical experience."[30] Though Swedenborg was following standard cosmological models of microcosm and macrocosm in imagining the whole of heaven as a human body, it was his own physiological learning that allowed him to detail with unusual precision the different organs of that Grand Man. The very "Form of Heaven," he noted trenchantly in *Heaven and Hell,* corresponded to "the structure of the human body, as viewed and examined by a skilful anatomist."[31] Swedenborg emerged from the anatomy theaters of the early Enlightenment and remade himself as the dissectionist of heaven's sensorium. His unrivaled ability to map that spiritual body, in turn, would deeply mark his American followers.

Swedenborg shared most of the assumptions about the senses current in the wider experimental philosophy. He was interested, for example, in how the bodily senses could be "sharpened"—that is, how they could be improved, trained, and managed. He was convinced of the utility of empirical demonstration and desired to provide just this sort of evidence of the spiritual realms. "I am well aware of the fact that many people will say nobody can possibly speak to spirits or angels as long as he is living in the body, and that many will call it delusion," Swedenborg confessed early on in the *Arcana Coelestia,* before offering his usual empiricist rebuttal. "But none of this deters me; for I have seen, I have heard, I have felt." The seer exuberantly affirmed the testimony of his own senses and took that sensationalism with him into heaven, pointing to a spiritual world where the senses were all the more delicate and vigorous: "Let people beware of falsely assuming that spirits do not possess far keener sensory powers than they did in the life of the body," Swedenborg warned. "From thousands of experiences I know that the reverse is true." As with hearing's grand enhancements among the angels, Swedenborg found in heaven the consummate refinement of the senses. "This spiritual body is most perfectly organized," one American adherent elaborated, "having all the organs and senses of the material body, but inconceivably more acute, exquisite, and perfect." In Swedenborgian circles, the careful education of the senses—not least the proper formation of the ear—became a given. "That the ear is highly susceptible of improvement," a writer in *New Jerusalem Magazine* concluded in 1838, "and that it will well repay a judicious cultivation, there can be no doubt."[32]

Like most of his Enlightenment contemporaries, Swedenborg's epistemology remained hybrid. Along with the experimental philosophy, he had also deeply imbibed a Neoplatonist as well as a Cartesian distrust of the bodily senses. The fallacies and illusions to which the senses were subject made reason's disciplines—the seasoned judgment that allowed for the correction of sensory error—extremely crucial, and Swedenborg rarely missed an opportunity to disparage the shortcomings of the bodily senses and the dangers of mere sensualism. Swedenborg so avidly pursued the body and the senses not as ends, but in search of a vehicle by which to refute all those "scientific and philosophic reasonings" that called "the life of a spirit or a soul" into question. "The senses are too strong for the soul. Our senses barbarize us"—so Emerson claimed, and it is not surprising that he and other American transcendentalists saw in Swedenborg a harbinger of their own revolt against "the despotism of sense." However analogous the bodily and spiritual senses were, Swedenborgian attention was ultimately riveted on cautioning the former against material illusions and opening up the latter to the really real.[33]

Perhaps Swedenborg was most in synchronicity with his philosophical colleagues in according particular privileges to the eye. At the outset of his treatise on the five senses, for example, he imagined all of knowledge in visual terms and made clear his desire for a panoramic view—the surveying of the world as if "from the top of a mountain" or "from a high tower." In the *Arcana Coelestia* he likewise elucidated the higher perfection of one spiritual realm over another by comparing sight's superior sweep to hearing's limits: "For that which hearing is able to take in through an hour of speech may be presented to the sight within a minute, such as for example, views of plains, palaces, and cities." Though Swedenborg cultivated a multi-sensory spiritual discipline, he often used the eye to stand for all the senses. In his memorable relations it was, first and foremost, his "spiritual sight" that was opened. "The eye is the noblest region of the face, and surpasses the other senses," Swedenborg wrote in his *Spiritual Diary,* and his American heirs readily embraced that incomparability. Caleb Reed, for example, echoed the seer's view in a lecture entitled "The Senses" in Boston in 1838, noting succinctly that "the sense of sight," corresponding to the understanding, "is the highest or noblest of the senses." Within the Swedenborgian sensorium—like its Aristotelian, Cartesian, Lockean, and Common-Sense counterparts—sight was the most honored sense.[34]

At the other end of the sensory hierarchy was taste, so thoroughly linked with the material body that it could not be freed for spiritual transformation. Taste, indeed, was the one sense that the angels did not have, at least not in any way comparable to its bodily counterpart. "Spirits have every sense except taste; but taste they have not," Swedenborg wrote in his *Spiritual Diary* in 1748. "It is now manifest to me that they are delighted with man's spiritual food, thus with the knowledges of truth and good. But they do not insinuate themselves into taste, which is a sense properly dedicated to corporeal food, or to the nourishment of the body, in which they have no delight."[35] The barring of taste from heaven suggested something of its earthly allure and power. One of the seer's earliest visions related to those who were "devoted to conviviality in eating" and to indulging "their appetites." "In the middle of the day at dinner an angel spoke to me, and told me not to eat too much at table," Swedenborg wrote. It was his own "unseemly appetite" for sumptuous dining that had to be "cast out of my body" like a demon; the craving had to be "burnt up" and "cleansed." This visionary lesson about taste and "overloaded stomachs" helped shape the bodily habits of temperance cultivated by Swedenborg's Anglo-American progeny. As Caleb Reed proclaimed in his Boston lecture, "taste is the lowest of the senses; and the love of indulging it is the grossest form of sensualism."[36]

Both smell and touch, falling in between vision and taste in the hierarchy of the senses, had a place in heaven. Following common anatomical models, Swedenborg considered touch the most comprehensive sense, the one underlying the rest, the very basis of all sensation. "The touch, therefore, which is extended over the whole body, is the common or universal sense, to which the others refer themselves," Caleb Reed averred in familiar terms. Though physical touch carried many of the same carnal dangers that hampered taste, the angels nonetheless retained this sense, often to an exquisite degree. Swedenborg himself was allowed repeatedly to witness the tactility of the spiritual world, including the delicate touch of spirit hands and the feel of angelic clothes (remember, only the celestial angels were naked). Despite the conventional denials of bodily cravings, the Swedenborgian spiritual world possessed a distinctly sensuous feel. Whether exercised in the intimacies of true marriage love or in the palpable enjoyments of otherworldly festivities, a transformed sense of touch clearly occupied a fundamental place in this angelic sensorium.[37]

Smell was packed with still greater import, especially because of the way its precise discriminations were joined to determinations of virtue and piety. In keeping with long-standing Christian perceptions of ethereal scents, Swedenborg's heaven abounded in pleasant fragrances—for example, floral perfumes of endless variety, and the redolence of those living in faith and charity. More than the aromatics, the very specific stenches by which the angels sniffed out dangerous spirits were especially critical to the social workings of the spiritual world. "The horrid stench of wall lice" revealed those who had persecuted the innocent; "that of a stinking mouse" corresponded to the avaricious; that of excrement, to adulterers. The smells of fetid water, vomit, carcasses, and burned bread all exhaled their own unmistakable character references as well. It was fitting that, according to Swedenborg's exegesis, the mark of Cain was not a visual emblem but an odor placed upon him that kept him eternally other—"such an odour so that there was nowhere that he could wander,

because men would want to drive him away." Odors were crucial to the social imagination of the Enlightenment and the rising bourgeois culture, and the spiritual senses
that Swedenborgians so eagerly anticipated showed how deep these sensory order-
ings of social, moral, and religious differentiation went. Spiritual odors, Caleb Reed
explained, allowed angels to judge "the quality of a spirit ... at a great distance"—that
is, to avoid proximity of those who were defiling or who were simply of a "lower"
sphere. The smells of heaven and hell were so loaded with nuances that Swedenborg
finally despaired of describing them fully, suggesting it would require a whole volume to set out the moral economy of odor.[38]

And then there was the ear, second to the eye in nobility, but showered with every
bit as much attention from Swedenborg as its more exalted counterpart. "How vast
a science and knowledge is this unique sense," he commented, and spared little of
his immense energy for anatomy in pursuing this organ. Knowledgeable about the
various acoustic experiments of his day—those on echoes, the velocity of sound,
the mathematics of harmony, and the physics of speaking trumpets, for example—
Swedenborg followed Hooke and Newton (among other natural philosophers) into a
speculative labyrinth in which sound vibrations were explored as a master key to the
animation of matter. "It is in the sense of hearing, above all other senses, that we may
most advantageously observe the real nature of tremulation," Swedenborg noted in
a treatise on the radiating force of vibrations in 1719. In his anatomical inquiries
into the ear, he even confronted (like Du Verney before him) the prospect of auditory illusions, the internal sounds that had no connection to external sensation: "In
fantastic imagination," he observed, "persons are able to hear various sounds and
connected conversations, so that they sometimes persuade themselves that a spirit
is speaking with them. I have spoken with a woman, who every day continually
heard the singing of hymns within her." Obviously undeterred by the auditory dangers of the enthusiastic imagination, Swedenborg would never waver in insisting on
the supreme verity of the internal sounds that he discovered through opening of his
spiritual hearing. Of this he was certain: the internal perceptions behind and beyond
bodily sensations belonged to a higher reality.[39]

Exploring the microscopic secrets of the ear's anatomy provided Swedenborg
with various tools for his religious imagination, one of which was conceiving the
actuality of the normally inaudible world of spirits:

I have spoken to spirits about the fact that few people probably are going to believe that
so many things exist in the next life, the reason for that unbelief being that man has no
more than a very general and hazy concept, amounting to none at all, about his life after
death, a concept which people have confirmed for themselves from the fact that they
do not see the soul or spirit with their eyes. ... Spirits whom I have spoken to have been
amazed that man should be like this, even though he knows that nature itself and each of
its kingdoms contain so many wonderful and varied things of which he is ignorant. Take
just the human ear, for example. A whole book could be written about the remarkable

and unheard of aspects of it, in whose existence everybody has faith. But if anything is said about the spiritual world, the source of every single thing in the realms of nature, scarcely anyone believes it.[40]

Swedenborg's explorations of the ear, a part of the body that was notorious for its minutely hidden mechanisms, prepared him for his soundings in the world of spirits and angels. Its elusive recesses, like the arcana of the human body more generally, served as one vehicle by which he moved from material to spiritual senses.

Throughout Swedenborg's vast corpus, the ear's primary associations were with the obedience of dutiful listening and with the will and the affections. While the ear also remained a conduit of rational learning, it was—at an almost structuralist level—the other with respect to the understanding and independence of the eye. Swedenborg made these correspondences recurrently, often with the simplicity of an equation: "By the ear and by hearing is signified hearkening and obedience; ... by 'giving ear to any one' is signified to obey," and the eye was, with equal terseness and repetitiveness, linked to rational understanding. As a universalized and cosmological anatomy, the opposition was inscribed in the very body of the Grand Man: those angels who resided in the eyes corresponded to analytic discernment; those in the ears, to hearkening obedience.[41] An American follower elaborated this basic sensory distinction in an article in *New Jerusalem Magazine* in 1834: "The two senses of seeing and hearing ... differ from each other in a manner corresponding to the difference between the understanding and the will." When the object of inquiry was critical appraisal, "the most direct way is through the eye," but when the hope was lifted affections, the best route was through the ear. Caleb Reed evoked the same correspondences in his lecture "The Senses" in 1838: "The sense of hearing has more relation to the will, and corresponds to obedience ... so the faculty of hearing is peculiarly a receptive faculty. And as such it is not active, investigating, questioning, penetrating, like the eye, but quiescent and passive." No more basic distinction existed in the Swedenborgian sensorium than this one, between the rational, inquisitive eye and the emotive, obedient ear.[42]

The opposition of the understanding and the will, along with that of the eye and the ear, was inevitably joined, in turn, to the differentiation of the male and the female. In the Swedenborgian economy of gender, the roseate vision was one of a grand, conjunctive union of the sexes in self-completing love, but that ultimate wholeness still presupposed, as one American follower put it in 1855, "a species of dominion belonging to the male over the female."[43] That privilege depended on the same advantage the eye enjoyed over the ear: in men, the understanding and rationality predominated; in women, the will and the affections—and such distinctions, however harmoniously conjoined, very much followed the couple into the blisses of the perfected marriage. As a corollary of these gendered assumptions, it was unimaginable within Swedenborg's vision that women might serve as preachers. Those women who invaded this public domain of masculine understanding lost their essential "feminine nature"—in this case, that of the affective yet obedient listener.[44] Given these classical oppositions at the heart of the Swedenborgian system, the eye appeared unassailable in its power and nobility; the ear, tied dangerously to passivity, irrationality, and femaleness.

Yet in the highest heaven, that of the celestial angels, hearing became the preeminent sense. "It is worthy of being noticed here," Swedenborg remarked in *Heaven and Hell,* "that the Angels of the Third Heaven advance in Wisdom by hearing, and not by sight; for what they hear from preaching enters not into the memory, but immediately into their perception and will, and so into the form of their life." In the most exalted heaven, for all its dazzling light, the ear was the perceptual center. There reasoning and understanding were absorbed into a higher wisdom; there the gap between reflection and action closed into immediate obedience and unquestioning love. These celestial angels, vastly excelling their counterparts in the spiritual kingdom in wisdom and glory, "know immediately by Influx (inspiration) from the Lord whether that which they hear be true or not." When the Lord's words come to them, they indulge in no rational calculation; "for as soon as they hear them, they immediately will and do them, without having any occasion to ... reason upon [them]." Hearing, precisely because of its associations with both the affections and submission, embodied this most inward way of angelic wisdom. And since in this Swedenborgian sensorium of the spirit all were to aspire toward this perfected practice of divine love, the hearkening of the celestial angels—the way they lent their ears to the Lord and to one another—served as an exalted model of Christian obedience in which listening and loving converged. For such a spiritual life, the reasoning, masculine eye was not so noble or so powerful or so enthroned, since all the celestial angels, male and female alike, progressed on notably feminine terms. In this Christian practice, in which obedience to God was ultimately more important than the understanding of God, the ear finally displaced the eye.[45]

Another acoustic model, that of musical harmony, provided the consummate representation of the unity, submission, and love that were dominant in the highest heaven. The ear's connection to the affections had always been marked most insistently through music, and the joys and delights of heaven were, for Swedenborg, as for most in the Christian tradition, dreamed especially through harmonious sounds. "Today, I heard angels of the interior heaven, of whom there were very many in consociation, forming a hymn which was plainly audible to me," Swedenborg noted in his *Spiritual Diary* in 1748. Through the alchemy of hymn singing, the angels "had been forming a golden crown with diadems about the head of our Saviour." What most caught Swedenborg's attention was not this bejeweling spectacle, but instead the wonders of how all the angels sang together: "No one leads the choir, but all together lead each other mutually." Such was the blessedness of this celestial harmony, Swedenborg discovered, that no one can be among the angels "who wants to act from himself and to command the others, and is unwilling to suffer himself to be led." Spontaneous in their affections, yet marked by unanimity, those who performed these canticles were utterly devoid of self-love. Sometimes the delights of these harmonies were so overwhelming as to be entrancing, leaving the angels in "a delightful stupor," one of utter stillness. In this representation of the heavenly choirs, Swedenborg offered a model of the self's engulfed subjection to the divine whole, and an exaltation of Christian mutuality over rational autonomy. Through devout listening Swedenborg imagined the soul's submission to God, as well as the rapt emotions of that obedience.[46]

Beyond the mystical enchantments of hearing, what Swedenborg and his progeny ultimately dreamed was a synesthesia of the eye and the ear, and, with that merging, a reunion of the understanding and the will as well as of the male and the female. That sensory recombination was made manifest in Swedenborg's shifting descriptions of angelic speech: the aural and the visual crossed each other in "a shining vibration." "The speech of angels," Swedenborg related, "is sometimes made to appear visually in the world of spirits, and thus before the interior sight, as shimmering light or a brilliant flame." On another occasion, he said, the spirits spoke to him "by means of purely visual representatives, by presenting flames varying in colour, by lights, [by] clouds rising and descending." These synesthesias of seeing and hearing mirrored the true marriages of heaven, in which the understanding of the husband joined in complete harmony with the will of the wife. Such heavenly unions, mutualities, and reciprocities were imagined in part through reconciling the gendered structures of the eye and the ear. With the advent of the New Jerusalem, one American writer explained in 1839, "the will and the understanding and the eye and the ear will not have separate interests and ends," but will be "made one," a restoration of the primordial unities of the Most Ancient Church. In Swedenborg's heaven, three interrelated marriages were performed—those of the understanding and the will, the male and the female, and the eye and the ear.[47]

Throughout all of his vast experiences, Swedenborg tested a mystical sensorium—Christian, kabbalistic, and Hermetic—in the crucible of the Enlightenment. By exhaustively exploring the spiritual senses in anatomical terms, he ushered a mystical strand of Christian devotionalism through the age of reason. To be sure, much of his vision was deeply traditional in its pietistic emphases, and this included the routine regulation of sensory pleasures. As one Swedenborgian pastor, John Clowes, noted in his *Letters on the Human Body* (1826), there was still a pressing need to impose order on "the otherwise uncontrollable, fascinating, and dangerous misrule of our *senses*"—that is, to place the dangerous seductions of the bodily senses in a *"state of submission"* to the purities of the spiritual senses. In a standard devotionalist conceit, Clowes pictured the bodily senses as animals that needed to be bridled before the spiritual senses could be spurred. One American New Churchman, likewise, praised Jeanne Marie Guyon for her contemplative teachings on the "death of the sensual," the mortification of the "outward senses," which "have always been among the chief occasions of sin." The spiritual senses of the mystic were still opened through a denial of the merely sensuous. Swedenborg's angels, after all, had been purged of the erotic allures of taste.[48]

But the seer's heaven was also one of floral gardens, brilliant colors, sumptuous homes, and ecstatic harmonies, so it remained easy for his followers to make him the broker of more indulgent sensibilities in which the spiritual senses invited not so much bodily renunciation as somatic celebration. Very much at home with genteel refine-ment, Swedenborg and his more affluent disciples comfortably blessed the pleasures that accompanied wealth, just so long as this love of the world did not eclipse the love of God (a notoriously difficult line to draw). With the coming of the New Church, Caleb Reed explained, Christians no longer needed to be "cut off" from their bodily senses, because the spiritual and the material, the internal and the external, could now be brought into harmonious correspondence. As the New Jerusalem progressively unfolded, Christians would "learn to cultivate the senses, and take pleasure in their perfection," by appreciating music, art, and architecture. The restored purity of the senses was a common Swedenborgian theme across a wide social spectrum; but for those, like Reed, who were especially concerned with respectability, the deliverance of the senses almost inevitably ended up being imagined in terms of genteel elegance. The taste of polite culture was fully redeemable, even in itself redemptive, and the refined senses of the New Jerusalem came to reflect those aesthetic sensibilities.[49]

Within the Swedenborgian restoration of Christian sensuousness hovered one especially momentous supposition. In the Most Ancient Church the bodily senses had been wholly at one with the spiritual senses, and, as a result, people had com-municated openly with angels, living in full awareness of "both worlds at the same time." And it was to this time of "open communication" that many in the New Church imagined returning—not just in heaven, but soon in a new era of "a more free intercourse with Heaven." In contrast to more temperate Protestant perspec-tives that treated the apparitions of angels as parallel to miracles—that is, phenom-ena useful to the foundation of the church, but now unnecessary and vulnerable to Catholic superstitions—many Swedenborgians hungrily pursued the ancient inti-macies with angels. "What then hinders our conversing with angels now, as the patriarchs and prophets did of old?" asked one expectant devotee. "That intercourse with the spiritual world is now becoming and will soon be more common than it has been, we have no doubt," wrote another in 1828. Any realization of such desires depended on an axial proposition about human perception—namely, that people are "endowed with spiritual senses, and that these senses may be opened by the Lord while man lives upon earth, so as to make him sensibly acquainted with the things of the spiritual world." But whose unlocked senses were to be trusted? Only Swedenborg's, or those of any and every mystic? In the heady atmosphere of antebellum America, the opening of the spiritual senses became an extremely contentious issue.[50]

Talking with Swedenborg; Or, the Problem of Authority

Swedenborg's followers had a love-hate relationship with immediate revelation. On the one hand, they celebrated the seer's heavenly conversations and the hovering nearness of angels, ever guiding and comforting. Some even rhapsodized about angels speaking to them in visions or in "the mystic land of dreams"; others told extraordinary tales of deathbed illuminations or epiphanic conversions. One Hoosier, for example, wrote to the *New Church Repository* in 1851 to recast his youthful conversion experience in a Swedenborgian light: with head bowed to "listen undisturbed" to a sermon, "I *lost* my *outer consciousness! My spiritual sight was opened!* ... With great wonder and astonishment I exclaimed—it is Jesus! Jesus! ... As I gazed intently upon the Divine, just above me, a little at the right, a voice, as of an angel, was heard in mine ear." More distinctively, a few devotees were even blessed with a manifestation of Swedenborg himself. One told of a "remarkable dream"—"so lively, so real, ... that I had some doubts whether I could pronounce it to be a dream"—in which he met Swedenborg as an angel of approval and blessing. Another humble devotee had the angelic Swedenborg thank him directly for going to the expense of displaying his framed portrait as "a family picture"—the image serving, in effect, as a materializing aid to the voice of Swedenborg's angel. As with Ann Lee's visionary presence among the Shakers, the seer was, on occasion at least, apotheosized into an angelic being of unsurpassed wisdom and beauty, a source of continuing inspiration.[51]

On the other hand, many Swedenborgians were defensive about their reputation for holding "a constant intercourse with angels and deceased persons," a "popular error," *New Jerusalem Magazine* lamented in 1829, that had made its way into the first volume of the first edition of the *Encyclopaedia Americana*. The same journal had complained the year before that misinformation of this sort was epidemic: How often had believers faced such misbegotten inquiries as to "whether we do not set chairs and dishes for our friends who have left the natural body"? It was all so galling, "for at the very threshold of the system we learn that it is impossible for spirits to be seen by the natural eye—to be heard by the natural ear—to sit in material chairs, and to eat material food."[52] Besides these basic affronts to their respectability and to their dualism of matter and spirit, American followers were also well aware of Swedenborg's more cautionary statements about the demonic dangers that shadowed direct spiritual intercourse. Evil spirits were just as real and prevalent as angels, and the ingrained fear of necromancy made many New Church leaders extremely harsh critics of Spiritualism. Most of all, the seer's devotees were apprehensive about maintaining the singular authority of his writings amid all this talk of spirits and angels. Here was the underlying dilemma: Was Swedenborg a final word or an open door?[53]

Long before the Rochester rappings effectively inaugurated the Spiritualist movement, Swedenborgians were enmeshed in a world of angels both eruptive and divisive. From early in the movement's rise in England, many followers were drawn to Swedenborg not only for the luminosity of his experiences but also as a bridge to their own mystical confirmations. "Several persons in Manchester," an observer noted of one of the foundational New Church societies in 1784, "are having open communication with the spiritual world and receive ocular and auricular proofs of the statements of Swedenborg."[54] The Anglican and Swedenborgian John Clowes, though himself of a visionary turn, was nonetheless alarmed in 1820 when a woman, "who was a receiver of the New Doctrines, asserted in the most solemn manner, that she had immediate open communication with heaven, that she frequently saw and conversed with the Lord Himself, and that she was expressly commanded by Him to establish a New Church, which was to be called the *New Church New,* to distinguish it from what was commonly called the New Church." The woman managed to gather a handful of converts before the official opposition of Clowes and others in the New Church silenced this oracle of the New Church New.[55]

The constitution of religious authority, everywhere a problem in antebellum America, was specifically refracted through the Swedenborgian senses. Take the vignette of Samuel Worcester and his circle of followers, for whom a small cache of manuscripts survive from the mid-1840s under the auspicious title, *Sundry Papers Regarding the Opening of the Spiritual Senses*. On a visit to New York in June 1844, six months before his death, Worcester, who was a prominent New Church minister from Massachusetts, reported having his spiritual senses opened, upon which he was enabled to see and converse with Swedenborg and other spirits. Going into a meditative state during worship in which the very light of his face and "the tones of his voice" made evident the nearness of "heavenly beings," Worcester was permitted to give "many truths direct from Swedenborg"—an angelic presence so "gentle and sweet" that it moved him to tears. Necessarily wary of the devil's illusions, he performed a battery of ritual tests, "calling the name of the Lord, repeating portions of the Word, making the sign of the Cross, &c &c," all of which these spirits passed. Soon others in the New York fellowship, quickly labeled the New Era movement, also had their spiritual sight and hearing opened. The conclusion these experiences pushed Worcester, family, and friends toward was that Swedenborg "is the *present* as well as the *past* revelator" to the New Church. For reasons large and small—for the Holy City to come down out of heaven, for the cure of rheumatism, for the right order of baptism, for the proper education of children, for the minute rules of Sabbath observance—Swedenborg had to become a living voice again.[56]

Many in the New Church were roused to excoriate Worcester and his circle for the supposed madness and indecorum of their "Necromantic Orgies," and the critics largely succeeded in shunting the group to the margins of an already small church.[57] Was not this, critics railed, the exact sort of auditory challenge to the anchor of canonical texts that should alarm anyone concerned about stabilizing church authority? The often accommodating George Bush warned against those who were "prone to say, 'I have a higher authority than that of any written record. I have a voice direct from the spirit-world itself. Is not this the head-quarters of truth? ... A new era is being ushered in.'" Within these subcultural debates, it was not natural philosophy, not theories of imposture and illusion, but ecclesial strictures that proved the gravest speech impediment that the angels faced. Though the flexible charges of insanity, hallucination, and priestly machination could still be invoked by one New Church-man against another (Richard DeCharms did this to Worcester, for example), the debate pivoted on ecclesiological concerns. Since within Swedenborgian circles the possibility of angels speaking was assumed, the question centered on the parameters and the trajectories of that communication. It was religious authority trying to main-tain some semblance of authority, not the acids of the Enlightenment, that set the sharpest limits on angelic speech.[58]

The Swedenborgian yearning for angels hardly led to a free-for-all, however eruptive the voices of these visitants seemed. The New Era advocates, as much as their opponents, had to draw discernible boundaries, had to police the line be-tween "orderly and disorderly open intercourse." The question was not whether, but when, to restrain the spiritual senses, how to close or narrow the openings. "You are all too desirous of new revelations, to permit those that are already given to do their work," so admonished Swedenborg the angel in one of the more ironic mes-sages that Samuel Worcester received. Read the Bible, read my writings—those are already filled with immediate presence, Swedenborg instructed from heaven. Once his spiritual hearing was opened, Worcester claimed that he spoke to no other spirits besides Swedenborg's without first getting permission from the seer. And the climax of Worcester's visionary experiences was his priestly ordination at the hands of the angelic Swedenborg, which he said that he received "spiritually kneel-ing." However dissolvent of authority the opening of the spiritual senses appeared, Worcester and company extended their perception only to underline the authority of Swedenborg and his ministers.[59]

The New Era coterie walked a tightrope. They needed the angels (especially the angelic Swedenborg) to bring form to a fellowship that was inchoate, as well as to confer authority on their priesthood and their sacraments, but they also dreaded the seductions of disorder that shadowed the spirits. As Silas Jones, a New Era defender, confessed in 1848, "It has pleased the Lord in his divine providence to lead the writer where he has seen much of open intercourse with the spiritual world. Much of what he has seen has been altogether disorderly." Still, Jones and Worces-ter, like others in this fellowship, desired the angels, longed to live "in perpetual society" with them, and dreamed of their consolation and love. They yearned, too, for the living presence of the absent dead (especially deceased family members, as well as Swedenborg himself); they sought to erase loss and separation. "Why should not the man of the church have open intercourse with angels?" Jones pined, even after all his sorting out of the unruly. He chided those "who are satisfied with their day of small things," those who did not seek "the opening of their internal sight and hearing," those who knew Swedenborg only as past and not a present revelator. Aware of the contradictions over authority he could hardly resolve, he nonetheless expressed bewilderment at those who "hatch out rules of order" and lose sight of this ultimate desire, "a state of oneness with an angel." The senses, their opening and closing, were fiercely embattled in these circles, vexed by questions of authority, yet ever laced with longing for "the privilege of hearing and conversing with those in heaven."[60]

That Swedenborg had come back to life as the angel of the New Era, speaking to people and performing ordinations, was not at all comforting to clericalists within the New Church. Always wary of the artful disguises of evil spirits, pastor Benjamin Barrett warned of hell-bent Swedenborg impersonators, those whose malignant design it was "to personate him in the most perfect and satisfactory manner" and thus to be all the more effective in leading people away from the true church. Filling the spiritual world with deceitful beings who eagerly wanted to assume Swedenborg's voice, Barrett warned that a fake Swedenborg would be likely to tell a self-conceited dupe "that the Lord had chosen him to be the medium of some new and important instruction to His church, and that his spiritual senses had been opened for that purpose." If a clerical hierarchy was to be sustained and routinized, the treacheries of the spiritual senses needed to be recognized and Swedenborg's angel kept quiet. Key New Church leaders, such as Richard DeCharms, were all too happy to sacrifice the hope of restored converse with angels to the requirements of ecclesiastical government, middle-class respectability, and intellectual solidity. Swedenborgians, DeCharms said, "are thought to be visionaries, enthusiasts, sight-keepers and sign-demanders," but against such "popular prejudice" he insisted that New Churchmen "are preeminent over all other men for cool-headed, common-sense intellection, and the utmostly practical utilitarianism." Keeping people from talking to Swedenborg's angel was part of creating that image of order, refinement, and rationality.[61]

The New Church was a small pond, and in the larger waters of American religion these particular ecclesial restraints made few ripples. Swedenborg's angelic form was a favorite guide among clairvoyants, mesmerists, and Spiritualists, and the New Church could do nothing to keep him quiet in those circles. Within the induced trances and clairvoyant healings of animal magnetism, the visions of Swedenborg were refracted through the hypnotic lens of Franz Anton Mesmer, the late eighteenth-century Austrian physician whose techniques proved so wonderfully popular in antebellum America. One wayfarer, Louisa Ogden, who moved from the Episcopal Church to the New Church in 1844, made her story of reidentification hinge on her witnessing the public exhibition of "a magnetic somnambulist." Ogden was soon conducting hypnotic experiments on her sister, and the sensory effects produced offered her "a proof that there existed a medium of communication to our spirits, other than that of our own material senses." It was through mesmeric sleep that Ogden was prepared for Swedenborg's sensorium, that she came to believe in "a still higher state of magnetism" in which people's "spiritual senses" were "so thoroughly opened, as to communicate with spirits." George Bush made the same correlations, joining Swedenborg to Mesmer and discussing Swedenborg's spiritual senses under the rubrics of "magnetic vision" and "magnetic hearing." Bush specifically credited Swedenborg with discovery of "the law of spiritual acoustics"—that is, his description of angelic speech corresponded to "the mode of hearing in the Mesmeric state." Swedenborg's understanding of the spiritual senses, closely bound to scriptural exegesis and contemplative practice, remained yoked to time-worn Christian emphases, but with these magnetic translations those ties were increasingly loosened.[62]

The ability of the New Church to control Swedenborg's angelic voice slipped all the more, once mesmerists had seized hold of the seer's understanding of internal perception. One of the most renowned clairvoyants and magnetic healers, Andrew Jackson Davis, featured Swedenborg prominently among his spirit guides (alongside the ancient physician Galen). Davis, known as the Poughkeepsie Seer, was led into Swedenborgian circles in the mid-1840s through his stage exhibitions of animal magnetism, in which he dictated wisdom from the spirits and offered medical diagnoses through his clairvoyant sight into bodies. A Pythagorean who listened for "the music of the spheres" and delved into "the secrets of harmony," Davis developed his own spiritual acoustics, which he termed "psychophonetics," and thus remade the Swedenborgian sensorium in the terms of his own system. "A most exquisite insight into the laws of psychophonetics is indispensable to a correct comprehension of the wonders heard by the spiritual tympanum," Davis instructed. Sailing on "a boundless ocean" of "soul-sounds" that were "absolutely inaudible to the physical ear," he filled his autobiography with episodes of mysterious voices and strange music. In a curious moment of reenchantment, he even taught himself "a sort of ventriloquism" by which he imitated the "Aeolian harmony" of the heavens, a "purling symphony" that he claimed to manage by "breathing through the epiglottis and pharyngeal passages."[63]

Davis was exactly the terror that New Churchmen like Richard DeCharms and Benjamin Barrett feared—a clairaudient for whom Swedenborg was one inner voice among several and who was not beholden to basic propositions of theirs about the Bible and the Trinity. For them, the Poughkeepsie Seer showed all that was wrong with talking with Swedenborg's angel: mediated through the mouths of such latter-day trance-speakers, the spirit of Swedenborg was regularly forced to acknowledge the errors in his own revelations, those that resulted from "the prevailing theology" and "the popular religion of his day." To Barrett and DeCharms, Davis and his ilk were no friends of Swedenborg; rather, they were a distraction, diminishing the true seer's "authority as the Lord's official expositor of his Word." "In all time past, and in all time to come," DeCharms exulted after debunking Davis's revelations, "there could not and cannot possibly be more than one Swedenborg, and no other man could or even can arrive at the same kind or degree of spirituality as his." The opening of the spiritual senses had become a minefield littered with the explosive issues of religious authority, and those who talked with Swedenborg's angel as well as those who refused this listening crystallized these problems as clearly as anyone did.[64]

Notes

1. Aubrey 1696, I: 82–86, 90–92, 133–138; Agrippa 1651: 412–413. The catalogue of Spiritualist sounds comes from Adin Ballou as quoted in Mattison 1855: 12. For the acoustic wonders of Spiritualism, see also Dewey 1850. On the importance of the invocation of angels within Renaissance occultism, see Yates 1979: 3–5, 20–21, 87.

2. For an analysis of the persistence of some of these Hermetic strands, see Brooke 1994. Most influential in my understanding of occultism has been the stellar work of Verter 1998.

3. For background on Swedenborg and the movement he spawned, see Brock 1988; Larsen 1988; Block 1932; Williams-Hogan 1985; Jonsson 1971; Toksvig 1948; Silver 1983. For Swedenborg's Hermetic, Masonic, and kabbalistic connections, see Schuchard 1988; Gabay 1997: 619–690; Garrett 1984: 67–81; Hitchcock 1865. For one inlet into how the Swedenborgian network of publishing and reading unfolded, see Carpenter 1839.

4. For Swedenborg's struggle with deism, see Kirven 1965: 16–24.

5. See, for example, Evans 1864; Presland 1884.

6. Swedenborg 1827: 15–19. For Swedenborg's devotional travails, see Swedenborg [1743–1744] 1986: 105–109, 121–122, 155–156.

7. Bush 1846a: iii, vii–viii; Bush 1846b: 69; Pond quoted in Bush 1847: 162–163; Rush 1812: 138.

8. Field 1879: 23.

9. Hayden 1846: 2–3; and various articles in *Precursor* 1 (March 1837): 75–76, *New Churchman* 1 (January 1842): 31–37, and *Medium* 2 (15 June 1850: 185). For a review of Wesley's role in medicalizing Swedenborg, see Kirven 1965: 164–173. There was an occasional positive evaluation of Swedenborg in the asylum circles of medical psychology, but such were the exception. See Taylor 1988: 156–158 n 171.

10. Hiller 1817: vii–ix.

11. Emerson 1987, IV: 58.

12. For Swedenborg's work in natural philosophy, see, for example, Acton 1939; Larsen 1988, section V. For a typical defense along these lines, see Fernald 1860.

13. Johnson and Jones 1818: vii, 15, 40–41; Worcester 1819: 12.

14. Swedenborg 1833: no. 798. Following the common scholarly convention, references are to Swedenborg's own numbering system, not to pages, here and subsequently.

15. For an American elaboration, see Hayden 1848.

16. *New Jerusalem Magazine* 27 (September 1854): 142–145.

17. Hiller 1817: viii. See also *New Jerusalem Magazine* 2 (July 1829): 360–361.

18. On Swedenborg's sales, see Mott 1947: 305–306.

19. Alley 1798: 6–10. The literature on this element of popular religion in the early republic is substantial. Among the best studies is Quinn 1987: 11–15, 25, 174–175.
20. "Preface by the Translator," in Swedenborg 1812: 3. This is the first American edition in what became a long run of them in the nineteenth century (seven of them between 1837 and 1854); this 1812 edition followed six British printings (the first in 1778).
21. Ibid.: 5–10.
22. Swedenborg 1812: nos. 234–236, 239; Paine 1998: 63, 68–69, 97–98. The early modern philosophical ambition for a universal language has received growing attention. For a still standard overview of the enterprise, see Knowlson 1975. For specific Swedenborgian contexts, see Jonsson 1971: 92–104; Wilkinson 1996.
23. Swedenborg 1812: nos. 259–262, 269. For a sampling of this "spiritual sense of numbers," indicative of the esoteric currents in which Swedenborg swirled, see Fernald 1860: 433–436; Swedenborg 1812: no. 263.
24. Swedenborg 1977: nos. 1149, 4309; Swedenborg 1812: nos. 236, 245, 269.
25. Swedenborg 1812: nos. 48, 462, 463.
26. Ibid., nos. 236–238.
27. Swedenborg 1983–1997: no. 1644. In the text, I have retained the eighteenth-century spelling *Arcana Coelestia*.
28. Swedenborg 1812: nos. 178–179, 280.
29. DeCharms 1856a: 8–9; Bush 1846a: 254. Swedenborg's understanding of the transparencies of angelic speech was widely reiterated and re-published on the American side. In addition to the various editions of *Heaven and Hell* (1812), see, for example, Fernald 1860: 194–198; and such articles as *New Jerusalem Magazine* 7 (December 1833): 123–124; *New Jerusalem Magazine* 12 (August 1839): 441–444; and Bush 1846a: 241–256.
30. Swedenborg 1914: no. 9; Jonsson 1988: 32–33; Jonsson 1971: 48–49.
31. Swedenborg 1812: no. 212.
32. Swedenborg 1914: nos. 64–65; Swedenborg 1983–1997: nos. 68, 322; and articles in *New Jerusalem Magazine* 44 (October 1871) and *New Jerusalem Magazine* 11 (February 1838). On Swedenborg's empiricism, see especially Kirven 1965:16–24.
33. Swedenborg 1829: 47; Emerson 1842: 377–378. See also Swedenborg 1914: no. 649; Massachusetts Association of the New Jerusalem Church 1858: 10–12, 35–36.
34. Swedenborg 1914: no. 3; Swedenborg 1983–1997: nos. 1642, 4407; Swedenborg 1977: no. 670; Reed 1838: 336. Much about Swedenborg's hierarchy of the bodily senses was conventionally positioned within Aristotle's long shadow—an ordering from high to low that ran sight to hearing, then with a marked drop-off for smell, taste, and touch. See Swedenborg 1914: nos. 56–57, 471. The more interesting mutations occurred in the spiritual senses (such as taste's loss and smell's enhancement).

35. Swedenborg 1977: no. 3567. See also Swedenborg 1983–1997: no. 1973; *New Jerusalem Magazine* 20 (December 1846): 148–149.

36. Reed 1838: 338. The antigluttony vision is from Swedenborg 1977: no. 397. It is didactically cited and applied in Wilkinson 1849: 76–77, and in Fernald 1860: 53, 108–109.

37. Reed 1838: 339; Swedenborg 1977: nos. 2386, 4093; Swedenborg 1812: nos. 181, 402, 462; Swedenborg 1983–1997: nos. 1883, 4622; Swedenborg 1840: no. 210. The sensuous, even material, quality of Swedenborg's heaven is explored in McDannell and Lang 1988: 181–227.

38. Swedenborg 1977: nos. 323, 1150; Swedenborg 1812: no. 385; Swedenborg 1983–1997: nos. 1514–1515, 4628–4631; Reed 1838: 338. The literature on the sense of smell is growing. See, for example, Harvey 1998: 109–128; Classen, Howes, and Synnott 1994; Corbin 1986.

39. Swedenborg 1914: nos. 97, 101–128; Swedenborg 1899: 61, 70. Also of note is George Bush's defense of this "internal hearing," in Bush 1846a: 242–243. On Swedenborg's work on vibration, see Jonsson 1971: 44–46.

40. Swedenborg 1983–1997: no. 946.

41. Swedenborg 1847: nos. 14, 808; Swedenborg 1812: no. 96.

42. *New Jerusalem Magazine* 7 (May 1834): 353–355. See also Fernald 1860: 310–315, 321; Worcester 1889: 273–316.

43. *New Church Repository* 8 (October 1855): 461–465 and 6 (September 1853): 403–405.

44. Swedenborg 1977: no. 5936. Swedenborg's views on gender are most fully developed in his treatise *Delights of Wisdom Concerning Conjugial Love*. For an American linkage of the obedience of the hearkening ear to the authority of the male minister, see "Science of Correspondences: The Eye and the Ear," *New Jerusalem Magazine* 12 (January 1839): 160.

45. Swedenborg 1812: nos. 25–26, 271; Swedenborg 1847: no. 14.

46. Swedenborg 1977 nos. 489, 491, 2108; Swedenborg 1983–1997: nos. 687, 690, 1648–1649. These ideas are picked up in Fernald 1860: 409; and various articles on music in *New Jerusalem Magazine* 44 (February 1872): 421–422; 33 (August 1860): 104–109; 15 (February 1842): 214–222; and 15 (April 1842): 281–290.

47. Swedenborg 1977: no. 4208; Swedenborg 1983–1997: nos. 1646, 1764; *New Jerusalem Magazine* 12 (January 1839): 155–156. On synesthesia, see Hollander 1975: 22–25, 42–43; Chidester 1992: 14–24, 53–72; Sullivan 1986: 1–33. Hollander is especially evocative on Romantic developments of what he calls "visionary sound."

48. Clowes 1826: 85–88; *New Church Repository* 7 (February 1854): 59.

49. Reed 1838: 334–335, 341. On the wider gospel of refined taste and bourgeois civility, see Bushman 1992.

50. "Preface by the Translator," in Swedenborg 1812: 10; Swedenborg 1812: nos. 87, 252–253; *New Jerusalem Magazine* 1 (March 1828): 218; Barrett 1852:

287; *New Jerusalem Magazine* 8 (March 1835): 243. For arguments about the ceasing of angelic apparitions, see Lawrence 1649: 16–19, 36; Saunders 1701: 192–198. Even within this framework, though, angelic powers, knowledge, and ministrations remained considerable, and Swedenborgian desires need to be seen as in keeping with much of Christian angelology.

51. *New Church Repository* 1 (May 1848): 319–320; 5 (January 1852): 30–32; 7 (September 1854): 402–404; Johnston 1866: 16–17.

52. *New Jerusalem Magazine* 3 (November 1829): 96; *Encyclopaedia Americana* 1829–1833, I: 244; *New Jerusalem Magazine* 6 (January 1833): 206–207.

53. On the wider ecclesiological crises in Swedenborgian circles that were brought to a head by Spiritualism, see Swank 1970; Carroll, 1997: 16–34.

54. John Tulk to James Glen, quoted in Block 1932: 70.

55. This English episode is discussed via a letter of John Clowes in Barrett 1845: 37–38.

56. Worcester n.d.

57. Ibid. For the internal containment, see Swank 1970: 197–205. The group's marginalization has had its counterpart in the quick dismissals of institutionally minded historians. See Odhner 1904: 500–501; Block 1932: 98–99.

58. Bush 1855: 248; DeCharms 1853: 38–42.

59. Jones 1848a: 23–27; Worcester n.d.; Worcester 1845: 2–3, 10.

60. Jones 1848a: 26–27, 31–34, 57; Worcester 1845: 7–10, 19–21; Jones 1848b: 5, 7. These desires, widely shared across the Swedenborgian subculture, were ones that the New Era's harsh critic Benjamin Barrett well understood: "It is not strange that we should desire," he said, to hear things "from the pure and loving lips of the angels." See Barrett 1845: 1–2.

61. Barrett 1845: 20–21; DeCharms 1856b: 44–51.

62. Ogden 1845: 14–17; Bush 1847: 104–120, 138–143. For the considerable play between religious vision and animal magnetism, see Taves 1999: 128–165.

63. Davis 1878: 14–17, 104–108; Davis [1858] 1871: 164–170, 191–192, 248, 324, 328–329, 424, 434, 441, 476.

64. DeCharms 1856b: 59; Bush 1855: 254–256.

References

Acton, A. (ed.) (1939), *The Mechanical Inventions of Emanuel Swedenborg,* Philadelphia, PA: Swedenborg Scientific Association.

Agrippa, H. C. (1651), *Three Books of Occult Philosophy,* London: R. W.

Alley, S. (1798), *An Account of a Trance or Vision of Sarah Alley,* Poughkeepsie, NY: Power.

Aubrey, J. (1696), *Miscellanies,* London: Castle.

Barrett, B. F. (1845), *Open Intercourse with the Spiritual World—Its Dangers and the Cautions Which They Naturally Suggest,* n.p.: n.p.

Barrett, B. F. (1852), *Lectures on the Doctrines of the New Christian Church,* Cincinnati: Michigan and Northern Indiana Association of the New Church.

Block, M. B. (1932), *The New Church in the New World: A Study of Swedenborgianism in America,* New York: Holt.

Brock, E. J. (ed.) (1988), *Swedenborg and His Influence,* Bryn Athyn, PA: Academy of the New Church.

Brooke, J. (1994), *The Refiner's Fire: The Making of Mormon Cosmology, 1644–1844,* Cambridge: Cambridge University Press.

Bush, G. (1846a), *Statement of Reasons for Embracing the Doctrines and Disclosures of Emanuel Swedenborg,* New York: Allen.

Bush, G. (ed.) (1846b), *The Memorabilia of Swedenborg; Or, The Spiritual World Laid Open,* New York: John Allen.

Bush, G. (1847), *Mesmer and Swedenborg; Or, The Relation of the Developments of Mesmerism to the Doctrines and Disclosures of Swedenborg,* New York: John Allen.

Bush, G. (1855), *New Church Miscellanies,* New York: McGeorge.

Bushman, R. L. (1992), *The Refinement of America: Persons, Houses, Cities,* New York: Knopf.

Carpenter, B. O. (1839), *Adventures of a Copy of Swedenborg's Treatise, Concerning Heaven and Hell,* Chillicothe, OH: n.p.

Carroll, B. E. (1997), *Spiritualism in Antebellum America,* Bloomington, IN: Indiana University Press.

Chidester, D. (1992), *Word and Light: Seeing, Hearing, and Religious Discourse,* Urbana, IL: University of Illinois Press.

Classen, C., Howes, D. and Synnott, A. (1994), *Aroma: The Cultural History of Smell,* London: Routledge.

Clowes, J. (1826), *Letters on the Human Body,* Warwick: W. Rose.

Corbin, A. (1986), *The Foul and the Fragrant: Odor and the French Social Imagination,* trans. M. L. Kochan, R. Porter and C. Prendergast, Cambridge, MA: Harvard University Press.

Davis, A. J. ([1858] 1871), *The Magic Staff,* Boston, MA: White.

Davis, A. J. (1878), *Views of Our Heavenly Home,* Boston, MA: Colby and Rich.

DeCharms, R. (1853), *An Introduction to Sermons against Pseudo-Spiritualism, Presenting Reasons for Their Delivery in New York,* Philadelphia, PA: New Jerusalem Press.

DeCharms, R. (1856a), *Apples of Gold in Pictures of Silver; Or, The True Rule of Scriptural Exegesis, and the Only Infallible Guide to the True Understanding of the Word of God,* Philadelphia, PA: n.p.

DeCharms, R. (1856b), *Sermons Three and Four of the Series of Five Preached to the First New York Society of the New Jerusalem, against the Pseudo-Spiritualism of Modern Times,* Philadelphia, PA: n.p.

Dewey, D. (1850), *History of the Strange Sounds or Rappings, Heard in Rochester and Western New-York, and Usually Called the Mysterious Noises!* Rochester: Dewey.

Emerson, R. W. (1842), "The Senses and the Soul," *The Dial*, 2 (January): 377–378.

Emerson, R. W. (1987), "Swedenborg; Or, The Mystic," in W. E. Williams and D. E. Wilson (eds), *The Collected Works of Ralph Waldo Emerson*, vol. 4, Cambridge, MA: Harvard University Press.

Evans, W. F. (1864), *The New Age and Its Messenger,* Boston, MA: T. H. Carter.

Fernald, W. M. ([1854] 1860), *Emanuel Swedenborg as a Man of Science,* Boston, MA: Otis Clapp.

Field, G. (1879), *Memoirs, Incidents and Reminiscences of the Early History of the New Church in Michigan, Indiana, Illinois, and Adjacent States, and Canada,* Toronto: Carswell.

Gabay, A. (1997), "Swedenborg, Mesmer, and the 'Covert' Enlightenment," *New Philosophy,* 100: 619–690.

Garrett, C. (1984), "Swedenborg and the Mystical Enlightenment in Late Eighteenth-Century England," *Journal of the History of Ideas,* 45: 67–81.

Harvey, S. A. (1998), "St. Ephrem on the Scent of Salvation," *Journal of Theological Studies,* 49: 109–128.

Hayden, W. B. (1846), *Review of the Rev. Dr. Pond on the Facts and Philosophy of Swedenborg,* Portland, ME: n.p.

Hayden, W. B. (1848), *On the History of the Dogma of Infant Damnation,* Portland, ME: Tucker.

Hiller, M. (1817), *Religion and Philosophy United; Or, An Attempt to Shew, that Philosophical Principles Form the Foundation of the New Jerusalem Church,* Boston, MA: Wells and Lilly.

Hitchcock, E. A. (1865), *Swedenborg, a Hermetic Philosopher,* New York: Miller.

Hollander, J. (1975), *Vision and Resonance: Two Senses of Poetic Form,* New York: Oxford University Press.

Johnson, J. and Jones, E. (1818), *An Interesting Discussion of the Fundamental Doctrine of the Christian Religion,* 4th edn, London: Hodson.

Johnston, J. (1866), *Last Legacy and Solemn Information Written in the Year 1826 by the Author of the Remarkable Manuscript, Entitled "Intercourse with Angels,"* n.p.: n.p.

Jones, S. (1848a), *Eras of the New Jerusalem Church, Being a Few Remarks on the Present State of the Church, and Showing the Necessity of Open Intercourse with Angels for Its Future Advancement,* New York: n.p.

Jones, S. (1848b), *Platform of the New Era of the New Church, Called New Jerusalem,* New York: Prall.

Jonsson, I. (1971), *Emanuel Swedenborg,* trans. C. Djurklou, New York: Twayne.

Jonsson, I. (1988), "Swedenborg and His Influence," in E. J. Brock (ed.), *Swedenborg and His Influence,* Bryn Athyn, PA: Academy of the New Church, pp. 32–33.

Kirven, R. H. (1965), "Emanuel Swedenborg and the Revolt against Deism," Ph.D. dissertation, Brandeis University.

Knowlson, J. (1975), *Universal Language Schemes in England and France, 1600–1800*, Toronto: University of Toronto Press.

Larsen, R. (ed.) (1988), *Emanuel Swedenborg: A Continuing Vision*, New York: Swedenborg Foundation.

Lawrence, H. (1649), *An History of Angells, being a Theological Treatise of our Communion and Warre with Them*, London: M.S.

Massachusetts Association of the New Jerusalem Church (1858), *The Pythonism of the Present Day*, Boston, MA: Phinney.

Mattison, H. (1855), *Spirit-Rapping Unveiled! An Exposé of the Origin, History, Theology and Philosophy of Certain Alleged Communications from the Spirit World*, New York: Derby.

McDannell, C. and Lang, B. (1988), *Heaven: A History*, New York: Random House.

Mott, F. L. (1947), *Golden Multitudes: The Story of Best Sellers in the United States*, New York: Macmillan.

Odhner, C. T. (1904), *Annals of the New Church*, Bryn Athyn, PA: Academy of the New Church.

Ogden, L. W. (1845), *Reasons for Joining the New Jerusalem Church*, New York: Douglas.

Paine, T. (1998), *The Age of Reason*, ed. Philip S. Foner, Secaucus, NJ: Carol Publishing Group.

Presland, J. (1884), *New Truths for a New Age*, London: Speirs.

Quinn, D. M. (1987), *Early Mormonism and the Magic World View*, Salt Lake City: Signature Books.

Reed, C. (1838), "The Senses," *New Jerusalem Magazine*, 11 (June): 336–51.

Rush, B. (1812), *Medical Inquiries and Observations upon the Diseases of the Mind*, Philadelphia, PA: Kimber and Richardson.

Saunders, R. (1701), *Angelographia; Or, A Discourse of Angels*, London: Parkhurst.

Schmidt, L. E. (2000), *Hearing Things: Religion, Illusion, and the American Enlightenment*, Cambridge, MA: Harvard University Press.

Schuchard, M. K. (1988), "Swedenborg, Jacobitism, and Freemasonry," in E. J. Brock (ed.), *Swedenborg and His Influence*, Bryn Athyn, PA: Academy of the New Church, pp. 359–379.

Silver, R. (1983), "The Spiritual Kingdom in America: The Influence of Emanuel Swedenborg on American Society and Culture, 1815–1860," Ph.D. dissertation, Stanford University.

Sullivan, L. E. (1986), "Sound and Senses: Toward a Hermeneutics of Performance," *History of Religions*, 26: 1–33.

Swank, S. T. (1970), "The Unfettered Conscience: A Study of Sectarianism, Spiritualism, and Social Reform in the New Jerusalem Church, 1840–1870," Ph.D. dissertation, University of Pennsylvania.

Swedenborg, E. (1812), *A Treatise Concerning Heaven and Hell, and of the Wonderful Things Therein, as Heard and Seen by the Honourable and Learned Emanuel Swedenborg*, Baltimore, MD: Miltenberger.

Swedenborg, E. (1827), *A Brief Account of the Life of Emanuel Swedenborg, a Servant of the Lord and the Messenger of the New-Jerusalem Dispensation,* Cincinnati: Looker and Reynolds.

Swedenborg, E. (1829), *The Doctrine of the New Jerusalem Church Concerning Angels and Spirits Attendant on Man, and Concerning Influx, and the Commerce of the Soul with the Body,* Philadelphia, PA: William Brown.

Swedenborg, E. (1833), *The True Christian Religion,* Boston, MA: John Allen.

Swedenborg, E. (1840), *Delights of Wisdom Concerning Conjugial Love,* Boston, MA: Otis Clapp.

Swedenborg, E. (1847), *The Apocalypse Explained according to the Spiritual Sense,* 5 vols, New York: John Allen.

Swedenborg, E. (1899), *On Tremulation,* trans. C. T. Odhner, Boston, MA: Massachusetts New-Church Union.

Swedenborg, E. (1914), *The Five Senses,* trans. Enoch S. Price, Philadelphia, PA: Swedenborg Scientific Association.

Swedenborg, E. (1977), *The Spiritual Diary,* 5 vols, London: Swedenborg Society.

Swedenborg, E. (1983–1997), *Arcana Caelestia,* trans. John Elliott, 11 vols, London: Swedenborg Society.

Swedenborg, E. (1986), *Swedenborg's Journal of Dreams, 1743–1744,* comment, W. Van Dusen, New York: Swedenborg Foundation.

Taves, A. (1999), *Fits, Trances, and Visions: Experiencing Religion and Explaining Experience from Wesley to James,* Princeton, NJ: Princeton University Press.

Taylor, E. (1988), "The Appearance of Swedenborg in the History of American Psychology," in E. J. Brock (ed.), *Swedenborg and His Influence,* Bryn Athyn, PA: Academy of the New Church, pp. 156–158.

Toksvig, S. (1948), *Emanuel Swedenborg: Scientist and Mystic,* New Haven, CT: Yale University Press.

Verter, B. J. (1998), "Dark Star Rising: The Emergence of Modern Occultism, 1800–1950," Ph.D. dissertation, Harvard University.

Wilkinson, J. J. G. (1849), *Emanuel Swedenborg: A Biography,* Boston, MA: Otis Clapp.

Wilkinson, L. R. (1996), *The Dream of an Absolute Language: Emanuel Swedenborg and French Literary Culture,* Albany, NY: State University of New York Press.

Williams-Hogan, J. (1985), "A New Church in a Disenchanted World: A Study of the Formation and Development of the General Conference of the New Church in Great Britain," Ph.D. dissertation, University of Pennsylvania.

Worcester, J. (1889), *Physiological Correspondences,* Boston: Massachusetts New-Church Union.

Worcester, S. (n.d.), *Sundry Papers Regarding the Opening of the Spiritual Senses of Rev. Samuel Worcester and Members of his Family,* Bryn Athyn, PA: Swedenborg Library, Bryn Athyn College of the New Church.

Worcester, S. H. (1845), *A Letter to the Receivers of the Heavenly Doctrines of the New Jerusalem*, Boston, MA: Otis Clapp.

Worcester, T. (1819), *A Discourse, Delivered before the New Jerusalem Church, in Boston, on Christmas Day, December 25, 1818*, Boston: Cummings and Hilliard.

Yates, F. (1979), *The Occult Philosophy in the Elizabethan Age,* London: Routledge and Kegan Paul.

8

The Erotics of Telepathy
The British SPR's Experiments in Intimacy
Pamela Thurschwell

At the end of the nineteenth century new ideas about communication technologies, new ideas about the mind and new ways of thinking about the supernatural help shape changing notions of intimacy and communication. Interest in telepathy can be seen as a focal point for these concerns. As a newly coined word (by F. W. H. Myers in 1882) telepathy is connected to other forms of tele-technology, and often imagined as functioning in the same way that these other technologies do, with the same popular "scientific" explanations or lack of them. Genealogically linked to the older concept of sympathy and the newer word *empathy,* telepathy is also related to love—the desire for complete sympathetic union with the mind of another. In this chapter I look at how telepathy was imagined during the 1880s and 1890s, when the Society for Psychical Research was conducting a series of thought transference experiments. What did it mean at that historical moment to have an interest in telepathy? I argue that championing of telepathy was not confined to a group of too-gullible Cambridge scientists, but rather that the popularity of the word, almost from its inception, indicates that as a cultural phenomenon, telepathy, whether disputed as myth or endorsed as reality, was effective beyond the confines of the *Journal* and *Proceedings of the Society for Psychical Research.* By contrasting the place of thought transference experiments within the workings of the Society to its other main experimental activity—séances with mediums—the significance of proximity (touch) and distance in what I am calling the erotics of psychical research becomes clear. I conclude by examining two novels which explore the threats as well as the promises of telepathy at the turn of the century.

The Society for Psychical Research

In Cambridge in 1874, Henry Sidgwick, F. W. H. Myers, Edmund Gurney, A. J. Balfour and Eleanor Balfour (soon to marry Sidgwick) began a systematic investigation of occult phenomena such as spiritualism and thought transference. These investigations eventually led to the founding of the Society for Psychical Research in 1882.[1] The stated aim of the Society was simply to study objectively claims for the existence of supernatural phenomena, such as spiritualism, but, as many have argued, its emotional impetus was towards countering the pessimism of a materialist and scientifically determined world view (Gauld 1968: 141). For Frederic Myers and others like him, the driving desire was to find scientific proof of survival after death, and thus ally the claims of nineteenth-century positivist science with the older claims of religious faith. The typical late nineteenth-century psychical researcher tended to-wards this combination of religious hopefulness and materialist scepticism. As Janet Oppenheim puts it: " ... it would not be an exaggeration to say that the early leaders of the SPR zealously explored the terra incognita of telepathy with the aim, whether purposeful or subconscious, of providing new, unassailable foundations for religious beliefs" (Oppenheim 1985: 111).

Psychical researchers' investigations fell somewhere between the new scientific and the old religious orthodoxies. Neither science nor the clergy was pleased with the claims of spiritualism and related phenomena:

> By and large the clergy discarded spiritualism on the grounds that it was either fraud or a work of the devil. With a few notable exceptions, including William Crookes, William Barrett, and mesmerism, telepathy, and spiritualism. Like the clergy, most scientists con-sidered the psychical occurrences fraudulent. A few actually did investigate séances. The scientific reductionism of others made them ill-disposed to consider the possibility that mind might exist separately from its physical organism. (Turner 1974: 54)

If one impetus of the Society for Psychical Research was to set the mind free of its materialist moorings, then another was to chart out a new map for understanding its intricacies. New phenomena in psychology such as hypnotism, hysteria, aphasias and multiple personalities, which suggested that the mind had unexplored regions, were of intense interest to psychical researchers. If the mind were structured like a haunted house, the hope was that science, stretched far enough, would be capable of exploring its hidden rooms.[2] Today psychical research is usually dismissed as a pseudo-science or looked on as a best-forgotten sideline to the careers of such nineteenth-century men of letters as Sidgwick and William James. Its inheritors are television shows such as *The X-Files* and the recent spate of alien abduction stories. I want to take a different, less dismissive approach to psychical research and read its concerns as coextensive with a late nineteenth-century fascination with the modus operandi of cultural transmission and communication. From its inception the Society for Psychical Research's primary concern was for communication that transgressed obvious boundaries. Spiritualism creates contact across inaccessible time, with the dead; telepathy creates contact across inaccessible space, with others who are out of the range of the usual forms of sensory communication.

The SPR set up the first of its six working committees to pursue thought trans-ference: "An examination of the nature and extent of any influence which may be exerted by one mind upon another, apart from any generally recognised mode of perception" (Anon. 1881–1882, I: 3–4). Its other committees were devoted to studying mesmerism, apparitions and haunted houses, the theories of Reichenbach (a German investigator who invented the theory of an odic force, a unifying fluid similar to Mesmer's magnetic fluid), the physical phenomena of mediums, and to collecting and collating information on the history of psychical occurrences.

The initial aim of the Society was to apply scientific methods to phenomena that the standard prejudices of scientists prevented them from investigating. As Henry Sidgwick put it in his presidential address to the Society in 1888, speaking of the Society's beginnings six years earlier:

> We believed unreservedly in the methods of modern science, and were prepared to accept submissively her reasoned conclusions, when sustained by the agreement of experts; but we were not prepared to bow with equal docility to the mere prejudices of scientific men. And it appeared to us that there was an important body of evidence—tending prima facie to establish the independence of soul or spirit—which modern science had simply left on one side with ignorant contempt; and that in so leaving it she had been untrue to her professed method, and had arrived prematurely at her negative conclusions. (Sidgwick 1888–1889: 272)

As a professor of moral philosophy at Cambridge, Henry Sidgwick's investment in psychical research was in large part an ethical one. He wanted to find a basis for an ethical relation to others in a world shorn of religious certainty. As he said in the same presidential address, "when we took up seriously the obscure and perplexing investigation which we call *Psychical Research,* we were mainly moved to do so by the profound and painful division and conflict as regards the nature and destiny of the human soul, which we found in the thought of our age" (Sidgwick 1888–1889: 272). While men of science such as Herbert Spencer looked to evolutionary models to ground their theories of human behavior, Sidgwick and other psychical researchers turned towards new expansive theories of the mind and consciousness to reconstruct an ordered, ethical universe.

In different ways, spiritualism and thought transference, the Society's main objects of interest, can both be seen to hold out the promise of new grounds for ethical relations. Alex Owen has indicated the connections between nineteenth-century spiritualism and various political reform movements. The desire to attain individual and social perfection on earth was seen as preparation for a progressive evolutionary drive towards the next world: "although there were certainly class tensions within the spiritualist movement, adherents across the spectrum of social class ... were committed to the amelioration of social abuses and working-class ills" (Owen 1990: 26). Organizations such as the British National Association of Spiritualists (BNAS), established in 1874, linked radical social politics with the promise of a spiritualist Utopia after death. The BNAS's prospectus "stated that the Association sought to reunite those who are now too often divided by seemingly material conflicting interests", and that it was dedicated to remedying the "excessive irregularity in the distribution of wealth" with its resulting "crying social evils" (Owen 1990: 26). Spiritualism, with its quest to form communities between the living and the dead, was an interest often shared by those who were committed to other radical reforms that aimed to stretch the boundaries, and assert the rights of other under-represented communities such as women, the working class, and, through vegetarianism and anti-vivisectionism, animals.[3]

The Society for Psychical Research's relationship to spiritualism shifted over the years. Some of the Society's original members were committed spiritualists, but by 1886 a rift had developed between the spiritualists and Sidgwick's more sceptical contingent. Most of the serious spiritualists left the Society in that year after taking offence at some of Eleanor Sidgwick's critical writings on the slate-writing of W. Eglinton (Gauld 1968: 138). Later in the chapter I will return to the ways in which class and gender divisions between the Society's members and the spiritualists contributed to stretching and delimiting the acceptable boundaries of interaction between living minds, living bodies and ghostly materializations. The methods of spiritualism and psychical research responded both to radical and conservative impulses, and to less easily discernible desires.

One person who embodied many of the conflicting impulses of the Society in its early years was F. W. H. Myers (1843–1901). Myers was obsessed with the possibility of life after death. His *magnum opus,* the enormous two-volume *Human Personality and Its Survival of Bodily Death,* is a tribute to his faith in survival, but it is also a testimony to his engagement with new materialist and anti-materialist psychological theories. In order to explain phenomena such as hypnotism and multiple personalities, Myers postulated the existence of a subliminal consciousness, similar in part to Freud's unconscious.[4] Myers conceived of human personality along the model of an iceberg, only a small percentage of which, the supraliminal "everyday" self, extended above the waterline. Like his friend and fellow psychical researcher William James, Myers believed that the greater portion of consciousness, the subliminal self, was submerged, elusive, and shifting:

> ... the stream of consciousness in which we habitually live is not the only consciousness which exists in connection with our organism. Our habitual or empirical consciousness may consist of a mere selection from a multitude of thoughts and sensations. ... I accord no primacy to my ordinary waking self, except that among my potential selves this one has shown itself the fittest to meet the needs of common life. (Myers 1891–1892: 301)

For Myers, the subliminal consciousness extended further than the supraliminal, opening up the possibility of engaging in "a far wider range both of physiological and of psychical activity" (Myers 1891–1892: 306). The supraliminal self could, under certain conditions, share the wealth of knowledge and insight that the subliminal self contained. The evidence of this communication between selves was what interested psychical researchers. According to Myers's theories, automatic writing, table-rapping, hallucinations, clairvoyance and dreams are all attempts by the subliminal self to deliver information to the supraliminal self (Oppenheim 1985: 258). In Myers's theories, as in Freud's, the human subject, in its combination of psychic and bodily automatisms and symptoms, is a relay station for information. For Freud, this information tends to be inward-looking, reflecting the subject's past history. For Myers, the information is more compelling when it is outward-looking, foreseeing the future, the possibility of surviving death, the potential for extra-sensory connections between minds. Myers's hope is for a human body and mind that would intimate immortality; Freud is looking for different things (the Oedipus complex, infantile sexuality, etc.), but both participate in versions of a late nineteenth-century hermeneutic project in which the subject is understood both as a text to be read and a space through which information flows.[5]

Myers was responsible for introducing Freud's work to England, delivering a paper on "Hysteria and Genius" to the Society in 1897, in which he gave an account of Freud and Breuer's *Studies on Hysteria* (see Jones 1955: 27).[6] Myers's work raises questions about the relationship between the dissolution of subjectivity and its conservation in the discourses of psychical research. *Human Personality and Its Survival of Bodily Death* encapsulates two contradictory strands of thought. On the one hand, human personality seemed infinitely more pliable, doubled, and easily broken down than had been previously suspected. Hypnotism, multiple personalities and hysteria all indicated a subject which was potentially not one and not always present to itself. On the other hand, spiritualism (and Myers) pinned its hopes on the possibility that human personality actually survived death. As Myers puts it in an introductory syllabus in his book: "The new evidence adduced in this book, while supporting the conception of the composite structure of the Ego, does also bring the strongest proof of its abiding *unity,* by showing that it withstands the shock of death" (Myers 1903). This breakdown of the subject, together with its simultaneous reassertion, anticipates a dynamic that recent critics have seen at work in psychoanalysis. Mikkel Borch-Jacobsen, for instance, suggests in *The Freudian Subject* that Freud finally preserves the unified subject at each moment when it seems most threatened, shifting its location from the conscious to the unconscious, or the individual to the crowd, but maintaining its basic unity. In Borch-Jacobsen's view, Freud needs to anchor the psychoanalytic subject firmly in his or her own egoistic identity in order to defend psychoanalysis from charges that it is indistinguishable from hypnotism, charges that while claiming to uncover psychic dynamics, it really installs its own predetermined structures and stories in a pliable, suggestible subject.

Although this dynamic of dispersed and reassembled subjectivity can be seen as endemic to the western philosophical tradition since Descartes,[7] as Kittler (1987) suggests, at the turn of the century the mind is imagined as inhabited, unified, dispersed and communicating in specific ways which are influenced by a nexus of scientific, literary and popular discussions. This account needs to be supplemented with what we might call a historical and affective understanding of fantasy. When we ask what factors contribute to late nineteenth-century ideas about the shape and configuration of the mind, subjectivity and communication, we need to think about what might compel people to want their minds to look certain ways. Whether we care about permanent metaphysical structures, the latest technologies or haunted houses, our explanatory models are bound to reflect these investments. Fantasies, especially site-specific academic fantasies of causal explanation, are often totalizing (i.e. the idea that this or that phenomenon is entirely the product of historical determinants, or entirely the product of a western metaphysics of presence); the appeal of the totalizing fantasy is as visible in the Society for Psychical Research's discussions of telepathy as in late twentieth-century literary theory. The point of the following discussion is not to endorse or critique these fantasies of totalization, but rather to try and understand how various imagined effects of collapse, communication and intimate contact with others' bodies and minds contributed to creating a permeable, boundary-crossing, potentially telepathic subject at the turn of the century.

Telepathy

In October 1884 Samuel Clemens wrote to the editor of the *Journal of the Society for Psychical Research* to express his appreciation of the experiments the Society had been conducting on thought transference:

> Dear Sir, I should be very glad indeed to be made a Member of the Society for Psychical Research; for Thought-transference, as you call it, or mental telegraphy as I have been in the habit of calling it, has been a very strong interest with me for the past nine or ten years. I have grown so accustomed to considering that all my powerful impulses come to me from somebody else, that I often feel like a mere amanuensis when I sit down to write a letter under the coercion of a strong impulse: I consider that the other person is supplying the thoughts to me, and that I am merely writing from dictation. ... I have been saved the writing of many and many a letter by refusing to obey these strong impulses. I always knew the other fellow was sitting down to write when I got the impulse—so what could be the sense in both of us writing the same thing? People are always marveling because their letters "cross" each other. If they would but squelch the impulse to write, there would not be any crossing, because only the other fellow would write. (Twain 1884: 167)

Clemens's engagement with the Society's work is recognized as at least partially ironic by the editors of the *Journal* who reproduce the letter with an introduction, "the following characteristic letter from Mr. S. L. Clemens (Mark Twain) will, doubtless, entertain many of our readers.—Ed" (Twain 1884: 167). Yet to dismiss Twain's interest in the Society as entirely facetious would be mistaken. He not only became a member of the Society but also corresponded with Frederic Myers, to whom he writes about subjects such as the functioning of consciousness and unconsciousness during an experience of blacking out.[8] In an 1891 article in *Harper's Magazine*

"Mental Telegraphy", Twain reiterates his early belief in telepathy and his support of the Society for Psychical Research: "Within the last two or three years they [the SPR] have penetrated toward the heart of the matter ... and have found out that mind can act upon mind in a quite detailed and elaborate way over vast stretches of land and water. And they have succeeded in doing, by their great credit and influence, what I could never have done—they have convinced the world that mental telegraphy is not a jest, but a fact, and that it is a thing not rare, but exceedingly common" (Twain 1963a: 71).[9] Twain's fascination with telepathy clearly dovetailed with his interest in new communication technologies such as the telephone line he early had installed, and the type-setting machine he invested in heavily (Seltzer 1992: 9).[10]

It appears from the letter to the Society that Twain's enthusiasm for thought transference is primarily for its money- and time-saving potential, as he makes clear when he describes a mental transaction which saves him the cost of a 50-cent telegram. He is not particularly interested in telepathy's metaphysical, spiritual or scientific consequences. Rather, for Twain it would be an economic advantage if mediation could be dispensed with and thought could be instantaneously shared:

> In my own case it has often been demonstrated that people can have crystal-clear mental communication with each other over vast distances. Doubtless to be able to do this the two minds have to be in a peculiarly favourable condition for the moment. Very well, then, why shouldn't some scientist find it possible to invent a way to create this condition of rapport between two minds, at will? Then we should drop the slow and cumbersome telephone and say "Connect me with the brain of the chief of police at Peking." We shouldn't need to know the man's language; we should communicate by thought only, and say in a couple of minutes what couldn't be inflated into words in an hour and a-half. Telephones, telegraphs and words are too slow for this age; we must get something that is faster. (Twain 1884: 167)

This is the American can-do version of thought transference. Telepathy promises to displace mediation and do away with the necessity for transmission, translation, even for language itself, in the service of efficiency. When Twain points out that words themselves, not just telephones and telegraphs, are too slow for this age, he takes telepathy towards its logical conclusion: a collapsing of communication upon itself. No communication would be necessary in Twain's Utopia, no transference of anything from one place to another, because there would be no distancing to begin with. To employ poststructuralist terminology, there would be no differentiation from the other, no loss, and no language needed to try to make good that loss. For Twain in this letter, lack of differentiation becomes entirely a matter of economics. No loss means nothing to pay in order to send one's message through.

In Twain's logics of media extension (reaching over farther and farther distances) and contraction (collapsing distance onto itself), telepathy is just a form of communication-enhancing technology that will make things faster, easier, better for market relations and productivity—a sort of Taylorization of the soul. At the turn of the century, telepathy, as has been pointed out, is only one in a whole series of new "tele" communications (Royle 1990). Recently, in the work of theorists such as Kittler (1990), Nicholas Royle (1990) and Avital Ronell (1989), "tele" or technology studies has formed an uneasy alliance with deconstructive theory. On the one hand, it seems that new communication technologies introduce, in a sort of epistemic break, new ways of conceiving of our relations to our minds and bodies, to other minds and bodies, and to time. But, on the other hand, deconstructive theory suggests that the modes of communication transmission employed by these new technologies are structural constants. Our forms of communication, inter- and intra-subjective, are now, and have always been, structured the same way that the telephone line is structured. Even with the knowledge that all communication is "tele", at a distance, the unfulfillable desire for the collapse of that distance, for "full" presence, remains. Hence Twain's ironic desire to do away with words.

The flip side of this collapse of communication on itself is the prosthetic extension of the senses into previously unimaginable realms, the fantasy that new technology could retrieve the absolutely lost. Twain's cheerful fantasies of immediacy resemble those of Thomas Edison, another relentlessly non-melancholic deployer of technological know-how. Edison, in his memoir, *The Diary and Sundry Observations of Thomas Alva Edison,* wants to bring science to the afterworld. The final chapter of Edison's musings is devoted to "The Realms Beyond" in which the scientist discusses the valve he is building to communicate with the dead, or at least to increase the volume level, so that if the dead are trying to get in touch with the living we'll have a better chance of hearing them: " ... if personality exists, after what we call death, it is reasonable to conclude that those who leave this earth would like to communicate with those they have left here. Accordingly, the thing to do is to furnish the best conceivable means to make it easy for them to open up communication with us, and then see what happens" (Edison 1948: 234).[11]

Twain and Edison assume a continuity between the teletechnology they are involved in inventing and deploying and the crossing over into a paranormal world. If you can talk to people at a distance on the phone, the logic runs, why shouldn't you be able to talk to the dead? Friedrich Kittler points out the connections between the nineteenth century's new forms of communication technology and the spiritual world:

> the tapping specters of the spiritualistic séances with their messages from the realm of the dead, appeared quite promptly at the moment of the invention of the Morse alphabet in 1837. Promptly, photographic plates—even and especially with the camera shutter closed—provided images of ghosts or specters which in their black and white fuzziness, only emphasized the moments of resemblance. Finally one of the ten uses Edison predicted ... for the recently invented phonograph was to preserve the "last words of the dying". (Kittler 1987: 111)

In other words there is always already a ghost in the machine, a telepath on the telephone wire. What is the force of this logic of extension? It may be grasped perhaps if we first consider the specific anxieties and hopes about telepathy within the Society for Psychical Research.

Although not such an obviously widespread cultural phenomenon as the mid-century craze for spiritualism, thought transference by the 1880s was a popular subject for debate. Rather like interest in the seemingly magical but less and less disputed powers of hypnotism and suggestion, at the end of the century telepathy begins to be taken for granted by some sections of the population. The Society for Psychical Research's interest in telepathy extended in several different directions. Chiefly through the early efforts of Myers and Edmund Gurney, the Society collected people's stories of their experiences of visual hallucinations and published them in the enormous *Phantasms of the Living* in 1886 (Gurney et al. 1886). The book told a repeated story of a dying person appearing to a loved one far away at the moment of death, which Gurney and Myers postulated was potentially caused by a telepathic projection. Whether these crisis apparitions were telepathic transferences sent out by the person at the moment before death or actual appearances of someone after death was a crucial question for members of the Society who accepted the evidence of *Phantasms* as proof of some sort of image transference. Was there survival after death, or could the evidence that pointed to it be explained away by that other extra-sensory, but comparatively mundane phenomenon, telepathy? For Myers and others, therefore, telepathy was double edged: both a step on the way towards proof of survival after death and a potentially less outlandish explanation for phenomena generated by mediums which might otherwise point towards proof of survival. It is in part because of this use of telepathy as the less radical explanation for spiritualists' evidence that telepathy itself comes to be assumed truly to take place, or at least to be plausible.

The Society's first and initially most successful thought transference experiments were carried out on the Creery sisters by the physicist William Barrett.[12] The 1881 successes with the Creery girls became the basis for a firm belief by Barrett, as well as other members of the Society, that thought transference was a proven phenomenon (Oppenheim 1985: 358). However, the Creerys were caught using a code when tested again in 1887. Other thought transference and hypnotic experiments carried out by Edmund Gurney in the 1880s, which seemed to point towards startling evidence for telepathy, were also partially discredited by doubts about the experimentees.[13] But the fact that many of the major experiments that acted as cornerstones for the Society's faith in telepathy were later shown to be untrustworthy is not my primary concern. Rather, I am more interested in the ways in which belief in telepathy was dispersed through the Society and outside it, despite lack of unimpeachable scientific evidence for its existence.

Henry Sidgwick thought that telepathy was still the most promising line of inquiry for the Society, even if there was not yet convincing evidence for its existence. In an 1888 journal entry he writes, "I have not much hope of our getting out positive results in any other department of inquiry, but I am not yet hopeless of establishing telepathy" (Sidgwick and Sidgwick 1906: 494). A theory of telepathy was what was needed to convince the rest of the scientific world. "If only I could form the least conception of the *modus transferendi!*" (Sidgwick and Sidgwick 1906: 473). Sidgwick's desire to believe but inability to understand how telepathy actually functioned indicates the role telepathy was fulfilling in the collective psyche of nineteenth-century psychical researchers. It was useful for explaining other phenomena, but seemed to have no explanation itself. Yet its popularity grew. Sidgwick's wife, Eleanor, another intrepid psychical researcher, writes, "telepathy ... had now become a catchword of the man in the street, who used it like 'electricity' to explain anything mysterious. Meantime telepathy had hardly moved an inch in the favour or respect, of the professional scientist" (Sidgwick 1938: 191).

As well as both being handy if mystifying explanations for transmission, telepathy and electricity share other characteristics. They both inspire fantasies of community—instant access to others. If the world becomes a smaller place because of telecommunication, telepathy too is imagined to create connections with even more startling potential effects. In his book *On the Threshold of the Unseen,* William Barrett, one of the staunchest supporters of the truth of telepathy, imagines a telepathic Utopia where social justice would follow inevitably from shared thoughts:

> If we were involuntarily sharers in one another's pleasures and pains, the brotherhood of the race would not be a pious aspiration or a strenuous effort, but the reality of all others most vividly before us; the factor in our lives which would dominate all our conduct. What would be the use of a luxurious mansion at the West End and Parisian cooks if all the time the misery and starvation of our fellow creatures at the East End were telepathically part and parcel of our daily lives? On the other hand what bright visions and joyous emotions would enter into many dreary and loveless lives if this state of human responsiveness were granted to the race! (Barrett 1917: 294)

In this scenario, the ethical consequences of telepathy would mean that the rich would have to think about the poor and the poor could telepathically share the privileges of the rich. For Myers as well, the existence of telepathy implied Utopian bonding. In his essay "Science and a Future Life", he claims: " ... that same direct influence of mind on mind" which telepathy revealed "*in minimis* would, if supposed operative *in maximis,* be a form of stating the efficacy of prayer, the communion of saints, or even the operation of a Divine Spirit" (Myers 1893: 40). Telepathy here becomes a dramatic and scientifically sanctioned method for transporting words such as sympathy or the recently coined *empathy* from the realm of the way things should be to the way things actually could be, the way things *will* be if thought is effectively shared.

Telepathy was imagined in a variety of ways. Both telepathy itself and the tendency to believe in it were subsumed by contemporary theories that posited what Robert Nye has called the two fallacies of nineteenth-century cultural anthropology:

"the presumption that modern savage societies represented carbon copies of their historical predecessors 'frozen' in time, and the notion that primitive institutions could be logically inferred from a study of their 'survivals' in contemporary social forms" (Nye 1975: 41). Telepathy was sometimes put in the service of Barrett's collective Utopia but it was also seen as a throw-back to a previous evolutionary state. Frank Podmore thought that telepathy was one of several "long lost but once serviceable faculties" which man, ages ago, used consciously, but which since had become involuntary residuals (Pierce and Podmore 1895: 332). Against telepathy, James Frazer and others argued that it was the *belief* in phenomena such as telepathy and ghosts, not the phenomena themselves, that was a survival of the superstitions of the savage mind which had not yet been ousted from the modern one (Stein 1968: 32). Henry Sidgwick mockingly described a *Pall Mall Gazette* article of 21 October 1882 which warned against the dangers of succumbing to belief in ghosts. The article "urged its readers to abstain from inquiring into ghost stories on account of the dangerous tendency to give them credence which, on the principle of evolution, must be held to exist in our brains. Owing to the many generations of our ancestors who believed in spirits, we retain, it seems in our nervous mechanism, 'innumerable connections of fibers', which will be developed into superstitious beliefs if we give them the slightest opportunity. ... The scientific attitude can only be maintained by careful abstention from dangerous trains of thought" (Sidgwick 1882–1883: 66).

The idea of telepathy as evolutionary survival was also used to connect humans to animals, particularly insects, who were pictured as employing forms of telepathic communication. Barrett suggests that, "the habits of ants and bees seem to indicate the possession of a mode of communication unknown to us. If our domestic animals are in any degree open to thought-transference, may we not get into somewhat closer communication with them?" (Barrett 1917: 293–294). Although lacking the desire to talk to the animals, Freud, in his article "Dreams and Occultism", is not far from Barrett when he suggests that telepathy might be an atavistic sense in humans, still at work in insects:

> ... it is a familiar fact that we do not know how the common purpose comes about in the great insect communities; possibly it is done by means of direct psychical transference of this kind. One is led to a suspicion that this is the original, archaic method of communication between individuals and that in the course of phylogenetic evolution it has been replaced by the better method of giving information with the help of signals which are picked up by the sense organs. (Freud [1911] 1953: 55)

Myers and others, however, saw telepathy as a progressive evolutionary step rather than a movement back towards a lost atavistic sense: "telepathy is surely a step in evolution. To learn the thoughts of other minds, without the mediation of the special senses, manifestly indicates the possibility of a vast extension of psychical powers" (Myers 1885: 32). In the emerging theories of crowd behavior, telepathy held an important if unexamined explanatory place. The crowd mind, often thought of as a primitive one, had to be imagined as telepathically created in order for it to act en masse. Gabriel Tarde postulates in *The Laws of Imitation* (1903) that sociality itself, in its most radical form, would be telepathic: "in its hypothetical form it would consist of such an intense concentration of urban life that as soon as a good idea arose in one mind it would be instantaneously transmitted to all minds throughout the city" (Tarde quoted in Borch-Jacobsen 1988: 266). Gustave LeBon, in his enormously popular *La Psychologie des foules* (1895) posits "*the law of the mental unity of crowds*", suggesting that crowds form themselves through contagion of a hypnotic order (LeBon 1976: 24–30). Although the unthinking, primitive crowd is for LeBon inferior to the reasoning individual, he also suggests that the crowd can at times rise above itself, somewhat in the manner of Myers's progressive evolutionary hopes for telepathy:

> So far as the majority of their acts are considered, crowds display a singularly inferior mentality; yet there are other acts in which they appear to be guided by those mysterious forces which the ancients denominated destiny, nature or providence, which we call the voices of the dead, and whose power it is impossible to overlook, although we ignore their essence. It would seem, at times, as if there were latent forces in the inner being of nations which serve to guide them. What, for instance, can be more complicated, more logical, more marvelous than a language? Yet whence can this admirably organised production have arisen except it be the outcome of the unconscious genius of crowds? (LeBon 1976: 6)

Language, LeBon suggests, is not developed through individual communicative interactions. Rather it arises spontaneously in the group mind, creating, amongst other things, national identity. If for Freud, telepathy is potentially an archaic, pre-linguistic method of communication, then for LeBon, language itself arises telepathically, instantaneously, contagiously in the mind of the crowd. Telepathy is imagined as the origin of language, sociality and nationhood.

Telepathy was clearly a contradictory creature. Sometimes imagined as the path towards spiritual or earthly Utopia through shared sensations, it could also be viewed as the mechanism behind a collapsing of all thought in the primitive, riotous, unthinking crowd mind. Physical explanations for its existence were often contradictory too. Telepathy was most often explained by recourse to analogies to electricity and other dematerialized, non-visible forms of transmission. The Society's "First Report on Thought-Reading" quotes a Dr T. A. McGraw from the *Detroit Review of Medicine* to support their beliefs about the plausibility of thought transference:

> It seems to me there is a hint towards the possibility of the nervous system of one individual being used by the active will of another to accomplish certain simple motions. There would be nothing inherently impossible in this when we recollect the strong similarities that exist between nervous and electrical forces; and as we know, it is possible to generate induced currents of electricity in coils of wire that are near to a primary electric

coil; so we can imagine the nervous current to be continued into ... another body and act there upon the automatic centres of action ... (Anon. 1882–1883: 15–16)

Such explanations borrow from older explanations of mesmerism, harkening back to come up with a new, technologically updated version of the bodily magnetism initially thought responsible for mesmeric effects. The "First Report on Thought-Reading" attempts to set thought transference in a continuum with other forms of dematerialized transmission once thought impossible but now scientifically accepted:

It is quite open to surmise some sort of analogy to the familiar phenomena of the transmission and reception of vibratory. ... One tuning-fork or string in unison with another will communicate its impulses through the medium of the air. ... A permanent magnet brought into a room will throw any surrounding iron into a condition similar to its own; and here the medium of communication is unknown though the fact is undisputed. Similarly, we may conceive ... that for every thought there is a corresponding motion of the particles of the brain, and that this vibration of molecules of brain-stuff may be communicated to an intervening medium, and so pass under certain circumstances from one brain to another, with a corresponding simultaneity of impressions. (Anon. 1882–1883: 33–34)

This desire to link mind and brain in a psycho-physical materialist explanation of the transference of thought goes hand in hand with the recognition of transmission's expansion into realms in which proximity or touch are not necessary to its workings. At the end of the nineteenth century science is severing the links between materiality, visibility and transmission, allowing for a sort of telepathic imaginary. In his 1886 novel *Tomorrow's Eve,* Philippe Villiers de l'Isle Adam has a fictional Thomas Edison deploy telepathy as well as a plethora of new technologies in the invention of an android woman. The book's hero, Lord Ewald, cannot understand how his robotic lover can be telepathically controlled and "electrified" from a distance. He says:

Just a minute. ... I'm sure it's already a remarkable thing that electric current can now transmit energy to great heights and over enormous, almost limitless distances. ... This trick is perfectly comprehensible, given the use of tangible conductors—magic highways—through which the powerful currents flow. But this INSUBSTANTIAL transmission of my living thought, how can I imagine it taking place, at a distance, without conductors or wires, even the very thinnest? (Villiers de l'Isle Adam 1982: 213)

Ewald's doubts suggest that one limit of conceiving of transmission at that particular moment in the historical development of electrical technology was materiality itself. Wires, even wisp thin ones, are still a substantial link between one thing and another. When these wires are snapped and transmission still takes place, then, for Ewald, we have crossed a line which divides science from the occult. Without a visual or substantial guarantee of the materiality of information flow, without some sort of promise about the empirical connection between cause and effect, we come face to face with the unknown. Anything can happen. Bring out your dead, bring on the mind-readers.

Rudyard Kipling's 1902 tale "Wireless" engages precisely this nexus of concerns about the line that divides science from the occult, but dispenses with Ewald's anxious tone. The story sets up an analogy between early wireless radio technology and spiritualist séances, and pictures both as untrustworthy methods of information transmission. "Wireless" rests on a simple conceit. In the back room of a chemist's shop an electrician sets up a wireless Morse conductor in order to receive signals from a friend in Poole. While the electrician waits for his signals to come through, in the front of the shop a young chemist's assistant, Mr Shaynor, falls into a drug-induced stupor and apparently begins channelling the spirit of John Keats by attempting to compose or transcribe "The Eve of St. Agnes". The narrator, who has come to witness the wireless communication, goes back and forth between the two scenes noting similarities between the two partially successful transmissions: the chemist gets a few verses almost right; the electrician fails to reach Poole but picks up the signals of two ships off the Isle of Wight which are unable to make contact with each other. The narrator surmises that the chemist's channelling of Keats, whom the chemist has not read, is due to a general resemblance in their situations. Like Keats, Shaynor is a tubercular chemist. He is also in love with Fanny Brand, a woman identified with modern commercial culture who, "distantly resembled the seductive shape on a gold-framed toilet-water advertisement"—a mass-produced, brand-named Fanny Brawne (Kipling 1920: 204).

The narrator of "Wireless" suggests that the electrician's inability to explain electricity—"Ah, if you knew *that* you'd know something nobody knows. It's just It— ... "—allows it to function both as an analogy to and explanation for the chemist's mediumistic trance. Here electricity is a "black box", a system in scientific discourse contained in such a way as to enable its utilization without understanding its components.[14] As Eleanor Sidgwick also pointed out, electricity functions as an explanation for which no explanation is required. The narrator "explains" to himself in terminology which could be a parody of a Society for Psychical Research explanation for séance phenomena: "it's the ... Hertzian wave of tuberculosis, *plus* Fanny Brand and the professional status which, in conjunction with the mainstream of subconscious thought common to all mankind, has thrown up temporarily an induced Keats" (Kipling 1920: 213). In "Wireless" this heady combination of a shared store of thought and "Hertzian waves"—a scientific-sounding phrase which purports to explain all sorts of transmission—makes for another example of the potential pleasures and dangers of severing wires, transgressing sense boundaries, and delivering unexpected messages through unintentional mediums (Oppenheim 1985: 379). Analogies between electricity and extra-sensory forms of communication such as telepathy and contact with the dead function in this story and in the writings of the Society for Psychical Research as the non-causal, causal ground for a range of desires and fantasies about new ways of knowing, both others and information.

"Wireless" makes no judgements about the potential truth or falsity of unconscious channelling of the dead; it simply observes the similarities between various forms of channelling. If Kipling's story rests on a straightforward analogy between science and séance, it is worth remembering that his sister, Alice Fleming, was a medium, who spent some time being dictated to by the deceased F. W. H. Myers amongst others (Haynes 1982: 61). In the period in which Kipling was writing "Wireless" it was not uncommon to have all sorts of media and mediums functioning in one house. Texts such as *Tomorrow's Eve* and "Wireless" point towards the structural analogies and the black-boxing of explanation which make these narratives of occult/technological transmission so compelling for turn-of-the-century culture. In experimenting with thought transference and searching for the *modus transferendi* of telepathy the Society for Psychical Research explored new relationships between the material and the psychic and between proximity and distance. The ways these turn-of-the-century experiments with and theorizations of telepathy become intertwined with an erotics of knowledge can be traced, in part, through the shift in the Society's experimentation from sittings with physical mediums to thought transference and mental mediums.

The Society's members, in general, quickly lost faith in the so-called physical mediums, nearly all of whom were discovered in trickery at some point during their careers.[15] Physical mediums were often paid for their performances and engaged in theatrical displays, moving tables and furniture and conjuring spirits while supposedly securely locked in a cabinet (Owen 1990). The later mental mediums the Society turned towards tended to be from a different class background from their predecessors. Studies of their automatic writing fed into psychical researchers' psychological interests in the subconscious or subliminal consciousness. William James in his presidential address to the SPR in 1896 expressed his relief at being able to discard the dubious displays of the physical mediums: "It is pleasant to turn from phenomena of the dark-sitting and rat-hole type (with their tragi-comic suggestion that the whole order of nature might possibly be overturned in one's own head, by the way in which one imagined oneself, on a certain occasion, to be holding a tricky peasant woman's feet) to the 'calm air of delightful studies'" (James 1896: 6).

"Holding a tricky peasant woman's feet" combines the class and sexual politics of the physical séance in one concise image. The Society's early séance experiments involved upper-class university-educated men locking themselves in rooms with working-class, sometimes foreign women, for hours on end.[16] In order to detect and prevent fraud, the mediums were often held on to during the sittings and searched thoroughly before and after. When physical mediums locked themselves in closets in order to provoke visible bodily spirit manifestations, they were kept under surveillance, through a series of complicated tests.[17] As Alex Owen has described, the body of the medium became a site of intense interest to the scientific investigators, and the séance became a site for transgressive contact between men and women of different classes (Owen 1990: 230–231).[18] When spirits materialized they were touched, embraced, kissed, in the name of testing the limits of their materiality, and they in turn touched, embraced and kissed their investigators. James's desire to turn away from the dubious job of holding a tricky peasant woman's feet should be read in this light.

But what exactly was he turning towards? If the erotics of the physical séance were centred around the physical manifestations of bodies which needed to be touched to ensure their materiality, is there an erotics of telepathy? From the first the goal of the Society's thought-transference experiments was to get away from physical contact: "The primary aim in all cases must be to get the results *without physical contact* or anything approaching it ... in no other way can the hypothesis of 'muscle-reading' be with certainty eliminated ... " (Anon. 1882–1883: 30). If any of the potential consequences, scientific, religious, metaphysical, Utopian, of telepathy were to be realized, it required that that wire, the physical connection, be severed. But in the popular imagination, this very severing became the source of new and intense imaginings of proximity. These are the erotics of mind melding.

In a letter to George Eliot in 1872 Myers wrote despondently:

> Life has come to such a pass—now that there is no longer any God or hereafter or anything in particular to aim at—that it is only coming into contact with some other person that one can be oneself. There is no longer anything to keep a [*sic*] isolated fire burning within one. All one can do is to feel the sparks fly from one for a moment when one strikes a kindred soul. Such contact in real life can make one feel for the moment immortal, but the necessary circumstances are so unusual. (Quoted in Turner 1974: 113)

Here Myers employs a metaphorics of physical contact, the striking of matches or flint to start a fire, to describe the contact of souls. Years later, after Edmund Gurney's death in 1888, Myers spoke of his grief in these terms: "For fifteen years we had been as intimate and as attached to each other as men can be;—every part of our respective natures found response by comprehension in the other. But I will not say more of that" (Gauld 1968: 182). Myers's response to his close friend's death is cast in the language of sentiment, friendship, homosocial bonding, but it is also in the language of telepathy as the desire for absolute knowledge and melding with another, inevitable perhaps between two friends who spent much of their time experimenting with thought transference. The type of rhetoric Myers uses to describe his relationship to Gurney moves us towards an explicitly erotic aspect of telepathy. The dematerialization, the lack of physical contact, required for scientific proof of telepathy in the Society seems to make it safe from a distracting erotics, untainted by desire. Minds should meet but not bodies, much to the relief of William James and the other scientists of the Society. But the types of investments in telepathy inside and outside the Society would indicate that the potential nature of the intimacy circumscribed by thought transference is not containable in these terms.

Two 1890s novels suggest how telepathy can signify dangerous proximity in this period. When one thinks of the perils of intimacy in Bram Stoker's *Dracula,* telepathy might not immediately spring to mind. Neither might the phonograph, for that matter, but both telepathy and phonographs threaten to invade and discover the secrets of the insides of minds in the novel, just as vampires threaten to suck dry the insides of bodies. When it becomes necessary for the vampire hunters to collect and process the information about Dracula's whereabouts that is contained in the various journals they all separately have been keeping, Mina Harker, who is trained in short-hand, agrees to listen to and transcribe the journal that Dr Seward had been record-ing on phonograph. Unfortunately, the phonographic recording contains, amongst other things, the record of his unrequited love for Lucy Westenra. Mina says to Seward: "That is a wonderful machine, but it is cruelly true. It told me, in its very tones, the anguish of your heart. ... I have copied out the words on my typewriter, and none other need now hear your heart beat as I did" (Stoker 1965: 229). Hear-ing someone's heart beat is, of course, a figurative expression for intimacy. But the phonograph, as a recording instrument, at least suggests the possibility of taking this literally, while simultaneously being entirely removed in space and time from the person to whom that heart belongs. Similarly, Mina, when under bodily attack from Dracula, becomes the victim of a telepathic or hypnotic attack on her mind. Dracula can gain access to her mind for information about the movements of the men who are pursuing him, because the sexualized, bodily enervating vampiric attack also creates a telepathic corollary. The mind is open to invasion, and bodily intimacy becomes impossible to extricate from "tele" intimacy: the all-knowing intimacy cre-ated by a machine like the telephone, the distant but penetrating access to another.

A final example of the dangers of the telepathic imagination comes from the anonymous pornographic novel *Teleny,* written by several people one of whom was probably Oscar Wilde. It was first published in a limited edition in 1893. The story of a tortured love affair between the pianist Teleny and the narrator Des Grieux, *Teleny* begins with a series of shared hallucinations between the two at a concert Teleny plays in: "Do you believe in the transmission of thought, of feelings, of sensations?" Teleny asks Des Grieux when they first meet (Wilde et al. 1986: 38). Teleny's very name conjures up tele-communication as well as his telepathic connection to Des Grieux. The love between Teleny and Des Grieux is described in terms of electri-cal currents and shocks (Wilde et al. 1986: 40). When Teleny spends a night with a woman, Des Grieux experiences the encounter simultaneously, as if he were there, explaining to his interlocutor: "There was, as I told you before, a strong transmission of thoughts between us. This is by no means a remarkable coincidence. You smile and look incredulous: well follow the doings of the Psychical Society, and this vision will certainly not astonish you any more" (Wilde et al. 1986: 79).[19]

In *Teleny* telepathy is radicalized towards narcissistic collapse, an economy of the same. When the Countess who spent the night with Teleny gives birth to a son nine months later he looks like Des Grieux. But then Des Grieux looks like Teleny, so who is to say who is the father, or who is who? In *Teleny* telepathy seems to function as trope and ground for a phantasmatic homosexual male sexuality based on narcissism and non-differentiation.[20] A few years later in his article "On Narcissism", Freud will reductively diagnose homosexuality as a disease of arrested auto-eroticism. Homosexuals, Freud asserts, are "plainly seeking *themselves* as a love-object" (Freud 1914: 88). At times *Teleny* reads like a textbook enactment of Freud's theories, for example when Des Grieux describes his embrace of Teleny: "As my hands wandered over his head, his neck, his shoulders, his arms, I could not feel him at all; in fact, it seemed to me as if I were touching my own body" (Wilde et al. 1986: 110). Telepathy, seemingly the most disembodied method of contact, can lead, as it does in *Teleny,* to an almost unbearably collapsed physicality.

As I hope I have amply indicated, desires for telepathic communication at the turn of the century were by no means necessarily sexual, nor were they inevitably solipsistic; the ultimate goal of telepathy was not necessarily speaking only to oneself. On the contrary, as a fantasy position, telepathy suggested a whole range of possibilities, from Mark Twain's cost-efficient replacement for the telegraph to William Barrett's dream of talking to the animals in a telepathic world of shared sensation and wealth. In the Society for Psychical Research in general, however, and certainly for someone such as Myers, telepathy seemed to fulfill two apparently contradictory functions. On the one hand, the Society's experiments in thought transference were a turn away from the dubious class and sexual connotations of séances with physical mediums towards scientifically reliable, dematerialized experiments within the confines of laboratory conditions. Crudely put, emphasizing thought transference rather than séances allowed the Society to move from touching (primarily) women to not touching (primarily) men.[21]

On the other hand, the Society's members who pinned their hopes for transcendent meaning on the SPR's findings were heavily affectively invested in thought transference experiments. Myers's desire to feel the sparks fly from his soul to another's is a fantasy which is imaginatively entwined with the image of a scientific laboratory filled with people not touching each other as they read each others' minds. One fantasy grounds itself in the other, and the hopes for what telepathy might mean both for other-worldly transcendence and for this world's intimate relations are bound up in that moment of scientific proof the Society felt was always so near and which always just eluded it.

Poststructuralist theory in the tradition of Derrida informs us that self-presence is the western metaphysical fantasy par excellence. What we want and what we can never have is plenitude and non-differentiation, a version of love that would be beyond language or make it unnecessary. Telepathy at the turn of the century can be read in the light of this overarching schema, but also more specifically in terms of the available cultural material around which these fantasies structure themselves. The ways in which new technologies of communication are severing the wire of visible, materialized transmission in the last decades of the nineteenth century help create a new metaphorics for imagining intimate relations with others. How a piece of information ("I'm thinking of a number from one to ten") gets from one place to another, and what that means in terms of the relationship between the bodies and minds that pass that information along is not as simple a problem as it may first appear. For psychical researchers, as for other commentators at the time, telepathy both promised and threatened that the mind was not necessarily a sealed and protected space. Critical interpretation of telepathy suggests that the mind's potential porousness was made to serve the purposes of the most erotically charged, as well as the most scientifically removed purposes, in a telepathic dialectic of touch and distance.

Notes

1. This chapter is not designed to be a history of the Society. Alan Gauld (1968), Frank M. Turner (1974) and Janet Oppenheim (1985) have covered the subject extensively. John Peregrine Williams's unpublished dissertation "The Making of Victorian Psychical Research" (1984) is an indispensable guide to situating psychical research amongst other medical and scientific discourses of the day.

2. See Castle (1995) for an explanation of how the mind came to be described in the language of haunting. Castle suggests that by the nineteenth century science had banished ghosts to the inside of the mind and consequently thought itself began to be conceived of as haunted, "as if there were, at the very heart of subjectivity itself, something foreign and fantastic, a spiritual presence from elsewhere, a spectre-show of unaccountable origin" (1995: 167). Although fascinating in many respects, Castle's thesis leaves aside the whole question of the craze for spiritualism which began in the mid-nineteenth century. I would maintain that ghosts have a more complicated, and more continuously externalized, history than Castle allows.

3. Logie Barrow (1986) confines the intersection of spiritualism and radical reform movements to the working-class spiritualists. In a footnote Alex Owen (1990: 250 n 27) argues that Barrow underestimates the crossing of interests between middle-class spiritualism and the working-class movement.

4. The fascination with the split and uncertain nature of the mind also surfaces in popular literature at the time in the many books about doubling written towards the end of the century, such as Robert Louis Stevenson's *Dr Jekyll and Mr Hyde* (1886) and Wilde's *The Picture of Dorian Gray* (1891).

5. See Carlo Ginzburg (1983) for an article which situates Freud in the context of other nineteenth-century interpretative sciences. By contrast the Lacanian return to Freud insists that psychoanalysis is not a hermeneutics and that the force of Freud's thought lies in its refusal of hermeneutics.

6. Joan Riviere and James Strachey both initially encountered Freud's thought via Myers and the Society for Psychical Research (King 1988: 124).

7. Jacques Derrida's body of work would be one place to look for the deconstructive tracing out of this dynamic. See especially *The Postcard* (1987).

8. Mark Twain, letter to F. W. H. Myers, 12 January 1892, Myers Papers, Wren Library, Trinity College, Cambridge University.

9. In his introduction to the article "Mental Telegraphy" (1963a), Twain explains that he has collected material on mental telegraphy for years but was afraid to publish it "for I feared that the public would treat the thing as a joke and throw it aside, whereas I was in earnest" (quoted in Neider 1963: 71).

10. Twain jokes about the difficulty of distinguishing between "magical" telepathic communication and the effects of the telephone in *A Connecticut Yankee in King Arthur's Court* (1982). Also see Twain's article "The First Writing-Machines" in *The Complete Essays of Mark Twain* (1963b).

11. Virginia Woolf invokes a similar fantasy in her story "Kew Gardens" in an overheard conversation about spiritualism. An old man explains the practical side of communicating with the dead in terms similar to Edison's: "You have a small electric battery and piece of rubber to insulate the wire—isolate?— insulate?—well, we'll skip the details, not good going into details that wouldn't be understood—and in short the little machine stands in any convenient position by the head of the bed, we will say, on a near mahogany stand. All arrangements being properly fixed by workmen under my direction, the widow applies her ear and summons the spirit by sign as agreed" (Woolf 1982: 36).

12. Thought transference experiments usually involved readers' attempts to correctly guess cards, numbers and names which were concentrated on by another. The records of these experiments make for gloriously dull reading, usually in the form of tables of guesses or narrative along the lines of "Expt. 2.—The same young lady, M.B., seated at the table with her eyes bandaged, pencil in hand. Her uncle, standing about twelve feet distance, asked "What word am I thinking of?" M.B. wrote "Homo." "This was right." (Anon. 1882–1883: 55). The tedium of psychical research in general is a point of scientific pride for many writers in the pages of the Society's *Journal* and *Proceedings*. Psychical researchers constantly insist that they are not engaged in frisson-producing activity: "Further we must warn future readers that the details of the evidence are in many cases not only dull, but of a trivial and even ludicrous kind; and that they will be presented for the most part in the narrator's simplest phraseology, quite unspiced for the literary palate. Our tales will resemble neither *The Mysteries of Udolpho* nor the dignified reports of a learned society. The romanticist may easily grow indignant over them; still more easily may the journalist grow facetious ... However caused, these phenomena are interwoven with the everyday tissue of human existence, and pay no more regard to what men call appalling than to what men call ridiculous" (Barrett et al., 1882–1883: 118).

13. See Trevor Hall (1964) for a highly speculative account of Gurney's death from an overdose of chloroform, in a Brighton hotel, in June 1888. Hall surmises that

Gurney must have discovered evidence of trickery, including that of his friend, experimentee and personal secretary, G. A. Smith, and therefore committed suicide. Hall provides no convincing evidence for Gurney's alleged discovery, but the verdict of accidental death was at least regarded by some at the time as a cover-up. The suicidally minded Alice James, invalid sister of Henry and William, writing in her diary in August 1889 says, "They say there is little doubt that Mr. Edmund Gurney committed suicide. What a pity to hide it, every educated person who kills himself does something towards lessening the superstition" (quoted in Edel 1964: 52).

14. See Latour (1987). Electricity is often portrayed at the time as simultaneously mysterious and commonplace, useful as an explanation for anything otherwise incomprehensible, but not easily explainable itself. "Perhaps the classic story in this vein was about the student who, asked to define electricity, said he used to know but had forgotten. 'How sad', replied his weary professor, 'the only man who knew what electricity was has forgotten'" (quoted in Marvin 1988: 47).

15. D. D. Home was the one medium who was never discovered in fraud of any kind. See Gauld (1968) for a discussion of the SPR's change from investigating physical mediums to investigating mental mediums.

16. Gauld reveals the assumptions underlying this scenario in his discussion of the medium Eusapia Palladino and sittings carried out at Myers's estate in Cambridge, Leckhampton House: "what points of contact could there possibly have been between the ignorant and earthy Eusapia, who was liable upon awakening from her trances to throw herself into the arms of the nearest male sitter with unmistakable intent, and a group of earnest and highly educated enquirers into the inmost secrets of the Cosmos?" (Gauld 1968: 240). It is precisely their literal, physical points of contact which interest me.

17. As Alex Owen describes it: "Mary Rosina Showers had a threaded needle passed through the pierced hole in her left ear and was thus attached via five yards of thread, to the outside of the cabinet where every movement of the cotton was visible. Florence Cook submitted to a test in which she completed an electric circuit so that any significant movement on her part would register on a galvanometer" (Owen 1990: 69).

18. Also see Con Coroneos (1995) for a fascinating analysis of Gesare Lombroso's investigations of Eusapia Palladino: "Not only was she subject to rigorous control throughout the séance (special ropes, continuous contact, etc.) but after the séance had ended she would be weighed and measured, internally examined, her temperature would be taken, her excreta checked and her perspiration examined for changes in chemical composition. Bodily abnormality could thus be read symptomatically, providing an index for understanding what was unavailable by direct examination" (Coroneos 1995: 12–13).

19. Wilde was familiar with the work of the SPR as he shows when he makes fun of *Phantasms of the Living* in "The Decay of Lying," first published January

1889. He complains about the drab nature that even hallucinations have taken on today: "why, even sleep has played us false, and has closed up the gates of ivory, and opened the gates of horn. The dreams of the great middle classes of this country, as recorded in Mr. Myers's two bulky volumes on the subject and in the Transactions of the Psychical Society, are the most depressing things that I have ever read. There is not even a fine nightmare among them. They are commonplace, sordid, and tedious" (Wilde 1994: 1089).

20. See Michael Warner (1990) for a brilliant critique of psychoanalytic thinking on homosexuality and its inevitable collapse into a solipsistic economy of the same. Elizabeth Guzynski's 1993 unpublished paper "'Homo-Narcissism' and the 1890s" extends Warner's ideas in an analysis of *Teleny* to which I am greatly indebted.

21. In an article called "A Thought-Reader's Experiences", Stuart Cumberland argues that women make bad thought transference subjects: " ... with the natural perversity of her sex, she will commence to think of everything or everybody in the room, or perplex herself with the thought what Mrs. A. thinks of her, or what Miss B. would do in her place, or whether Mr. C. is of opinion she is making an exhibition of herself. With such thoughts running like wild-fire through her mind there is no room for that dominant idea which the operator is in search of" (Cumberland 1886: 883). Cumberland's methods were disdained by the Society for Psychical Research as he relied on physical contact with his subjects and thus opened himself up to the suspicion of muscle-reading. But his supposition that women's minds are too full of other subjects, primarily their own narcissism, to concentrate on one subject for long enough to be effectively "read" is a fascinating one in the light of my somewhat schematic assignment of the séance as a primarily feminine space and the telepathy experiment as a primarily masculine one.

References

Anon. (1881–1882), "Objects of the Society," *Proceedings of the Society for Psychical Research,* I: 3–4.

Anon. (1882–1883), "First Report on Thought-Reading," *Proceedings of the Society for Psychical Research,* I: 13–34.

Barrett, W. (1917), *On the Threshold of the Unseen,* 2nd edn, rev, London: Kegan Paul.

Barrett, W., Massey, C. C., Moses, R. W. S., Podmore, F., Gurney, E. and Myers, F. W. H. (1882–1883), "Report of the Literary Committee," *Proceedings of the Society for Psychical Research,* I: 116–155.

Barrow, L. (1986), *Independent Spirits: Spiritualism and English Plebeians, 1850–1910,* London: Routledge & Kegan Paul.

Borch-Jacobsen, M. (1988), *The Freudian Subject,* trans. C. Porter, Stanford, CA: Stanford University Press.

Castle, T. (1995), *The Female Thermometer: Eighteenth Century Culture and the Invention of the Uncanny,* Oxford: Oxford University Press.

Coroneos, C. (1995), "The Cult of *Heart of Darkness,*" *Essays on Criticism,* 45: 1–23.

Cumberland, S. (1886), "A Thought-Reader's Experiences," *Nineteenth Century,* 20: 867–885.

Derrida, J. (1987), *The Postcard,* trans. A. Bass, Chicago, IL: University of Chicago Press.

Edel, L. (ed.) (1964), *The Diary of Alice James,* Middlesex: Penguin Books.

Edison, T. A. (1948), *The Diary and Sundry Observations of Thomas Alva Edison,* New York: Philosophical Library.

Freud, S. ([1911] 1953), "Dreams and Occultism," in *The Standard Edition of the Complete Psychological Works of Sigmund Freud,* ed. and trans. J. Strachey, vol. 22, London: Hogarth Press, pp. 31–56.

Freud, S. (1914), "On Narcissism," *SE,* XIV: 67–102.

Gauld, A. (1968), *The Founders of Psychical Research,* London: Routledge & Kegan Paul Ltd.

Ginzburg, C. (1983), "Morelli, Freud and Sherlock Holmes: Clues and Scientific Method," in U. Eco and T. A. Sebeok (eds), *The Sign of Three: Dupin, Holmes, Pierce,* Bloomington, IN: Indiana University Press, pp. 81–118.

Gurney, E., Myers, F. W. H. and Podmore, F. ([1886] 1970), *Phantasms of the Living,* 2 vols, Gainesville, FL: Scholars' Facsimiles & Reprints.

Guzynski, E. (1993), "'Homo-Narcissism' and the 1890s," unpublished paper.

Hall, T. (1964), *The Strange Case of Edmund Gurney,* London: Gerald Duckworth & Co. Ltd.

Haynes, R. (1982), *The Society for Psychical Research,* London: Mcdonald & Co.

James, W. (1896), "Presidential Address," *Proceedings of the Society for Psychical Research,* XII: 4–7.

Jones, E. (1955), *The Life and Work of Sigmund Freud,* vols II and III, New York: Basic Books Inc.

King, P. (1988), "Early Divergences between the Psycho-Analytical Societies in London and Vienna," in E. Timms and N. Segal (eds), *Freud in Exile: Psychoanalysis and Its Vicissitudes,* New Haven, CT: Yale University Press, pp. 124–133.

Kipling, R. (1920), "Wireless," in *Traffics and Discoveries,* New York: Doubleday, Page & Co.

Kittler, F. (1987), "Gramophone, Film, Typewriter," *October,* 41: 101–118.

Kittler, F. (1990), *Discourse Networks, 1800/1900,* trans. Michael Metteer with Chris Gullens, Stanford, CA: Stanford University Press.

Latour, B. (1987), *Science in Action,* Cambridge, MA: Harvard University Press.

LeBon, G. (1976), *The Crowd,* London: Penguin Books Ltd.

Marvin, C. (1988), *When Old Technologies Were New*, Oxford: Oxford University Press.

Myers, F. W. H. (1885), "Automatic Writing," *Proceedings of the Society for Psychical Research*, III: 1–63.

Myers, F. W. H. (1891–1892), "General Characteristics of Subliminal Messages," *Proceedings of the Society for Psychical Research*, VII: 298–355.

Myers, F. W. H. (1893), *Science and a Future Life, with Other Essays*, London: Macmillan.

Myers, F. W. H. (1903), *Human Personality and Its Survival of Bodily Death*, London: Longmans, Green & Co.

Neider, C. (ed.) (1963), *The Complete Essays of Mark Twain*, New York: Doubleday & Company, Inc.

Nye, R. (1975), *The Origins of Crowd Psychology: Gustave LeBon and the Crisis of Mass Democracy in the Third Republic*, London: Sage Publications Ltd.

Oppenheim, J. (1985), *The Other World: Spiritualism and Psychical Research in England, 1850–1914*, Cambridge: Cambridge University Press.

Owen, A. (1990), *The Darkened Room: Women, Power and Spiritualism in Late Victorian England*, Philadelphia, PA: University of Pennsylvania Press.

Pierce, A. H. and Podmore, F. (1895), "Subliminal Self or Unconscious Cerebration?" *Proceedings of the Society for Psychical Research*, XI: 317–332.

Ronell, A. (1989), *The Telephone Book*, Lincoln, NE: University of Nebraska Press.

Royle, N. (1990), *Telepathy and Literature*, Oxford: Basil Blackwell Ltd.

Seltzer, M. (1992), *Bodies and Machines*, New York: Routledge.

Sidgwick, A. and Sidgwick, E. M. (1906), *Henry Sidgwick: A Memoir*, London: Macmillan & Co, Ltd.

Sidgwick, E. (1938), *Mrs Henry Sidgwick*, London: Sidgwick and Jackson, Ltd.

Sidgwick, H. (1882–1883), "President's Address," *Proceedings of the Society for Psychical Research*, I: 65–69.

Sidgwick, H. (1888–1889), "President's Address," *Proceedings of the Society for Psychical Research*, V: 271–278.

Stein, R. D. (1968), "The Impact of the Psychical Research Movement on the Literary Theory and Literary Criticism of Frederic W. H. Myers," Ph.D. dissertation, Northwestern University.

Stevenson, R. L. ([1886] 1981), *Dr Jekyll and Mr Hyde*, New York: Bantam Books.

Stoker, B. ([1897] 1965), *Dracula*, New York: Signet Classics.

Tarde, G. (1903), *The Laws of Imitation*, trans. E. C. Parsons, New York: Henry Holt and Co.

Turner, F. M. (1974), *Between Science and Religion: The Reaction to Scientific Naturalism in Late Victorian England*, New Haven, CT: Yale University Press.

Twain, M. (1884), "Mark Twain on Thought Transference," *Journal of the Society for Psychical Research*, I: 166–167.

Twain, M. (1892), "Letter to F. W. H. Myers, 12 January," Myers Papers, Wren Library, Trinity College, Cambridge University.

Twain, M. (1963a), "Mental Telegraphy," in C. Neider (ed.), *The Complete Essays of Mark Twain,* New York: Doubleday & Company, Inc., pp. 70–87.

Twain, M. (1963b), "The First Writing-Machines," in C. Neider (ed.), *The Complete Essays of Mark Twain,* New York: Doubleday & Company, Inc., pp. 324–326.

Twain, M. (1982), *A Connecticut Yankee in King Arthur's Court,* R. A. Ensor (ed.), New York: Norton.

Villiers de l'Isle Adam, P. A. M. (1982), *Tomorrow's Eve,* trans. R. M. Evans, Urbana, IL: University of Illinois Press.

Warner, M. (1990), "Homo-Narcissism; or, Heterosexuality," in J. A. Boone and M. Cadden (eds), *Engendering Men: The Question of Male Feminist Criticism,* New York: Routledge, pp. 190–206.

Wilde, O. ([1891] 1994), *The Picture of Dorian Gray,* in *The Complete Works of Oscar Wilde,* Glasgow: HarperCollins.

Wilde, O. (1994), *The Complete Works of Oscar Wilde,* Glasgow: HarperCollins.

Wilde, O., et al. (1986), *Teleny,* London: GMP Publishers Ltd.

Williams, J. P. (1984), "The Making of Victorian Psychical Research: An Intellectual Elite's Approach to the Spiritual World," Ph.D. dissertation, Cambridge University.

Woolf, V. ([1944] 1982), *A Haunted House and Other Short Stories,* London: Harper Collins.

9

Intuition and Reason in the New Age
A Cultural Study of Medical Clairvoyance
Ruth Barcan

In 2005, the U.S. comedian Stephen Colbert popularized the term *truthiness,* using it to describe a culture in which "perception is everything" (2006: np). Facts, he claimed, "matter not at all" to a culture in which the intuitive and the instinctive have come to dominate: "It used to be, everyone was entitled to their own opinion, but not their own facts. But that's not the case anymore" (2006: np). As a form of "gut" knowledge, truthiness is, he claimed, a selfish, emotional quality. He is not alone in identifying or lamenting the rise of a new emotionality in the public sphere and linking it to a resurgence of superstitious, magical, or religious thinking or to a decline in the rational basis of democracy. Al Gore, for example, published *The Assault on Reason* (2007)—an attack on the forces that he alleges "dumbed down" U.S. democracy in the time of Bush. He pointed, as Colbert did, to a presidency based on a hostility to reason and a preference for feel-good falsehood and to a media and public that have largely lost the will for facts and for critical interrogation. Gore's book can be seen as part of a widespread public lament about the status of reason in the modern world, in which the threats to reason are seen as widespread and disparate—ranging from fundamentalism to relativism. On the one hand, public figures like the author and journalist Christopher Hitchens (2007) and the biologist Richard Dawkins (2006) argue that belief in God is both delusional and dangerous. But so too, it seems, is relativism. The philosopher Roger Scruton claims that we are witnessing an assault on reason, led, in a bitter irony, by "the gurus of the new university establishment" (1999: 88)—postmodernists and poststructuralists. The writer and journalist Francis Wheen broadens the list of culprits to include economic rationalists and New Agers, among others, who, alongside fundamentalist Christians, form "an incongruous coalition" (2004: 7) driven by "mumbo jumbo" rather than reason. Clearly, the purveyors of mumbo jumbo don't have much in common. Indeed, they may even be actively hostile to each other, as in the case of New Agers, Christians, and poststructuralists. But they are easily identifiable place-holders for a whole range of contemporary phenomena that are often pointed to only via slippery and, it must be noted, feminized terms like intuition, emotionality, and gut feelings—qualities summed up in Wheen's catastrophic phrase "the sleep of reason" (2004: 7).

This chapter is about one of those terms (intuition) as understood in one of those contexts (the New Age). I am treating the New Age less as a specific religious movement than as a pervasive popular spirituality inextricably interwoven with (though not reducible to) alternative medicine.[1] I focus on a particular metaphysical healing practice—medical intuition, also known as medical clairvoyance—in order to explore the New Age's version of the "sixth sense," and its relation to reason. Many might wonder why I have chosen to explore such a fringe form of alternative therapy. I do so not in order to debunk it (a skeptical critique being commonsensical and therefore redundant), nor to judge its medical effectiveness, but because I think the popular discourse of the "sleep of reason" makes it an important time to put reason in dialogue with its supposed others, in specific contexts. Here, I want to consider how the practice of medical intuition configures relations between reason and intuition and, further, to understand how this configuration in turn relies on a particular body and sensory model that Westerners are finding increasingly appealing, as evidenced by the escalating public participation in alternative medicine. I have considered the social workings of intuitive medicine as a clandestine medical practice elsewhere (Barcan 2006). Here, I am interested in its conceptual and epistemological underpinnings, which are important because they make visible assumptions that are at play, perhaps more subtly, in other forms of alternative medicine. And since they are at play in alternative medicine they are, in fact, tacitly implicated in a huge array of medical encounters, since alternative medicine is increasingly intermeshed with the medical mainstream. Medical intuition, then, is worthy of study in its specific context (the rise of alternative medicine), where it is symbolically, if not substantively, central,[2] as well as in a broader context—public debates about the place of reason in postmodernity.

While medical intuition remains relatively clandestine, alternative medicine more generally is a highly visible and significant phenomenon, involving transformations right across the social fabric—medically, economically, philosophically, spiritually, and culturally. The use of so-called CAM (Complementary and Alternative Medicine) is expanding exponentially in the West. Surveys in the United States, the United Kingdom, and other Western nations consistently show that almost half the population uses CAM, and that there are more visits annually to alternative therapists than to orthodox primary carers (Institute of Medicine 2005: 34). At the same time, then, that critics and skeptics denounce the rise of the New Age as the triumph of irrationality and the burgeoning of alternative therapies as a "pernicious" trend (Donnelly et al. 1985: 539), millions of people in the West make use of them. My interest in the New Age/alternative conception of intuition has arisen both out of my own often enthusiastic experiences of alternative medicine (both as an amateur practitioner of reiki and as a client of many therapies, including intuitive medicine) and out of a larger research project on alternative therapies, in which I focus on them as sensory practices. The analysis that follows is based on a series of interviews with medical psychics and spiritual healers that I carried out as part of this broader project, as well as on readings of a number of New Age texts.[3]

I begin with a brief outline of the practice in question. Medical intuition is a specific clairvoyant practice: the use of clairvoyance for the purposes of "medical" diagnosis and/or treatment or healing. While most clairvoyants answer questions about health and illness, not all specialize in health. Those who do may call themselves medical intuitives, medical clairvoyants, or medical psychics, or other perhaps more euphemistic titles like intuitive counselor. Medical intuitives give a clairvoyant "reading" of their clients' health, whether in general terms or focused on a particular issue. The client may be present in the room or the process may occur *in absentia*—for example, over the telephone or by email. Physical touch is not required. Medical intuitives detect medical problems; they carry out intuitive "diagnosis," whether or not they use orthodox anatomical or medical labels. Some, though not all, also suggest treatment regimes (e.g., by "prescribing" naturopathic remedies) and some also carry out healing techniques as part of the consultation, for example, by using visualization, which is where the process may overlap with spiritual healing. Some practitioners see their central role as the passing on of information; others integrate information and healing. Some even work alongside orthodox practitioners, albeit usually discreetly. Intuitive practitioners share a set of principles that include a commitment to holism, a goal of "client" empowerment, the according of a central role to the emotions, and, most important for my purposes here, the valorizing and centralizing of intuition as a mode of knowing and as a diagnostic and healing tool.

As a New Age healing practice, intuitive medicine is bound up in a broader project of personal and ultimately "planetary" transformation, a dual project that many consider to be the defining characteristic of the New Age (Melton 1990: xiii). The ultimate claim of the New Age movement is (or perhaps *was*)[4] that we are witnessing an epochal shift—the dawning of a new consciousness that will result in a new era of harmony. This transformation, it is argued, can come about only through the transformation of the *self,* through a shift in individual consciousness. Altering one's consciousness is understood to involve not just changing one's beliefs, but also unlearning habitual modes of perception, and cultivating new forms, through practices such as meditation, bodywork, or other forms of spiritual apprenticeship.

The transformative project of the New Age is thus bound up in a reformation of the body and, as Jay Johnston (2008) argues, of perceptual practice. Self-transformation comes about as a result of ritual, meditative, or other spiritual practices in which the subject's self-knowledge and his or her ability to "apprehend invisible exchanges and interrelations" (Johnston 2008: 89) are slowly enhanced, via the development of the intuitive faculty. The idea of perceptual (re)training emanates from a model of embodiment in which the body is understood not as singular, but as a hierarchically organized set of bodies, most of which are invisible to ordinary perception. This so-called subtle model of the body and the centralizing of intuition go hand in hand, since "subtle bodies have traditionally been presented as apprehended by intuitive modes of knowledge" (Johnston 2008: 1). Such perceptual faculties need to be patiently cultivated by a lifetime of spiritual practice. A model of anatomy, a mode of perception, and a project of self-realization are thus inextricably intertwined. The main conduit for subtle body models into the modern West was the Theosophical Society in the late nineteenth century, which is commonly thought to have adopted and adapted Hindu and Buddhist esoteric teachings and body schemas. The influence of Eastern religions on Theosophy is perhaps a little less direct than commonly suggested, however; religious scholar Wouter Hanegraaff argues that the debt of its founder, Helena Blavatsky, to an "Oriental perspective" is "more apparent than real" (1998: 455). His account of the genesis of the Theosophical Society's conception of subtle bodies suggests that Eastern sources were initially incorporated at one remove, via a "synthesis" of three components: esoteric traditions, especially the occult sciences; nineteenth-century science; and the new mythography (1998: 455). The Theosophical approach was, then, "basically eclectic" (1998: 455)—like that of the New Age it was so heavily to influence. The Theosophical and Anthroposophical versions of subtle anatomy provide the direct source for the New Age (Hanegraaff 1998: 222), which has promulgated them in a typically "eclectic" and "unsystematic" way (1998: 223), with the result that there is no consensus in the New Age literature about the details of subtle anatomy, and even less in contemporary popular culture, where the idea of a body made of "energy," along with some elements of the lexicon, such as "auras" and "chakras," now circulates quite widely. Moreover, within New Age literature, intricate anatomical schemas may at times coexist uneasily with the dualist schemas of Western metaphysics that their advocates have ostensibly abandoned.

A similar looseness characterizes the New Age conception of intuition, which wavers between the spiritual and the psychological, reflecting what is, for Hanegraaff, a distinctive feature of the New Age—its rupturing of what is normally the "absolutely crucial" distinction between religion and psychology (1998: 196). Hanegraaff describes this blurring as a "strong tendency towards a *psychologizing of religion combined with a sacralization of psychology*" (1998: 197, original italics). New Age writings on intuition may reflect elements of Eastern mysticism, Western occultism, Freudian psychoanalysis, and contemporary psychology. A loose idea of "gut feelings," for example, connects to favored psychological themes of communication and expressivity. But New Age ideas of the expressive body go far beyond the idea of a knowing gut. In New Age metaphysics, the *entire body* is imagined as inherently expressive, receiving, storing, and transmitting information. "The body is always talking to us, if we will only take the time to listen," says New Age self-help guru Louise L. Hay (1987: 127). It both speaks and hears: "Every cell within your body responds to every single thought you think and every word you speak" (1987: 127). The New Age alternative health project thus becomes one of listening to, translating, and interpreting the "messages" sent by every single cell in your body (and of trying to send only positive messages in return). For proponents of this metaphysical view of the body and illness, health becomes a lifelong project of cultivating the skills necessary to interpret one's body, with varying degrees of external help. Hay has produced a minutely detailed dictionary of the metaphorical "meanings" of bodily symptoms and illness (*Heal Your Body* [1988]). But ultimately, most practitioners believe that the highest goal is to cultivate one's *own* intuition. In this, spiritual ideas of enlightenment as a lifelong path intersect with the American ethic of individual self-reliance. But understanding the body may also require the aid of skilled transla-tors. The kind of "gut" knowledge clients hope to receive from these translators is not some touchy-feely hunch, some communication from a chatty gut, but precise answers to precise questions like "Do I have any food allergies?", "How are my thy-roid levels?", "What is the source of my back pain and how can it be helped?" These are questions too significant, and too precise, for any old gut to answer.

This intuition, then, is not at all the same as Stephen Colbert's "truthy" intuitive-ness, where facts no long matter. Rather, it is a quest to access "higher" truths, a quest that sits somewhat at odds with the New Age's notorious "epistemological individualism" (Wallis 1979: 45)—that is, the belief in personal rather than objec-tive or universal truth, most infamously summed up in the New Age dictum that we "create our own reality." The tension between the New Age's individualism and relativism on the one hand and its holism on the other leaves it with a somewhat contradictory idea of truth. Despite this, it is problematic to assume that the contem-porary New Age search for enlightenment is a *complete* repudiation of that "other" Enlightenment, and that the New Age's infamous valorization of emotions and intu-ition is tantamount to the abandonment of reason. Indeed, Hanegraaff argues against the "common assumption" that occult or mystical traditions and phenomena are "not only opposed to, but *incompatible* with the values of the Enlightenment" (1998: 411, original italics).[5] He notes that despite the Enlightenment's seeming emphasis on "reason as the *exclusive* foundation for reliable knowledge," its doctrines none-theless maintained "an unshaken belief in the reality of natural law and of eternal principles which apply to humanity in all times and places" (1998: 411, original italics). In a more popular vein, Francis Wheen, paraphrasing Foucault, reminds us that the Enlightenment "was not so much an ideology as an attitude": "a presumption that certain truths about mankind, society and the natural world could be perceived, whether through deduction or observation, and that the discovery of these truths would transform the quality of life" (2004: 3).

The New Age concept of enlightenment shares three of these four characteristics: a belief in an ultimate reality and natural laws (a belief nonetheless complicated by the notorious relativism and individualism of the New Age)[6]; a faith that truths are know-able (hence the injunction to discover one's true self); and a hope that this knowledge will transform the quality of life. Where it differs, crucially, is in the value attached to reason as the best means of accessing truth. Reason is understood as a useful tool, but one that needs to be complemented or even overruled by intuition.

As this chapter will make clear, clients of intuitive medicine are still seeking facts—indeed, one might claim they are seeking the kind of *certainty* even biomed-icine rarely claims to provide—but they don't see reason or logic as always the best means to access those facts. While this search for certainty might sound like fundamentalism, I suspect that for many users of alternative medicine it represents less a wholesale overthrow of reason than a philosophical and/or cognitive strategy involving the relativization of reason—its relegation to being one faculty among many. This can be thought of as a form of philosophy in the everyday—a practical process involving complex mental negotiations to determine, for example, *when* it is best to prioritize reason over other modes of knowing, when one should visit a medical intuitive and when a GP, or how to discriminate between "divine" intuition and any old gut feeling. Which faculty or faculties one uses to *make* such negotiations is, of course, part of the conundrum. This is why the *training* of intuitive perception is a core part of spiritual and religious systems in which intuition features. But the broadening of the New Age into popular culture and the marketization of alternative therapies mean that many engagements with metaphysical/spiritual healing techniques take place as discrete commodified transactions, sometimes experimental, rather than in the context of systematic lifelong pedagogies. Thus, the place of reason in making medical choices in a pluralist medical environment is hard to determine.

The remainder of this chapter explores the New Age understanding of intuition in detail, by addressing three questions about how intuition is conceived and mobilized in intuitive medicine: How is intuition conceived in these practices? What is its relation to reason? What is its relation to "everyday" or rationally conceived intuition? There are two further questions I don't have space to canvass in depth here, but which are important to flag. The first is intuition's relation to the other bodily senses, a complex topic that I will explore at length in the larger project from which these current reflections have emerged. The other, which is connected to the first, and which I do touch more on here, though still not in as much detail as I would like, is the importance of gender. [7] For at the heart of the problematic I have set out to address are questions about different modes of acquiring truth and the relative usefulness and reliability of different forms of knowledge, questions that are, as it is commonplace but not insignificant to point out, deeply gendered. As Genevieve Lloyd (1984: 2) states, in the mainstream Western philosophical tradition, the feminine has been "associated with what rational knowledge transcends, dominates or simply leaves behind." Reason has thus played an important role in this tradition not only in excluding women, but in actually constituting femininity through that exclusion (Lloyd 1984: 106).

The New Age Conception of Intuition

For New Agers and alternative health advocates, "living without intuition is like living without the east point on your compass" (Schulz 1998: 360). Intuition is the "autopilot" (Schulz 1998: 24) that steers us, a faculty that is simultaneously sacred ("divine revelation" [Shumsky 1996], "the language of the soul" [Schulz 1998: 116]), and practical, the "commonest sense" of all (Schulz 1998: 17). It makes sense that clairvoyants and healers tend to think of intuition as a practical capacity. After all, people come to them with problems to be fixed—from sick bodies, to broken cars, to businesses gone wrong. The physician, neuroscientist, and medical intuitive Mona Lisa Schulz, author of a popular book on intuition, frequently emphasizes this practical, useful, nature of intuition. She is clearly keen to demystify it:

> It's counterproductive to think of intuition and intuitiveness in terms of separateness or superiority, or in terms of the supernatural, or even of the offbeat and bizarre. Intuition is simply a sense that's common to each and every one of us. It's neither a magic power nor just the crazy hunches of eccentrics. It's a real down-to-earth capacity that is available to anyone willing to tune in his transmitter and listen in to what's being broadcast. The information it offers us is practical, and it can immeasurably improve and enrich our lives. In this light, intuition is common sense operating on the most fundamental, spontaneous level. (1998: 26)

According to its advocates, the advantages of intuition are that it is accurate,[8] may work against habitual thinking, and is faster. For example, one medical psychic I interviewed ("Mary") considers that medically it is often "a fast track to finding the answers." Intuition, then, is understood as providing *accurate* information by non-rational means: "Intuition occurs when we directly perceive *facts* outside the range of the usual five senses and independently of any reasoning process. As one scientist defined it, intuition is 'the process of reaching accurate conclusions based on inadequate information' (Schulz 1998: 19, my emphasis).

So when critics accuse New Agers of trying to demonstrate that "objective truth is the unattainable bugaboo of thick-headed rationalists" (Schultz 1988: 342), they are only partly correct. For despite the centrality of philosophical relativism to New Age thought (we all create our own reality; things are true because, and only if, we believe them to be so), other elements in the discourse assume the existence of objective truths and celebrate the human ability to access them via intuition. This willingness to accommodate contradiction (we create our own reality but a clairvoyant can help us access the truth of ourselves) points not only to the eclecticism of the New Age, a "movement" comprising "a bewilderingly diverse array of practices and beliefs" (Basil 1988: 11), but also to the pragmatic tenor of the U.S. cultural milieu in which it developed. (It may also, as I suggest in the conclusion, typify a more pervasive postmodern skepticism about the existence of universal truths that results in more contingent and contextual philosophical "performances.")

The conjoining of the sacred and the practical is not just a recent grafting but has been a feature of many of the spiritual movements that helped give rise to the New Age, especially in the United States. Gordon Melton's history of the New Age stresses the "scientific" pretensions of the major nineteenth-century U.S. traditions that fed into it—Swedenborgianism, mesmerism, spiritualism—and the pragmatic vein of another of its precursors, the Transcendentalism of Ralph Waldo Emerson

(1988: 36–9). Emerson integrated Eastern idealist metaphysics with prime American values like "individualism, personal responsibility, and the drive to get ahead in life," creating in the process "a workable mysticism" (1988: 38). Other American variants of spiritualism, namely Christian Science and its offshoot Free Thought, also turned metaphysics to practical purposes—first healing, then material wealth and happiness (1988: 39). According to Melton, the last major nineteenth-century influence, Theosophy, broadened its scope back out from health, wealth, and happiness into the aim of producing "a vast panoramic vision of the cosmos" (1988: 35).

Today, interplay between the universalism of esoteric metaphysics and the individualism of the modern West is found in the widespread understanding of intuition as an innate and universal gift—but one that is able to be developed in some people more than others. The intuitive counselor Mary, for example, says:

> I feel that everybody has the ability to tap into this universal unconsciousness as it were. I think that given a certain amount of focusing as in training, these gifts can be developed within each and every one of us. I think it's like with any gift, there are some brilliant artists, they have a natural talent. ... So I think that some people will take more naturally to it once they're fine-tuned and finely honed and others could spend all of their life trying to achieve it and wouldn't. But basically I think everybody has the potential for developing this sort of ability. Because I think it's an innate part of human beings. And I don't think we use it.

Jonas Salk, inventor of the polio vaccine and author of a book on the nature of reality, conceives of intuition as something that can be "developed and cultivated" (1983: 79) through training. The notion of spiritual practice as a lifelong project of gradual enlightenment, usually in relationship to "a beloved teacher" or guru (Cope 1999: 143), is a feature of many Eastern spiritual traditions. Spiritual techniques are understood as potentially dangerous, needing to be nurtured in relationship rather than in solitary practice (1999: 144). At the turn of the twentieth century, the British Theosophist Charles Webster Leadbeater, author of a book on clairvoyance, lamented the fact that the vast majority of European clairvoyants were untrained. He claimed that lack of training meant that they usually "fall very far short" of what systematically learned clairvoyance can achieve (1918: 50). He pointed to shortfalls in the degree of clairvoyance, the variety of ways it can manifest, its permanence, and above all its precision (1918: 50). The idea of training fitted very well with ascetic U.S. values like patience, discipline, and hard work, and with Theosophy's evolutionary narrative of progressive human spiritual development. This narrative occasionally took a racist form within Theosophy (its goal of developing a universal brotherhood of humanity notwithstanding), though the nature and extent of this racism is much disputed.[9] Either way, the New Age has taken up the humanist strand of Theosophy's evolutionary narrative rather than its racist potential. Intuition is seen as a universal human potential, and those seeking enlightenment are urged to "let go of all critical judgments about race, sex, physical characteristics, and so forth, and just see the divine beauty in each person" (Shumsky 1996: 91).[10]

As a popular, commodified, and heterogeneous set of practices, the contemporary New Age is, almost by definition, much slipperier about the question of training than its esoteric forebears. Participants in New Age culture may encounter intuition in a quite specialist way as a discipline requiring years of training or in a looser form more friendly to the market and to pop psychology—as a kind of gut feeling. Yoga and meditation are the most obvious places to find it in its former guise, but some New Age writers do emphasize the need for training. Susan Shumsky, for example, writes that you need training to differentiate the voice of spirit from other "inner" voices (1996: 24), and her book is a set of techniques that include some for telling the difference between "true intuition" and the myriad of other internal voices that characterize mental processes. Other New Age–inspired accounts of intuition, however, are quite casual—reducing it to a question of whether something "feels right." By focusing on moments where everyday hunches proved true, some writers erode (intentionally or otherwise) the distinction between a trained and disciplined capacity and one always at the ready. Mona Lisa Schulz's book *Awakening Intuition,* for example, even while it makes use of subtle anatomy, which signals its debt to spiritual traditions in which apprenticeship plays a large role, occasionally veers toward a more popular understanding of intuition, as when she says that "hunches, gut feelings, senses, or dreams" are "all the same thing" (1998: 19). Since this slipperiness is found even among the advocates of intuition, it naturally appears among its critics, who deride the individualism, relativism, and irrationality of the New Age and/or pop psychological advocacy of intuition over rationality as a basis for decision making: "How easy would life be if we could 'trust our gut' whenever we face a problem. No need for logic or rationality. Just act on instincts and everything will work out fine. But as anyone who's ever given their computer or television a good thump knows, your gut is a moron" (Lallo 2007: 9).

The sloppy advocacy of "gut feeling" is part of a quick-fix culture, and reflects the decontextualization and cultural translation of spiritual concepts and practices that occurred when Eastern concepts were brought to the West from the nineteenth century on. It also reflects the more recent changes brought about by the diffusion of the New Age project of personal and planetary transformation into a broader popular culture (Sutcliffe 2006: 160). This diffusion has been inseparable from their increasing marketization, and hence from a host of familiar processes of abstraction, reduction, and proliferation, including the separation of specific spiritual practices from their religious contexts and their circulation more freely as "methodologies" (Melton 1988: 42).

In this context, it becomes too easy for popular discussions of intuition to imply that what is at stake is the ability of any old gut to answer any old question. So, enjoyable and heartening as rationalist rejoinders to New Age banality can sometimes be, it's important to recognize that they do not in reality address the question of whether all New Age practices and conceptions of intuition are the same as this easily satirizable "gut feeling"—whether, to put it differently, our moronic gut is one and the same as the New Age's wise inner guide, let alone the highly trained perception of the yogi or the experienced meditator. Here, I will go out on an academic limb and state that, based on my own experiences over twenty years of sustained interest in alternative therapies, I do in fact believe that there are non-rational ways of knowing—including accurate, factual ways of knowing—whose origins are not clear but that aren't reducible to what Hubert and Stuart Dreyfus call "pattern recognition" (quoted in Benner and Tanner 1987: 24). When it comes to debates about intuition, I am intellectually and politically concerned less by the positing of some as yet little understood perceptual capacity (for which spirit may or may not be an appropriate metaphor) than by the populist elision of the cultural in the name of the universal. I see intuition as (mysteriously) non-, extra-, or supra-rational, but not supra-*cultural*. I do think there are ways of accurate knowing whose mechanisms, including biological mechanisms, are as yet poorly understood, but I wouldn't for a moment think they are acultural. So I'd agree heartily with those critics of the New Age who point to the fatuousness of the idea of something "simply" feeling right:

> Unfortunately for the "if it feels good it must be true" school of New Age philosophy, we've all had experiences in life with ideas that sounded and felt good only to turn out to be either wrong or only partly true. The flat earth theory felt just fine to millions of ancient Babylonians, all of whom turned out to be in error. (Schultz 1988: 350)

In addition to the question of the cultural production of knowledge in this broad sense, it's also obvious that even on a psychoanalytical level the ability to discriminate between accurate, if mysteriously obtained, information and all the other products of psyche—emotions, rationalizations, projections, assumptions—must clearly lie at the heart of any project of perceptual retraining. In this, intuitive ability is not, ironically, so different from reason. We spend years learning how to reason, including being trained in specific forms, styles, and vocabularies of reasoning. Even so, no one, when they reason, can be absolutely certain that their conclusions have been derived free of the workings of habit, assumptions, prejudice, cultural limitations, or, for that matter, "intuition." There may be no pure intuition, but there is no pure reason either—and here, perhaps, my poststructuralist and alternative leanings intersect, making me, in fact, *doubly* culpable as an instrument of mumbo jumbo. But I have not yet abandoned reason.

Intuition and Reason

In the Introduction to the collection *Not Necessarily the New Age,* Robert Basil baldly states that the New Age represents a "flight from the premises of science and materialism" (1988: 22). A few pages later, however, his lead contributor, Gordon Melton, states that the New Age, as merely the latest phase in the Western occult/ metaphysical tradition, is actually the by-product of the Enlightenment—not, as one might expect, because it is a form of resistance to it, but because the occult tradition, largely destroyed by Protestantism, needed a new vehicle after the demise of alchemy, and found it in the science of the eighteenth and nineteenth centuries (1988: 36). The contemporary New Age is not, as Basil argues, "a large-scale re-nunciation of science" (1988: 21)—at least, not in any straightforward sense. On the contrary, it uses science as "a major vehicle" (Melton 1988: 36).[11] Anyone with the most passing acquaintance of New Age literature would be familiar with its selective and strategic uptake of any science that seems to suit its purposes—be that psychoneuroimmunology, neuroscience or, most infamously, quantum phys-ics. The relation of the New Age with rationality itself is therefore quite complex. Hanegraaff, for example, considers that New Age religion is not consistently anti-intellectual so much as "trans-intellectual" (1998: 221).

On the surface, intuitive medicine appears simply to invert the valuation of the mainstream binary between reason and intuition. Intuitive knowledge is considered the highest knowledge of all. The knowledge it provides is universal, non-judgmental, true—all the attributes traditionally associated with reason. Rationality is seen at best as useful, at worst as deceptive, an *impediment* to higher knowledge. Knowledge acquired intuitively may contradict the seeming truths arrived at by reasoning. The intuitive counselor Mary claims that insights derived from intuition frequently go *counter* to logic, rationality, or experience:

> Everything that I know about the psychic realm or the spiritual realm or healing or health or whatever you call it—probably 99 percent of what I actually know, logically know—is given psychically. Often I have to unlearn what I think I knew from other means. I mean, I've learned so much about who we are physically and mentally and emotionally and the intricate workings of how we're put together which no textbook could ever teach.

That reason might be a limited means of accessing truth and, moreover, that of all things it should be intuition that is seen as the channel for universal, impartial knowledge, is, to paraphrase Genevieve Lloyd, a philosophical scandal and a gender outrage, since in the mainstream Western philosophical tradition we aspire "to a Reason common to all, transcending the contingent historical circumstances which differentiate minds from one another" (Lloyd 1984: ix), but which has been associ-ated with masculinity. Lloyd's study of reason in the mainstream Western philo-sophical tradition begins with Plato, whose early works, those in which Socratic influence is strongest, were marked by a stark binary between a unitary soul and the body (1984: 6). The soul is depicted as trapped in a burdensome body, longing for freedom. The senses drag the soul back down into the life of confusion, but Reason can aid the soul to regain its final immortality:

The soul which cultivates Reason during life can expect at death to be released from error, folly, fear and fierce passions, living with the "divine, and the immortal, and the wise." The soul which does not pursue this "deliverance and purification" during life is in contrast, defiled by contact with the body and is at death "weighed down and dragged back to the visible world," taking root in another body "like a seed which is sown." During life, Plato concluded, the god-like rational soul should rule over the slave-like mortal body. (1984: 6)[12]

In Plato's later work, the struggle is not between a rational soul and the distracting senses, so much as a struggle *internal* to the soul—between its superior and inferior parts. But in both these versions, life is characterized by an internal struggle for dominance between warring tendencies. These tendencies were deeply and explicitly gendered: "From the beginnings of [Western] philosophical thought, femaleness was symbolically associated with what Reason supposedly left behind" (Lloyd 1984: 2). Not that this gendering was without complexity (see Spelman 1982). But it was entrenched, especially as Christian thinkers elaborated the theme of the divided soul's struggle in ways that "connected it explicitly with the theme of man's rightful domination of woman" (1984: 7).

Lloyd's discussion of Plato makes it clear that his view of reason is connected to a gendered model of the body, of knowledge, and of power. The New Age view of intuition is likewise connected to a model of the body—in this case, a non-dualist one. For despite a commonsensical framing of reason and intuition as *opposites,* intuitive medicine is, as mentioned earlier, actually based on a more complex model of the body and of knowledge than this—a non-dualist model of the body, in which the self is an organized assemblage of many interpenetrating layers rather than a binary between mind and body. In practices based on this so-called subtle body model, the binary between reason and intuition is therefore caught up in a much more complex epistemological/anatomical system.

The subtle body model, which exists in various forms across a range of religious traditions, including both Western occultism and Eastern religions, such as Sufism, Buddhism, and Hinduism, is an energetic conception of the body in which the body is understood as "comprised of numerous sheaths of matter-consciousness that interpenetrate, overlay, and exceed one another" (Johnston 2008: 3). Perhaps its most well-known lexicon in the modern West is that of *auras,* a term used in this sense since the late nineteenth century, but popularized by the New Age. In recent decades, the countercultural uptake of yoga and Tantric philosophy meant that Sanskrit terms like *chakras* (energy centers in the body) and *kundalini* (the coiled energy at the base of the spine) have become increasingly known in the West. Precise body schemas differ between traditions, but usually outline a body system made up of between five and seven sheaths or bodies arranged hierarchically from the gross physical body to some form of highly spiritual body. In one common Hindu schema, for example, "the" body is made up of five sheaths or *koshas* organized into three bodies or *shariras:* the *annamayakosha* (sheath of food); the *pranamayakosha* (sheath of vital airs); the *manomayakosha* (sheath of mind); the *vijnanamayakosha* (sheath of causal intellect); and the *anandamayakosha* (sheath of pure bliss) (Cope 1999: 68). These bodies are understood to expand outward from the most dense, physical body, but they interpenetrate one another. It is beyond the scope of what I can do here to outline this model in any detail, since there are so many variants (for detailed studies, see Johnston 2008; Tansley 1977). The important point for my purposes is that in any subtle body schema, different ways of knowing are intimately bound up in anatomy itself (as names such as "the emotional body," "the mental body," or "the knowledge body" suggest). Though these bodies, and hence the mode of knowledge they embody, are valued hierarchically (more highly spiritual bodies being "higher" than the gross physical body), each is valued for its place in a *system* rather than a binary opposition. All levels of reality are "conscious" (Brennan 1988: 137). Hence the body is a *knowing* organism and, likewise, modes of knowledge are understood as inherently embodied.

Such schemas complicate the straightforward gendering of different perceptual and cognitive faculties. They have, however, been taken up into a context in which reason and emotion are distinctly gendered, and as a result a gendered dualism permeates alternative discourse (as it arguably existed also in Theosophical discourse itself.)[13] Thus, in the New Age, as in popular culture more broadly, women are commonly seen to be more intuitive than men, a stereotype supported and furthered by the fact that almost all medical intuitives and their clients are women. This would seem simply to signal a classic inversion of value between reason and intuition, with its gendered qualities remaining intact. The following quotation from the intuitive counselor Mary, however, makes it clear that the gendered picture can be a little more complex than that, owing to the influence of the non-dualistic subtle body scheme. In her understanding, emotional and intuitive ability are not the same thing, and a developed intuitive ability is how one is able to be "objective":

> Men make really wonderful psychics. They're so black and white. They don't have the emotional component that a lot of women have to get through before they can deliver the information. ... [F]or example, if we are dealing with somebody who's very ill, got cancer or something, as a female I think we have very highly developed emotional bodies and we tend to empathize probably a bit more than men do. So you really kind of open your heart and you take in the suffering as it were. And you've got to deal with that before you can rise above it and deliver the information to the client. Whereas men can be more objective I think. They don't let their emotions get involved so much. They're just likely to deliver the information—although I'm not really aware of male medical intuitives.

In this account, traditional gender attributes are maintained, but not in a traditional binary. Emotional skill is still seen as a feminine trait, and one that in certain contexts needs to be transcended in the name of objectivity, but it is not conflated with intuition; nor is it seen as the simple Other of reason. Rather, the subtle body schema within which most clairvoyants work, which envisages the self as comprising a multiplicity of mostly invisible bodies rather than a binary opposition between body and mind or body and soul, means that emotion is understood in relation to a hierarchy of ways of being and knowing, rather than as part of a binary. Thus, Mary spoke not of women being "more emotional" than men, but of having "very highly developed emotional bodies"—a concept from the subtle anatomy schema that, it should be noted, recognizes emotionality as an achievement, with its own legitimate part in a complex embodied perceptual schema.[14] Not all medical intuitives separate out emotionality and intuition in quite this way, however. Mona Lisa Schulz, for example, sees emotions as crucial to intuition, considering them a "major component" (1998: 10) of the intuitive network, allied closely with empathy (1998: 30).[15] Even though this alliance of emotion, empathy, and intuition reconnects in a conventionally gendered way the capacities that Mary kept analytically more distinct, Schulz still argues for the necessary interdependence of different cognitive and perceptual faculties. There is no point being good at emotions, she says, if you can't analyze them (1998: 337). Schulz considers intuition a mode of perception rather than a mode of thought (1998: 22), and she argues that a whole range of perceptual and cognitive faculties need to co-operate in the "intuition network."

Residues of dualist thought certainly persist in New Age discourse, reflecting a struggle between the holistic (if hierarchical) subtle body model and the dualism underpinning the predominantly Christian culture into which it has been translated. A gendered metaphor of the *complementarity* of reason and intuition is quite widespread in New Age discourse (see Hanegraaff 1998: 152–3), even in accounts that strive to move beyond binary divisions, such as that of Mona Lisa Schulz. Writing in the late 1990s, Schulz uses the emerging metaphor of the network, but also makes significant use of the conventionally gendered and binary concept of complementarity. But in its more elaborated formulations, New Age metaphysics is often based on something more subtle and more complex than a simple valorization of intuition over reason, or even a model of complementarity. Rather than seeing intuition in dualistic terms as the feminized and denigrated Other to reason, the subtle body model imagines *all* forms of knowing (cognition, intuition, emotions) as inherently embodied and as located less in a simple hierarchy of value than in a complex matrix of ways of knowing. Cultivating intuition thus involves learning to discriminate intuition not just from rational thought but also from *all* elements of "the mental world" (Shumsky 1996: 168)—beliefs, ideologies, subconscious fears, the "ego-chatter of the surface mind" (1996: 168)—as well as from other-worldly communications, such as those coming from "astral entities" (1996: 174). It is precisely such a vision of a manifold anatomy inextricably enmeshed in a complex mix of cognitive and perceptual faculties and situated in a wider cosmos that makes the cultivation of intuition in spiritual traditions as difficult and lifelong a task as the cultivation of intellect is in rationalist institutions, such as the academy.

The upshot of this is that any serious advocate of intuitive medicine does not seek to overthrow reason, but to work with it. Reason is understood as just one human cognitive faculty, undoubtedly an important one, but one with imperialistic tendencies. In therapeutic or spiritual settings (but not necessarily in all life contexts), it should be "managed."[16] All my interviewees argued that the specificity and advantages of different modes of thought should be recognized. They saw intuition as working holistically, especially in contrast to the way that reason has traditionally been understood, as operating via compartmentalization or the breaking down of a problem into its component parts. Jonas Salk considers intuition to be both faster and more sensitive than reason (but not, clearly, to replace it): "Our subjective responses (intuitional) are more sensitive and more rapid than our objective responses (reasoned). This is in the nature of the way the mind works. We first sense and then we reason why" (1983: 79).

As I have argued in detail elsewhere (Barcan 2006), the nature of the Western medical landscape means that all professional medical clairvoyants have had to actively consider, negotiate, and operationalize their relations to orthodox medicine and to the rationality on which it reposes. Their modes of doing this vary, but the practitioners I found most fascinating were those who actively (if largely invisibly) worked across both systems. The clairvoyant Mary thought that it was best to think of medical intuition and orthodox medicine as different areas of competence rather than as directly in competition. She has a number of medical specialists who consult her regularly, mostly for their own ailments but occasionally in relation to their patients. Mainstream medicos would no doubt find this absolutely horrifying—to me it's both intellectually and medically fascinating, despite the host of ethical, intellectual, and political problems it so obviously invites. Mary's vision of an ideal medical system is one in which we could "have the best of both worlds," and in which the advantages and limitations of different medical paradigms could be recognized and accommodated:

Mary: You've got to work with the strictly scientific medical arena as well. I think so.

Ruth: So you think that medical psychics should belong in a separate sphere, as it were, like separating consulting rooms?

Mary: Yes, but possibly working in harmony with each other. Like if I break my leg I'm not going to rush off to a psychic for healing. I'm going to go to a doctor; I want it set. That sort of thing. So there are areas. I think psychics can work well with emotions as long as they're the right psychics. I think they can do a lot of healing with the emotional body and the mental body and I also think that for lots of illnesses psychics can diagnose. I had a client ... who had a son who was very ill so he rang me and asked me what could I see was the cause of the boy's problem. And I tuned in and I said, look he's got glandular fever. So he went and asked for a test for glandular fever and it showed up that's what he had. So it can be something which can be very useful in speeding up the process of diagnosing.

What we see here is the renunciation neither of orthodox biomedicine nor of the scientific rationality on which it is founded, but rather a professional practice based on the active negotiation of different modes of knowing and different institutional contexts.

Special versus Everyday Intuition

Having considered how the New Age conceives of the relation between intuition and reason, I turn now to another way we might interrogate intuition through reason— that is, by a rational analysis of the concept itself. To a rationalist, intuition, if it exists at all, is the name we give to a series of patterns learned through cultural conditioning and experience, and perhaps augmented by heightened empathic abilities. In the words of Miller and McHoul, it "is no more than the inference-making machine used by every member of 'rational society'" (1998: 126). Psychological or spiritual discourse "super-adds" intuition to the sociocultural rules of everyday life, thus turning the ordinary, learned process of daily living into "something extraordinary" (1998: 126). Intuition rationally conceived is a set of naturalized, embodied, largely unrecognized skills able, when analyzed, to be broken down into particular subsets of skills. For example, Hubert and Stuart Dreyfus, in their study of human intuition in the computer age, isolated six discrete aspects of what they term *intuitive judgment:* pattern recognition, similarity recognition, commonsense understanding, skilled know-how, sense of salience, and deliberative rationality (quoted in Benner and Tanner 1987: 23).

This rational conception of intuition has been studied within the nursing literature as part of an implicitly feminist attempt to recognize and validate the skills and experience of expert nurses (see, for example, Benner and Tanner 1987; Schraeder and Fischer 1987).[17] These advocates of intuition do share some features with the New Age writers. For example, nursing theorists Benner and Tanner see intuition as an essential component of humanness, using machines (which infamously lack intuitive ability) as a commonsense pointer to its largely unrecognized centrality in human judgment (1987: 23). They conclude that academic training of nurses has focused on rational calculation to the detriment of intuitive judgment, and that "skilled pattern recognition can be taught" (1987: 30). Moreover, they argue that holistic rather than overly segmentist approaches are the best way to do this (1987: 30). Despite this call for a greater understanding of and respect for expert intuitive judgment, Benner and Tanner differ from the alternative advocates of intuition in that they see intuition as a habitual, embodied form of knowledge born of experience and sensitivity, rather than an innate, sacred perceptual capacity able to be augmented by training. For Benner and Tanner, intuition is non-rational rather than supra-rational.

Perhaps, then, one should argue, as most skeptics do, that the clairvoyant's skill is best understood rationally, as the ability to be particularly subtle and acute at picking up signals from their clients. When I asked my interviewees about the role of experience and "everyday" (by which I mean acquired) intuition in their perceptual abilities, they gave a variety of answers, but unsurprisingly none agreed that their brand of intuition could be reduced to a super-nuanced attention to body language, tone of voice, and so on. At one end of a continuum was Mary, who saw clairvoyant intuition and everyday "intuition" as having nothing in common. She understands her special insights as a spiritual gift that arose, mysteriously, after a major traumatic life event, and they came, to use her metaphor, as a complete package. She sees herself as simply "delivering" information to her clients. Her everyday intuitive and empathic abilities might help her sympathize with clients, and are not without their use in the therapeutic encounter, but they are distinct from her special, "psychic," perception. Indeed, as we have seen, she felt that such sympathies can actually be a hindrance to the clear transmission of psychically given information. But isn't there perhaps some silent, subtle unconscious communication between client and clairvoyant that might explain the feeling of recognition and confirmation experienced by clients? I asked this of Mary:

Ruth: Do you ever think that what you're doing is mirroring something that the client unconsciously knows? Or do you see yourself strictly as channeling information from another realm to this?

Mary: Yes, that's how I see myself. I don't see that I'm reading the client's subconscious mind or whatever. I feel the information is given externally from the universal energies and so that's how I deliver it.

For others, the waters were muddier. A medical intuitive, Glen Margaret, agreed that clairvoyance and everyday intuition were distinct capacities, but on reflection she considered that she probably used a variety of perceptual modes more or less simultaneously. For the intuitive counselor Rhondda, the picture was even more complicated, with her clairvoyant abilities subject to psychological mechanisms like interference, blockage, or projection on the part of both herself and client. For her, intuition worked most easily and most accurately when there is "a good connection between myself and the client." This doesn't always happen: "A person can be a little bit blocked or a bit fearful and they block you and therefore the message doesn't come through clear enough. It doesn't mean you don't get anything at all; it's just that sometimes it's more profound than others."

Whereas some of my interviewees felt they could very easily distinguish everyday intuition from clairvoyant intuition, Rhondda's description of the process suggests one in which client and clairvoyant, everyday and clairvoyant intuition, are thoroughly commingled:

I think sometimes what happens is that the confirmation [i.e., a bodily sensation that tells her the insight is coming from "somewhere else"] comes through quite strongly because

I need to confirm that that's what I'm feeling or that that's the truth. So whether it's my own intuition that I'm questioning—that can happen as well. So much goes on under the surface you know. When you are really fired up then you are not really sometimes aware of what's going on. It's just coming through thick and fast.

Despite these differences, there was no interviewee at all who thought that her special mode of intuition could be explained as or reduced to the kind of expert, habitual, embodied knowledge that Benner and Tanner (1987), following the Dreyfuses, call intuitive judgment. Even those for whom clairvoyance was a somewhat messy process agreed that while professional and life experience, heightened empathy, context, and so on might account for some proportion of the knowing, there was a clear-cut, palpable difference between (for want of a better distinction) capital-I Intuition and lower-case intuition. They believe their intuition derives clearly from the spirit realm because it often involves knowledge they couldn't possibly infer or guess (e.g., proper names), because it sometimes involves precognition, or, for some, because they experience different bodily sensations as they pass it on. Rhondda, for example, describes the bodily sensations she experiences when this kind of intuition, in her words, "drops in": "Everybody gets their intuition in lots of different ways. But the way it happens for me, it's like a touch. It's like your whole body becomes alive. I get a feeling going all the way down my back and it's like goose bumps and it gets so strong."

In sum, whatever surface similarities exist between these and more everyday conceptions of intuition, there is underneath them a key and insuperable difference between a purely rational conception of intuition and a supra-rational one, whether intuition is conceived of as a psychological/mental capacity or an ultimately spiritual one, and whether it is imagined as a deep interiority ("inner self") or an external intervention ("divine revelation"). This is a seemingly incommensurable gap between intellectual paradigms, and yet thousands of people move across it every day, a boundary crossing instantiated in daily medical choices.

Conclusion

Here then is the point to which my interviews (and experiences) with medical intuitives have led me. I wonder about the medical possibilities—and dangers—of "admitting" medical intuition to any extent at all. And I wonder about the hidden philosophical work going on every day by people engaged in a kind of transit between a state-sponsored biomedicine and an ever-increasing panoply of "alternatives." What are the cognitive processes by which people negotiate stark paradigmatic differences on the level of the everyday, and the philosophical negotiations they use to accommodate such differences? And is the popular discourse on the threat to reason a relevant frame for thinking about this practice?

To begin to consider these questions, we need to draw together a number of salient features of how medical intuition functions *systemically* in Western consumer societies. As I argue elsewhere (Barcan 2006), it is part of a pluralist medical envi-ronment where it often functions as a medicine of last resort for first-time clients and then becomes accepted and naturalized to the point where it may be chosen in paral-lel or in combination with more orthodox treatments, even functioning for some as a medicine of first resort (cf. Goldstein 2004: 940). Despite this, its workings are still largely hidden to the medical mainstream. Moreover, intuitive techniques may be en-countered as part of a long-term project of self-cultivation, supported by mentors and teachers, a philosophical tradition, and a community (e.g., the yoga or meditation class, or the reiki group) and/or as a commodified transaction more or less discon-nected from such communal and pedagogical contexts. What this means is that pow-erful and potentially dangerous techniques are regularly mobilized in unsupervised and unregulated situations—a fact that may be delicious to political romantics and can certainly add to the pleasure and frisson of the experience, but which can also potentially be medically or psychologically dangerous.

The paradigmatic differences and the relatively hidden nature of medical intu-ition in the medical landscape also mean, however, that medical intuition is likely to be quite consciously *chosen*. The bigger question, then, is *how* clients of medical intuition choose whether, how, when, and with whom to use it. In choosing medical clairvoyance over biomedicine in a given instance, people aren't necessarily being irrational at all, if by irrational we mean unthinkingly swayed by emotions or illogic. They may be quite consciously opting for a particular model of the body—making a philosophical and/or political choice, which, while it may be based on beliefs in non- or supra-rational faculties, is not necessarily irrationally *made*. This is likely to be the case with someone who identifies strongly with the New Age, for whom the choice to use medical intuition would sit comfortably within an explicit worldview in which reason is understood as the complementary counterpart to intuition and in which "the intellect is good and useful as long as it does not dominate its intuitive counterpart" (Hanegraaff 1998: 221).

But perhaps only a minority of people are so philosophically consistent. Per-haps for every ardent New Ager there are a dozen more people whose medical choices are more pragmatically, strategically, or inconsistently made—founded less on philosophical certainty than on doubt, ambivalence, openness, desperation, or hope. After all, most users of alternative medicine are also users of biomedicine (Goldstein 2004: 927). This would suggest that there are clearly times when a lot more is going on in mainstream medical encounters than is visible on the surface. Stark paradigmatic differences are being negotiated by patients, largely privately and invisibly.[18]

So while practices such as medical intuition do indeed represent "epistemological disruptions of the rational order" (Sutcliffe 2006: 161), there will be some people for whom they are part of a radical epistemological overhaul, and other instances in which they are "only local, contingent and temporary" (2006: 161). That is, while medical intuition *as a medical paradigm* may well be a radical reconfiguration if not a complete subversion of (modern Western accounts of) reason, and while it may be starkly intellectually incompatible with a medical system based on scientific rationality, these subversions occur as particular instances or engagements. Rather than seeing the systematic overturning of reason, we are seeing that an increasing number of people use instrumental rationality selectively, contextually, and sometimes strategically. As Steven Sutcliffe argues, New Age practice, however "mystical," "depends upon the promise of achieving release through utilizing accessible practices in everyday life settings" (2006: 161). It involves not so much irrationality as a "strategic use of the logic of instrumental rationality in pursuing a practical, given end" (2006: 161).

In this, New Agers may in fact resemble a broader section of modern Westerners—those for whom the potential failure of any coherent philosophical principle is taken as a matter of self-evidence, and for whom the infamous "incredulity toward metanarratives" (Lyotard 1984: xxiv) is an established feature of everyday personal and intellectual life. For such people, why *not* cross paradigmatic boundaries and experiment with practices that are simultaneously intellectually and medically novel and which might even prove of practical benefit? Perhaps in our increasingly pluralistic world many users of alternative medicine do not seek philosophical coherence but actively "paradigm surf." Judging from the large number of (female) academics I know who regularly use not just homeopaths and masseurs but also clairvoyants and healers, this may well be so. The commonsensical assumption that in a putatively rational society people seek choices that match with or confirm a more or less fixed worldview is perhaps untrue. Perhaps some people make strategic use of philosophies—picking them up and putting them down as it suits them. Perhaps the value placed within the academy on philosophical coherence is not popularly shared. These are questions that can be explored only through qualitative research, and even then only with difficulty.[19] But they are questions that are worth pursuing. After all, in times when we hear the refrain of the assault on reason almost daily, it is easy to panic. But those who value reason should surely use it to analyze more systematically those practices and beliefs that seem on the surface to challenge or subvert reason. If now is the time to defend reason, it is also, clearly, the time to better understand it, along with the things that threaten it, and even, perhaps, the things that might amplify it.

Notes

1. Though the New Age and alternative medicine are not one and the same phenomenon, they are deeply interwoven historically and philosophically.
2. The clandestine nature of medical intuition makes it harder to track than other, more visible, forms of alternative medicine, so it is hard to know whether it is a relatively stable practice—a constant but more or less minor corner of alternative medicine—or a growing phenomenon.

3. To be published by Berg Publishers, and provisionally titled *The Body in Alternative Therapies: Cultural Practice and the Boundaries of the Senses*. Interviewees for this particular section included clairvoyants and medical psychics, spiritual healers, and a "psychic masseuse." I would like to thank them for their participation. Some names are pseudonyms.

4. Gordon Melton considers that the New Age as a religious movement came to an end in the late 1980s, "dissolv[ing] back into the ethers from which it had emerged" (2001: 9). Having transformed and mainstreamed the occult, "it left behind a measurably changed situation" (2001: 1).

5. Hanegraaff's view is heavily influenced by a study by Joscelyn Godwin, *The Theosophical Enlightenment* (1994). Godwin argues that Blavatsky's Theosophy "owed as much to the sceptical Enlightenment of the eighteenth century as it did to the concept of spiritual enlightenment" (Godwin, cited in Hanegraaff 1998: 443).

6. The New Age is somewhat paradoxical in this regard. One of its ultimate truths is, precisely, that we create our own reality. Hanegraaff describes this "ambiguity" thus: "On the one hand, the experience of ultimate wholeness must be *universal,* which suggests that all human beings have access to one and the same fundamental reality; on the other hand, the emphasis on the value of *individuality* combined with the irreducible character of individual experience means that *all* personal experiences must be fully honoured and respected" (1998: 329).

7. On the connection between the other bodily senses and gender see Classen (1998).

8. Advocates of intuition are thus presented with the problem of how to explain fallibility. Are failures of intuition to be understood as failures of mediation, or as part of an always-infallible higher order, where mistakes might be a necessary part of the journey? "Sometimes the mind gets in the road; so you try to intellectualize something," says a clairvoyant I interviewed, Rhondda. "[N]o study is perfect," says the disclaimer inside Schulz's book: "There are limitations to any scientific inquiry" (1998: np).

9. Critics point to the anti-Semitism of the Theosophist Alice Bailey, for example. Leadbeater discusses the lesser quality clairvoyance in the "savage, whether of Central Africa or of Western Europe" (1918: 22), in contrast to the fully developed but rarely used astral bodies of "most cultured people of the higher races of the world" (1918: 25).

10. Jonas Salk's study of intuition and reason is also underpinned by an evolutionary narrative, a secular one, in which he argues that the human mind is "part of an evolutionary continuum" (1983: 81). Such ideas are discussed in Hanegraaff (1998: 223–4).

11. Melton argues that it is based on "the full acceptance of science" (1988: 36). I'd be hesitant to agree. Rather, it seems to be based on strategic and selective use of science.

12. The quotations come from the *Phaedo,* in which Socrates prepares for death.
13. Jay Johnston (2008: 86) argues that theosophical discourse "demonized" one of its own seven subtle bodies—the astral or desire body, seeing its "selfish," emotional content as needing to be cleansed and controlled. But in this formulation, intuition and emotions are not conflated. Rather, both mind and intuition are needed to control emotions (Johnston 2008: 87).
14. My interviews with practitioners have revealed that good practitioners, even when they may well work with fairly popular notions, especially about gender, have more nuanced and interesting views than a cursory reading of New Age books might suggest. For another example concerning women and emotionality, I was quite struck by a passing comment made by a naturopath—that women were "more analytical about emotions" than men, an observation that I found to be much more subtle and enabling than the more conventional description of women as "more emotional" than men.
15. Schulz in fact makes a distinction between medical intuitives who see clients in relation to energy fields, and those, such as herself, who are emotional intuitives (1998: 10).
16. Steven Sutcliffe also uses the paradigm of "management," arguing that New Agers can be better understood as *"managing* the dominant epistemic order, rather than *transcending* or *overthrowing* it" (2006: 161). Sutcliffe points to the dual senses of the word *manage*—both adjusting oneself to a dominant order and subverting it.
17. I became aware of this literature within nursing through a discussion in Schulz (1998: 21–2).
18. Most users of complementary and alternative medicine do not disclose it to their doctors (Eisenberg et al. 2001: 348).
19. In 2007 I attempted a small-scale pilot qualitative research project aimed at exploring the basis on which regular users of alternative therapies make such choices, and the way they negotiate the incommensurability of medical paradigms in a pluralist consumer environment. I discovered that it is easier to persuade alternative *therapists* to engage in long interviews than it is to ask patients to give up the kind of time necessary to elicit a nuanced understanding of complex practices. For the difficulties in involving the "consumer" in research on CAM, see Paterson (2007).

References

Barcan, R. (2006), "Spiritual Boundary Work: How Spiritual Healers and Medical Clairvoyants Negotiate the Sacred," paper presented to *Negotiating the Sacred: Medicine, Religion and the Body,* Centre for Cross-Cultural Cultural Research, Australian National University.

Basil, R. (1988), "Introduction," in R. Basil (ed.), *Not Necessarily the New Age: Critical Essays,* Buffalo, NY: Prometheus, pp. 9–32.

Benner, P. and Tanner, C. (1987), "How Expert Nurses Use Intuition," *The American Journal of Nursing,* 87(1): 23–31.

Brennan, B. A. (1988), *Hands of Light: A Guide to Healing through the Human Energy Field: A New Paradigm for the Human Being in Health, Relationship, and Disease*, Toronto: Bantam Books.

Classen, C. (1998), *The Color of Angels: Cosmology, Gender and the Aesthetic Imagination*, New York: Routledge.

Colbert, S. (2006), Interview with Nathan Rabin, *AV Club* (January 25), www.av club.com/content/node/44705, accessed 7 March 2007.

Cope, S. (1999), *Yoga and the Quest for the True Self*, New York: Bantam Books.

Dawkins, R. (2006), *The God Delusion*, London: Bantam.

Donnelly, W. J., Spykerboer, J. E. and Thong, Y. H. (1985), "Are Patients Who Use Alternative Medicine Dissatisfied with Orthodox Medicine?" *Medical Journal of Australia,* 142(10), 13 May: 539–41.

Eisenberg, D. M., Kessler, R. C., Van Rompay, M. I., Kaptchuk, T. and Wilkey, S. A. (2001), "Perceptions about Complementary Therapies Relative to Conventional Therapies among Adults Who Use Both: Results from a National Survey," *Annals of Internal Medicine,* 135(5): 344–51.

Goldstein, M. S. (2004), "The Persistence and Resurgence of Medical Pluralism," *Journal of Health Politics, Policy and Law,* 29(4–5): 925–45.

Gore, A. (2007), *The Assault on Reason,* New York: Penguin.

Hanegraaff, W. J. (1998), *New Age Religion and Western Culture: Esotericism in the Mirror of Secular Thought*, Albany: State University of New York Press.

Hay, L. L. (1987), *You Can Heal Your Life*, Concord, CA: Specialist Publications.

Hay, L. L. (1988), *Heal Your Body: The Mental Causes for Physical Illness and the Metaphysical Way to Overcome Them*, Concord, CA: Specialist Publications.

Hitchens, C. (2007), *God Is Not Great: How Religion Poisons Everything*, Crows Nest, NSW: Allen and Unwin.

Institute of Medicine of the National Academies (2005), *Complementary and Alternative Medicine in the United States*, Washington, DC: National Academies Press.

Johnston, J. L. H. (2008), *Angels of Desire: Esoteric Bodies, Aesthetics and Ethics,* London: Equinox.

Lallo, M. (2007), "Seven Biggest Self-Help Myths," *Sydney Morning Herald, Essential Style + Home + Health* [supplement], February 8: 8–9.

Leadbeater, C. W. (1918), *Clairvoyance,* 4th edn, London: Theosophical Publishing House.

Lloyd, G. (1984), *The Man of Reason: "Male" and "Female" in Western Philosophy,* London: Methuen.

Lyotard, J.-F. (1984), *The Postmodern Condition: A Report on Knowledge*, Minneapolis: University of Minnesota Press.

Melton, J. G. (1988), "A History of the New Age Movement," in R. Basil (ed.), *Not Necessarily the New Age: Critical Essays*, Buffalo, NY: Prometheus, pp. 35–53.

Melton, J. G. (1990), "Introductory Essay: An Overview of the New Age Movement," in J.G. Melton, J. Clark and A.A. Kelly, *New Age Encyclopedia,* Detroit: Gale Research, pp. xiii–xxxviii.

Melton, J. G. (2001), "New Age Transformed," http://religiousmovements.lib.virginia.edu/nrms/newage.html, accessed 3 February 2007.

Miller, T. and McHoul, A. (1998), *Popular Culture and Everyday Life,* London: Sage.

Paterson, C. (2007), "Involving the Consumer in CAM Research," in J. Adams (ed.), *Researching Complementary and Alternative Medicine,* London: Routledge, pp. 133–51.

Salk, J. (1983), *Anatomy of Reality: Merging of Intuition and Reason*, New York: Columbia University Press.

Schraeder, B. D. and Fischer, D.K. (1987), "Using Intuitive Knowledge in the Neonatal Intensive Care Nursery," *Holistic Nursing Practice,* 1(3): 45–51.

Schulz, M. L. (1998), *Awakening Intuition: Using Your Mind-Body Network for Insight and Healing,* New York: Harmony Books.

Scruton, R. (1999), "What Ever Happened to Reason?" *The City Journal* [New York] 9(2): 88–96.

Schultz, T. (1988), "A Personal Odyssey through the New Age," in R. Basil (ed.), *Not Necessarily the New Age: Critical Essays,* Buffalo, NY: Prometheus, pp. 337–58.

Shumsky, S. G. (1996), *Divine Revelation,* New York: Fireside.

Spelman, E. V. (1982), "Woman as Body: Ancient and Contemporary Views," *Feminist Studies,* 8(1): 109–31.

Sutcliffe, S. J. (2006), "Practising New Age Soteriologies in the Rational Order," in L. Hume and K. McPhillips (eds), *Popular Spiritualities: The Politics of Contemporary Enchantment,* Aldershot: Ashgate, pp. 159–74.

Tansley, D. V. (1977), *Subtle Body: Essence and Shadow*, London: Thames and Hudson.

Wallis, R. (1979), "Reflections on *When Prophecy Fails,*" in *Salvation and Protest,* New York: St. Martin's Press, pp. 44–50.

Wheen, F. (2004), *How Mumbo-Jumbo Conquered the World: A Short History of Modern Delusions*, London: Harper Perennial.

–10–

Refusing to Give Up the Ghost
Some Thoughts on the Afterlife from
Spirit Photography to Phantom Films
Pamela Thurschwell

We might think that today disembodied spirits are more likely to haunt the aesthetic realm than the religious; the meanings of the modern specters we find in the contemporary photographs in "The Disembodied Spirit" exhibit (Bowdoin College Museum of Art, 2003) may appear to differ in kind and motivation from the spirit photography of the latter half of the nineteenth century, and they may indicate some very different beliefs about ghosts. Yet in this chapter I hope to trace some paths from those early photos through to some popular modern films in which the dead return, by considering the investment in the ghost as both a tool for mourning and as a spectral shield against the reality of loss. The spirit photography represented in "The Disembodied Spirit" exhibit takes us back to the double origins of modern spiritualism as both a way of satisfying a culture's yearning for a recognizable afterlife, and a new form of popular entertainment. The enormous upsurge of interest in the supernatural in Britain and America from the middle of the nineteenth century is usually attributed to the work of two resourceful American sisters, Kate and Margaret Fox, who began to experience mysterious knockings and rappings in their upstate New York home in 1848. Very soon the girls figured out how to talk to the spirits who were haunting their house through a code of raps; their investigations revealed that the trouble was caused by the ghost of a peddler who had apparently been murdered in their house. Under the management of an older sister, the Fox girls began performing. As the rapping spirits conveniently followed them everywhere, they had soon launched a new craze for spiritualism in Britain and America and launched themselves in successful careers as spirit mediums. The possibility that the dead were literally still available to be communicated with was a reality in Victorian era Britain and America. From the 1850s onwards the intelligentsia, as well as the working and middle classes, were, some reluctantly, some enthusiastically, attending séances. Dickens, Tennyson, the Brownings, George Eliot, and G. H. Lewes amongst others all found themselves participating in spiritualist displays. Not everyone was impressed by the spirits they experienced (Robert Browning wrote a damning poem "Mr Sludge the Medium" in response to his wife's enthusiasm for spiritualism), but almost everyone experienced them. Sometimes no more than a good party game, sometimes the basis for an organized alternative religious belief, spirit rapping, table turning and full medium materializations (in which mediums would lock themselves in cupboards, in dark lighting and create spirits who would appear and entertain the assembled company) were an integral part of Victorian culture.

Spirit photography, which emerged as a profitable business in the 1860s, helped bring spiritualism out of the aural and into the visual realm both as evidence and as entertainment.[1] The spirit photograph, as Tom Gunning (1995) has convincingly argued, combined the possibility of communicating with the elusive dead with the tempting accuracy of new technologies of reproduction. The photograph promised a certain kind of apparently irrefutable scientific evidence—the exact likeness. And yet that new "science" of photography was shadowed from the beginning by uncanny doubles and disturbing repetitions, both in theory and practice:

> In 1856 Sir David Brewster in his book describing his new invention, the stereoscope, advised his readers that "[f]or the purposes of amusement the photographer might carry us even into the realm of the supernatural," since it was quite possible "to give a spectral appearance to one or more of his figures and to exhibit them as 'thin air' amid the solid realities of the stereoscopic picture" (Stereoscope 205) ... that such images could display the iconic accuracy and recognizability of photographic likenesses and at the same time the transparency and insubstantiality of ghosts seemed to demonstrate the fundamentally uncanny quality of photography, its capture of a specter-like double. (Gunning 1995: 47)

The popularity of spirit photography was inseparable from the mourning practices of Victorians who were struggling to grasp the significance of new scientific theories that seemed to dislodge so many of the received doctrines of Christianity. A poem such as Tennyson's *In Memoriam* for instance was both an act of mourning for the loss of a much loved friend and an act of mourning for the loss of a world where heaven was assured. Allaying these anxieties, the familiar photographed spirit could be seen as guaranteeing an afterlife to even the most skeptical. The viewers confronted with the spirit image could console themselves about their own mortality; eventually they too might be hovering benignly above the heads of their still living relatives.

But as Gunning indicates, the spirit photograph also explicitly revealed the paradoxically doubled nature of any photographic image. Photography insisted upon the accuracy of its reproductive and mimetic powers, and yet also immediately conjured up the realm of magic and spectres. On a day to day level every photographic portrait of a person worked to evade death by appearing to stop time. By reproducing what seemed like the essence of the individual life, the photographic portrait of the living promised to circumvent mortality in a way similar to that of the spirit photograph. With the perfect likeness ostensibly guaranteed by the photograph you might always have an image of your deceased mother, husband, or son available to you, frozen at a certain age. So in a sense photography, as Julia Margaret Cameron's works elegantly display, didn't need to be explicitly of the corpse to signify death, and it didn't need to indulge in the double exposures of spirit photography to refer to the disembodied. According to Roland Barthes (2000) the photo leads us inexorably towards death, our own and others.[2]

The photograph, insofar as it always gestures towards both the embodiment of the real and the disembodied spirit, can be seen as ambivalently placed in relation to mourning. Insofar as the photograph arrests memory and can be used to deny loss, it may conceivably prolong mourning indefinitely—you may never escape that haunting image of the dead in a modern world in which it is literally always available to you. The protracted public mourning over Princess Diana was certainly inseparable from the ubiquity of her image in the papers. But on the other hand the photograph may also aid the processes of mourning—loss may not be so unconquerable if you can disassociate your own ego from that of your lost loved one, one step at a time, using the photograph as a sign that the loved one is and was essentially different from yourself. In this scenario, eventually you put that photograph away in a box under the bed and get on with the world of the living. The photograph can safely contain the past for the mourner or it can make it impossible to escape. It can be a small *memento mori* or a permeating image of the past that seems to threaten the continued existence of the self. The power of the photograph is in its referentiality—we imagine it refers to the truth of what was—but also in its insubstantiality—it's a two dimensional attempt to capture life, endlessly reproducible perhaps, but essentially flimsy. If an image is disembodied to begin with it may be that much more difficult to effectively destroy.

The dynamic I'm exploring here comes from Freud's "Mourning and Melancholia" (1917), an essay that I think is as least as important for disentangling the meanings of the disembodied spirit as captured by photography or film in our modern culture as his other influential musing on ghosts, doubles and repetition in "The Uncanny" (1919). In "Mourning and Melancholia" Freud analyses the ways in which people react to the death of a loved one or the loss of a cherished idea. He claims that a normal state of mourning may involve an extended period of distress and depression but will eventually heal itself in time. Melancholia, although it resembles mourning in many ways, is a different creature. Symptoms of melancholia include "a profoundly painful dejection, cessation of interest in the outside world, loss of the capacity to love, inhibition of all activity, and lowering of the self-regarding feelings to a degree that finds utterance in self-reproaches and self-revilings, and culminates in a delusional expectation of punishment" (Freud 1917, 11: 252). The melancholic resembles the normal mourner in everything but his self-hatred and expectation of punishment.

Mourning, for Freud, is a process; while melancholia, although driven by a ceaseless psychic activity, only finally signifies stasis—caught in an inexorable and inescapable relation to the lost object, the ego of the melancholic is in a constant state of damage and disintegration. In normal mourning, "when the work of mourning is completed the ego becomes free and uninhibited again" (Freud 1917, 11: 253). Not so for melancholia—the work of melancholia eats away at the self. "In mourning it is the world which has become poor and empty; in melancholia it is the ego itself" (Freud 1917, 11: 254). The basic mechanism is a reversal; the melancholic cannot relinquish the object because he or she had conflicting feelings of love and hate towards it to begin with. The guilt of living with these feelings after the object's death makes the melancholic feel responsible for the death of the object; melancholics unconsciously believe themselves to be murderers—in a sense they have created their own loss. To deal with the guilt of this situation, the melancholic reacts by literally not letting the loved one go, often to the point of unconsciously taking on the traits of the other person in an extreme identification, designed to deny the fact that a loss has taken place. In a vampiric dynamic, the self is emptied out to keep the dead alive. As Freud (1917, 11: 258) poetically puts it "the shadow of the object [falls] upon the ego."

The questions that Freud's psychic economy raises are replete with the language of haunting. They also seem to suffuse the psychic work of both spirit photography and photography more generally. How did the spirit photograph function for those who participated in them? As melancholic signifier or consoling step on the way to an acceptance of loss? How far away or how near are the dead in these works; hovering about the heads of the living or invading their souls? Where do disembodied spirits stop and embodied ones (ourselves) begin? On the one hand, these images might be seen as killing the dead yet again—by taming death and reducing its otherness until it becomes just a rather banal extension of life. (At the best spirit photography studios your apparition would be guaranteed.) On the other hand these images go about continually resurrecting the dead in a realm that hovers uncertainly between the terrifying and the consoling.

Our culture today may not seem as suffused in the belief in ghosts as the Victorian era was and yet disembodied spirits continue to make their presence felt. One place ghosts have found a spiritual home, if you can forgive the pun, is at the movies. We now know that seeing dead people sells films even apart from the endless serial resurrections of the horror genre. From *Ghost* (1990) to *The Sixth Sense* (1999) the dead have, in recent years, reappeared in Hollywood in commercially and critically successful forms. What Theodor Adorno (1986) once referred to, in reference to postwar Germany's relationship to the Holocaust, as "coming to terms with the past," has become the stuff of popular entertainment, and this dynamic is often represented by the handy cinematic image of the ghost. In afterlife films such as *Ghost* and *Truly, Madly, Deeply* (1991) living characters who have lost loved ones are forced, in the space of two hours, to recognize that that loss is unrecoverable; yet simultaneously, the magic of the flickering screen also denies, or at least defers, this necessary emotional lesson, because their unrecoverable dead are still hanging around the frame finishing up their own unfinished business. In more recent films such as *The Sixth Sense* and *The Others* (2001) the dead simply don't know they are dead. In all these films mourning, or relinquishing the past is a two-way street; the dead must release the living just as the living must release the dead. Unlike the ghost of Hamlet's father, who makes only a few brief appearances towards the beginning of the play as catalyst, modern day cinematic ghosts are usually only banished at the end of the film when everyone, including the still living characters, also dissolve into the final credits. Modern ghost films create an apparently unbridgeable gap between the living and the dead and then soothingly bridge that gap by representing the dead, both to the audience and to other characters in the film, and endorsing the possibility of contact between the two realms. Not coincidentally, these films tend to employ a minimal amount of special effects to disembody their ghosts for the screen. In *Ghost* the dead Patrick Swayze appears on screen for most of the film as his usual beefcake self but we the audience are the only ones who can see him. Dismayed by the fact that he can no longer make any impact on the outside world and wanting to rescue his girlfriend Demi Moore from the clutches of the business associate who had him killed, he takes lessons from another ghost in how to be corporeal. Beginning by moving a penny and kicking a tin can he eventually learns to kick ass (and operate a computer) to see that justice is done. Simultaneously, materiality is achieved.

The plots of *The Sixth Sense* and *The Others* hinge on the fact that the thickly corporeal actor, Bruce Willis, and Nicole Kidman, sporting a Grace Kelly body to match her Grace Kelly hair, have no sense of their own post-death disembodiment and neither should the cinema audience (My apologies to those who haven't yet seen the films. But to continue what I've begun, I suppose I should also tell you that Rosebud was his sled). We are given little or no access to the ghostliness of the ghost in recent cinema excursions despite film's eminent suitability for ghosting; instead the dead are shown to be still with us. This is appropriate perhaps to the quotidian religious atmosphere of modern day America in which, some polls claim, more than 70 per cent of the population believes in angels.[3] Spirits can and are readily pictured by the popular cultural imagination in all kinds of forms from the most mundane and material—the dead wife still puttering around the kitchen—to the most spectacular and spectral—the heavenly choir at the end of the long tunnel. Perhaps it is the case that the dead have once again come to have a comfortable presence in our shared mass culture imaginary. But what shifts in the form and meanings of disembodied spirits can we find from the Victorian period to our current era? Is it that new kinds of compensatory magic might be needed to heal a world that's rife with postmodern loss? These afterlife films function to allay anxieties and, in the more interesting cases, refuse to allay anxieties, that are inextricable from the technologies of reproduction that create their ghosts; they are films that are in part about the fantasies and fears that are created by film's promise of cinematic immortality. In a larger (and, I'm sure, largely unanswerable) sense these movies pose the question of what forms of melioration make sense in modernity?

Cinema has, not surprisingly, tarried with disembodied spirits from its very beginnings. The new and potentially manipulable techniques of film were deployed practically from the form's invention to create ghosts, just as the tricky techniques and fortuitous double exposures of photography had been used from early on to create the spirit photography that you find in this exhibit. Georges Méliès's 1897 film

Enchanted Hotel showed a confused hotel dweller watching his boots walk away without him and his furniture mysteriously collapse, while the following year saw the British director G.A. Smith *Photographing a Ghost* (in a print that has, unfortunately, not survived). This was followed in 1901 by a ten minute film of Dickens's *A Christmas Carol,* called *Scrooge or Morley's Ghost* (Merck 1999: 168). It seems clear that these early cinematic ghosts were created in part because the technology available motivated their production (as the technology available has also inspired a slew of metaphors of haunting that have attached themselves to the language of film and photography).[4] But recent ghost films often resist the path that film technology seems to lead towards; instead of making an image appear transparent or fleeting these movies make the dead past appear as embodied as the fictional filmic present. When we watch a film, on some level of course, we know, even as we disavow that knowledge, that everyone on the screen is really simply a flickering two dimensional image, but for the space of the film, the ghosts share the material reality of the living. The dead are with us again; the past can be reassuringly restored. Romantic comedies used to guarantee their audiences a united couple at the end; modern romantic ghost stories agree to break up the couple, sending one off towards life (and often a new partner) and the other towards death, but they do so by portraying an interlude, the space of the movie, in which nothing ever dies and the past can be resolved. There is, in these films, a happy marriage between life and death, an acceptance of loss made easy by an unexpected if temporary return of the dead used finally to help one or both parties through the transition. And it's usually pretty clear that that for the dead, the transition is towards some place else (in *Ghost* for Patrick Swayze, a shaft of light in contrast to the cartoonish black demons who come to bear the bad dead characters away). Either way the dead are not headed towards utter extinction. But of course, this ambiguous transition applies to the audience as well—films that initially seem geared towards getting us to negotiate our way through proper mourning to an acceptance of death actually function to promise that we may all continue to live in the continuous present of screen time.

Seemingly tilted towards the processes of mourning—the moment of recognition, the releasing of the past—perhaps these films really make available a kind of warm fuzzy cultural melancholia in the sense that the *work* part of the work of mourning seems to drop out. Death is too easily processed by refusing to process it as difference; we see the live Patrick Swayze as continuous with the dead Patrick Swayze; he's still the slightly inarticulate man who loves his Demi and beats up on bad guys. I'm arguing that films like *Ghost* encourage, in the realm of fantasy, the sense that death is just another version of life, with a few more communication difficulties. On one level the audience is made successfully and happily melancholic by phantom-rom-com films. Like the endless resurrections of the serial form more generally (I've just seen a poster for *Final Destination II* with the tag line, "It's not over yet"), ghost films let us believe that nothing ever dies, not really. *The Sixth Sense* and *The Others* appear to buck this trend by suggestively shifting the locus of melancholia away from the living and towards the dead who do not know and cannot accept their own status. We as audience become implicated in their melancholia by similarly not knowing that they are dead. There's a double education that needs to take place for the work (both the film and the work of mourning) to be complete. In both films the ghosts must learn to accept their condition—coming to terms with loss is coming to terms with the loss of their living selves as well as coming to terms with the loss of their loved ones. The child psychologist character played by Bruce Willis in *The Sixth Sense* must initially learn to accept the claim of the troubled young boy, Cole, he is attempting to treat, that he sees dead people. Interestingly, he only does so because he identifies Cole's problems as similar to an old patient of his (in fact the disturbed patient who shoots Bruce Willis and then himself at the beginning of the film). He goes back and listens closely to a tape of his conversation with this earlier patient as a child and turns up the volume on a point when he had left the room for a few minutes leaving the child alone; soon he can hear another voice muttering something about death in Spanish. Like the spirit photo, the tape recorder is a guarantor of mimetic accuracy. Recording media bear witness to the continued existence of the dead where the human eye and ear cannot.

In the course of the film, Bruce Willis must learn that what he thought was a failing marriage—he's incapable of communicating with his wife—is actually a marriage that has been terminated more definitively because he is very much a late husband. He must learn to let her go, relinquish her to another man and to the world of the living. At the very end of *The Sixth Sense,* when Bruce Willis has finally recognized his own ex-existence and accomplished this letting go, we see a flash of white and then a brief image of a wedding photo; a juxtaposition of his (perhaps heavenly, perhaps blank) future with his (happily coupled) past. Throughout the film we periodically see Bruce Willis's wife lying on a couch in their house watching home movies of their wedding. If we are alert viewers we might suspect from this that he is dead; that she is using the filmic image as a tool for prolonging mourning into melancholia. For the audience Bruce Willis is literally next to her on the couch; for her he is still alive on the TV. Again it is notable the ways in which, in these films, technologies of reproduction—the photo, the home movie, the tape recorder—function both to ratify the continuing presence of the dead among the living, and to disavow loss. Earlier we saw Cole's mother look at a series of photos of him hanging on her wall. We and she notice that in every photograph there is the faintest of spectral glimmers hovering next to him. The photograph registers, ever so slightly, the possibility of another world. It seems that the spiritual supercharge of photography has not changed drastically since the Victorian period; the photograph is still imagined as bearing witness to the ineffable, just as film can still keep us in communication with the dead.

The Others also features photographs as part of its process of recognizing and accepting death. The film is set in the 1940s shortly after World War II. In one scene, Grace, played by Nicole Kidman, discovers an eerie album of photos from the late nineteenth century all showing people in various poses with their eyes closed. Her somewhat creepy housekeeper informs her that these are mortuary photos, photos of the dead, a practice which was popular in England and America from at least the American Civil War to the end of the nineteenth century and which has continued, although often unacknowledged, into the present day.[5] (Again the link between death and photography is historical as well as theoretical; because early exposures took so long, dead people made the best, and at first, only human subjects for portraits. Alexander Gardner, one of the earliest and best known photographers of war dead, actually moved dead soldiers and weapons into more aesthetically satisfying positions in order to photograph them for the newspapers (Ruby 1995: 13).) Later in the film Grace discovers another mortuary photo, this time of her housekeeper, maid and gardener dated 1897; the servants she has recently hired are dead already as the photographic evidence shows. But it is only still later, at the end of the film, when she stumbles upon a séance being given by the current owners of the house (the supposed spectres she believes are tormenting her and her children) that she is forced to acknowledge her own death and that of her children. We might see the acknowledgement of a kind of death in life as coming earlier in the film as well. On the one hand, Grace's pale-complexioned son and daughter are metaphorically linked to photographs; they are photo-sensitive and cannot be exposed to the light. They must be kept in a kind of darkroom. On the other hand they are also linked to death; the house is kept shrouded in darkness and the children cannot leave it; they behave like ghosts before we or they know that they are. When we realize that the children are already dead their photosensitivity makes sense; they are more two dimensional than three, already the disembodied spirits that photography promises to capture. Again we return to the photograph as a kind of privileged metonym and metaphor for the dead—that which reveals the disembodied spirit and preserves the past but does so by killing it and freezing it at one moment in time.

The Others ends with another version of the education of the dead; Grace takes on the knowledge of their deathly status, but the film makes no comforting gesture towards successful mourning by having the dead relinquish the realm of the living. Instead what Grace has to relinquish is her rabid Catholicism—early in the film she is shown to be fanatical in her faith, forcing her children to read the bible continuously and learn many lessons steeped in hellfire and damnation. However at the end of the movie her daughter asks her where limbo is and she replies, "I don't know. I don't know any more than you do." The only thing she knows is that whatever happens they must never leave the house. *The Others,* unlike the other films I've discussed, gives us a portrait of death as real otherness. The interactions between the dead and the living are never made easy, never tamed. By continuing to haunt the house one might argue that the Nicole Kidman character chooses melancholia; by insisting that they will share a space with the living, she maintains a grasp on her past and refuses to countenance loss. But paradoxically this melancholic dynamic may be the best way of respecting death in its unknowability; she and her children will be proper ghosts from now on—they have become the Others of the title, they can no longer pretend to themselves that they are the same.

One final film, which is not precisely a ghost movie but is all about the attractions of the ghost as embodied in the cinematic image, also participates in a melancholic dynamic. In Woody Allen's *The Purple Rose of Cairo* the romantic lead of the eponymous film within the film played by Jeff Daniels comes down off the screen to romance audience member Mia Farrow, an inveterate movie-goer who uses the silver screen to escape her own unhappy marriage and the poverty of the Great Depression. When Farrow finally is forced to decide between love offered by the real actor (also played by Jeff Daniels) and the fictional character, she mistakenly chooses the real person and the heart-broken movie character returns to the screen. When her living lover then deserts her Farrow is left with nothing but the remains of a flickering and elusive vision of cinematic happiness and luxury. In the final scene she is back in the same theatre, watching Fred Astaire and Ginger Rogers dance cheek to cheek in a world she can never again reach. Allen's film suggests that the disembodied image is actually better than the real thing, that the "real" coming to life of the past or the lost or the missing may not satisfy your every desire for closure and narrative conciliation. Unlike most of these other films which assume that coming to terms with the dead or the lost and then putting them tidily away will make "real" life better, Allen's film actually exhorts its audience to choose the ghost, and by so doing, I would argue, portrays the romance of "real" loss more poignantly.

It is Woody Allen of course who is the modern master of the art of disavowing death: "I don't want to achieve immortality through my work, I want to achieve immortality through not dying" or alternatively, "I don't want to live on in the hearts and minds of my countrymen, I want to live on in my apartment." The modern ghost films that appeal most to our culture, on one level, portray a version of mourning's work— the return of the dead allows both the living and the dead to work through unfinished business—come to terms with the past. And yet these films simultaneously seem unable to countenance the nature of their own disavowals—they promise their audiences that perhaps death is simply like watching a film; that all losses can be restored onscreen. Films that insist on denying death in favor of a world of filmic fantasy or the continuing presence of the ghost may have something more interesting to tell us both about our attitude towards death, and those spectral modern forms, the film and the photograph, that maintain and shape those attitudes. Perhaps in this version of modern melancholia disembodied spirits may find their natural home. What we need, perhaps, is a way of confronting death that respects the ghost without pretending to know his contours—in a sense, that lets him live on in his own apartment.

Notes

1. See Connor (1999) for more on the early importance of sound to the séance.
2. See Barthes (2000: 79) on the strange temporality of the photograph: "For the photograph's immobility is somehow the result of a perverse confusion between

two concepts: the Real and the Live: by attesting that the object has been real, the photograph surreptitiously induces belief that it is alive, because of that delusion which makes us attribute to Reality an absolutely superior, somehow eternal value; but by shifting this reality to the past ('this-has-been'), the photograph suggests that it is already dead."

3. According to Michael Shermer (2000), a Gallup poll of American adults showed that 72% believed in angels. A similar poll conducted by *Time* magazine in 1993 plumped for 69%.

4. Gunning (1995) provides many instances of spectral language being used from early on to describe photography. For film's fascination with the spectral see for instance Eisner (1969) and O'Brien (1993).

5. See Ruby (1995) for a history of representing the dead photographically, as well as analysis of why these photos, unlike the contemporaneous spirit photography, might seem particularly creepy to us now in a culture in which death has become a taboo subject. With spirit photography we now feel assured that we are not actually looking at images of the dead; with mortuary photography we are certain that we are.

References

Adorno, Theodor W. (1986), "What Does Coming to Terms with the Past Mean?" in Geoffrey H. Hartman (ed.), *Bitburg in Moral and Political Perspective,* Bloomington: Indiana University Press, pp. 114–29.

Barthes, R. (2000), *Camera Lucida: Reflections on Photography,* trans. Richard Howard, London: Vintage.

Connor, S. (1999), "The Machine in the Ghost: Spiritualism, Technology and the 'Direct Voice,'" in Peter Buse and Andrew Stott (eds), *Ghosts: Deconstruction, Psychoanalysis, History,* Houndmills: Macmillan Press Ltd., pp. 203–25.

Eisner, Lotte (1969), *The Haunted Screen,* Berkeley: University of California Press.

Freud, Sigmund (1917), "Mourning and Melancholia," in *Penguin Freud Library,* Vol. 11, Harmondsworth, Middlesex: Penguin Books, pp. 245–68.

Freud, Sigmund (1919), "The Uncanny," in *Penguin Freud Library*, Vol. 14, Harmondsworth, Middlesex: Penguin Books, pp. 335–76.

Gunning, Tom (1995), "Phantom Images and Modern Manifestations: Spirit Photography, Magic Theater, Trick Films, and Photography's Uncanny," in Patrice Petro (ed.), *Fugitive Images: From Photography to Video,* Bloomington: Indiana University Press.

Merck, Mandy (1999), "The Medium of Exchange," in Peter Buse and Andrew Stott (eds), *Ghosts: Deconstruction, Psychoanalysis, History,* Houndmills: Macmillan Press Ltd., pp. 163–77.

O'Brien, Geoffrey (1993), *The Phantom Empire,* New York: W. W. Norton.

Ruby, Jay (1995), *Secure the Shadow: Death and Photography in America,* Cambridge, MA: MIT Press.

Shermer, Michael (2000), *How We Believe: The Search for God in an Age of Science,* New York: W. H. Freeman and Co.

Part III
Uncanny Sensations

–11–

The Sense of Being Stared At
Rupert Sheldrake

For a long time, I have had a feeling of telepathy with my two daughters who I am very close to. I start thinking about them just before the phone rings. It happens too with friends. I'm always saying "I was just thinking about you" when I answer the phone to them.

(Janet Ward)

William Carter was leading a patrol of Gurkhas on an anti-terrorist operation in Malaya in 1951 when they came across a camp that had obviously just been abandoned. "While we were examining the bits and pieces left lying around, I had an uncanny feeling that someone was watching me. I had this sense of danger. I felt the sensation of something almost gripping me at the back of the neck. I turned around and there, about twenty yards away, was a chap in uniform with a red star on his cap gazing hard at me. He was bringing his rifle up and I knew one of us was going to be killed. I shot him before he shot me, so I have lived to tell the tale." He says he does not doubt the existence of a sense of being stared at. "But for it, I wouldn't be alive today" (Matthews 1996).

Telepathy, premonitions and the sense of being stared at are currently unexplained in scientific terms. Indeed their very existence is controversial. They *appear* to happen, but if all possible kinds of forces, fields and information-transfer are already known to science, then they ought not to exist. Is our scientific understanding of fundamental principles already more or less complete? Have all the big questions been answered? Some scientists believe they have (Horgan 1996).

On the other hand, if these phenomena do in fact occur, they show that current science is incomplete. When they are taken seriously within the scientific community, the effects will be revolutionary. They will enlarge our ideas about minds and brains, about animal nature and human nature, and about space and time.

In the book *The Sense of Being Stared At* (2003) I discuss a large body of evidence and summarize recent research that shows that telepathy, the sense of being stared at and precognition occur both in non-human animals, such as dogs and cats, and in people. They are not "paranormal" or "supernatural". They are normal and natural, part of our biological nature.

Different groups of people refer to these phenomena by different names. Some call them psychic, implying that they are related to the psyche, or soul, or call them psi phenomena, for short. Some describe them as forms of extrasensory perception, or ESP, meaning forms of perception beyond the senses. (Here the word *extra* means "beyond", in its original Latin sense, not "additional" as in the modern English sense.) Some prefer to call them paranormal, meaning beyond the normal (the Greek *para* means "beyond"), or parapsychological, meaning beyond psychology. Other people think of them as aspects of a "sixth sense," an additional sense over and above the five familiar senses of seeing, hearing, smelling, tasting and touching.

The fact that so many different terms are used is confusing. And all these terms carry different implications. *Psychic* implies a dependence on the psyche, or soul. This shifts the problem back one stage, because no one knows how the psyche could account for these experiences. To do so it would have to stretch out beyond the brain. But how?

The term *extrasensory perception* restates the problem in different words. It tells us that these phenomena cannot be explained in terms of the known senses, but says nothing about how they can be explained.

The word *paranormal* raises the question of what is normal. The sense of being stared at and telepathy are normal in that they are common. Most people have experienced them. But they seem paranormal from the point of view of the materialist theory of the mind, still taken for granted within institutional science. According to this theory, the mind is just an aspect of the activity of the brain. A mind confined to the inside of the head cannot account for psychic phenomena. Hence, from a materialist point of view, they ought not to happen. But what if science took a broader view of the mind?

As science progresses, it continually changes the boundaries of the scientifically "normal". Television and mobile phones would have seemed miraculous to an eighteenth-century physicist, knowing nothing of electromagnetic fields. Seeing things at a distance or hearing the voices of people far away would have seemed like the work of witches or the delusions of lunatics. Now they are everyday experiences, thanks to television, radio and telephones.

Likewise, hydrogen bombs would have been unthinkable for nineteenth-century physicists. In the age of steam and gunpowder, such devices would have sounded like an apocalyptic fantasy. Lasers would have sounded like mythic swords of light. They only became conceivable for twentieth-century physicists through the scientific revolutions wrought by relativity theory and quantum theory.

These enlargements of science did not contradict or invalidate what was already known, but built on it. The recognition of electromagnetic fields in the nineteenth century supplemented rather than overthrew classical Newtonian physics. The twentieth-century revolutions in physics brought about by quantum and relativity theory and modern cosmology did not destroy the achievements of nineteenth-century physicists, but added to them. In biology, Darwin's theory of evolution illuminated rather than eclipsed the classification of living organisms by the great eighteenth-century biologist Linnaeus.

Historians of science, most notably Thomas Kuhn (1970), have recognized that at any given stage in the history of science, phenomena that do not fit into the prevailing model, or paradigm, are dismissed or ignored or explained away. They are anomalies. Yet they refuse to go away. To the embarrassment of the reigning theories, they persist. Sooner or later science has to expand to include them.

To cite one of many examples, meteorites were anomalies in the eighteenth century. In the perfect mathematical universe of Newtonian physics, there was no possibility of stones falling from the sky seemingly at random. So when people claimed to have seen such things happen, scientists felt they had to deny them, explain them away as illusions, or dismiss them as superstitions.

In one celebrated example, on 13 September 1768, in Maine, France, several villagers heard a noise like a thunderclap, followed by a whistling sound, and saw something falling into a meadow. It turned out to be a stone too hot to touch. A local priest sent part of it to the Academy of Sciences in Paris for identification. The chemist Lavoisier ground it up, did some tests, and claimed he had proved it had not fallen from the sky, but instead was an ordinary stone that had probably been struck by lightning (Inglis 1977: 148–9). He told the academy: "There are no stones in the sky. Therefore stones cannot fall from the sky" (Michell and Richard 1977: 16). Now, of course, meteorites present no theoretical problem, and their existence is no longer disputed.

Materialism as a philosophy keeps evolving as scientific ideas about physical reality change within science. The boundaries of the "normal" are not fixed, but shift according to changes in scientific orthodoxies. In the course of the twentieth century, materialism "transcended itself" through physics, as the philosopher of science Karl Popper remarked (Popper and Eccles 1977). Matter is no longer the fundamental reality, as it was for old-style materialism. Fields and energy are now more fundamental than matter. The ultimate particles or matter have become vibrations of energy within fields.

The boundaries of scientific "normality" are shifting again with a dawning recognition of the reality of consciousness. The powers of the mind, hitherto ignored by physics, are the new scientific frontier.

The Sixth Sense and the Seventh Sense

Of all the terms used to describe phenomena such as telepathy, "sixth sense" seems to me a better starting point than any of the others. This has a more positive meaning than "ESP" or "the paranormal", in that it implies a kind of sensory system over and above the known senses, but a sense just the same. As a sense, it is rooted in time and place; it is biological, not supernatural. It extends beyond the body, though how it works is still unknown.

An even better term is "seventh sense". The sixth sense has already been claimed by biologists working on the electrical and magnetic senses of animals. Some species of eels, for example, generate electrical fields around themselves through which they sense objects in their environment, even in the dark (McFarland 1981). Sharks and rays detect with astonishing sensitivity the body electricity of potential prey (Downer 1999). Various species of migratory fish and birds have a magnetic sense, a biological compass that enables them to respond to the Earth's magnetic field (Baker 1980).

There are also a variety of other senses that could lay claim to being a sixth sense, including the heat-sensing organs of rattlesnakes and related species, which enable them to focus heat and track down prey by a kind of thermographic technique (Droscher 1971). And there is the vibration sense of web-weaving spiders, through which they can detect what is happening in their webs, and even communicate with one another through a kind of vibratory telegraph (Droscher 1971).

The term "seventh sense" expresses the idea that telepathy, the sense of being stared at and premonitions seem to be in a different category both from the five normal senses, and also from so-called sixth senses based on known physical principles.

Extended Minds and Modern Physics

In the book *The Sense of Being Stared At* I have suggested that minds are not confined to the insides of heads, but stretch out beyond them. The images we experience as we look around us are just where they seem to be.

Our intentions likewise extend beyond the brain. They are generally directed towards people, things and places in the outer world, in accordance with our needs, appetites, desires, loves, hates, duties, ambitions and, sometimes, ideals.

Through attention and intention, our minds stretch out into the world beyond our bodies. I have suggested that these extensions of the mind take place through morphic fields. Here I suggest that these extended fields of the mind help to account for the sense of being stared at and for telepathy.

A metaphor that helps in thinking about the extended mind is provided by one of the simplest forms of animal life, the single-celled amoeba. Some species of amoeba live in ponds and feed by engulfing bacteria. The prototypical amoeba of biology textbooks is *Amoeba proteus,* named after the classical sea god Proteus, a shape-shifter.

Amoebas move around by sending out projections into the world around them. These are called pseudopodia, literally meaning "false feet". (The singular of this Greek word is pseudopodium.) The pseudopodia project out in any direction. Some projections can be retracted while others form, stretching out in a different direction.

Although amoebas are very primitive animals, amoeba-like, or "amoeboid", cells are part of our own cellular make-up. As in all other complex animals, amoeboid cells are vital for our survival.[1] For example, some of the white blood cells, the macrophages, are amoeboid and send out pseudopodia that engulf bacteria and other foreign bodies, just as free-living amoebas in ponds gobble up bacteria by engulfing them. The most extreme examples of amoeboid cells are the nerves (Wilmer 1970). Some nerve cells have enormously elongated pseudopod-like projections, which serve as the nerve fibres that conduct nerve impulses. These pseudopodia, called axons, can be several feet in length, such as those in the sciatic nerve linking your toes, feet and legs to the sacral plexus, at the base of the spinal column. As axons grow, they send out many thin, hair-like projections (called filopodia) that explore the area around the tip of the growing axon.

Nerve cells have many axons, some of which project out towards the surface of other nerve cells, forming a network of interconnections. Some stretch out from the brain or spinal cord into the sense organs; and some stretch out and make contact with the muscles and glands, whose activity they can trigger.

It is no coincidence that the mind is rooted in networks of nerve cells, with pseudopod-like axons stretching out far beyond the main part of the cell body. The mind in turn is capable of sending out mental pseudopodia into the world beyond the body, and is forming networks of interconnections with other minds.

In visual attention, the mind is focused on a particular person, animal, plant, machine, place, object or field of view. A visual pseudopodium reaches out from the body to touch the object of attention and, by doing so, affects it. Of course visual pseudopodia shoot out very fast, in the twinkling of an eye. Other people and animals may detect this attention through their own extended fields, and sense that they are being stared at.

Through social fields, the pseudopodia of attention and intention link one person to another. The bonds between people serve as channels of thought transference. They are the medium of telepathic calls (Chapters 3 and 6 of *The Sense of Being Stared At*), telepathic detection of intention (Chapter 5), and telepathic sensing of distant distress and death (Chapter 4).

Through a combination of attention and intention, the pseudopodia of the mind may also reach out to distant places and objects, and make contact with them, beyond the range of the senses. One result may be clairvoyance, or remote viewing. Another may be psychokinesis, the influence of mind over matter at a distance.

In the book *The Sense of Being Stared At* I have not discussed the evidence for "mind over matter" effects, because my focus is on the seventh sense. Suffice it to say that there is much evidence from well-controlled experiments that people can influence physical events, like the activity of random-event generators, at a distance through their intentions (Radin 1997; Jahn and Dunne 1987). Exactly how these intentions bring about their effects is obscure; but, in general terms, psychokinesis is consistent with the idea of the extended mind focused on physical systems at a distance, and linked to them through pseudopodia of intention.

In addition to the experimental evidence for psychokinesis, there is a growing body of evidence for the beneficial effects of prayer at a distance. In several independent series of experiments, some patients in hospitals were prayed for while others were not. These experiments were conducted according to standard "double blind" procedures, as in clinical trials. The patients themselves did not know they were being prayed for, nor did their physicians. Nevertheless, those who were prayed for without their knowing it tended to survive better or heal more quickly than those who were not prayed for (Dossey 1993, 2001; Astin, Harkness and Ernst 2000). But the healing effects of prayer may involve more than psychokinesis, or even telepathic hypnotic suggestion. Those who pray do not think that the healing power comes from themselves, but from God. But most would probably agree that the focusing of their intention provides a channel for healing grace or divine power.

Finally, one of the most intriguing fields of contemporary research is the study of the possible effects of shared experience on the patterns of activity in random-event generators. Such devices produce random "noise" as a result of quantum processes. On several occasions these "random" patterns have shown large, statistically significant changes all over the world at times when billions of people's minds were focused on the same events at the same time, such as the verdict of the O. J. Simpson trial (in which he was unexpectedly found not guilty of murder), and the cataclysmic events in New York and Washington on 11 September 2001.[2]

Intentions Projecting into the Future

Precognition is the most puzzling of all psychic phenomena. In so far as it implies that future events reach backwards in time to influence minds in the present, it seems to defy all our normal ideas about causality, in which causes precede effects. How could we possibly sense something that has not yet occurred?

We could do so either if an influence worked backwards in time, or if our minds in some way extended forwards in time, connected to their own future states. Could our minds in the present in fact be connected to themselves in the future? We already know that minds are connected to themselves in the past, through memory. But perhaps these two alternatives, a working backwards in time or a projection forward of the mind, are not really alternatives, but different aspects of the same process.

Our minds project forwards into the future through our intentions, which extend outwards not only in space, but also in time, towards future aims. By their very nature, intentions extend into the future. Say, for example, that I form an intention to take the train with my family from London to Edinburgh to attend a friend's wedding next month. I make plans, buy tickets, and so on. My intention stretches out both in space, from London to Edinburgh, via the Great North Eastern Railway, and also in time, from now to the time and place of the ceremony. I also have many other future plans. Some, like my plan to go to Edinburgh, are formal arrangements entered in my diary; others are more vague ambitions and hopes, and others more implicit and habitual, like my intentions to sleep tonight, get up tomorrow at a normal time, have breakfast, work, have lunch, and so on. All these pseudopodia of intention stretch out from my mind now into the future, towards various places, times and events.

Say that one or more of these intentions is interrupted, for example by a disaster. If the disaster affects my intentions, perhaps it can in some way be sensed by the mental pseudopodia that it interrupts, even though these are in the future from the point of view of the present moment. This change in the future may be detected through my fields of intention. It may affect me first of all physiologically and emotionally. I may remain unaware of it, or I may become aware of this impending change either through a vague feeling of unease or foreboding, or through a more specific intuition, or through a dream. The connection from the future event to me now takes place through my intentions, extended outwards in space and time, like mental filaments in the future, more in the near future, and fewer in the remote future.

Freedom and Determinism

Precognition inevitably raises deep questions about freedom and determinism. If we know that something is going to happen, does that mean the future is fixed? And if the future is fixed, does that mean that free will is an illusion?

These problems are not as bad as they seem. First, precognition is not definite. Any premonition or precognition can be recognized only in retrospect (see Chapters 15 and 16 of *The Sense of Being Stared At*). Hence, before the event to which it refers, it has an indeterminate status, at best a probability.

Second, the usual theoretical contrast between a future that is entirely determined or entirely undetermined is unrealistic and artificial. The view of an entirely determined future admits no freedom or choice, or even chance. By contrast, the view of an entirely undetermined future implies that in the present there is a sudden collapse of all undetermined possibilities into determined facts the instant they enter the present, a vertical drop from total indeterminism to total determinism. As the mathematician Ralph Abraham has pointed out, a more plausible view is that there are intermediates between those extremes. One simple model is that there is a gradient of determination. The immediate future is more determined than the remote future.

Immediately, much is indeed more or less fixed. For example, for the straightforward physical reasons like inertia and acceleration due to gravity, the moon will continue in its orbit, and a stone dropped a second ago from the top of a cliff will continue to fall until it reaches the ground at the bottom. Animals and people will continue to act in accordance with their already formed intentions. The closer the future is to the present, the more determined it seems, and the more predictable—except for unexpected disasters or accidents, or surprising decisions, or creative acts. The further away the future is from the present, the less determined and the less predictable.

Even the relatively determined near future is predictable only in terms of probabilities. We are used to this kind of probabilistic prediction from everyday life, for example in weather forecasts, or in economic forecasts, or in the life-expectancy calculations of insurers. Indeed, actuaries in insurance companies were among the first people in the world of business to use mathematical theories of probability, starting in the late seventeenth century. These theories of probability originated in a correspondence between the mathematician and philosopher Blaise Pascal (1623–1662) and the mathematician Pierre de Fermat (1601–1665) about the mathematics of games of chance, the throwing of dice and the value of bets.

At the beginning of the twentieth century, most scientists believed that messy and inexact predictions in terms of probabilities were simply a result of limited human knowledge and limited capacities to carry out calculations. All events in the physical world were fully determined. The future was in principle entirely predictable, although in practice most things could not be predicted with any accuracy. Nevertheless it was believed that everything would be predictable if there were a mathematical intelligence vastly superior to our own. In the early nineteenth century, the French physicist Pierre-Simon Laplace epitomized this ideal in a kind of thought experiment:

> Consider an intelligence which, at any instant, could have a knowledge of all forces controlling nature together with the momentary conditions of all the entities of which all nature consists. If this intelligence were powerful enough to submit all these data to analysis it would be able to embrace in a single formula the movements of the largest bodies in the universe and those of the lightest atoms; for it nothing would be uncertain; the future and the past would be equally present before its eyes. (Laplace [1819] 1951: 4)

Physicists have now abandoned this fantasy. Indeterminism lies at the heart of quantum physics. Predictions are possible only in terms of probability, even in principle. In addition, through the rise of chaos and complexity theories, many natural processes are now modeled in terms of chaotic dynamics.

Old-style determinism is no longer a fundamental principle of physics, though it may be useful as a mathematical abstraction in technologies like rocket science. Mechanistic determinism works best when it is applied to machines, which are specifically made and designed to act in a predictable way, such as computers. The last thing we want to happen is for our machines to work capriciously, subject to random errors or fluctuating probabilities. But they go wrong anyway, and break down unpredictably.

The pseudopodia of intention that project into the future from people, and from other animals, are projected into a realm not of complete determinism or of complete indeterminism, but of probability. They themselves contribute to the probabilities of what will happen. My intentions affect the future. Other people's intentions, and what is probably going to happen, also affect my intentions.

Can pseudopodia of intention themselves interact in the future? For example, because of my intention to take the train from London to Edinburgh, I need to be at King's Cross station on a particular day at a particular time. Someone I know may be planning to take a different train from King's Cross, and our plans mean that we are likely to meet at the station. Our intentions overlap or intersect. Shortly before we actually meet, I may start thinking about this other person, or that person may start thinking of me. And then we actually meet. Such anticipations of meetings are quite common (see Chapter 17 of *The Sense of Being Stared At*).

The idea of pseudopodia of intention reaching into the realm of future probabilities is not a full and complete theory of precognition, or of other aspects of the seventh sense; rather it is a preliminary attempt to think about the seventh sense in terms of the extended mind, using a biological metaphor. We can see the "sense organs" of the seventh sense as the pseudopodia of the mind stretching out into the external world, and into the future.

Theories of Psychic Phenomena

Before discussing in more detail my own ideas about the extended mind, I briefly survey a variety of other theories of psychic phenomena, to give an idea of the alternatives (Stokes 1987).

1. First of all, there is the standard viewpoint of dogmatic sceptics, who claim that there is nothing to explain. All apparent "paranormal" phenomena are illusions, errors, chance coincidences, the products of subtle sensory cues, or even the result of fraud and deceit. All the evidence without exception can be denied, dismissed or ignored. The mind is nothing but the activity of the brain, and there are no new fields or kinds of information transfer that are not already recognized by orthodox physics.

2. For many decades, some psychic researchers have adopted dualistic theories of mind and matter, following the extreme dualism of Rene Descartes. The world of matter is entirely separate from the world of consciousness or spirit, which is non-material and exists outside space and time. Descartes himself thought of the mind as essentially spiritual, and thought that humans were the only mortal beings to have this spiritual nature. They were also the only spiritual beings to have a bodily nature. All other kinds of spiritual beings were non-material, like angels and God.

   A non-material consciousness unlimited by space and time, or rather outside space and time, might help explain how psychic phenomena take place at a distance. But unfortunately no one has been able to suggest exactly how it might interact with brains or anything else material, given that it is essentially outside space (Smythies 2000). Another problem is that much of the mind is unconscious, not conscious. And where is the unconscious located? Is it material and inside space, or spiritual and outside space?

Last but not least, Cartesian dualism limits consciousness to human beings, and denies it to non-human animals. Hence it cannot explain the biological nature of the seventh sense.

A form of disembodied consciousness outside space and time might be ideal for understanding eternal abstract ideas and mathematical equations. It would be entirely rational and impersonal. But these kinds of disembodied rational thoughts would not be much help to a mother in picking up her baby's needs telepathically, or to a dog in knowing when its owner is coming home.

3. A variety of theorists have proposed that in addition to the familiar three dimensions of space and one of time, there are extra dimensions that might help to explain psychic phenomena. In the 1920s when researchers like John Dunne (1958) suggested the existence of a single extra dimension it seemed extremely daring. In the 1970s, Gertrude Schmeidler (1972) suggested that the universe contains an extra dimension that permits "topological folding", so that two regions that appear to be widely separated might be in immediate contact through this extra dimension. A few years later an eight-dimensional model of space-time was proposed to explain ESP (Targ, Puthoff and May 1979).

Within mainstream physics extra dimensions now come cheap. The equations of quantum physics involve numerous extra dimensions. So does the branch of mathematics called dynamics. In modern dynamics, processes of change are modeled in "phase spaces" in which the system moves towards a goal, called an attractor. Such attractors are an essential aspect of chaos theory, which, in the 1980s, revolutionized scientific thinking about complex systems. Complex systems may have dozens of dimensions, or even hundreds or thousands, in their phase spaces (Gleik 1988).

In superstring theory, a branch of physics that combines cosmology and fundamental particle physics, the universe is supposed to be embedded in eleven dimensions, ten of space and one of time (Davies 1984; Greene 1999). Brane theory, as advocated by Stephen Hawking in his book *The Universe in a Nutshell* (2001), has ten or eleven dimensions.

In this context, it is not surprising that some researchers have suggested that extra dimensions might help explain psi phenomena. Some have also proposed that numerous independent space-time systems may coexist and interact with each other (Smythies 2000). The problem is that such suggestions are very vague. They do not make it clear how these extra dimensions might help explain telepathy, for example or precognition.

4. Jon Taylor (2000) has recently proposed a theory of ESP in which information transfer occurs between living brains by a kind of resonance between similar patterns of nervous activity. He accounts for precognition by supposing, first, that future events already exist and, second, that resonance can occur through time. His theory is based on the special theory of relativity. "Einstein's special theory of relativity combines the three co-ordinates of space with one of time, to create a frozen-block universe of four-dimensional space-time. The model implies that all events, future as well as past, already exist on the space-time continuum" (Taylor 2000). One problem with this theory is that even within physics itself, the Einstein block-universe seems incompatible with quantum physics, in which the future is not fixed. Another problem is that the block-universe seems to be incompatible with any form of free will.

5. In the 1970s the parapsychologist Rex Stanford (1978) put forward a general theory of psi phenomena that he called "conformance behavior". Although this theory was vague, it focused attention on two essential features of psychic phenomena: first, that psi effects occur in accordance with the goals or needs of living organisms and, second, that organisms, through their goals and needs, affect random processes. One of the strengths of Stanford's theory was that it did not require conscious intention, in good agreement with the observation that psi phenomena often occur unconsciously.

6. The parapsychologist William Braud (1981) has made an important contribution to theories about psi, even though it is not a theory in itself. He contrasted conditions of "lability" and "inertia". Lability is the ready capacity for change, "the ease with which a system can move from one state to another, the amount of 'free variability' in the system." Inertia is the opposite, the tendency to resist change.[3] Braud proposed that psychokinesis should be related directly to the amount of randomness in the target system: the more lability, the more the capacity for psi effects; conversely, the more inertia, the lower the capacity for psi effects. In relation to telepathy and other aspects of ESP, labile minds should be more receptive than minds with a strong inertia. In dreaming, meditation and relaxation, the mind is more labile; it can flit quickly from one idea or image to another, and in such states, minds do indeed seem more open to psychic influences. Novelty also facilitates receptivity to psi; by definition, it involves a change from an old pattern. By contrast, when attention is focused on the external physical and social worlds, their stability and inertia usually make the mind less labile, and less receptive to subtle psychic influences (see Hansen 2001).

7. For more than forty years, some researchers have suggested that quantum physics may help provide an explanation for psychic phenomena.

Among quantum physicists there is a long-standing controversy about what constitutes a "measurement" or "observation". Some physicists argue that consciousness plays an essential role, interrelating the observer and the observed. A few, most notably Evan Harris Walker (1975, 1984), have gone further and proposed that consciousness interacts with quantum processes not only in the external world, leading to psychokinesis, but also within the brain itself. According to this theory, consciousness imposes coherence, meaning, order or information on what would otherwise be random noise within the brain and in the external world (see Hansen 2001).

Another aspect of quantum theory is quantum "non-locality", also known as "non-separability" or "entanglement". According to quantum theory, when a quantum system (such as an atom) breaks up into parts, these parts remain "entangled" with each other in such a way that a change in one is instantaneously coupled to a change in another, even though they may be many miles apart. For example, when a pair of photons are emitted from the same atom, their polarization is undetermined, although one is obliged to have a polarization opposite to the other. As soon as the polarization of one is measured, the other has the opposite polarization instantaneously. Albert Einstein was deeply unhappy about this aspect of quantum theory precisely because it appeared to allow a "spooky action at a distance". But experiments have shown that quantum non-locality is indeed a fundamental feature of reality (Davies and Gribbin 1991).

Several quantum physicists have suggested that phenomena like telepathy and psychokinesis involve quantum non-locality. Through quantum physics, there really may be a spooky action at a distance, by which minds affect other minds or physical systems on which they are focused.

Brian Josephson and his colleague Fotini Pallikari-Viras, in a paper entitled "Biological Utilization of Quantum Nonlocality", have proposed that focusing in relation to goals may change quantum probability distributions, and that this focusing would become more effective as learning took place:

> The kind of focussing process involved can be illustrated with a simple example. This consists of a coil attached by a length of wire to an ammeter a short distance away. The meter needle can be caused to deflect by moving a magnet in the vicinity of the coil. A person who does not understand the facts of magnetism and attempting to produce a meter deflection in a particular direction will at first move the magnet randomly and hence produce deflections in a random direction. But he may in time discover the principle that is involved and utilise the magnet in a non-random way, and gain the ability to produce deflection in the prescribed direction at will. In exemplification of the processes described above, his learning process changes an initially random distribution of magnet movements into one focussed with regard to the goal, the principles referred to above. The proposal being made here is that mechanisms of a similar kind may be operative at a microscopic level in biosystems. (Josephson and Pallikari-Viras 1991)

This is not a complete review of all the various theories of psi, but it illustrates the main ideas in this field. It also shows how far we are from understanding these unexplained phenomena. My own hypothesis resembles some of the ideas proposed above, but it starts neither from quantum physics nor from theories of human consciousness, but from biology. As a biologist, I see psychic phenomena as rooted in our biological nature. I suggest they arise from fields of a kind that are fundamental to all living organisms, namely morphic fields.

Mental Fields

I first became convinced that living organisms were organized by fields when I was doing research at Cambridge University on the development of plants. How do plants grow from simple embryos inside seeds into foxgloves, sequoias or bamboos? How do leaves, flowers and fruits take up their characteristic forms? These questions are about what biologists call morphogenesis, the coming into being of form (from Greek *morphe* = form + *genesis* = coming-into-being). The same problems arise in understanding how fertilized egg cells in animals give rise to fruit flies, goldfish or elephants.

The naive answer is to say that everything is genetically programmed. Somehow each developing plant or animal follows the instructions coded in its genes. The problem with this theory is that we actually know what genes do: they code for the sequence of building blocks, called amino acids, that make up protein molecules. Also, some genes are concerned with the control of protein synthesis. This is a very different matter from "programming" morphogenesis or instinctive behavior.

Genes enable cells to make the right proteins at the right times as the organism develops. But how does having the right proteins explain the shape of a flower, or the structure of a mouse? No one knows. This is one of the major unsolved problems of biology. Sydney Brenner, one of the most perceptive of molecular biologists, summarized the situation in 2001 as follows:

> If you simply say, "Development is just a matter of turning on the right genes in the right place at the right time and that's the answer" that's absolutely true. But it's absolutely useless, because somewhere deep down what we'd really like to do is to actually go on and make a mouse. ... Of course no one will build a real mouse, but we'd like to be able to make a gedanken (imaginary) mouse. (Brenner 2001)

Over the last forty years an enormous effort has gone into studying genes and the control of gene activity. A vast amount of detailed information is now available, but as Brenner points out, this does not amount to understanding the development of a mouse or any other organism. Turning on genes and making the right proteins in the right cells and at the right times is only the first of many steps.

To say that cells, tissues and organs simply assemble themselves automatically is like saying that if all the materials were delivered to a building site at the right times, the building would automatically assemble itself in the right shape as a result of blind physical forces. Obviously this is not the case. Buildings do not construct themselves, and they are built to a plan. Moreover, the plan is not contained in the building materials. It is more like a spatial idea, a pattern of information. Nevertheless it has real effects, and determines how the building materials are put together, and what form the building takes.

Since the 1920s, many biologists who have studied the development of plants and animals have been convinced that in addition to the genes, there must be organizing fields within the developing organism, called morphogenetic fields. These fields contain, as it were, invisible plans or blueprints for the various organs and for the organism as a whole. In mathematical models of morphogenetic fields, the goals of morphogenetic process are represented as *attractors*. These attractors lie within "basins of attraction" in a multidimensional phase space, and draw the developing organism towards developmental aims or goals (Thom 1975, 1983). The development of a mouse is shaped by mouse fields, and the development of a pine tree by pine fields.

These fields help to explain not only normal development, but also regeneration. If you cut a willow tree or a flatworm into pieces, each piece can regenerate to form an entire new organism. Like other kinds of field, morphogenetic fields are intrinsically holistic. The isolated parts retain the capacity to re-form a whole organism, because each part is still associated with the field of the whole organism.

If you cut a magnet up into parts, each part is a complete magnet, with a complete magnetic field. Systems organized by fields are very different from purely mechanistic systems, such as computers. Computers do not assemble themselves; they are put together in factories according to external designs. If you cut a computer up into parts, all you get is a broken computer.

In systems organized by fields, the parts all interact through the field of the whole system. For example, the planets and the sun all interact through the gravitational field of the solar system. Magnetic fields are within and around magnets, and interact with other magnetic fields nearby, and also with electrical currents. Likewise, morphogenetic fields are within and around the plants and animals they organize, and interrelate their parts (Sheldrake 1981, 1988).

The trouble is that no one knows exactly what morphogenetic fields are, or how they work. Most biologists assume that they will eventually be explained in terms of conventional physics and chemistry. For a variety of reasons, I do not agree. I think they are a new kind of field, of a kind not yet recognized by physics. In my two books on this subject, *A New Science of Life* and *The Presence of the Past,* I discuss the nature of these fields in detail, and also the supporting experimental evidence (Sheldrake 1981, 1988). Here I will only summarize three of their main characteristics.

First, morphogenetic fields work by imposing patterns or structures on otherwise random or indeterminate processes in the systems under their control. Second, they contain attractors, which draw systems under their influence towards future goals. Third, they evolve, along with living organisms themselves. The morphic fields of all species have history, and contain inherent memory given by the process I call morphic resonance. This resonance occurs between patterns of activity in self-organizing systems on the basis of similarity, irrespective of their distance apart. Morphic resonance works across space and across time, from the past to the present.

Through morphic resonance, each member of a species both draws upon and contributes to a collective memory of the species. For example, as a mouse embryo develops, it is shaped by mouse morphogenetic fields containing a spatial memory of countless previous mice, and of the organs, tissues and cells within them.

Morphogenetic fields not only shape cells, tissues, organs and living organisms, but also work at the molecular level. For example, the morphogenetic fields of protein molecules shape the way that chains of amino acids fold up in the right way to give the proteins their characteristic form. Genes specify the sequence in which amino acids are strung together, but they do not determine how these chains of amino acids fold up. A given chain could potentially fold up into an astronomical number of different forms. A typical chain of 100 amino acids has trillions of possible three-dimensional forms. If it folded up by "exploring" these at random until it found the most energetically stable form, it could take longer than the entire age of the universe to do so (Creighton 1978). (This is sometimes called the Levinthal paradox, after the molecular biologist Cyrus Levinthal; see Karplus 1995.) In fact the folding process may take only a few seconds or at most a matter of minutes. Worse still, proteins do not have only a single possible form with a minimum energy; many alternative minimum-energy forms are possible, according to calculations. In the literature on protein folding, this is called the "multiple minimum problem" (Anfinsen and Scheraga 1975). Despite thirty-five years of intensive research, the folding of proteins is still one of the major unsolved problems in molecular biology (Zhou and Karplus 1999).

The most successful mathematical models of the folding process take the final form of the protein as an attractor, or "basin of attraction" (D. Baker 2000). These models are consistent with the idea that folding is determined by a morphogenetic field that greatly restricts otherwise random or indeterminate processes (Sheldrake 1988).

Morphogenetic fields are part of a larger class of fields, called morphic fields, all of which contain inherent memory given by morphic resonance. Other kinds of morphic fields include the behavioral fields that underlie the behavior and instincts of animals. As a kitten grows up, its instincts and behavior are shaped by morphic resonance from countless cats in the past. Its morphic fields contain a collective memory of the species. These fields interact with nervous systems and brains by imposing pattern and order on otherwise indeterminate or chaotic processes within them, as I discuss below.

In addition, the morphic fields of social groups, or social fields, coordinate the behavior of animal groups, such as termite colonies, flocks of birds, schools of fish and packs of wolves (see Chapter 17 of *The Sense of Being Stared At*).

Morphic fields also underlie our perceptions, thoughts and other mental processes. The morphic fields of mental activities are called mental fields. Through mental fields, the extended mind reaches out into the environment through attention and intention, and connects with other members of social groups. These fields help explain telepathy, the sense of being stared at, clairvoyance and psychokinesis. They may also help in the understanding of premonitions and precognitions through intentions projecting into the future.

Mental Fields and Brains

The morphic fields of perception, behavior and mental activity are rooted in the activity of brains, but they are far more extensive than brains. A crude analogy is provided by a mobile phone. The transmissions it sends out are rooted in the electrical activity in its circuits and electronic components. Yet the radio transmissions travel in electromagnetic fields that extend far beyond the material structure and electrical circuitry of the phone. Analogously, I suggest that mental fields of perception and behavior are intimately related to the activity of the brain, but they extend beyond it, through attention and intention.

A few decades ago, scientists thought of brains as like telephone exchanges, with nerves linked to sense organs transmitting signals to the central switchboard, where switches connected them to other neurons that stored memories, or that triggered muscular or glandular activity. Old-style telephone exchanges have now been replaced by the computer metaphor: brains are like computers, and nerve cells work like transistors in an electronic network. But research on brain activity does not support these computer models, with their hard-wired circuits.

Instead, there are complex patterns of activity in large populations of neurons. These patterns of activity can be detected either through brain imaging techniques, where different parts of the brain "light up" as a result of the increased activity within them, or by measuring patterns of electrical activity through electrodes placed over the surface of the brain.

The neuroscientist Walter Freeman, at the University of California at Berkeley, has spent many years investigating these patterns of activity, especially in relation to the perception of smells. He and his colleagues have found that these patterns are not fixed, but change in accordance with the animal's experience. "Brain activity patterns are constantly dissolving, reforming, and changing, particularly in relation to one another. When an animal learns to respond to a new odor, there is a shift in all other patterns, even if they are not directly involved with the learning. There are no fixed representations, as there are in computers; there are only meanings" (Freeman 1999: 117).

Freeman argues that these meanings depend on intentions, which are often unconscious. He models the interpretation of meaning in terms of attractors, using the language of dynamics (Freeman 1999: 107). He proposes that the activity of the brain is modified by meanings and intentions, precisely because it is chaotic, in the sense of chaos theory. "[B]rains are drenched in chaos" (Freeman 1999: 117).

My suggestion is that morphic fields help impose order and pattern on this sensitive chaos, and interact with the brain through their ordering activity. They contain an inherent memory, through morphic resonance. They also project out far beyond the brain through attention and intention.

Extended Minds and Personal Experience

In the book *The Sense of Being Stared At* I have suggested that our minds extend beyond our brains. They do so even in the simplest act of perception. Images are where they seem to be. Subjects and objects are not radically separated, with subjects inside heads and objects in the external world. They are interlinked.

Through vision, the external world is brought into the mind through the eyes, and the subjective world of experience is projected outwards into the external world through fields of perception and intention.

Our intentions stretch out into the world around us, and also extend into the future. We are linked to our environment and to each other.

Likewise, our minds pervade our bodies, and our body images are where we experience them, in our bodies, not just in our heads.

At first it may seem shocking to take our most direct and immediate experience seriously. We are used to the theory that all our thoughts, images and feelings are in the brain, and not where they seem to be. Most of us picked up this idea by the time we were ten or eleven. Although Francis Crick called this theory the Astonishing Hypothesis, it is not usually treated as a testable scientific hypothesis. Within institutional science and medicine, it is generally taken for granted and most educated people accept it as the "scientifically correct" view. Yet the mind-equals-brain theory turns out to have very little evidence in its favor. It contradicts immediate experience. And it rules out the possibility of the seventh sense, forcing believers in the brain theory to deny or ignore all the evidence that goes against it.

The idea of the extended mind enables us to take seriously the evidence for the seventh sense in people and in animals. It helps us recognize that the seventh sense is part of our biological nature. And it opens up vast new areas of the natural world for research and exploration. In Appendix A to *The Sense of Being Stared At* I suggest how anyone interested can take part in this new research programme.

Above all, the recognition that our minds extend beyond our brains liberates us. We are no longer imprisoned within the narrow compass of our skulls, our minds separated and isolated from each other. We are no longer alienated from our bodies, alienated from our environment, and alienated from other species. We are interconnected.

Notes

1. Amoeba-like cells are called amoebocytes, and form one of the three main families of cell types in multicellular animals, according to the classification of the cytologist E. N. Wilmer (1970).
2. For details, see the Web sites http://noosphere.princeton.edu and http://www.boundaryinstitute.org/randomness.htm.
3. Braud understood that lability was related to randomness, and in this sense his ideas were in close agreement with Stanford's and with theories based on quantum physics.

References

Anfinsen, C. B. and Scheraga, H. A. (1975), "Experimental and Theoretical Aspects of Protein Folding," *Advances in Protein Chemistry,* 29: 205–300.

Astin, J. A., Harkness, E. and Ernst, E. (2000), "The Efficacy of 'Distant Healing': A Systematic Review of Randomized Trials," *Annals of Internal Medicine,* 132(11): 903–10.

Baker, D. (2000), "A Surprising Simplicity to Protein Folding," *Nature,* 405: 39–42.

Baker, R. (1980), *The Mystery of Migration,* London: McDonald.

Braud, W. (1981),"Lability and Inertia in Conformance Behaviour," *Journal of the American Society for Psychical Research,* 74: 297–318.

Brenner, S. (2001), *My Life in Science,* London: BioMed Central.

Creighton, T. E. (1978), "Experimental Studies of Protein Folding and Unfolding," *Progress in Biophysics and Molecular Biology,* 33: 231–97.

Davies, P. (1984), *Superforce,* London: Heinemann.

Davies, P. and Gribbin, J. (1991), *The Matter Myth,* London: Viking.

Dossey, L. (1993), *Healing Words,* San Francisco: Harper.

Dossey, L. (2001), *Healing beyond the Body,* Boston: Shambhala.

Downer, J. (1999), *Supernatural: The Unseen Powers of Animals,* London: BBC.

Droscher, V. B. (1971), *The Magic of the Senses,* London: Panther.

Dunne, J. W. (1958), *An Experiment with Time,* 3rd edn, London: Faber and Faber.

Freeman, W. J. (1999), *How Brains Make up Their Minds,* London: Weidenfeld and Nicholson.

Gleik, J. (1988), *Chaos: Making a New Science,* London: Heinemann.

Greene, B. (1999), *The Elegant Universe,* London: Cape.

Hansen, G. P. (2001), *The Trickster and the Paranormal,* Philadelphia, PA: Xlibris Corporation.

Hawking, S. (2001), *The Universe in a Nutshell,* London: Bantam.

Horgan, J. (1996), *The End of Science: Facing the Limits of Knowledge in the Twilight of the Scientific Age,* London: Little, Brown and Co.

Inglis, B. (1977), *Natural and Supernatural: A History of the Paranormal from Earliest Times to 1914,* London: Hodder and Stoughton.

Jahn, R. and Dunne, B. (1987), *Margins of Reality: The Role of Consciousness in the Physical World,* New York: Harcourt Brace Jovanovich.

Josephson, B. D. and Pallikari-Viras, F. (1991), "Biological Utilization of Quantum Nonlocality," *Foundations of Physics,* 21: 197–207.

Karplus, M. (1995), "The Levinthal Paradox Yesterday and Today," *Folding and Design,* 2: 569–76.

Kuhn, T. S. (1970), *The Structure of Scientific Revolutions,* 2nd edn, Chicago: University of Chicago Press.

Laplace, H. ([1819] 1951), *A Philosophical Essay on Probabilities,* New York: Dover.

Matthews, R. (1996), "Sixth Sense Helps You Watch Your Back," *Sunday Telegraph,* 14 April, p. 17.

McFarland, D. (ed.) (1981), *The Oxford Companion to Animal Behaviour,* Oxford: Oxford University Press.

Michell, J. and Richard, R. (1977), *Phenomena,* London: Thames and Hudson.

Popper, K. and Eccles, J. (1977), *The Self and Its Brain: An Argument for Interactionism,* Berlin: Springer.

Radin, D. (1997), *The Conscious Universe,* San Francisco: Harper Edge.

Schmeidler, G. R. (1972), "Respice, Adspice and Prospice," *Proceeding of the Parapsychological Association,* No. 8, Durham, NC: Parapsychological Association.

Sheldrake, R. (1981), *A New Science of Life: The Hypothesis of Formative Causation,* London: Blond and Briggs.

Sheldrake, R. (1988), *The Presence of the Past: Morphic Resonance and the Habits of Nature,* New York: Times Books.

Sheldrake, R. (2003), *The Sense of Being Stared At and Other Aspects of the Extended Mind,* London: Arrow Books.

Smythies, J. (2000), "The Theoretical Basis of Psi," *Journal of the Society for Psychical Research,* 64: 242–4.

Stanford, R. T. (1978), "Toward Reinterpreting Psi Effects," *Journal of the American Society for Psychical Research,* 72: 197–214.

Stokes, D. M. (1987), "Theoretical Parapsychology," *Advances in Parapsychological Research,* 5: 77–189.

Targ, R., Puthoff, H. E and May, E. C. (1979), "Direct Perception of Remote Geographical Locations," in C. T. Tart, H. Puthoff and R. Targ (eds), *Mind at Large,* New York: Praeger, pp. 78–106.

Taylor, J. (2000), "Information Transfer in the Space-time," *Journal of the Society for Psychical Research,* 64: 193–210.

Thom, R. (1975), *Structural Stability and Morphogenesis,* Reading, MA: Benjamin.

Thom, R. (1983), *Mathematical Models of Morphogenesis,* Chichester: Horwood.

Walker, E. H. (1975), "Foundations of Paraphysical and Parapsychological Phenomena," in L. Oteri (ed.), *Quantum Physics and Parapsychology,* New York: Parapsychology Foundation, pp. 1–51.

Walker, E. H. (1984), "A Review of Criticism of the Quantum Mechanical Theory of Psi Phenomena," *Journal of Parapsychology,* 48: 227–32.

Wilmer, E. N. (1970), *Cytology and Evolution,* 2nd edn, London: Academic Press.

Zhou, Y. and Karplus, M. (1999), "Interpreting the Folding Kinetics of Helical Proteins," *Nature,* 401: 400–3.

–12–

Tactility and Distraction
Michael Taussig

Now, says Hegel, all discourse that remains discourse ends in *boring* man.

Alexander Kojève, *Introduction to the Reading of Hegel*

Quite apart from its open invitation to entertain a delicious anarchy, exposing principles no less than dogma to the white heat of daily practicality and contradiction, there is surely plurality in everydayness. My everyday has a certain routine, doubtless, but it is also touched by a deal of unexpectedness, which is what many of us like to think of as essential to life, to a metaphysics of life, itself. And by no means can my everyday be held to be the same as vast numbers of other people's in this city of New York, those who were born here, those who have recently arrived from other everydays far away, those who have money, those who don't. This would be an obvious point, the founding orientation of a sociology of experience, were it not for the peculiar and unexamined ways by which "the everyday" seems, in the diffuseness of its ineffability, to erase difference in much the same way as do modern European-derived notions of the public and the masses.

This apparent erasure suggests the trace of a diffuse commonality in the commonweal so otherwise deeply divided, a commonality that is no doubt used to manipulate consensus but also promises the possibility of other sorts of nonexploitative solidarities which, in order to exist at all, will have to at some point be based on a common sense of the everyday and, what is more, the ability to sense other everydaynesses.

But what sort of sense is constitutive of this everydayness? Surely this sense includes much that is not sense so much as sensuousness, an embodied and somewhat automatic "knowledge" that functions like peripheral vision, not studied contemplation, a knowledge that is imageric and sensate rather than ideational; as such it not only challenges practically all critical practice, across the board, of academic disciplines but is a knowledge that lies as much in the objects and spaces of observation as in the body and mind of the observer. What's more, this sense has an activist, constructivist bent; not so much contemplative as it is caught in *media res* working on, making anew, amalgamating, acting and reacting. We are thus mindful of Nietzsche's notion of the senses as bound to their object as much as their organs of reception, a fluid bond to be sure in which, as he says, "seeing becomes seeing *something*" (Nietzsche 1989: 119). For many of us, I submit, this puts the study of ideology, discourse, and popular culture in a somewhat new light. Indeed, the notion of "studying," innocent in its unwinking ocularity, may itself be in for some rough handling too.

I was reminded of this when as part of my everyday I bumped into Jim in the hallway of PS 3 (New York City Public School Number Three) where he and I were dropping off our children. In the melee of streaming kids and parents, he was carrying a bunch of small plastic tubes and a metal box, which he told me was a pump, and he was going to spend the morning making a water fountain for the class of which his daughter, age eight, was part. She, however, was more interested in the opportunity for the kids to make moulds of their cupped hands and then convert the moulds into clam shells for the fountain. I should add that Jim and his wife are sculptors, and their home is also their workplace, so Petra, their daughter, probably has an unusually developed everyday sense of sculpting.

It turned out that a few days back Jim had accompanied the class to the city's aquarium in Brooklyn which, among other remarks, triggered the absolutely everyday but continuously fresh insight, on my part as much as his, that here we are, so enmeshed in the everydayness of the city that we rarely bother to see its sights, such as the aquarium. "I've lived here all of seventeen years," he told me, "and never once been there or caught the train out that way." And he marveled at the things he'd seen at the station before the stop for the aquarium—it was a station that had played a prominent part in a Woody Allen film. He was especially struck by the strange script used for public signs. And we went on to complete the thought that when we were living in other places, far away, we would come to the city with a program of things to see and do, but now, living every day in the shadow and blur of all those particular things, we never saw them any more, imagining, fondly, perhaps, that they were in some curious way part of us, as we were part of them. But now Jim and Petra were back from the visit to the aquarium. He was going to make a fountain, and she was going to make moulds of hands that would become clam shells.

"The revealing presentations of the big city," wrote Walter Benjamin (1973: 69) in his uncompleted *Passagenwerk,* "are the work of those who have traversed the city absently, as it were, lost in thought or worry." And in his infamously popular and difficult essay, "The Work of Art in the Age of Mechanical Reproduction," written in the mid-1930s, he drew a sharp distinction between contemplation and distraction. He wants to argue that contemplation—which is what academicism is all about—is the studied, eyefull, aloneness with and absorption into the "aura" of the always aloof, always distant, object. The ideal-type for this could well be the worshipper alone with God, but it was the art-work (whether cult object or bourgeois "masterpiece") before the invention of the camera and the movies that Benjamin had in mind. On the other hand, "distraction" here refers to a very different apperceptive mode, the type of flitting and barely conscious peripheral vision perception unleashed with great vigor by modern life at the crossroads of the city, the capitalist market, and modern technology. The ideal-type here would not be God but movies and advertising, and its field of expertise is the modern everyday.

For here not only the shock-rhythm of modernity so literally expressed in the motion of the business cycle, the stock exchange, city traffic, the assemblyline and Chaplin's walk, but also a new magic, albeit secular, finds its everyday home in a certain tactility growing out of distracted vision. Benjamin took, as a cue here Dadaism and architecture, for Dadaism not only stressed the uselessness of its work for contemplation, but that its work "became an instrument of ballistics. It hit the spectator like a bullet, it happened to him, thus acquiring a tactile quality." He went on to say that Dadaism thus promoted a demand for film, "the distracting element of which," and I quote here for emphasis, "is also primarily tactile, being based on changes of place and focus which periodically assault the spectator" (Benjamin 1969: 238).[1] As for architecture, it is especially instructive because it has served as the prototype over millennia not for perception by the contemplative individual, but instead by the distracted collectivity. To the question "How in our everyday lives do we know or perceive a building?" Benjamin answers through usage, meaning, to some crucial extent, through touch, or better still, we might want to say, by proprioception, and this to the degree that this tactility, constituting habit, exerts a decisive impact on optical reception.

Benjamin set no small store by such habitual, or everyday, knowledge. The tasks facing the perceptual apparatus at turning points in history, cannot, he asserted, be solved by optical, contemplative, means, but only gradually, by habit, under the guidance of tactile appropriation. It was this everyday tactility of knowing which fascinated him and which I take to be one of his singular contributions to social philosophy, on a par with Freud's concept of the unconscious.

For what came to constitute perception with the invention of the nineteenth-century technology of optical reproduction of reality was not what the unaided eye took for the real. No. What was revealed was the optical unconscious—a term that Benjamin willingly allied with the psychoanalytic unconscious but which, in his rather unsettling way, he so effortlessly confounded subject with object such that the unconscious at stake here would seem to reside more in the object than in the perceiver. Benjamin had in mind both camera still shots and the movies, and it was the ability to enlarge, to frame, to pick out detail and form unknown to the naked eye, as much as the capacity for montage and shocklike abutment of dissimilars, that constituted this optical unconscious which, thanks to the camera, was brought to light for the first time in history. And here again the connection with tactility is paramount, the optical dissolving, as it were, into touch and a certain thickness and density, as where he writes that photography reveals "the physiognomic aspects of visual worlds which dwell in the smallest things, meaningful yet covert enough to find a hiding place in waking dreams, but which, enlarged and capable of formulation, make the difference between technology and magic visible as a thoroughly historical variable" (Benjamin 1979a: 44). Hence this tactile optics, this physiognomic aspect of visual worlds, was critically important because it was otherwise inconspicuous, dwelling neither in consciousness nor in sleep, but in waking dreams. It was a crucial part of a more exact relation to the objective world, and thus it could not but problematize consciousness of that world, while at the same time intermingling fantasy and hope, as in dream, with waking life. In rewiring seeing as tactility, and hence as habitual knowledge, a sort of technological or secular magic was brought into being and sustained. It displaced the earlier magic of the aura of religious and cult works in a pretechnological age and did so by a process that is well worth our attention, a process of demystification and reenchantment, precisely, as I understand it; Benjamin's own self-constituting and contradictorily montaged belief in radical, secular, politics *and* messianism, as well as his own mimetic form of revolutionary poetics.

For if Adorno reminds us that in Benjamin's writings "thought presses close to its object, as if through touching, smelling, tasting, it wanted to transform itself" (Adorno 1981: 240),[2] we have also to remember that mimesis was a crucial feature for Benjamin and Adorno, and it meant both copying and sensuous materiality— what Frazer in his famous chapter on magic in *The Golden Bough,* coming out of a quite different and far less rigorous philosophic tradition, encompassed as imitative or homeopathic magic on the one side, and contagious magic, on the other. Imitative magic involves ritual work on the copy (the wax figurine, the drawing or the photograph), while in contagious magic the ritualist requires material substance (such as hair, nail parings, etc.) from the person to be affected. In the multitude of cases that Frazer presented in the 160-odd pages he dedicated to the "principles" of magic, "these principles of copy and substance are often found to be harnessed together, as with the Malay charm made out of body exuviae of the victim sculpted into his likeness with wax and then slowly scorched for seven nights while intoning, 'It is not wax that I am scorching, it is the liver, heart, and Spleen of So-and-so that I scorch'" (Frazer 1911, I: 57), and this type of representation hitching likeness to substance is borne out by ethnographic research throughout the twentieth century.

This reminder from the practice of that art form known as "magic" (second only to advertising in terms of its stupendous ability to blend aesthetics with practicality), that mimesis implies both copy and substantial connection, both visual replication and material transfer, not only neatly parallels Benjamin's insight that visual perception as enhanced by new optical copying technology has a decisively material, tactile, quality, but underscores his specific question as to what happens to the apparent withering of the mimetic faculty with the growing up of the Western child and the world historical cultural revolution we can allude to as Enlightenment, it being his clear thesis that children, anywhere, any time, and people in ancient times and so-called primitive societies are endowed by their circumstance with considerable miming prowess.[3] Part of his answer to the question as to what happens to the withering-away of the mimetic faculty is that it is precisely the function of the new technology of copying reality, meaning above all the camera, to reinstall that mimetic prowess in modernity.

Hence a powerful film criticism which, to quote Paul Virilio quoting the New York video artist, Nam June Paik, "Cinema isn't I see, it's I fly," or Dziga Vertov's camera in perpetual movement, "I fall and I fly at one with the bodies falling or rising through the air," registering not merely our sensuous blending with filmic imagery, the eye acting as a conduit for our very bodies being absorbed by the filmic image, but the resurfacing of a vision-mode at home in the pre-Oedipal economy of the crawling infant, the eye grasping, as Gertrude Koch (2001) once put it, at what the hand cannot reach.[4]

And how much more might this be the case with advertising, quintessence of America's everyday? In "This Space For Rent," a fragment amid a series of fragments entitled *One Way Street and Other Writings* (Benjamin 1979b), written between 1925 and 1928, Benjamin anticipated the themes of his essay on mechanical reproduction, written a decade later, claiming it was a waste of time to lament the loss of distance necessary for criticism. For now the most real, the mercantile gaze into the heart of things, is the advertisement, and this "abolishes the space where contemplation moved and all but hits us between the eyes with things as a car, growing to gigantic proportions, careens at us out of a film screen." To this tactility of a hit between the eyes is added what he described as "the insistent, jerky, nearness" with which commodities were thus hurtled, the overall effect dispatching "matter-of-factness" by the new, magical world of the optical unconscious, as huge leathered cowboys, horses, cigarettes, toothpaste, and perfect women straddle walls of buildings, subway cars, bus stops, and our living rooms via TV, so that sentimentality, as Benjamin put it, "is restored and liberated in American style, just as people whom nothing moves or touches any longer are taught to cry again by films." It is money that moves us to these things whose power lies in the fact that they operate upon us viscerally. Their warmth stirs sentient springs. "What in the end makes advertisements so superior to criticism?" asks Benjamin (1979b: 86). "Not what the moving red neon sign says— but the fiery pool reflecting it in the asphalt."

This puts the matter of factness of the everyday on a new analytic footing, one that has for too long been obscured in the embrace of a massive tradition of cultural and sociological analysis searching in vain for grants that would give it distance and perspective. Not what the neon says, but the fiery pool reflecting it in the asphalt; not language, but image; and not just the image but its tactility and the new magic thereof with the transformation of roadway parking-lot bitumen into legendary lakes of fire-ringed prophecy so that once again we cry and, presumably, we buy, just as our ability to calculate value is honed to the razor's edge. It is not a question, therefore, of whether or not we can follow de Certeau and combat strategies with everyday tactics that fill with personal matter the empty signifiers of postmodernity, because the everyday is a question not of universal semiotics but of capitalist mimetics. Nor, as I understand it, is this the Foucauldian problem of being programmed into subjecthood by discursive regimes, for it is the sentient reflection in the fiery pool, its tactility, not what the neon sign says, that matters, all of which puts reading, close or otherwise, literal or metaphoric, in another light of dubious luminosity.

This is not to indulge in the tired game of emotion versus thought, body versus mind, recycled by current academic fashion into concern with "the body" as key to wisdom. For where can such a program end but in the tightening of paradox; an intellectual containment of the body's understanding? What we aim at is a more accurate, a more mindful, understanding of the play of mind on body in the everyday and, as regards academic practice, nowhere are the notions of tactility and distraction more obviously important than in the need to critique what I take to be a dominant critical practice which could be called the "allegorizing" mode of reading ideology into events and artifacts, cockfights and carnivals, advertisements and film, private and public spaces, in which the surface phenomenon, as in allegory, stands as a cipher for uncovering horizon after horizon of otherwise obscure Systems of meanings. This is not merely to argue that such a mode of analysis is simpleminded in its search for "codes" and manipulative because it superimposes meaning on "the natives' point of view." Rather, as I now understand this practice of reading, its very understanding of "meaning" is uncongenial; its weakness lies in its assuming a contemplative individual when it should, instead, assume a distracted collective reading with a tactile eye. This I take to be Benjamin's contribution, profound and simple, novel yet familiar, to the analysis of the everyday, and unlike the readings we have come to know of everyday life, his has the strange and interesting property of being cut, so to speak, from the same cloth as that which it raises to self-awareness. For his writing, which is to say the very medium of his analysis, is constituted by a certain tactility, by what we could call the objectness of the object, such that (to quote from the first paragraph of his essay on the mimetic faculty) "His gift of seeing resemblances is nothing other than a rudiment of the powerful compulsion in former times to become and behave like something else" (Benjamin 1978: 333). This I take to be not only the verbal form of the "optical unconscious," but a form which, in an age wherein analysis does little more than reconstitute the obvious, is capable of surprising us with the flash of a profane illumination.

And so my attention wanders away from the Museum of Natural History on Central Park, upon which so much allegorical "reading," as with other museums, has been recently expended, back to the children and Jim at the aquarium. It is of course fortuitous, overly fortuitous you will say, for my moral concerning tactility and distraction that Jim is a sculptor, but there is the fact of the matter. And I cannot but feel that in being stimulated by the "meaning" of the aquarium to reproduce with the art of mechanical reproduction its watery wonderland by means of pumps and plastic tubes, Jim's tactile eye and ocular grasp have been conditioned by the distractedness of the collective of which he was part, namely the children. Their young eyes have blended a strangely dreamy quality to the tactility afforded the adult eye by the revolution in modern means of copying reality, such that while Jim proffers a fountain, Petra suggests moulds of kids' hands that will be its clam shells.

Notes

This chapter originally was written for the conference "Problematics of Daily Life," organized by Marc Blanchard, Director, Critical Theory, University of California, Davis, November, 1990.

1. In emphasizing the tactile in the reorganization of the human sensorium in the early twentieth century, Benjamin was echoing not only Dada but even earlier statements, such as that of the Russian, Tatlin, in 1913 " ... the eye should be put under control of touch." Benjamin Buchloh, from whose article, "From Faktura to Factography" (1987: 81), I take this quotation, adds to it Marcel Duchamp's "famous statement" that he wanted to "abolish the supremacy of the retinal principle in art."

2. I have used Susan Buck-Morss's translation of this passage from her *Origin of Negative Dialectics* (1977: 83).

3. Take the opening paragraph of Benjamin's 1934 essay, "On the Mimetic Faculty," which reads:

Nature creates similarities. One need only think mimicry. The highest capacity for producing similarities, however, is man's. His gift of seeing resemblances is nothing other than a rudiment of the powerful compulsion in former times to become and behave like something else. Perhaps there is none of his higher functions in which his mimetic faculty does not play a decisive role. (Benjamin [1934] 1978: 333)

Adorno had much to say about the relation between alleged origins of mankind, mimesis, and magic, in his posthumously edited *Aesthetic Theory* (Adorno [1970] 1984). A good place to begin is with Appendix II, "Thoughts on the Origins of Art—An Excursus," pp. 447–55.

4. See also Sergei Eisenstein's 1935 lecture, "Film Form; New Problems" (1977: 133–45).

References

Adorno, T. W. (1981), "A Portrait of Walter Benjamin," in *Prisms,* Cambridge, MA: MIT Press, pp. 227–41.

Adorno, T. W. ([1970] 1984), *Aesthetic Theory,* London and New York: Routledge and Kegan Paul.

Benjamin, W. (1969), "The Work of Art in the Age of Mechanical Reproduction," in *Illuminations,* New York: Schocken Books, pp. 217–51.

Benjamin, W. (1973), "The Paris of the Second Empire in Baudelaire," in *Charles Baudelaire: Lyric Poet of High Capitalism,* London: New Left Books, pp. 9–106.

Benjamin, W. ([1934] 1978), "On the Mimetic Faculty," in *Reflections,* New York: Harcourt, Brace, Jovanovich, pp. 333–36.

Benjamin, W. (1979a), "A Short History of Photography," in *One Way Street and Other Writings,* London: New Left Books.

Benjamin, W. (1979b), "This Space For Rent," in *One Way Street and Other Writings,* London: New Left Books.

Buchloh, B. (1987), "From Faktura to Factography," in *October: The First Decade; 1976–1986,* Annette Michelson (ed.), Cambridge, MA: MIT Press, pp. 76–113.

Buck-Morss, S. (1977), *Origin of Negative Dialectics,* New York: The Free Press.

Eisenstein, S. (1977), "Film Form; New Problems," in *Film Form,* trans. Jay Leyda, New York: Harcourt, Brace, Jovanovich, pp. 122–49.

Frazer, J.G. (1911), "The Golden Bough, Part I," in *The Magic Art and the Evolution of Kings*, vol. 1, 3rd edn, London: Macmillan.

Koch, G. (2001), "Mimesis and the Ban on Graven Images," in H. de Vries and S. Webber (eds), *Religion and Media,* Stanford, CA: Stanford University Press, pp. 151–62.

Nietzsche, F. (1989), *On the Genealogy of Morals,* W. Kauffman (ed.), New York: Vintage.

Part IV
Cross-Cultural Investigations

–13–

Sense-Experience
and Mystical Experience
Mircea Eliade

Preliminary Remarks

In societies still at the ethnographic stage, mystical experience is generally the prerogative of a class of individuals who, by whatever name they are called, are *specialists in ecstasy.* The shamans, the medicine-men, magicians, healers, the ecstatic and the inspired of every description, are distinguished from the rest of the community by the intensity of their religious experience. They live the sacred side of life in a profounder and more personal manner than other people. In most cases they attract attention by some unusual behavior, by the possession of occult powers, by having personal and secret relations with divine or demonic beings, by a style of life, or dress, by insignia and ways of speaking, which are theirs alone. By general agreement, these individuals are regarded as, the equivalents, among "primitives", of the religious elites and the mystics in other and more highly evolved cultures.

If it be true that the shamans and the medicine-men represent the richest and most authentic mystical experience of humanity at the ethnographic stage, we have a keen interest in finding out what function they ascribe to sensory activity in their quest for sanctity. In other words, it would be interesting to know how far sense-experience as such can be charged with religious meaning or value; or to what degree, among "primitives", the attainment of a condition regarded as superhuman may be reflected in the senses.

Let us begin with two observations about method.

1. Our having decided here to enlarge upon the various forms of shamanism and upon the techniques of ecstasy, does not at all imply that these privileged beings are the only ones in whom sensory activity is capable of taking on religious value or significance. On the contrary; among primitives as well as among the civilised, religious life brings about, in one way and another, a religious use of "sensibility". Broadly speaking, there can be no religious experience without the intervention of the senses; all hierophany represents a new incursion of the sacred into the cosmic environment, but hierophany in no

way interferes with the normality of sense-experience. When the collective religious life is centred in a "sensory experience"—such as, for instance the communion of the first-fruits, which lifts the tabus on food-stuffs and makes it possible to eat the new harvest—the act in question is at once a sacrament and a physiological action. Moreover, among "primitives" every responsible action is charged with a magico-religious value and meaning: one need only recall the cosmological implications and, in the last analysis, the mystiques, of sex-activity, of fishing and agriculture; nutrition, like sexuality and work, is at one and the same time a physiological activity and a sacrament. In short, throughout religious history, sensory activity has been used as a means of participating in the sacred and attaining to the divine. If we have chosen to speak only of the "mystics" of primitive societies, it is because their experiences more readily afford us glimpses of the processes which lead up to the transformation of sensory activities in contact with the sacred.

2. Our second observation bears upon the actual experience of the mystics. When we speak of their "sensory activity" we are using this term in its widest and least technical sense; not implying any judgment at all about the actual nature of that activity. The "sensibility" is always and continually integral with a kind of behavior, and consequently participates in the collective psychology, as well as in the underlying ideology, in any society, at whatever stage of evolution. Needless to add that, in taking our stand upon the plane of the history of religions, we do not mean to pursue the analysis of the psychological facts further than their magico-religious significance. We are only seeking to find out to what extent, among the "primitives", sensory experience comes to assume religious values—that and nothing more.

Illness and Initiation

One becomes a shaman (a) by spontaneous vocation—the "call" or "election"; (b) by hereditary transmission from the shamanist profession; and (c) by personal decision or, more rarely, by the will of the clan. But whatever the method of his selection, a shaman is only recognised as such at the end of a twofold instruction: first, of the ecstatic order (dreams, visions, trances, etc.) and, secondly, of the traditional order (shamanic techniques, names and functions of the spirits, mythology and genealogy of the clan, secret language, etc.). This dual instruction, for which the spirits and the old master-shamans are held responsible, is equivalent to an initiation. The initiation may be public, and constitute an autonomous ritual in itself. But lack of a ritual of this kind does not at all imply lack of the initiation; for this may very well be brought about in dreams or in the ecstatic experience of the neophyte.

It is, above all, the syndrome of the mystical vocation with which we are concerned. The future shaman marks himself off progressively by some strange behavior: he seeks solitude, becomes a dreamer, loves to wander in woods or desert places, has visions, sings in his sleep, etc. (see Eliade 1951: 26ff, 30ff). Sometimes this period of incubation is characterised by rather grave symptoms; among the Yakuts, the young man occasionally becomes violent and easily loses consciousness, takes refuge in the forests, feeds upon the bark of trees, throws himself into the water or the fire or wounds himself with knives. According to Shirokogorov, the future shamans of Tonga undergo a hysteric or hysteroid crisis at the approach of maturity, but the vocation may declare itself in more tender years: the boy may flee into the mountains, remaining there for seven days or more, living upon animals "that he catches directly with his teeth" and then returning to the village, dirty, blood-stained, with his clothes torn and his hair disheveled "like a savage" (quoted in Eliade 1951: 114). It is only after about another ten days that the neophyte begins to stammer some incoherent words.

Even when the office is hereditary, the election of a new shaman is preceded by a change of behavior: the souls of shaman ancestors choose a young man out of the family; he becomes absent-minded or dreamy, is seized with a desire for solitude, he has prophetic visions and, in some cases, attacks that leave him unconscious. During that time, as the Buriats think, his soul is carried away by spirits, is welcomed in the palace of the gods, and receives instruction from ancestor shamans in the secrets of the craft, the forms and names of the gods, the cult and the names of spirits, etc. It is only after this first initiation that the soul re-enters the body. Among the Altaians, the future *kam* manifests himself from infancy by a frail constitution, by solitary and contemplative inclinations. If, in a family, one young man is subject to fits of epilepsy, the Altaians are convinced that one of his ancestors was a shaman.

One may also become a shaman in consequence of an accident, or of some unusual event: thus, among the Buriats, the Soyotes and the Eskimos, if one has been touched by lightning, or has fallen from a tree, or if one has undergone with impunity any trial comparable to an initiatory ordeal (such an Eskimo, for instance, spent five days in ice-cold water without wetting his garments, etc.).

The strange behavior of future shamans has not failed to attract the attention of the learned, and several times since the mid-nineteenth century they have tried to explain the phenomena of Arctic and Siberian shamanism as a mental ailment (e.g. Krivoshapkin in the 1860s, Bogoraz, Vitashevskij and Czaplicka in the 1910s). The last advocate of this theory that shamanism was an Arctic hysteria, A. Ohlmarks (1939), went so far as to distinguish an Arctic from a sub-Arctic shamanism, by the degree of neuropathic disturbance in their representatives. According to this author, shamanism was normally an exclusively Arctic phenomenon, essentially related to the influence of the geographical situation upon the nervous instability of the inhabitants of Polar regions. The excessive cold, the long nights, the desert solitudes, shortage of vitamins, etc., took their toll of the nervous constitution of the Arctic populations, producing either mental illnesses (Arctic hysteria, the *meryak*, the *menerik,* etc.) or the shamanic trance. The only difference between a shaman and an epileptic was that the latter could not bring about a trance at will (Ohlmarks 1939: 1, 100 ff, 122 ff).[1]

But the hypothesis "shamanism is an Arctic phenomenon" will not stand up to more careful analysis. There are no special geographical zones where the shamanic trance is a spontaneous and organic phenomenon; we find shamans here and there all over the world, and everywhere observers have noted the same relationship between their mystical vocation and nervous instability; shamanism cannot, therefore, be a consequence of Polar physical surroundings. G.A. Wilken (1887) asserted that Indonesian shamanism had originally been a real illness, and it was only later that people began to make dramatic representations of the genuine trance.[2]

This problem, in our view, has been wrongly stated. In the first place, it is not correct to say that shamans are, or must *always* be, neuropaths: on the contrary, a great many of them are perfectly sound in mind. Moreover, those who had previously been ill have *become shamans just because they succeeded in getting well.* Very often, when the vocation reveals itself in the course of an illness or an attack of epilepsy, the initiation is also a cure. The acquisition of the shamanic gifts indeed presupposes the resolution of the psychic crisis brought on by the first signs of this vocation. The initiation is manifested by—among other things—a new psychic integration.

This explains, furthermore, the social prestige of the shaman and his considerable status in the cultural life of the tribe. Far from being neuropaths or degenerates, shamans are, from the intellectual point of view, evidently superior to those around them. They are the principal custodians of the rich oral literature: the poetic vocabulary of a Yakut shaman comprises some 12,000 words, whilst his ordinary speech—all that is known to the rest of the community—consists of only 4,000. Among the Kasakh-Kirghizes the *baqça,* "singer, poet, musician, seer, priest and doctor, seems to be the guardian of the popular religious traditions, the custodian of legends several centuries old". The shamans exhibit powers of memory and of self-control well above the average. They can perform their ecstatic dance in the very restricted space in the middle of a yourt crowded with spectators; and this without touching or hurting anyone, though they are wearing costumes loaded with from thirty to forty pounds of iron in the form of discs and other objects.

There have been analogous observations about the shamans of other regions. According to Koch-Grünberg, "The Taulipang shamans are, as a general rule, intelligent individuals, sometimes artful, but always of a great force of character; for in their training, and in the exercise of their functions, they are obliged to give proof of energy and self-mastery" (quoted in Eliade 1951: 41 ff). And A. Métraux writes of the shamans of the Amazon, that "No physical or physiological anomaly or peculiarity would seem to have been chosen as the symptom of a special predisposition to the exercise of shamanism" (quoted in Eliade 1951: 41 ff). As for the Sudanese tribes studied by Nadel, there can be no shaman who, in his everyday life, is an "abnormal" individual, a neurasthenic or a paranoiac; if he were, he would be numbered among the fools, not respected as a priest. All things considered, shamanism cannot be put down to abnormality, nascent or latent; I cannot remember a single shaman whose professional hysteria degenerated into serious mental disorder.

One cannot, then, say that

shamanism absorbs the mental abnormality diffused throughout the community, nor that it is founded upon a marked and prevalent psychopathic predisposition. Beyond all question, shamanism is not to be explained simply as a cultural mechanism designed to deal with abnormality or to exploit a hereditary psychopathological predisposition. (Nadel quoted in Eliade 1951: 42 ff)

The Morphology of "Election"

But though we cannot ascribe shamanism to psychopathology, it remains true that this mystical vocation often enough involves a profound crisis, sometimes touching the borderline of "madness". And since one cannot become a shaman until one has resolved it, this crisis evidently plays the part of a *mystic initiation.* Indeed, as we have shown in detail in a previous work, the shaman is consecrated by a long and often difficult initiation centred in the experience of the mystical death and resurrection. Now, every initiation, of whatever order, includes a period of isolation and a certain number of trials and ordeals. The illness produced in the future shaman by the agonising feeling that he has been "chosen" is, by that very fact, turned to advantage as an "initiatory illness". The precarious state and the solitude incident to every illness are, in this special case, aggravated by the symbolism of the mystical death: for to assume the supernatural "election" is to be filled with the sense of being abandoned to the divine or demonic powers; that is, doomed to imminent death.

Very often, the syndrome of the "illness"—that is, as we have just seen, of the psychopathology exhibited by the future shaman—closely follows the classic ritual of initiation. The sufferings of the "elect" are in every way similar to the tortures of initiation; just as the candidate was slain by the demons—"masters of the initiation"—so the future shaman sees himself being cut to pieces by the "demons of the illness". The specific rites of shamanic initiation include a symbolic ascent to Heaven by means of a tree or a post (see Eliade 1951: 116 ff, 125 ff); the sick man "chosen" by the gods or the demons[3] sees himself, in a dream or in a series of dreams, upon his celestial journey right to the foot of the Tree of the World. The ritual death, without which no initiation is possible, is passed through by the "patient" in the form of a descent into Hell. He is present, in a dream, at his own dismemberment, sees the demons cut off his head, tear out his eyes, etc.

This whole set of procedures is highly important for a correct understanding of the shamanic psychopathology: these "crises", these "trances" and this "madness" are not anarchic; in other words, not "profane", they do not belong to ordinary symptomatology; *they are of an initiatory pattern and meaning.* The future shaman sometimes takes the risk of being mistaken for a "madman"—that is often the case among the Malays—but in reality his "madness" fulfils a mystic function; it reveals certain aspects of reality to him that are inaccessible to other mortals, and it is only after having experienced and entered into these hidden dimensions of reality that the "madman" becomes a shaman.

In studying the symptomatology of the "divine election" we are struck by the pattern of all these pathological experiences; their structure is always the same, and the symbolism is always that of initiation. Too much has been made of the psychopathological character of the first symptoms of being "chosen": we are presented, in effect, with a total crisis, very often leading to disintegration of the personality. The "psychic chaos" has its value, within the horizon of archaic spirituality, as a replica of the "pre-cosmogonic chaos", the amorphous and indescribable state which precedes all cosmogony. But we know that, for the archaic and traditional cultures, the *symbolic return to chaos is indispensable to any new Creation,* upon whatever plane of manifestation it may be: every new sowing and every new reaping is preceded by a collective orgy which symbolises the re-integration of the "pre-cosmogonic chaos"; every New Year brings with it a number of ceremonies which signify the repetition of the primordial chaos and of the cosmogony. The "return to chaos" is, for a man of the archaic culture, equivalent to the preparation for a new "Creation".[4] Now, *the same symbolism is discernible in the "madness" of the future shamans, in their "psychic chaos"; it is a sign that the profane man is on the way to dissolution, and that a new personality is about to be born.* All the tortures, trances or initiatory rites that accompany and prolong this "return to chaos" represent, as we have seen, stages in a mystical death and resurrection—in the last analysis, the birth of a new personality.

For our purpose, we want to know to what extent the shamanic vocation and initiation give an additional value to sensory experience, by rendering it capable of more directly apprehending the sacred. Broadly speaking, one might say that the process to which we have just been referring—that of the "illness" as an *initiation*—leads to a change of sensibility, a qualitative alteration in the sensitivity: from being "profane" it becomes "chosen". During his initiation the shaman learns how to penetrate into other dimensions of reality and maintain himself there; his trials, whatever the nature of them, endow him with a sensitivity that can perceive and integrate these new experiences. The psychopathological crisis registers the break-up of normal, profane experience. "Chosen" by supernatural powers, the future shaman no longer resists, with his previous "sensibility", the initiatory experience. One might almost say that, thanks to all these trials, the sensory activity of the "elect" tends to become a hierophany: through the strangely sharpened senses of the shaman, the sacred manifests itself.

Illumination and Interior Vision

Sometimes, the change of organisation of sensory experience brought about by supernatural "election" is easily understandable. The man who has survived being struck by lightning acquires a "sensibility" not attainable at the level of ordinary experience; the revelation of the divine "choice" is manifested by the destruction of all the anterior structures: the "elect" becomes "another"; he feels himself to be not only dead and re-born, but *born into existence* which, while it is lived to all appearances in this world of ours, is framed in other existential dimensions. In terms of traditional shamanic ideology, this experience is expressed as the combustion of the flesh and the breaking-up of the skeleton. Struck by lightning, the Yakut Bükes Ullejeen is shattered and scattered in a thousand fragments; his companion hurries to the village and returns with several men to collect the remains for burial; but finds Bükes Ullejeen safe and sound. "The God of Thunder came down from Heaven and cut me into little pieces," Bükes tells them: "Now I have come back to life, a shaman; and I can see what is happening all around to a distance of thirty versts" (Ksenofontov 1930: 76 ff).

Bükes passed in the space of an instant through the initiatory experience which, for others, takes a fairly long time, and includes the cutting up of the body, the reduction to a skeleton and the renewal of the flesh. No less does initiation by lightning modify the sensory experience. Bükes is straightway gifted with clairvoyance. To "see at a distance of thirty versts" is the traditional term for clairvoyance in Siberian shamanism: during a séance, when the shaman begins his ecstatic journey, he announces that he can see "at thirty versts".

Now, this modification of the sensibility, acquired spontaneously by the shock of an extraordinary event, is what is laboriously sought for during the apprenticeship of those who are working to obtain the shamanic gift. Among the Iglulik Eskimos, the young men or women who aspire to become shamans present themselves before a master they have chosen, declaring: "I come to you because I want to see." Instructed by the master, the apprentice passes many hours in solitude: he rubs one stone against another, or remains seated in his cabin of snow, meditating. But *he has to have the experience of the mystical death and resurrection;* he falls down "dead" and remains inanimate three days and three nights; or he is devoured by an enormous white bear, etc. "Then the bear from the lake or from the glacier in the interior will come forth, he will eat all the flesh and make a skeleton of you, and you will die. But you will find your flesh again, you will awaken and your garments will fly towards you" (Eliade 1951: 267). (The "flight" of the garments is a characteristic feature of the séances of Eskimo shamans; see Eliade 1951: 267 ff.)

The neophyte ends by obtaining the "flash" or "illumination" (*qaumaneq*), and this mystical experience both lays the foundation of a new "sensibility" and reveals to him capacities of extra-sensory perception. The *qaumaneq* consists of a mysterious light that the shaman suddenly feels in his body, in the interior of his head, at the very centre of the brain, an inexplicable guiding light; a luminous fire which makes him able to see in the dark, literally as well as figuratively, for now he is able, even with eyes closed, to see through the darkness and see things and events of the future, hidden from other human beings. In this way he can see into the future as well as into the secrets of others.

When the candidate experiences this "illumination" for the first time, it is

as though the house in which he is were suddenly lifted up; he can see very far in front of him, right through the mountains, exactly as if the earth were one great plain and his sight reached to the ends of the earth. Nothing is now hidden before him. Not only is he now able to see a long way, but he can also discover the stolen souls, whether they are guarded, hidden in strange distant places, or whether they have been carried away up on high, or down below into the land of the dead. (Rasmussen quoted in Eliade 1951: 69)

This mystical experience is related to the *contemplation of his own skeleton,* a spiritual exercise of great importance in Eskimo shamanism, but which is also found in Central Asia and in Indo-Tibetan Tantrism. The ability to see oneself as a skeleton implies, evidently, the symbolism of death and resurrection; for, as we shall not be slow to see, the "reduction to a skeleton" constitutes, for the hunting peoples, a symbolico-ritual complex centred in the notion of life as perpetual re-newal. Unfortunately, the information that we have about this spiritual exercise of the Eskimo shamans is rather lacking in precision. Here is what Rasmussen reports of it:

Although no shaman can explain how or why, he can, nevertheless, by the power that his thought receives from the supernatural, divest his body of flesh and blood, so that nothing of it remains but the bones. He then has to name all the parts of his body, mentioning each bone by name; and for this he must not use ordinary human language, but only the special and sacred language of the shamans that he has learned from his instructor. While seeing himself thus, naked and completely delivered from the perishable and ephemeral flesh and blood, he dedicates himself, still in the sacred language, to his great task, through that part of his body which is destined to resist, for the longest time, the action of sun, wind and weather. (Quoted in Eliade 1951: 71)

Such a spiritual exercise implies the "exit from time", for not only is the sha-man, by means of an interior vision, anticipating his physical death, but he is finding again what one might call the non-temporal source of Life, the *bone*. In-deed, for the hunting peoples the bone symbolises the ultimate root of animal Life, the matrix from which the flesh is continually renewed. It is starting with the bones that animals and men are re-born; they maintain themselves awhile in carnal existence, and when they die their "life" is reduced to the essence concentrated in the skeleton, whence they will be born anew according to an uninterrupted cycle that constitutes an eternal return. It is duration alone, *time,* which breaks and separates, by the intervals of carnal existence, the timeless unity represented by the quintessence of Life concentrated in the bones. By contemplating himself as a skeleton, the shaman does away with time and stands in the presence of the eternal source of Life. So true is this, that in the ascetic technique of mysticisms as highly developed as Tantric Buddhism and Lamaism, meditation upon the image of one's skeleton, or divers spiritual exercises done in the presence of corpses, skeletons or skulls, still play an important part; such meditations, among others, reveal the evanescence of temporal duration and, consequently, the vanity of all incarnate existence. But evidently this "going out of time" by means of the contemplation of one's own skeleton is differently evaluated among the shamans of hunting and pastoral peoples, and among the Indo-Tibetan ascetics; for the former, its aim is to re-discover the ultimate source of animal life and thence to participate in Being; while, for the Indo-Tibetan monks, it is to contemplate the eternal cycle of existences ruled by *karma;* and hence to dispel the Great Illusion (*mâyâ*) of Cosmic Life, striving to transcend it by placing oneself in the unconditioned, symbolised by Nirvâna.

The Change in the Organisation of Sensory Experience

As we have just seen, the attainment of a state higher than "profane sensibility" is preceded by the experience of the initiatory death. Spontaneously, as in the case of the shaman "elected" by lightning, or laboriously as among the Eskimo shaman-apprentices, one comes out upon a level of experience where clairvoyance, clairaudience and other kinds of extra-sensory perception become possible. Sometimes the symbolism of the mystical agony, death and resurrection is conveyed in a brutal manner, aiming directly at the "change of sensibility": certain operations of the shaman-apprentices disclose the aim of "changing the skin" or of radically modifying the sensibility by innumerable tortures and intoxications. Thus, the Yagan neophytes of Tierra del Fuego rub their faces until the second or even the third skin appears, "the new skin" visible only to initiates.

> The old skin must disappear and give place to a new, delicate and translucent layer. If the first weeks of friction and painting have at last rendered this apparent—at least to the imagination and the hallucinations of the *yékamush* (medicine-man)—the old initiates have no longer any doubt about the capacities of the candidate. From that moment, he must go on, with redoubled zeal, delicately rubbing his cheeks until a third skin, still more fine and delicate, is revealed; it is so sensitive that it cannot be touched without causing the most acute pain. When the learner has at last reached this stage, the regular instruction is ended. (Gusinde quoted in Eliade 1951: 63, n. 3)

Among the Caribs of Dutch Guiana, the apprentice shamans undergo a progressive intoxication by tobacco-juice and the cigarettes which they smoke quite incessantly. Instructresses massage their bodies every evening with a red liquid; they listen to their masters' lessons after their eyes have been well rubbed with pimento-juice; and, lastly, they dance in turn upon tightropes at various heights, or swing suspended in the air by their hands. They finally attain the ecstasy upon a platform "suspended from the roof of the hut by several cords twisted together, which, as they untwine, make the platform revolve more and more rapidly" (Métraux quoted in Eliade 1951: 128).

The aberrant and infantile side of these operations is of no interest to us; it is their end and aim that we find revealing. The symbolism of the mystical death—which, moreover, is attested, among the same peoples, in other rites of shamanic initiation—expresses itself in the cases we have cited as a *will to change the sensibility*. Now, as we have already said, such a change seeks, in effect, to "hierophanise" all sensory experience: through the senses themselves the shaman discovers a dimension of reality which remains inaccessible to the uninitiated. To obtain such a "mystic sensitivity" is equivalent to surpassing the human condition. All the traditional shamanic practices pursue this same end: to destroy the "profane" kinds of sensibility; the monotonous chants, the endlessly repeated refrains, the fatigue, the fasting, dancing, the narcotics, etc., end by creating a sensory condition that is wide-open to the "supernatural". This is not only, of course, a matter of physiological techniques: the traditional ideology directs and imparts values to all these efforts intended to break the frame of profane sensibility. What is above all indispensable, is the absolute belief of the subject in the spiritual universe which he desires to enter; nothing can be attained without the "faith". In the cases of apprentices who have no vocation—that is, of those who have not had the experience of "election"—the voluntary quest for shamanic powers implies formidable efforts and tortures.

But whatever the point of departure—supernatural election or a voluntary quest for magico-religious powers—the personal labor which precedes and follows initiation leads of necessity to a change of sensibility: *the apprentice endeavours to "die" to profane sensibility so as to be "re-born" with a mystical sensibility.* This is manifested by a considerable expansion of the sensory capacities, as well as by the acquisition of paranormal extra-sensory faculties. The Eskimos call the shaman *elik,* "he who has eyes" (Rasmussen 1932: 27), thereby emphasising his clairvoyance. The shamanic visual power is described, among the Selk'nam of Tierra del Fuego, as "an eye which, stretching out of the magician's body, goes in a straight line towards the object that it has to observe while still remaining united with the magician" (Gusinde 1931: 751). This occult power, say the Fuegians, stretches out like "a thread of gum", and the image corresponds to a genuine ability to see at a distance; and of this the neophyte has to give proof by describing, without moving from his place, objects hidden some distance away from him (Gusinde 1937: 784 ff).

Extra-Sensory Perception and Paranormal Powers

We now touch upon a problem of the greatest importance, one which cannot be altogether avoided although it exceeds the range of the present study—that is, the question of the *reality* of the extra-sensory capacities and paranormal powers ascribed to the shamans and medicine-men. Although research into this question is still at its beginning, a fairly large number of ethnographic documents has already put the authenticity of such phenomena beyond doubt. Recently, an ethnologist who is also a philosopher, Ernesto de Martino, subjected the testimonies of explorers concerning extra-sensory perception to a searching criticism and concluded that they were real.[5] From among the best-observed cases, let us recall those of clairvoyance and thought-reading among the shamans of Tonga, recorded by Shirokogorov: some strange cases of prophetic clairvoyance in dreams among the Pygmies, as well as cases of the discovery of thieves with the aid of a magic mirror; some very concrete instances concerning the results of the chase, also aided by a mirror; examples of the understanding, among these same Pygmies, of unknown languages (Trilles 1932: 144 ff, 180 ff, 193; de Martino 1942: 25 ff); cases of clairvoyance among the Zulus (Leslie quoted in Lang 1909: 68; de Martino 1942: 28); and, lastly—attested by a number of authors and by documents that guarantee its authenticity—the collective ceremony of fire-walking in Fiji (de Martino 1942: 29–35). Several other paranormal phenomena have been noted among the Chukchee by W. Bogoraz, who has even made disc-records of the "voices of the spirits" of the shamans; these sounds had previously been ascribed to ventriloquism, but this seems improbable, for the voices clearly came from a source far from the apparatus in front of the shaman (Bogoraz 1907: 435; de Martino 1942: 46; Eliade 1951: 229). Rasmussen, among the Iglulik Eskimos, and Gusinde, among the Selk'nam, have collected many cases of premonitions, clairvoyance, etc., and this list could easily be extended (de Martino 1942: 71; Eliade 1951).

This problem belongs to parapsychology; hence it cannot usefully be discussed in the perspective of the history of religions, to which we have adhered from the beginning of this study. Parapsychology examines the conditions under which certain paranormal phenomena occur, and endeavors to understand, and even to explain them; whereas the historian of religions is concerned with the *meanings* of such phenomena, and seeks to reconstitute the ideology in which they are assumed and given value. To confine ourselves to a single instance: parapsychology seeks primarily to establish the authenticity of the concrete case, such as one of levitation, and studies the conditions of its manifestation; the history of religions tries to elucidate the symbolism of ascension and of the magical flight, in order to understand the relations between the ascensional myths and rituals and, finally, to define the ideology which gave them their value and justification.

To succeed in his task, the historian of religions is not bound to pronounce upon the authenticity of this or that particular case of levitation, nor to limit his enquiry to study of the conditions under which such a case may really occur. Every belief in the "magical flight", every ritual of ascension, every myth containing the motif of a possible communication between Earth and Heaven, is equally of importance for the historian of religions: each one represents a spiritual document of very great value, for these myths, rites and beliefs express existential predicaments of man in the Cosmos, and at the same time disclose his obscure desires and longings. In one sense, all these things are real for such a historian, for each represents an authentic spiritual experience in which the human soul has found itself profoundly involved.

For our purpose, what is important is to underline the perfect *continuity of paranormal experience* from the primitive right up to the most highly evolved religions. There is not a single shamanic "miracle" which is not also well attested in the traditions of the Oriental religions and in Christian tradition. This is true, above all, of those most shamanic of all such experiences, the "magical flight" and the "mastery of fire". The essential difference between the archaic world and certain religions of Asia, to say nothing of Christianity, has to do with the *value that one attaches to such paranormal powers.* Buddhism and classical yoga, just like Christianity, are careful never in any way to encourage the quest for "marvelous powers" (*siddhi* or, in Pali, *iddhi*). Patañjali, although he speaks at length about the *siddhi,* allows them no importance for the attainment of deliverance (*Yoga Sutra* III, 35 *et seq.*) The Buddha knew them, too, and his description of them follows the pan-Indian magical tradition, as well as the immemorial tradition of the shamans and primitive "sorcerers". The *bhikku,* Buddha tells us,

> enjoys marvelous power (*iddhi*) in its different modalities: from being one, he becomes several; having become several, he again becomes one; he becomes visible or invisible; he passes, without feeling any resistance, through a wall, a rampart or a hill as if it were air: he dives from on high down through the solid earth as through water; he walks upon water without sinking in it, as though upon firm land. With his legs crossed and folded under him, he voyages in the heavens as do birds upon the wing. The Moon itself and the Sun, strong and powerful though they are, he touches, he feels them with his hand; while remaining in the body, he attains even unto the heaven of Brahma ...
>
> With that clear, celestial hearing that surpasses the hearing of men, he senses both human and heavenly sounds, either far or near ...
>
> Penetrating the hearts of other men by his own, he knows them ... With his heart thus tranquil, etc., he directs and inclines his attention to the knowledge of his previous lives. (*Samañña Phalla Sutta,* 87 *et seq.*; *Dîghanikâya,* I, 78 ff; see Eliade 1969: 178)

There is not a single one of these *siddhi* evoked by the Buddha that we do not meet with in the shamanic traditions; even the knowledge of previous lives, a specifically Indian "mystical exercise", has been reported among the shamans of North America (see Hultkrantz 1953: 418 ff). But Buddha is very well aware of the vanity of such acts of magical prowess, and most of all of the dangers they may portend in minds that are ill-advised. After an exhibition of such *siddhi,* the unbeliever might retort that they were not obtained through the excellence of Buddhist teaching and practice, but were gained by mere magic; that is, by a vulgar and useless fakirism.

> If a believer (a Buddhist) claimed the possession of mystical powers (*iddhi*) whilst in a state of multiform becoming, the unbeliever would say to him, "Why, yes, sir, there is a certain charm called the *gandharva* charm. That is the power by which he does all this!" "Indeed, Kevaddha! It is just because I see the danger of performing mystical marvels (*iddhi*) that I execrate, abominate and am ashamed of them!" (*Kevaddha Sutta*, 4 *et seq.*; *Dîghanikâya*, I, 212 ff; Eliade 1969: 179 ff)

However, for Buddha, as well as for Patañjali, the *siddhi* are paranormal powers *the possession of which cannot be avoided.* In the course of their ascetic and contemplative labors the yogi and the *bhikku* necessarily come to a plane of experience on which extra-sensory experience and all the other "wonderful powers" are given to them. Buddha, Patañjali and others drew attention not only to the danger of "exhibiting" such "marvelous powers" but to the dangers that they present to their possessor; for the yogi is in danger of yielding to the temptation of magic; of being content to enjoy the marvelous powers instead of sticking to his spiritual work and obtaining the final liberation.

Let us remember this fact: that the *siddhi* follow automatically from success in the ascetic and mystical techniques undertaken. If we take account that, in yoga as in Buddhism, liberation amounts to an actual surpassing of the human condition—in other words, that one has to "die" to the profane "natural" existence constituted by the law of endless "conditionings" (*karma*) and be re-born into an "unconditioned", that is, a perfectly free and autonomous existence—we recognise here again the same archaic and universal symbolism of an *ontological mutation through the experience of death and resurrection.* Yoga and Buddhism, with the ascetic and mystical practices related to them, are continuations—although of course on another plane and directed to quite a different end—of the immemorial ideologies and techniques which endeavored to change the condition of man by a change in his psychosomatic structures. At the end of long and painful exercises in mystical physiology, the Indian apprentice attains a radical modification of his "sensibility". If one reads the yoga texts attentively one can follow the successive stages leading up to this final ontological mutation. We cannot analyse them here; but we know that, from the beginning of the apprenticeship, one is trying to break down the structures of the "profane sensibility", to make way for extra-sensory perception (clairvoyance, clairaudience, etc.) as well as for an almost unbelievable control over the body. The exercises of Hatha yoga, in the first place those of rhythmic respiration (*prânâyâma*), refine the sensory experience and introduce it to planes inaccessible under normal behavior. And in other ways, one undergoes a progressive "reversal" of normal behavior: in the words of the texts, the senses are made to "withdraw themselves from objects" (*pratyâharâ*) and to turn in upon themselves. The ordinary profane condition being characterised by movement, disordered breathing, mental dispersion, etc., the yogi sets himself to reverse it by practising just the opposite: immobility (*âsana*), controlled breathing (*prânâyâma*), concentration of the psycho-mental flux upon a single point (*ekâgratâ*), etc. This aim, of "reversing" the natural behavior, can be seen even in the Tantric-yoga practice of erotic mysticism: the normal sensitivity is progressively abolished; the yogi trans-forms himself into a god and his partner into a goddess; the sexual union becomes a ritual and all the normal physiological reactions are "inverted": not only is the seminal emission arrested, but the texts emphasise the importance of the "return of the semen" (see Eliade 1969: 270 ff). Once again: all these efforts are directed to "the death of the profane man", and the symbolism of yogi or Tantric initiation continues the symbolism of the shamanic death and resurrection, even though the aim of yoga is quite other than that of a "primitive" mystic or magician.

The "Magical Heat" and the "Mastery of Fire"

Since it would be impossible to study all the "wonderful powers" (*siddhi*) which are as prominent in the Indian—and the general Asiatic—traditions as they are in the primitive, let us be content to observe one type only: the class of paranormal powers which includes the "magical heat" and the "mastery of fire". Their study is instruc-tive, because the documents available derive from every cultural level, from the most archaic to the most highly developed.

One of the initiatory ordeals of shamanism demands a capacity to endure extreme cold, as well as the heat of embers. Among the Manchurians, for instance, the future shaman has to undergo the following trial: in the winter, nine holes are made in the ice; the candidate has to plunge into one of these holes, swim under the ice and come out at the next one, and so on to the ninth hole (Eliade 1951: 114). And there are certain Indo-Tibetan initiatory ordeals which consist precisely in testing a disciple's progress by his ability, during a winter night and under falling snow, to dry both his naked body and a number of wet sheets. This "psychic heat" is called in Tibetan *gtûm-mo* (pro-nounced *tumo*). "Sheets are dipped in icy water, each man wraps himself up in one of them and must dry it on his body. As soon as the sheet has become dry, it is again dipped in the water and placed on the novice's body to be dried as before. The opera-tion goes on in that way until daybreak. Then he who has dried the largest number of sheets is acknowledged the winner of the competition" (David-Neel 1931, ch. 6).

This *gtûm-mo* is an exercise of Tantric yoga well known in the Indian ascetic tradition. As we shall see in another connection (Eliade 1960: 146 ff), the awakening of the *kundalini* is accompanied by a sensation of great warmth. That discovery is not to be credited to the Tantric yogis: as early as the *Rig Veda* the ascetic effort in general (*tapas*) was regarded as productive of "heat". Here we are in the presence of a very ancient mystical experience; for a number of primitive traditions represent the magico-religious power as "burning". Moreover, this magico-religious power is not a monopoly of the mystics and magicians; it is also obtained in the "excitement" of initiatory military combats.

The "magical heat" is related to another technique that may be called the "mastery of fire", that which renders its practitioners insensible to the heat of live embers. From almost everywhere in the shamanic world we have accounts of such exploits, reminding us of those of the fakirs. In preparation for his trance, the shaman may play with live coals, swallow them, handle red-hot iron, etc. During the festivities at the "ordination" of an Araucanian shaman, the masters and the novices walk barefoot over fire, without burning themselves or setting fire to their clothes. Throughout Northern Asia the shamans gash their bodies, and they are able to swallow burning coals or to touch red- or white-hot iron. The same feats are attested among the shamans of North America. Among the Zuni, for example, the shamans play all kinds of tricks with fire: they are able to swallow glowing coals, to walk upon fire, touch red-hot iron, etc. Matilda Coxe Stevenson relates, among her personal observations, that a shaman kept hot embers in his mouth for up to sixty seconds. The *wâbêne* of Ojibwa are called "handlers of fire", and they manipulate blazing coals with impunity (quoted in Eliade 1951: 63, 285 ff).

Such exploits are sometimes collective. Thus, in China, the *sai-kong* leads the march over the fire: the ceremony is called "walking on a road of fire", and takes place in front of a temple; the *sai-kong* is the first to step out upon the embers, followed by his younger colleagues, and even by the public (see Eliade 1951: 400). The most striking example, which has also been the best observed, of collective walking upon white-hot stones, is the well-known ceremony of Fiji. Certain families possess this "power" and pass it on to their posterity. During the ceremony a great number of the non-initiated, and even of strangers, walk over the glowing embers with impunity: but for this, it should be noted, a degree of "faith" and respect for a particular ritual symbolism are necessary: at Rarotonga, one of the Europeans, who had turned back after starting on the walk, had his feet burned (see Gudgeon 1899; see also de Martino 1948: 29 ff). Similar ceremonies occur sporadically in India. At Madras, a yogi made this fire-walk possible for a considerable number of spectators who were not only unprepared, but some of them frankly sceptical; among them the Bishop of Madras and his attendants (see the detailed report in Leroy 1931).

The "mastery of fire" is attested, together with other shamanic marvels—ascension, magical flight, disappearances, walking upon water, etc.—among the mystics of Islam. One tradition of the dervishes tells us that "the séyyd, while listening to the teachings of the sheik and understanding the mysteries of them, became so excited that he put both feet into the hearth, and took pieces of glowing coal out of it with his hand ... " (Huart quoted in Eliade 1951: 361). Lastly, let us remember that a collective ritual of walking on fire still survives in some places in Greece: although integrated with popular Christian devotion, this rite is incontestably archaic; not only pre-Christian, but perhaps pre-Indo-European. One point of importance to us is that the insensibility to heat and the incombustibility are obtained by prayer and fasting: "faith" plays the essential part, and sometimes the walk over the embers is achieved in ecstasy (Romaios 1945: 84 ff).

Thus there exists a perfect continuity of these mystical techniques, from cultures at the paleolithic stage right up to the modern religions. The true meaning of the "magical heat" and the "mastery of fire" is not difficult to guess: these "marvelous powers" indicate the attainment of a known condition of ecstasy, or, upon other cultural levels (in India, for instance), access to a non-conditioned state of perfect spiritual freedom. The "mastery of fire" and the insensibility both to extreme cold and to the temperature of live embers are material expressions of the idea that the shaman or the yogi has surpassed the human condition and already participates in the condition of the "spirits" (see also Eliade 1960: 72).

The Senses, Ecstasy and Paradise

Upon the plane of the archaic religions, participation in the condition of the "spirits" is what endows the mystics and the magicians with their highest prestige. No less than the spirits, the shamans are "fireproof", they fly through the air and become invisible. Here we must direct attention to the important fact that the supreme experience of the shaman ends in the ecstasy, in the "trance". It is during his ecstasy that the shaman undertakes, *in the spirit,* long and dangerous mystical journeys even up to the highest Heaven to meet the God, or up to the Moon or down into Hell, etc. In other words, the supreme experience of the shaman, the ecstasy, is reached *beyond the realm of the sensorial;* it is an experience that brings into play and engages only his "soul", not the whole of his being, body and soul; his ecstasy manifests the separation of the soul; that is, it anticipates the experience of death.

This is no more than we might expect: having already, in his initiation, passed through death and resurrection, the shaman is able to enter into the discarnate condition with impunity; he can exist, in his capacity as a "soul", without its separation from the body being fatal to him. Every "trance" is another "death" during which the soul leaves the body and voyages into all the cosmic regions. Yet, although the shamanic ecstasy is universally regarded as the conclusive proof of "sanctity", it represents, none the less, in the eyes of the primitive, a *decadence compared with the primordial status of the shamans.* Indeed, the traditions speak of a time when the shamans set out on their travels to Heaven *in concreto;* they claim remembrance of an epoch when shamans *really* flew up above the clouds. Moreover the ecstasy, that mystical ecstasy realised only in the spirit, is regarded as inferior to his earlier situation, when the shaman *in his own body* realised all his miracles—magic flight, ascension to Heaven and descent into Hell. The mastery of fire remains one of the rare concrete proofs of a "real" miracle worked in our carnal condition—which, moreover, is why such great importance is attributed to this phenomenon in all shamanic circles. *It is the proof that the shaman participates in the condition of the "spirits" while still continuing to exist in the flesh:* the proof that the "sensibility" can be transmuted without being abolished; that the human condition has been surpassed without being destroyed, that is, that it has been "restored" to its primordial perfection. (We shall shortly return to this mythic motive of a primordial perfection.)

But even the "mastery of fire" is alleged to be decadent in comparison with earlier manifestations. The Maoris declare that their ancestors could traverse a great trench full of burning coals: but in our days this ritual has disappeared. At Mbenga, it is said that the trench used to be much wider, and that the crossing was repeated three or four times (de Martino 1948: 174–75). The Buriats say that "in the old times" the blacksmith shaman touched the fire with his tongue and held melted iron in his hand. But Sandschejev, when he attended a ceremony, did not himself see anyone do more than touch red-hot iron with the feet (Eliade 1951: 410). The Paviotso still speak of the "old shamans" who put burning coals in their mouths and handled red-hot iron with impunity. The Chukchee, the Koryak and the Tongans, as well as the Selk'nam of Tierra del Fuego are all agreed that the "old shamans" had much greater powers and that the shamanism of today is in decline. The Yakuts recall with nostalgia the time when the shaman flew right up to heaven upon his courser; one could see him, dressed all in iron, soaring through the clouds, followed by his drum (Eliade 1951: 271, 227, 231 ff. and 212).

The decadence of the shamanism of today is a historical phenomenon to be explained partly by the religious and cultural history of the archaic peoples. But in the tradition to which we have just been alluding, something else is in question; namely, a myth *about* the decline of the shaman; since they claim to know there was a time when the shaman did not fly to heaven in ecstasy but in physical fact. *In illo tempore* this ascension was not made "in the spirit" but bodily. The "spiritual" state therefore signifies a fall in comparison with the earlier situation, in which the ecstasy was not necessary because no separation between body and soul was possible; which means that there was no death. It was the appearance of Death that broke up the unity of the whole man by separating the soul from the body, and limiting survival to the "spiritual" principle. To put it another way: for primitive ideology present-day *mystical experience* is inferior to the *sensory experience of primordial man.*

Indeed, according to the myths, as we have already seen (Eliade 1960: 59 ff), the Ancestor or primordial Man knew nothing of death, suffering or work: he lived at peace with the animals and had easy access to Heaven for direct encounter with God. A catastrophe occurred and interrupted communications between Heaven and Earth; and that was the beginning of the present condition of man, limited by temporality, suffering and death.

So, during his trance, the shaman seeks to *abolish this human condition* —that is, the consequences of the "fall"—and to *enter again into the condition of primordial man* as it is described in the paradisiac myths. The ecstasy re-actualises, for a time, what was the initial state of mankind as a whole—except that the shaman no longer mounts up to Heaven in flesh and blood as the primordial man used to do, but only *in the spirit,* in the state of ecstasy.

We can understand, then, why the shaman's ecstasy is looked upon as something decadent; it is a purely "spiritual" experience, not to be compared with the powers of the "shamans of old" who, though they did not manage completely to surpass the human condition, were nevertheless capable of working "miracles" and, in particular, were able to fly up to the Heaven *in concreto.* Thus, the "shamans of old" themselves were already representatives of a decadent humanity, striving to get back into the paradisiac state of things before "the fall".

This depreciation of the ecstasy accompanied by a high esteem for the "powers" does not, in our view, signify disrespect for "spirituality" nor the wondering fear aroused by "magic", but the nostalgia for a lost paradise, the longing to know Divinity, as well as the unattainable realms of reality, *with our very senses.* In other terms, one might say that the primitive man longs once more to meet with the sacred in the body and therefore *easily accessible,* and this it is that explains his view of the Cosmos as a hierophany, the fact that any and every object may become an embodiment of the sacred. We have no right to infer from this any "mental inferiority" on the part of the primitive, whose powers of abstraction and speculation have now been attested by so many observers. The "nostalgia for Paradise" belongs, rather, to those profound emotions that arise in man when, longing to participate in the sacred with *the whole of his being,* he discovers that this wholeness is only apparent, and that in reality the very constitution of his being is a consequence of its dividedness.

Notes

1. See the criticisms of the methods of Ohlmarks in our *Le Chamanisme* (Eliade 1951: 36 ff).

2. But later researches into Indonesian shamanism have not confirmed this hypothesis; the phenomenon is infinitely more complex. See our *Le Chamanisme* (Eliade 1951: 304 ff).

3. Within the spiritual horizons of shamanism, this term does not necessarily imply a negative value-judgment. Demons, more often than not, are shaman-ancestors and, therefore, the Masters of Initiation. Their "demonic" character is due to the fact that they torture the neophyte and put him to death; but these sufferings and this "death" are those of initiation, leading to the transmutation of the profane condition into the superhuman.

4. Upon this symbolism, see our *Patterns in Comparative Religion* (Eliade 1958: 358ff, 398ff., and *The Myth of the Eternal Return* (Eliade 1971: 17ff).

5. See de Martino, 1942: 1–19, 19–20 and 1948. See also Leroy 1927: 141 ff; and Humphrey (1944). There is a bibliography of works on paranormal psychology in the volume of writings edited by Greenwood et al. (1940) and in Madou (1954).

Bibliography

Bogoraz, W. (1907), "Chukchee Mythology," *Jesup North Pacific Expedition,* 1st part, Leiden-New York: American Museum of Natural History.

David-Neel, A. (1931), *With Mystics and Magicians in Tibet,* London: Penguin Books.

de Martino, E. (1942), "Percezione extrasensoriale e Magismo etnologico," *Studie Materiale di Storia delle Religione,* XVIII: 1–19.

de Martino, E. (1948), *Il Mondo Magico. Prolegomeni a una storia del Magismo,* Turin: Einaudi.

Eliade, M. (1951), *Le Chamanisme et les techniques archaïques de l'extase,* Paris: Payot.

Eliade, M. (1958), *Patterns in Comparative Religion,* trans. R. Sheed, London: Sheed and Ward.

Eliade, M. (1960), *Myths, Dreams and Mysteries: The Encounter between Contemporary Faiths and Archaic Realities,* trans. Philip Mairet, New York: Harper & Brothers.

Eliade, M. (1969), *Yoga, Immortality and Freedom,* Princeton, NJ: Princeton University Press.

Eliade, M. (1971), *The Myth of the Eternal Return: Cosmos and History,* Princeton, NJ: Princeton University Press.

Greenwood, J. A., Rhine, J. B., Pratt J. G., Stuart, C. E. and Smith, B. M. (1940), *Extra-Sensory Perception after Sixty Years,* New York: Henry Holt.

Gudgeon, W. E. (1899), "The Umu-ti, or Fire-walking Ceremony," *Journal of the Polynesian Society,* 8: 273–6.

Gusinde, M. (1931), *Die Feuerland Indianer. Band I: Die Selk'nam,* Vienna: Anthropos.

Gusinde, M. (1937), *Die Feuerland Indianer. Band II: Die Yamana,* Vienna: Anthropos.

Hultkrantz, A. (1953), *Conceptions of the Soul among North American Indians: A Study of Religious Ethnology,* Stockholm: The Ethnological Museum of Sweden.

Humphrey, B. (1944), "Paranormal Occurrences among Pre-literate Peoples," *Journal of Parapsychology,* 8: 214–29.

Ksenofontov, G. W. (1930), *Legendy i raskazy o shamanach u jakuto, burjat i tungusov,* Moscow.

Lang, A. (1909), *The Making of Religion,* London: Longmans.

Leroy, O. (1927), *La raison primitive,* Paris: Librairie Orientaliste Paul Geuthner.

Leroy, O. (1931), *Les Hommes salamandres. Sur l'incombustibilité du corps humain,* Paris: Brouwer & Cie.

Madou, R. A. (1954), *La Parapsychologie,* Paris: PUF.

Ohlmarks, A. (1939), *Studien zum Problem des Schamanismus,* Lund-Kopenhagen: Sleerup.

Rasmussen, K. (1932), "Intellectual Culture of the Copper Eskimos," *Report of the Fifth Thule Expedition, 1921–24,* Copenhagen: Gyldendalske Boghandel, Nordisk Forlag.

Romaios, C. A. (1945), *Cultes populaires de la Thrace,* Athens: np.

Trilles, R. G. (1932), *Les Pygmées de la forèt equatorial,* Paris: np.

Wilken, G. A. (1887), *Het Shamanisme bij de volken van den Indischen Archipel,* The Hague: Martinus Nijhoff.

–14–

Peyote and the Mystic Vision
Barbara G. Myerhoff

The Huichol Indians realize the climax of their religious life in Wirikuta, a high desert plateau several hundred miles from their mountain homeland, conceived of as their sacred land of origin. Wirikuta may well represent a historical as well as mythical site of Huichol beginnings. In Wirikuta, the First People, quasi-deified ancient ancestors, once dwelled in harmony and freedom as nomadic hunters. According to their legends, they were driven out, into mortality, into a life of sedentary agriculture in the Sierra Madre Occidental. Every year, small groups of Huichols, men and women, young and old, are led by a shaman-priest, the *mara'akame,* in a return to Wirikuta to hunt peyote (*Lophophora williamsii;* Huichol, *hikuri*), a hallucinogenic cactus growing in the high central plateau of northern Mexico between the Sierra Madre Oriental and Sierra Madre Occidental. Although peyote hunts differ, depending on a variety of factors, such as the composition of the hunt party, *mara'akame* leadership, and the like, it is nonetheless a very stable event.

To reenter this sacred land these pilgrims, or *peyoteros,* must be transformed into the deities. The complex cluster of ceremonies and rituals which prepares them for this return includes a rite wherein the *mara'akame* dreams their names and the names of the Ancient Ones and thus determines their godly identities. The peyote-hunt pilgrimage is a return to paradise, for Wirikuta is the place where, as they say, "All is one, it is a unity, it is ourselves." There they "find their lives" and dwell in primordial unity until the *mara'akame* leads them back to ordinary time and life. The climax of the pilgrimage is the hunting of peyote.

For the Huichols, peyote as a sacred symbol is inseparable from deer and maize. Together, deer, maize, and peyote account for the totality of Huichol life and history. The deer is associated with the Huichols' idealized historical past as nomadic hunters; the maize stands for the life of the present—mundane, sedentary, good and beautiful, utilitarian, difficult, and demanding; and peyote evokes the timeless, private, purposeless, aesthetic dimension of the spiritual life, mediating between former and present realities and providing a sense of being one people, despite dramatic changes in their recent history, society, and culture.

The actual pilgrimage lasts several weeks. Each step along the way is highly ritualized, and in retracing the steps of the Ancient Ones, the pilgrims perform numerous actions attributed to the First People at specific locations, reenacting the feelings and attitudes as well as the behavior of the deities. They rejoice, grieve, celebrate, and mourn appropriately as the journey progresses. They do so as a profoundly integrated community. For the hunt to succeed, they must pledge their entire loyalty and affection to each other and to their *mara'akame*. Unless they are in complete accord, their venture will fail and they will not find the peyote. The journey is a very dangerous undertaking. The pilgrims may lose their souls, conceptualized as fuzzy threads (*kupuri*) that connect each *peyotero* to the deity who gave him or her life. If the *mara'akame* is to protect them from the danger of soul loss, the pilgrims must unconditionally give their hearts to him and to the others. Such trust and intensity of affection cannot be sustained in the everyday world, and once the peyote hunt has ended, it is dissolved. The unity and its disbandment are symbolized by a ritual in which each pilgrim makes a knot in a cord which the *mara'akame* keeps during the journey. When the pilgrimage has been completed, the cord is unknotted and the unity terminated. In a statement of great sociological acumen, Ramon Medina Silva said, "It is true that I receive my power from Tatewari, our Grandfather Fire, but I could not use it without the complete trust of my peyote comrades."

As deities, the pilgrims endure many privations. They forgo or minimize physiological needs: sleep, sexual relations, excretion, eating, and drinking are actually or ritually foresworn during this period, for these are activities of humans, not gods. In becoming gods, the pilgrims are cleansed of their mortality, symbolized by sexual relations. Ritually they confess to all illicit adventures; even children must participate, and the *mara'akame* as well. After this confession, they are reborn and renamed, and the godly character so received is maintained throughout the pilgrimage.

Sometime before reaching the sacred land, everything is equated with its opposite and reversed. The known world is backward and upside down: the old man becomes the little child; that which is sad and ugly is spoken of as beautiful and gay; one thanks another by saying "You are welcome"; one greets a friend by turning one's back and bidding him or her good-bye. The sun is the moon, the moon the sun. It is said:

> When the world ends, it will be like when the names of things are changed, during the peyote hunt. All will be different, the opposite of what it is now. Now there are two eyes in the heavens, Dios Sol and Dios Fuego. Then, the moon will open his eye and become brighter. The sun will become dimmer. There will be no more difference. No more man and woman. No child and no adult. All will change places. Even the *mara'akame* will no longer be separate. That is why there is always a *nunutsi* [Huichol, little baby] when we go to Wirikuta. Because the old man, the tiny baby, they are the same.

These oppositions, like the godly identities and like the hunt of the peyote, are not merely stated; they are acted out. For example, an old man, now having become a *nunutsi*—a little baby—does not gather firewood in Wirikuta, for such work is not fitting for an infant.

Primeros, those making their first peyote pilgrimage, have their eyes covered on arriving at the periphery of Wirikuta so as not to be blinded by the glory and brilliant light of the sacred land. Their blindfolds may be safely removed only after proper preparation, which involves a kind of baptism with sacred water by the *mara'akame* and a description of what they may expect to see when their eyes are bared to the sight of Wirikuta.

Once arrived, the party camps and begins to search for the peyote, which is tracked by following its deer tracks. When the tracks are sighted, the *mara'akame* stalks the peyote-deer, and cautiously, silently drawing near, slays it with bow and arrow. Blood gushes upward from it in the form of an arc of rays. (Blinding light, flashing colors, and the general intensification of visual imagery are, of course, constants in psychedelic experiences, and indeed the presence of the divine is most commonly signified by dazzling luminosity.) With his sacred plumes, the *mara'akame* gently strokes the rays back into the body. The *peyoteros* weep with joy at having attained their goal and with grief at having slain their brother; his "bones," the roots of the peyote plant, will be cut away and saved, to be buried in the brush so that he may be reborn. The peyote is removed from the earth, and the resultant cavity surrounded with offerings. The cactus is then sliced by the *mara'akame,* who gives a segment to each of the peyote companions. Then, a pilgrim acting as the *mara'akame's* assistant in turn administers a segment of the peyote to the leader.

This moment marks the fulfillment of the highest goal in Huichol religious life. Unity has been achieved on every level; social distinctions have been obliterated: male and female, old and young, have been treated and have behaved as though they were alike. The otherwise profound distinctions between the *mara'akame* and the followers are deliberately eradicated when the former becomes one of them by receiving the peyote from their hands. The separation of the natural and the supernatural order has been overcome, for the *peyoteros* are the deities. The plant and animal realms have likewise merged, for the deer and the peyote are one. And the past and present are fused in the equation of deer-maize with the peyote. All paradoxes, separations, and contradictions have been transcended. Opposites have become identical. Time itself has been obliterated, for Wirikuta is not only the world as it existed before Creation, but it is also the world that will reappear at the end of Time, after this epoch has ended. Ramon stated this explicitly in saying, "One day all will be as you have seen it there in Wirikuta. The First People will come back. The fields will be pure and crystalline. ... One day the world will end and that beauty will be here again." The past and future are the same, and the present is but a human interlude, atypical and transitory, a mere deviation from the enduring reality represented by Wirikuta. This moment of unity is a foretaste of paradise and eternity.

The rest of the day is spent in gathering more peyote, to be eaten later. On the evening following the ritual slaying and token consumption of the first peyote, the pilgrims seat themselves before the fire surrounded by their companions and eat several segments of their best peyote. This generally quiet affair is the first release they have had from the earlier intense camaraderie and demanding conformity to ritual. Each one is now alone in his or her inner world, for it is not the custom, as the Huichols say, to talk of one's visions. Ramon explained:

> One eats peyote and sees many things, remembers many things. One remembers every-
> thing which one has seen and heard. But one must not talk about it. You keep it in your
> heart. Only one's self knows it. It is a perfect thing. A personal thing, a very private thing.
> It is like a secret because others have not heard the same thing, others have not seen the
> same thing. That is why it is not a good thing to tell it to others.

All that is said is that ordinary people see beautiful lights, lovely vivid shooting colors, little animals, and peculiar creatures. These visions have no purpose, no message: they are themselves.

The year before the peyote hunt in which I participated, before I understood the need for secrecy, Ramon had given me some peyote and watched over me while I had my vision. Afterward, I attempted to elicit from Ramon an explanation or interpretation of what I had seen. It took me some time to understand his reluctance as he attempted tactfully to steer me away from questions about its meaning to observations about its beauty. We continued in this fashion for a while, until at last he said, "It means itself—no more!" Each experience is personal, and only the vaguest references are made to this part of the ceremony. The visions are always good. If one has followed the *mara'akame* and done all with a pure heart, the experience can only be happy, even joyous. Neither nausea nor terror is experienced, with one exception: When peyote is eaten by one who has not properly prepared himself, not truly confessed, or not gathered "good peyote" under the direction of a *mara'akame,* conventional bad visions are said to occur.

Only the *mara'akame* has routinized visions. They are concerned with lessons and messages from Tatewari. He or she sees Tatewari in the fire and communicates directly with him. Thus the *mara'akame* brings back information from other worlds, information of value and meaning to the people. In classical shamanic fashion, the Huichol *mara'akame* undertakes a magic flight to help the people understand the regions of the unknown. But ordinary pilgrims need not be concerned with such cares; for them peyote brings only extravagant, purposeless beauty and release into the realm of pure aesthetic and spiritual delight. The peyote experience constitutes that part of a person's life which is private, beautiful, and unique. As such, it constitutes that part of religion which has nothing to do with shared sentiments, morals, ethics, or dogma. It is within the religious experience but separate from it. In some philosophical systems such experiences are considered the most elevated and most intensely spiritual known to humankind, providing liberation from structure within a structure, allowing for a voyage into subjectivity, into the unknowable, within a fixed framework.

Peyote may be viewed as the Huichol provision for that dimension of religious experience which can never be routinized and made altogether public—that sense of awe and wonder, the *mysterium tremendum et fascinans,* without which religion is mere ritual and form. It provides the ecstatic and enormous moment when the soul departs, flies upward, and loses itself in the other reality. The darkness explodes into dancing colors. The Huichol pilgrims have nothing to fear; knowing that their flight will not last, they can fling themselves into it with impunity. They are protected by the wealth of Huichol tradition, ritual, symbol, and mythology, and by the certain knowledge that the *mara'akame* is guarding them, that they are pure in their hearts. They are at one with their comrades. The religious culture of peyote can be thought of as a strong resilient net that allows for ever higher ascent and greater and greater freedom.

What does the *peyotero* actually see? The *mara'akame* described an ordinary vision and his own contrasting didactic vision of Tatewari:

> And then, when one takes peyote, one looks upward and what does one see? One sees darkness. Only darkness. It is very dark, very black. And one feels drunk with the peyote. And when one looks up again it is total darkness except for a little bit of light, a tiny bit of light, brilliant yellow. It comes there, a brilliant yellow. And one looks into the fire. One sits there, looking into the fire which is Tatewari. One sees the fire in colors, very many colors, five colors, different colors. The flames divide—it is all brilliant, very brilliant and very beautiful. The beauty is very great, very great. The flames come up, they shoot up, and each flame divides into those colors and each is multicolored—blue, green, yellow, all those colors. The yellow appears on the tip of the flames as the flame shoots upward. And on the tips you can see little sparks in many colors coming out. And the smoke which rises from the fire, it also looks more and more yellow, more and more brilliant.
>
> Then one sees the fire, very bright, one sees the offerings there, many arrows with feathers, and they are full of color, shimmering, shimmering. That is what one sees.
>
> But the *mara'akame,* what does he see? He sees Tatewari, if he is chief of those who go to hunt the peyote. And he sees the Sun. He sees the *mara'akame* venerating the fire and he hears those prayers, like music. He hears praying and singing.
>
> All this is necessary to understand, to comprehend, to have one's life. This we must do so that we can see what Tatewari lets go from his heart for us. One goes understanding all that which Tatewari has given one. That is when we understand all that, when we find life over there.

Wirikuta is no less magnificent than the pilgrims had been led to expect in the stories they had heard all their lives. Yet after gathering sufficient peyote to take home and plant in house gardens and for use throughout the year, they leave Wirikuta precipitously. It is said, "It is dangerous to remain." Not a moment of lingering is permitted, and the pilgrims literally run away, following the *mara'akame* beyond the boundaries of the sacred area as speedily as their bundles and baskets of peyote permit. They leave behind their offerings, their deity names, the reversals, their intense companionship, and all physical traces and reminders of Wirikuta. Cactus spines, bits of earth, dust, matchsticks, cigarette stubs, pieces of food—everything that was part of or was consumed or used in Wirikuta—is discarded and scraped and shaken into the fire. The things of the everyday world and the things of the sacred are kept rigidly apart.

Returning to ordinary reality, the pilgrims are left grief-stricken, exhausted, and exhilarated by the experience. An enormous undertaking has been accomplished. They have traveled to paradise, dwelled there as deities for a moment, and returned to mortal life. In their lifetime they achieved the most complete intention of religion: the experience of total meaning and coherence in the universe. If, as Bertrand Russell has suggested, a minimal definition of religion consists of the relatively modest assertion that God is not mad, the maximum definition of religion might be said to be the insight and knowledge of utter harmony and meaning, the participation in the alleged coherence of the cosmos. The distinction between appearance and reality is not merely blurred; the two are the same. It is impossible to put it any better than the Huichols' own description of the peyote hunt and the pilgrimage: "It is one, it is a unity, it is ourselves." Through the *mara'akame* and peyote, the pilgrim has found his or her place in the divine scheme of things: the *peyotero* is of the divine and the divine is in the *peyotero*.

The Structure of the Mystic Vision as Revealed in Wirikuta

Scholars and writers generally agree on the nature of the mystical experience, whether the phenomenon is called transcendence, peak experience, poetic vision, ecstasy, or mysticism; whether it is described in religious or secular terms; whether it is induced by drugs, occurs spontaneously, or is facilitated by techniques that produce bodily changes—altered respiration, fasting, special diets, flagellation, sensory deprivation, rhythmic behaviors such as drumming, chanting, dancing, and physical exercise. Several writers, among them Dobkin de Rios (1975), Walter Pahnke (1966), Alan Watts (1971), Bernard Aaronson and Humphrey Osmond (1971), intrigued by the obvious relationship between religion and psychedelic drugs, have suggested typologies for common constituents of the mystical and the psychedelic experience. I have drawn upon these schemes selectively in analyzing the Huichol peyote hunt as an excellent example of the mystical experience elaborated into a world view.

The most significant theme in the peyote hunt is the achievement of total unification on every level. This sense of unity is the most important characteristic of the mystical experience according to Pahnke, who distinguishes between internal and external unity. Internal unity refers to the loss of the ego or self without the loss of consciousness and to the fading of the sense of the multiplicity of sensory impressions. External unity consists of the disappearance of the barriers between self and object.

Mircea Eliade, in *The Myth of the Eternal Return* (1949), terms this most fundamental experience of unity "the pan-human yearning for paradise." Paradise is the archetype for the primordial bliss which preceded Creation. The feeling accompanying this condition is variously characterized as beatitude, peacefulness, bliss, blessedness, a sense of melting, and an oceanic flowing into the totality. Images of flowing and blending are a common part of mystic experiences, according to Marghanita Laski's *Ecstasy* (1961), a content analysis of ecstatic imagery. Many explanations have been offered for this yearning toward paradise. Freudian interpretations conceptualize it as a desire to return to the womb or as the wish never to have been separated from prenatal dependence. Jungians see it as a form of incest, a reluctance to individuate and take on the demands of adulthood, for after Creation the human being must be born, die, suffer, feel pain and confusion. The human being works, struggles, is vulnerable and ultimately alone; in short, he or she is mortal. The dangers of attempting to reenter Eden are couched in many idioms. The Huichols say that one's soul may be lost in Wirikuta, that the *kupuri* may be severed. It may be called the loss of ego, rationality, volition, or sanity. The awareness of danger and transience is regularly cited as part of the mystic vision, most dramatically portrayed in the *peyoteros'* flight from Wirikuta—an explicit recognition that ecstasy cannot be a permanent way of life.

Also regularly mentioned are feelings of brotherly love and camaraderie more intense than everyday feelings of friendship and affection. Victor Turner (1969) has suggested that these feelings may be called *communitas;* Martin Buber (1965) referred to them as *Zwischenmenschlichkeit,* the I-Thou intimacy that knows no boundaries, when people stand alongside one another, naked, shorn of the guidelines and expectations of role and persona, a seamless, skinless continuity which is the most intense kind of community conceivable. Watts, in *The Joyous Cosmology,* calls the feelings between those who together undertake the mystical voyage "a love which is distinctly eucharistic, an acceptance of each other's natures from the heights to depths" (Watts 1965: 51). Among the Huichols this acceptance is conceptualized, symbolized, and ritualized. The knotted cord binds the *peyoteros* together, but the bonds cannot and should not be carried back to everyday life. Just as the things of the sacred land and the home are separated by leaving behind that which belongs to Wirikuta, so are the human connections undone after the peyote hunt. The *mara'akame* aids the Huichols in relinquishing ecstasy and shows them that they must leave it behind for another year. *Communitas,* like internal and external unity, is also an experience of wholeness, a form of flowing together, the all is One manifested in social relationships.

Transcendence of time and space is cited by Pahnke and others as a universal constituent of the mystical experience. Space does not appear to be treated with special significance by *peyoteros,* except that the usual spatial categories clearly do not obtain. The entrance to Wirikuta through crashing rocks is known as the Vagina. Transit through these portals is perilous, and shamans must typically pass through such dangerous doorways in the course of their magical flights. Clearly, Wirikuta is not in everyday space.

More significant is the notion of time during the peyote hunt. Mythic time prevails. The single moment contains all that was and will yet be, history is obliterated and the present elongated to imply the beginning and the end of the world. The seamless flow into which the peyote pilgrim slips is eternity, a stable feature in mystical visions.

Also significant is the manner in which individuals dwell, behave, and recognize themselves in the sacred realm. Knowledge of this is provided by the ritualization of reversals on the peyote hunt, which serves several distinct purposes. To know how to act in paradise is not a simple matter; being designated a god is one thing, acting like one is more difficult. How does one remain in character for an entire day or evening or even weeks? How does one treat one's fellow deities? Surely not by following ordinary norms. The upside-down quality of life in Wirikuta serves as a kind of mnemonics, providing a basic metaphor by which the pilgrims can coordinate their behaviors and attitudes and understand exactly what is transpiring. If the sacred realm is just the opposite of the real world, one can picture it in detail and relate to it very concretely and precisely, but not just any metaphor will serve. The recourse to the reversals is a way of stating that despite appearances, all indeed is One. Not only are differences and multiplicities of form illusory, but things which appear to be the very opposite of each other are shown to be identical, to be completely interdependent, to be part of each other. Subject-object, left-right, male-female, old-young, figure-ground, saint-sinner, police-criminal—all these are definable only in terms of each other. Paradoxes are resolved in this experience; formulations that tax the rational mind to its limits are managed comfortably and lucidly. The deer, peyote, and maize are one. A logic prevails, though not the Aristotelian logic which holds that A cannot be B. Eliade (1962) has called this the *coincidentia oppositorum* and regards it as the eschatological image par excellence. Indeed, it occurs in countless societies, in folklore, and in the worlds of dream and imagination, always suggesting the mystery of totality.

Ineffability is consistently cited as part of this vision. The experience is essentially nonverbal. In spite of attempts to relate or write about the mystical experience, mystics insist either that words fail to describe it adequately or that the experience is beyond words. "Perhaps," Pahnke (1966) suggests, "the reason is an embarrassment with language because of the paradoxical nature of the essential phenomenon." Another interpretation for the ineffable nature of the mystic vision may be added to that of paradoxicality. As poets have always known, in order to evoke an intense emotional response, effective symbols must be ambiguous to a degree. This notion has been called the multireferential feature of symbols by Turner (1969). The broad spectrum of references embraced by symbols permits one to find in them particulars sufficiently personal to elicit a subjective response. A detailed discussion of individual ecstatic experiences would make it clear to those within a mystical community that each person's vision is distinctive. It is more important for each person to have an intense and private experience and at the same time a sense of sharing it with others. Specific language would diminish the sense of communitas among the Huichol pilgrims; this is implied in these words of the *mara'akame:* "It is like a secret, because others have not heard the same thing, seen the same thing."

Finally, one of the recurring explanations of the power of drugs is their ability to loosen cognitive social categories. Conceptualizations are socially provided and given in language. One of the sources of wonder and ecstasy in the mystic experience is the direct perception of the world, without the intervention and precedence of language and interpretation. The mystic experience is nonverbal precisely because it takes one back behind the word, or more accurately, before the word, to the stunning immediacy of sense data. The Huichols are surely correct when they say that to talk about one's visions is not good.

Peyote Outside of Wirikuta

To discuss peyote only in connection with Wirikuta would be misleading, for it is also part of ordinary Huichol life, and is used on many occasions. One of the most significant features of peyote use among the Huichol is its integration within the society and culture. This notion is especially relevant from the perspective of contemporary American youth culture, in which drug use by comparison is haphazard and promiscuous; with few exceptions, psychedelic drugs, although possibly producing similar visions, are not integrated into a system of meaning which may be regarded as a world view.

Among the Huichols, peyote itself is called "very delicate" and generally regarded as sacred. But to be sacred it has to have been gathered in the proper fashion, that is, under the leadership of a *mara'akame* in Wirikuta. Peyote purchased in Mexican markets is not sacred, according to Ramon, who comments: "That other peyote, that which one buys, it did not reveal itself in the Huichol manner. One did not hunt it properly, one did not make offerings to it over there [in Wirikuta]. That is why it is not good for us." In order to be sure that they always have a supply of peyote from Wirikuta, the Huichols bring some back from the peyote hunt to plant in their gardens.

The references to "that other peyote," the one that can be purchased, is explained by Huichol ethnobotanical classification, which specifies the existence of two kinds of peyote, "good and bad." Peter Furst, in *Flesh of the Gods,* identified bad peyote as *Arioscarpus retusus,* a member of the same cactus subgroup as *Lophophoro williamsii* (Furst 1972). They are very similar in appearance, and only someone experienced, usually a *mara'akame,* can be certain of collecting the good kind. One may accidentally purchase the bad kind, called *tsuwiri.* The results of eating *tsuwiri* are indeed terrible: "If one eats one of those, one goes mad, one goes running into the barrancas, one sees scorpions, serpents, dangerous animals. One is unable to walk, one falls, one often kills oneself in those barrancas, falling off the rocks"—effects are similar to those attributed to *Datura*. The hallucinations described due to eating *tsuwiri* are conventional; a common one is the experience of encountering a huge agave cactus in the desert, thinking it is a woman, and making love to it.

Eating *tsuwiri* may occur not only as a result of mistaking it for peyote; it may be a supernatural sanction, punishment for going to Wirikuta without prior confession. "It is said that if one comes there not having spoken of one's life, if one comes not having been cleansed of everything, then this false *hikuri* will discover it. It is going to bring out that which is evil in one, that which frightens one. It knows all one's bad thoughts." Not only will the *tsuwiri* read one's thoughts, but those who have not confessed honestly or completely will probably behave oddly. The pilgrim who knows that he has lied to his companions will eat his peyote in secret "because he does not have good thoughts, he knows he has not spoken honestly with his companions." When such a person hunts for peyote, he will find the *tsuwiri*, which "only has the appearance of peyote," and when he returns to his companions after his harrowing visions, the *mara'akame* knows at once what has occurred. The man must confess, and then he will be cleansed by the *mara'akame*.

Peyote, like maize, can "read one's thoughts" and punish one for being false or evil. The peyote rewards or punishes a person according to his or her inner state and moral standing. The sanction is immediate, just, and certain, a most effective regulator of behavior in a small, well-integrated society.

Peyote is eaten or drunk ritually only during dry-season ceremonies, but may be eaten casually at any time of the year. It is used medicinally in a multitude of situations—to relieve pain, as a poultice applied to wounds. It may also be taken for energy, endurance, or courage. In fact, it is a panacea. The quantity taken ritually is usually insufficient to obtain visions and must in this context be regarded as having the specific symbolic purpose of achieving communion with the deities.

Peyote-eating for the purpose of experiencing a vision thus constitutes but one relatively narrow part of a larger set of purposes. It is nonetheless quite an important part, though more for the *mara'akame* than for ordinary folk. When peyote is eaten for visions, nonritually, it is taken in a relaxed and convivial atmosphere, much in the manner of the Westerner's use of liquor. Concerning one's first experiences with peyote early in life, Ramon had this to say:

> The first time one puts the peyote into one's mouth, one feels it going down into the stomach. It feels very cold, like ice. And the inside of one's mouth becomes dry, very dry. And then it becomes wet, very wet. One has much saliva then. And then a while later, one feels as if one were fainting. And one begins to yawn, to feel very tired. And after a while one feels very light. One feels sleepy, but one must not go to sleep. One must stay awake to have the visions.

In at least one context peyote may be used in prophecy. If a very young child, upon being given a small amount of peyote, finds it pleasant-tasting, this may be construed as a sign that he or she would make a good *mara'akame*. The interpretation of the taste of peyote is itself an interesting matter; the Huichols insist that peyote is "sweet." "Chew it well," they tell each other, "it is sweet, like tortillas." This may be a reversal brought back from Wirikuta; clearly, though no one vomits after eating peyote, neither is it savored. Huichols eating it look like anyone else with a mouthful of peyote: they grimace, sucking in their cheeks and moving their eyebrows up and down in a most uncharacteristic manner—a reaction to the shockingly sour taste of the cactus.

Cleaning the peyote is not an elaborate process: the roots are usually cut off and the dust and earth brushed away. The little tufts of hair on the top, called *tsinurawe* (the eyebrows of the peyote), are especially delicate and are always eaten. Different peyotes are said to differ in flavor, texture, and color, and one of the pleasurable pastimes in Wirikuta is comparing peyotes and their aesthetic attributes. The most highly valued are those with five segments, five being the Huichol sacred number. These five-segment peyotes are often strung together as a necklace and may be used to adorn the antlers of Tatewari. Peyote is often referred to affectionately as "*ti peyote*" (our peyote) and even spoken to in baby talk. Often its attributes are likened to stages in the growth of maize. "It is new, it is soft like the ripening maize, how fine, how lovely."

Before being consumed, the first peyote eaten in Wirikuta is touched to the forehead, eyes, breast, voice box, and cheeks. The gesture is not repeated after this first ceremonial eating. Peyote brought out of Wirikuta is carefully packed into baskets in concentric circles from the bottom up to prevent its being jostled en route, for, as is said, it is delicate and the trip is long.

Peyote may be eaten fresh or it may be dried and ground and drunk. It may be taken along on trips and given as a gift to a host, to eat or plant. It is sometimes traded for various items with other Indians, especially the Cora and Tarahumara, who regard Huichol peyote as very desirable. It is always in demand and must be available throughout the year, since all major religious ceremonies require the presence of peyote, maize, and deer meat or blood. The ceremonies form an interlocking cycle. The peyote hunt is preceded by the drum-and-calabash ceremony and followed by the deer hunt; substitutes for deer meat and blood are acceptable, but nothing can take the place of properly gathered peyote.

Peyote is no less important as an artistic motif. As Carl Lumholtz has shown, peyote is a theme with numerous variations in embroidery and weaving, a key source of inspiration (Lumholtz 1900).

The Huichol World View

The Huichol world view in several important features represents a cultural inflection of what appears to be a highly regular human production: the mystic vision. If dreams and myths are structured, as Freud and Lévi-Strauss have persuasively demonstrated, it should come as no surprise to find that one of the most private, subtle, ineffable, mysterious, and elusive human experiences—the mystic vision—is also structured. Still, it is easier by far to deal with cultural regularities in matters of an instrumental nature, pertaining to subsistence and survival, environmental requirements, and similar events where utility and efficiency dictate a fixed number of possible alternatives. In the realms of the imagination, metaphysics, the arts, religion, areas which are not identifiably rational undertakings, we expect variation rather than uniformity. Our explanatory concepts are taxed when we find specific similarities in very different cultural settings where history and diffusion cannot be evoked. We may then fall back on old concepts—memory traces, collective unconscious, instinct, racial memories, and the like—or on the as yet incomplete formulations about universal characteristics of the human mind and human nature. Most anthropologists have had to content themselves with mere descriptions of social processes, falling short of earlier hopes for the discovery of genuinely lawful regularities. Nowadays, only the intrepid take up problems of psychic unity and common human experience, though these issues, if hazardous, are among the most important and interesting.

From this perspective, recent studies on the relationship between hallucinogenic drugs and religion may be regarded as a significant development in the attempt to enlarge our understanding of universals in human social phenomena. Osmond (1957), Schultes (1972), and Wasson (1969) have demonstrated that the origins and history of religion are inseparable from the use of psychedelic plants. More recently, Aaronson and Osmond (1971), Pahnke (1966), Watts (1965), and Dobkin de Rios (1975) have developed typologies which draw our attention to the highly regular factors in psychedelic drug experiences. Watts (1971), Pahnke (1966), and Marsh (1965) have been concerned specifically with isolating the effects of a drug experience which appear to be the same as those associated with the mystical vision—the "Fourth Way," as it is called in the *Mandukya Upanishad,* the way that is neither waking dreaming nor dreaming sleep, but "pure unitary consciousness, wherein awareness of the world and of multiplicity is completely obliterated. ... It is One without a second."

The Huichols offer a fine example of this experience; more than that, they provide a case in which the mystic vision is extended and elaborated into a world view, much of which can be explained by reference to their use of peyote. That hallucinogenic drugs produce regular experiences is now an established fact: what interests us is how these Indians use those experiences. To say that peyote is the direct cause of the Huichol world view would be an oversimplification. Peyote use produces the raw material which is built into a system of thought, a *Weltanschauung.* The individual peyote eater's expectations precede and profoundly influence perceptions and interpretations of personal visions. But these expectations are not random; they are shaped by the regularly recurring results of eating peyote. Thus do culture and individual interlock.

Peyote is the touchstone for the Huichol world view. In the basic psychedelic experience we find the source of much of their version of the ideal—in human relations, in the relationship of men and women to the natural world, in the understanding of human history and ultimate destiny.

The Huichol world view may be understood as a combination of several layers of belief: the mystic vision, classical shamanism, and a hunting ideology. Many features typically associated with the last of these include the continuity between man and animal; the belief that the animal (deer-peyote) is reborn from its bones; the deer as the *mara'akame's* familiar spirit; the shamanic flight through dangerous passages to the other world; the shaman's access to direct knowledge of the supernatural realm, and so forth.

Perhaps in the present context the most significant lesson of the Huichol use of peyote is a fuller understanding of a hallucinogenic drug in a sacred context. Peyote produces certain biochemical changes to some degree uniform in their effects. What is done with these effects, what meanings they are given, and how they are integrated and elaborated into a context of significance, coherence, and beauty, is the concern of anthropologists. Simply stated, we see peyote used as a means. Clearly, its effects per se are valued, but they are a relatively small part of the entire picture. To discuss Huichol peyote use in terms of "kicks," "highs," "escapes," and all the other terms used to describe the goals of individualistic drug-taking outside of an integrated cultural setting would be a profanation. Peyote is woven into every dimension of Huichol life. It is venerated for its gifts of beauty and pleasure. But this projection is Durkheimian; with it we see with the Huichols venerating their own customs and traditions, the sense and pattern of a way of life which uses this little plant, this part of its natural environment, so wisely and so well.

Acknowledgments

A shorter version of this paper was prepared for and presented to a conference on Cross-Cultural Perspectives on Cannabis, convened in Chicago, August, 1973, during the IXth International Congress of the International Union of Anthropological and Ethnological Sciences, coordinated by Dr. Vera Rubin. It appeared in the volume issuing from that conference, *Cannabis and Culture* (Rubin 1975). Grateful acknowledgment is made to the publisher for permission to use it in this context.

Field work on which this article is based was conducted during 1965 and 1966, and was partially funded by a Ford International and Comparative Studies Grant administered through Professor Johannes Wilbert of the University of California at Los Angeles, Latin American Center. My colleague Professor Peter T. Furst worked with me in Mexico and collaborated in subsequent interpretations of the data. Many of the Huichol texts were translated by Professors Joseph E. Grimes and Barbara Grimes. I acknowledge gratefully this assistance, and especially that of the late

Ramon Medina Silva, Huichol *mara'akame,* his wife, Guadalupe, and the Huichols who shared so much of their time, their knowledge, and their lives. Ramon led the peyote hunt in which Furst and I participated in 1966; to my knowledge this was the first time anthropologists had an opportunity for firsthand observation of this event.

References

Aaronson, B. and Osmond, H. (eds) (1971), *Psychedelics: The Uses and Implications of Hallucinogenic Drugs,* Cambridge, MA: Schenkman.

Buber, M. (1965), *Between Man and Man,* New York: Macmillan.

Dobkin de Rios, M. (1975), "Man, Culture and Hallucinogens: An Overview," in V. Rubin (ed.), *Cannabis and Culture,* The Hague: Mouton, pp. 401–16.

Eliade, M. (1949), *The Myth of the Eternal Return,* New York: Pantheon.

Eliade, M. (1962), *The Two and the One,* New York: Harper Torchbooks.

Furst, P. (ed.) (1972), *Flesh of the Gods,* New York: Praeger.

Laski, M. (1961), *Ecstasy: A Study of Some Secular and Religious Experiences,* Bloomington: Indiana University Press.

Lumholtz, C. (1900), *Symbolism of the Huichol Indians,* Memoirs of the American Museum of Natural History, 1, New York: American Museum of Natural History.

Marsh, R. P. (1965), "Meaning and Mind-Drugs," *ETC,* 22: 408–30.

Osmond, H. (1957), "A Review of the Clinical Effects of Psychotemimetic Agents," *Annals of the New York Academy of Sciences,* 66: 418–34.

Pahnke, W. N. (1966), "Drugs and Mysticism," *International Journal of Parapsychology,* 8: 295–313.

Rubin, V. (ed.), (1975), *Cannabis and Culture,* The Hague: Mouton.

Schultes, R. (1972), "An Overview of Hallucinogens in the Western Hemisphere," in P. Furst (ed.), *Flesh of the Gods,* New York: Praeger, pp. 3–54.

Turner, V. (1969), *The Ritual Process: Structure and Anti-Structure,* Chicago: Aldine Publishing.

Wasson, R. G. (1969), *Soma: Divine Mushroom of Immortality,* New York: Harcourt, Brace, Jovanovich.

Watts, Alan. (1965), *The Joyous Cosmology: Adventures in the Chemistry of Consciousness,* New York: Vintage Books.

Watts, Alan. (1971), "Psychedelics and Religious Experience," in B. Aaronson and H. Osmond (eds), *Psychedelics: The Uses and Implications of Hallucinogenic Drugs,* Cambridge, MA: Schenkman, pp. 131–45.

–15–

The Embodiment of Symbols and the Acculturation of the Anthropologist
Carol Laderman

Symbolic systems exist on a number of interpenetrating levels, ranging from the most abstract to the most concrete. All contribute to the maintenance of the system. The most abstract level reflects and gives coherence to a world view. Its language and theory are logically consistent throughout a number of conceptual domains. A middle level of abstraction provides metaphors for reasoning in the mundane world. The most concrete level is direct sensory experience which moors the system at strategic points to empirical reality and acts as a structural support to the symbolic edifice. Its "proof" of the system's validity is most persuasive when it occurs in the context of illness or other situations perceived as dangerous, and when effect appears to follow closely after cause. The symbolic structure makes experience meaningful, but without an input from sensory reality the edifice would crumble.

Four salient aspects of the embodiment of Malay symbolism were explained to me by informants, and became, as well, part of my personal experience. According to Malay theory, we are all born with four bodily humors, varieties of Inner Winds (*angin*) that determine personality, and the spirit of life (*semangat*). Some people have, as well, a tendency towards disharmony that only manifests after eating certain foods (*bisa*). These components of the self must be protected from the harm that occurs when, through loss of inner balance, they are depleted, become overabundant, or are seriously skewed. Balance is the key to well-being in the individual, the community, and the universe—the harmonious interaction of the microcosm and the macrocosm, the person and society, the internal and the external.

The first section of this chapter will discuss the embodiment of Malay symbolism. The second section will discuss the acculturation of this embodiment as it was experienced by the anthropologist.

The Humors

Humoral reasoning, based upon belief in the universality of four basic elements— earth, air, fire, and water—and their manifestations in the cosmos, the body politic, and the human person, pervades contemporary Malay thought. Its metaphors center around notions of heat and coolness which, in a humoral system, refer to intrinsic qualities rather than merely thermal temperatures, i.e., alcohol is always "very hot" humorally speaking, even when served on ice; steaming hot squash is still humorally "cold."

Malay identification of heat with destruction and coolness with well-being, a mirror image of ancient Greek humoral doctrine which equated heat with vitality and coolness with ill-health, is reflected in daily language. *Sejuk* ("coolness") can be used as a synonym for "healthful, energetic, and pleasant." *Menyejukkan* ("to make cool") can mean "to calm, revive, repair, amuse." A person whose liver (the Malay seat of emotions) is cool is tranquil and carefree. In contrast, *panas* ("heat") can be a synonym for unlucky, ominous, disastrous. Those with *panas rezeki* ("hot livelihood") are poor unfortunates. An ill-tempered person is described as a "glowing ember," a person quick to anger has a "hot liver" or "hot blood." "To cause the liver to become hot" means to instill hatred in one's breast. Black magic is called "the hot science" because it carries out a mission of hatred (Hairul and Khan 1977; Iskandar 1970; Wilkinson 1959).

The power of the Malay ruler to keep or restore peace and harmony within his kingdom rests, metaphorically, in his ability to provide the coolness that balances destructive heat threatening the body politic. If his rule is harmonious, the heat of war will not destroy the nation, the heat of anger will not cause internal dissension, and the heat of nature will not destroy the crops. Within his own person, the successful ruler embodies this coolness, made explicit by such expressions as "*Perentah-nya sejuk,*" usually translated as "His reign was full of benign influences," but literally meaning "His reign was cool" (Zainal-Abidin 1947: 43).

In order to maintain harmony, the invisible disembodied spirits must not be allowed to encroach upon the human domain. Historically, the ruler was considered to be not only the defender of Islam but also a harborer of friendly familiar spirits and controller of spirits whose heat puts the kingdom at risk, spirits incomplete in the universal scheme of things, lacking the earthly and watery elements of which the human body is made. Control of these spirits, on the national level, was the duty of the state shaman, usually a brother of the sultan. Commoners also contributed to the maintenance of national harmony by their daily recitation of the "blessed cooling prayers" of Islamic obligation (Zainal-Abidin 1947: 43).

On a personal level, Malays depend upon their traditional healers (*bomoh*) to deal with illnesses brought on by spirit attacks, as well as those with more mundane causes. Spirits most often afflict human victims by blowing superheated breath on the victim's back, upsetting his humoral balance. The *bomoh* has several methods of increasing cold and wet (earthy and watery) elements of the patient's body. Spells are recited with the patient's back to the healer. At strategic times during his recitation the *bomoh* blows on the patient's back. His breath, cooled by the incantation, counteracts the spirits' hot breath. Illness due to spirit attacks is rarer than the fevers, respiratory ailments, and digestive upsets which are believed to result from a humoral imbalance. These might occur because of improper management of diet, work, sleep, because one's body has not adjusted to changes in the weather, or other problems of daily life. Malays generally agree on criteria for classifying ordinary sicknesses, which interpret sensory evidence on the basis of humoral reasoning. Humoral concerns are very salient in contemporary life. Within days after I arrived at my research site I was warned that eating durian fruit together with hospital-type medicines was dangerous since their combined heat might cause madness or even death.

There are several rules of thumb Malays use to decide which foods are humorally hot or cold, or belong to a third category, *sederhana,* neutral or the proper mean (see Laderman 1983). Hot foods include fats, oils, animal flesh, spices, salty and bitter foods, and alcohol. Most cold foods are juicy, slimy, sour, or astringent. The ultimate test is the effect on the body, but while a majority claimed they could feel some heating or cooling effects of food, not everyone is sensitive enough to perceive subtle differences. Appealing to sensory perceptions is further complicated by the dynamic nature of the humoral system whose model incorporates variability. Individuals differ physically and temperamentally; all change as they pass through stages of life, seasons of the year, and hours of the day. Thus, a person who tends toward the hot polarity would classify as neutral a food considered "cold" by most people, since his own body does not feel its cooling effects as strongly as others might.

Empirical observation reinforces the humoral world view in the eyes of its adherents. Western science, while rejecting humoral reasoning, has provided some support for these "folk" observations. Most "cold" foods contain large amounts of indigestible roughage, so one would expect they would irritate some people's digestive tracts while leaving others unscathed. Eating only "cold" foods is likely to lead to weakness, since their composition does not provide complete proteins, concentrated food energy, or fat-soluble vitamins. Fats and oils, humorally "hot," make people feel satiated since they provide nine calories per gram, compared with four per gram for carbohydrates. Animal proteins, also "hot," contain all essential amino acids necessary for the maintenance of health, compared with the incomplete amino acids provided by "cold" fruits and vegetables. After ingestion of proteins, the body's heat output is increased by 20 to 30 percent over intake, compared with 5 percent for ingestion of carbohydrates (Burton 1965: 25). Salt, and foods high in sodium, have been shown to aggravate hypertension in many susceptible sufferers. In an interesting experiment (Ramanamurthy 1969), four individuals were put on "hot" diets, according to Indian humoral conceptions, for ten days, and then placed on "cold" diets for the same length of time. Subjective feelings reported during the "hot" diet were burning eyes, burning urination, and a general feeling of warmth in the body. Analysis of urine and feces showed that those on the "hot" diet displayed higher urine acidity and sulfur excretion and lower retention of nitrogen.

Bisa

Less pervasive than the humoral system but even more important within its narrow range is the concept of *bisa.* Like the humoral system, it is strengthened by sensory phenomena that, through their force, carry along the belief system as a whole. The dictionary definition of *bisa* is "blood-poison, anything that gives a septic wound, venomous. Of the stings of hornets, scorpions and centipedes; the bites of snakes; the poison used on darts; the septic nature of bites of tigers and crocodiles, and of wounds from krises of laminated steel" (Wilkinson 1959: I: 145). This definition leaves out the core meaning of the term and neglects its most common usage. Malays refer to power, whether used for good or evil, as *bisa.* The words of the *bomoh,* neutral when he is not speaking in his professional capacity, become *bisa* when he chants an incantation. The words of the sultan are always *bisa* to his subjects. No moral judgment is implied: the *bomoh*'s *bisa* words are usually used for their curative power, although he may also use them to harm; the ruler's *bisa* speech is for the well-being of the nation, although it may prove painful to some of his subjects.

The most frequent everyday use of *bisa* in rural Malay society is in connection with foods and food avoidance. It has been treated by social and medical scientists as symbolism about impure food "succinctly expressive of the patient's dilemma as a social being" (Provencher 1971: 188–9), or as superstitious beliefs detrimental to health (Wilson 1970, 1971; Mills 1958: 141). Rural Malays, on the other hand, believe that avoiding *bisa* foods has a beneficial effect on health. Knowledge of which foods are *bisa* is common; people act upon it during illnesses and in other vulnerable conditions, particularly the postpartum period. Beliefs about *bisa* foods accord well with what is known about allergies. Allergic reactions occur only after the patient has been sensitized to a particular allergen, and may be lifelong or transient. Malays believe that *bisa* foods exacerbate preexisting disharmonies in individuals who may have been unaware of this condition. Illness may hide unknown within a person's body, emerging only after *bisa* food is eaten. It would be a mistake, however, to assume that *bisa* and allergen are synonymous. Many of my Malay neighbors developed red itchy welts after eating albacore or Spanish mackerel and immediately classified these fish as *bisa.* Their welts may have been due to scombroid poisoning. Fish normally contain a chemical constituent called histadine, found in varying amounts in different species. When histadine is acted upon by bacteria it changes into saurine, a histamine-like substance which can cause an illness resembling severe allergy. Scombroid fish are especially prone to become toxic when left to stand in the sun, or even room temperature in the tropics (Halstead 1959: 112; 1967), but do not cause illness when fresh. It is significant that *bomoh* advise patients not to eat stale fish. Their dietary recommendations may be grounded in the reality, as well as the symbolism, of impure food.

The concept of *bisa* is most complete during postpartum and postcircumcision periods. Until the wound of circumcision is healed, a boy adheres to the same diet prescribed for the postparturient woman. They avoid "cold" fruits and vegetables, fried foods, mollusks, crustaceans, and an extensive list of fish. The midwife refers to these fish in particular when she cautions patients against eating *bisa.* The fact that some women in the puerperium have eaten these fish without experiencing problems does not affect a general belief in the validity of the system. Malays reason that some people are so strong, or lucky, they can get away with dangerous actions. The epidemiology of scombroid, ciguatera, and other fish poisoning offers ideal support for these beliefs. Scombroid poisoning does not invariably occur when one eats scombroid fish, and does not affect every victim with equal severity; ciguatera is not invariable after eating implicated species. The incidence and severity of these illnesses depend on the potential victim's prior state of health as well as the level of toxicity in the individual fish and the amount eaten. Although more than 300 different species have been incriminated in ciguatera, its occurrence is unpredictable and therefore exceedingly difficult to control (Halstead 1959: 117). An occasional health problem associated with specimens of a particular species can be enough to place the entire species, and possibly related species, in the *bisa* category. Within any species, only some individuals are toxic. Of two caught simultaneously in the same place, one could be eaten without ill effects and the other could produce agonizing symptoms (Gordon 1977: 223). The variable nature of this input from sensory perception supports rather than vitiates Malay belief regarding the wisdom of avoiding *bisa* fish during vulnerable periods.

Semangat

Maintenance of good health requires more than just a proper diet and sensible life style. Following a world view that harmony and balance support the health of the cosmos, the body politic, and the human body, one must not only guard against tipping oneself too far toward a humoral polarity; one must also protect one's self against depletion or overabundance of other component parts. The person, in the Malay view, is composed of more than a thinking mind, a body that decays after death, and a soul that lives on in Heaven or in Hell. Some of its parts are common to all of creation, some shared with the animal kingdom, others restricted to humans, and others particular to individuals.

Human beings, like all God's creatures, must inhale the Breath of Life at birth. This *nyawa,* containing the elements of air and fire, animates the watery, earthy body; without it the body must die. It drives the blood in its course; its effects are felt within the body and its presence is obvious to observers when it emerges as breath, just as a breeze, itself invisible, is signaled by the rustling of leaves and the feeling it produces as it blows on the skin.

Semangat (Spirit of Life) is not limited to animals. It permeates the universe, dwelling in man, beast, plant, and rock. The universe teems with life: the life of a fire is swift; a rock's life is slow, long, and dream-like. *Semangat* strengthens its dwelling place, whether the human body or a stalk of rice, and maintains health. It is extremely sensitive, however, and can be depleted: it may even flee, startled, from its receptacle. The vulnerability of *semangat* governs the conduct of the traditional

Malay rice harvest. Modern methods may be more efficient, but they are not calculated to spare the feelings of the Rice Spirit (*semangat padi*). To a traditional Malay, the field of rice is like a pregnant woman, and the harvest is equivalent to the birth of a child. It is inaugurated by the taking of the Rice Baby, a stalk of rice swaddled like a human child after being cut from its plant with a small, curved blade concealed in the hand, so as not to frighten the Rice Spirit by its brutal appearance. The harvested rice crop is stored in a special bin with a coconut, coconut oil, limes, *beluru* root shampoo, bananas, sugar cane, water, and a comb, all for the use of the Rice Spirit, personified as a timid young woman (see also Firth 1974: 192–5). Since she is easily frightened, the rice must be brought back to the storeroom and left there in silence for three days.

Semangat in humans is similarly timid and must be protected. It can be summoned by spells such as thwarted lovers use to regain their beloved, or called by a *bomoh,* using the same sound Malays use to call their chickens (*kurrr*). The timidity of *semangat* makes it prone to leap and fly at the approach of a frightening object or unexpected noise. The effect of the startle reaction is most serious in people who are already in a vulnerable condition, such as pregnant women whose fear may be communicated to their unborn children, resulting in infantile abnormalities. *Semangat* loss is felt as loss of energy, loss of confidence, a weakness in body and mind.

Although most people live secure within the "gates" of their individuality, some people's boundaries are riddled with tiny openings, more like a permeable membrane than a wall. At times, such people find their thoughts becoming confused, their actions less than voluntary. The extraordinary permeability of some individuals was offered to me by many Malays as an explanation of *latah,* a condition in which being startled by a loud noise or an unexpected event triggers a spate of obscene language or imitative behavior. This startle reaction in turn increases the permeability of the membrane, allowing the thoughts of others to mix with those of the *latah* victim's own and to govern his actions.

Angin

Inner Winds (*angin*) determining the child's personality, drives and talents are already present at birth. Their presence, type and quality can be deduced from the behavior of their possessor, but they are palpable neither to observers nor to their owner, except in trance, when they are felt as high winds blowing within the possessor's breast.

Angin is a word with multiple meanings, many of which are connected with notions of sickness and treatment. It can refer to the wind that blows through the trees, a wind that may carry dirt and disease. A strong cold wind can make you sick if it chills your body, upsetting your humoral balance and causing upper respiratory symptoms and pains in the joints. *Angin* in the stomach is produced spontaneously when a person overeats, making his belly swell and producing heartburn and nausea. Diseases that are not suspected of being a result of spirit attacks but are not readily diagnosed are often called wind sickness, meaning essentially, "I don't know what it is."

Another meaning of *angin,* capricious desires, is closer to its core meaning within the shaman's séance. If these whims are not indulged, the whimsical one may feel a sadness known as wind within the liver. The concept of *angin,* however, goes far beyond the whimsical, and the thwarting of these Inner Winds can result in consequences more serious than sadness.

The Inner Winds, as understood by east coast Malays, are close to Western concepts of temperament, both in the medieval sense of the four temperaments and as artistic temperament. They represent the airy part of the four universal elements, as shown in the shaman's divination. He counts out grains of popped rice into three piles. If the count in any pile ends on fire, the diagnosis points to a hot illness and may implicate the hot breath of spirits or the hot anger of humans as a cause of the patient's suffering; earth implies a cold illness, possibly caused by spirits of the earth; water points to a phlegmy condition, possibly contracted near the river or ocean. Wind in the divination refers to problems with the Inner Winds. All people are born with *angin,* the traits, talents and desires representing their ancestors' heritage, but some have more, or stronger, *angin* than the common run. If they are able to express it, they can lead untroubled lives and be respected for their strong and gifted characters. If they cannot, their *angin* is trapped inside them where it accumulates and produces *sakit berangin,* sickness due to blockage of the Inner Winds. Euro-Americans recognize this problem in artists and writers whose creativity is blocked, or whose art is insufficiently appreciated, and would not find it difficult to understand why Malays say that musicians, actors and puppeteers are attracted to their professions because of *angin,* and could not succeed without it. Malays do not recognize a split between the arts, the sciences, and sports; what we call artistic temperament refers to a wider range of behavior among east coast Malays than it does in Euro-American culture. Most of the healers are also performers in the Malay opera (*Mak Yong*) or shadow play, or are masters of the art of self-defense. Healers of all types must possess *angin* specific to their calling and suffer when their talents are ignored. A *bomoh* whose patients have forsaken him, a midwife with limited mobility, even a masseur without a steady call on his services can develop *sakit berangin.* Malays take the concept yet further. Everyone who hopes to be successful in any of the specialized roles that Malay village society provides must not only study diligently but also have the *angin* specific to that role. No amount of study can substitute for *angin.* Those whose *angins* are not appropriate to their roles may be particularly at risk of *sakit berangin,* such as a man who has inherited the *angin* of a midwife but has no opportunity to assist a woman in childbirth.

The meaning of *angin,* and the problems it may entail, extend beyond professional temperament to the basic personality. The majority of conditions treated by *Main Peteri,* the shamanic performance which cures by means of singing, dancing, trance, and dramatic characterizations of spiritual forces (Laderman 1991), are *sakit berangin,* and the most prevalent variety is due to thwarting of the personality type known as *Angin Dewa Muda* (The Wind of the Young Demigod), whose needs are those of royalty: fine clothing, delicate food, aromatic perfumes, comfortable living, and the love and respect of kin, friends and neighbors. Many people have inherited *Angin Dewa Muda* but few can satisfy its demands. Such people need to be pampered and admired, provided with life's luxuries and reassured often of their worth. Malay village society, where neither material goods nor overt expressions of affection and admiration are in plentiful supply, is a difficult setting for this personality. It is not enough to say that the expression of strong emotions is frowned upon in rural Malaysia. Most people deny that they have any. Women suffer through prolonged labors without raising their voices, and mourners at funerals remain dry-eyed. Married couples normally exhibit no signs of connubial affection or public aggression.

I would never have known that my next-door neighbor was almost strangled to death one night by her mistakenly jealous husband had she not shown me his finger marks on her throat. No tell-tale sound had broken the peace of the night. Her husband is a classic example of *Angin Hala,* the Wind of the Weretiger, which makes one quick to anger and heedless of its consequences. *Angin Hala* is difficult to express unless its possessor is a fighter or occupies a social position that allows him to vent his aggression without fear of retaliation. Those with tigerish personalities may prove dangerous to others if they express their *angin,* and dangerous to themselves if they do not.

Angin Dewa Penchil, an archetype from the Malay opera, is the heritage of nobility dissatisfied with their lives and homes. They wander in foreign parts and dress and behave like people of lower status, confusing the rules and etiquette of proper society. This kind of inappropriate behavior, whether it concerns the denial of special prerogatives by aristocrats or, even more worrisome, the dangerous presumptions of equality by those of humble origins, has been discouraged by Malay law and custom. In the past it was a punishable offense for commoners to use royal language when referring to themselves. Aside from legal sanctions against transgressing the prerogatives of royalty, commoners who dared break the social barrier or disobey royal commands might expect to fall ill with an incurable skin disease, or suffer in other respects from the curse that accompanies the flouting of royal power (Osman 1976).

People may be heir to one or several types of *angin.* Their strength can range from a mild breeze to gale force. These Winds, freely blowing or sublimated in ways that satisfy both possessor and society, keep the individual healthy and enrich his community. A person with *Angin Dewa Muda* may try to earn the love and admiration he so desperately needs. A man with *Angin Hala* may cover himself with glory on the playing field or battlefield. Powerful *angin,* ignored or repressed, will make its effects felt in the mind and body. Its symptoms include backaches, headaches, digestive problems, dizziness, asthma, depression, anxiety; in short, a wide range of what we call psychosomatic and affective disorders. Asthma in particular represents a graphic example of repressed *angin*—Wind locked within, choking its possessor.

The Inner Winds of *Main Peteri* patients who have been diagnosed as suffering from *sakit berangin* must be allowed to express themselves, released from the confines of their corporeal prison, enabling the sufferer's mind and body to return to a healthy balance. The band strikes up appropriate music as the shaman retells the story of the *angin*'s archetype. When the correct musical or literary cue is reached, the patient achieves trance, aided as well by the percussive sounds of music and the rhythmic beating of the shaman's hands on the floor near the patient's body. The essential differences between the patient's trance and that of the shaman are (1) the patient's trance does not make him or her a conduit for spirits, but, rather, puts patients in touch with their inner being; and (2) shamans control the alterations of their own consciousness, while the patient's consciousness is controlled by the shaman.

In shamanic ceremonies of other cultures, whose primary aim is to remove demonic influence from human sufferers, the patient's trance is "the peak moment [at which] the object of the demonic enters into direct communion with the subject" (Kapferer 1983: 195). For Malay patients, trance does not occur during exorcistic parts of the *Main Peteri*. The communication is not with the demonic, but with their own inner nature. While in trance, if a patient has *angin* for *silat* (the Malay art of self-defense), he will rise and perform its stylized moves and stances; if she has *angin* for *Mak Yong,* she will dance with the grace of a princess; *Angin Hala* can cause a trancing patient to roar and leap like a tiger. Patients are encouraged to act out the repressed portions of their personalities until their hearts are content and their *angin* refreshed. Coming out of trance, into the awareness of an enthusiastic, approving audience, the patient experiences a wonderful feeling of relaxation and satisfaction. Headaches and backaches have disappeared, and asthma sufferers find they can once again breathe freely.

Embodiment and the Acculturation of the Anthropologist

Anthropologists use their own bodies and minds as primary tools for the investigation of cultures. They participate as deeply as possible in the lives of those they study, at the same time maintaining sufficient distance to observe the workings of culture. They become insider-outsiders, observing with cool eyes and participating with a warm heart. Anthropologists who have achieved rapport find that they have become acculturated to some degree to their informants' beliefs and behaviors. Signs of this process are changes in bodily movements and postures, as when I assumed the squatting position used by Malay women while preparing foods for cooking. I hardly realized I was squatting rather than sitting at a table to perform this action as I had done throughout my life, until my husband laughingly remarked on it, calling me his "Malay wife." Another sign is change in habits of the mind: many of the characters in my dreams, including myself, spoke in Malay, and the symbols of my night theater were symbols of Malay, rather than Freudian, thought.

My neighbors were so convinced of the empirical reality of humoral doctrine that, when I sent off foods to be analyzed by the Institute for Medical Research, they assumed that they would not only be tested for nutrient content but scientific procedures would finally put to rest disagreements as to their humoral qualities. This insistence on the reality of humoral reasoning led me to observe my own physiological reactions to foods. I found "cold" foods refreshing, especially in the hot weather. Unlike some of my neighbors, I was able to eat them in large quantities at any time of the day or year without ill effects. According to the Malays, this was due to my body's unusually high intrinsic heat. This became obvious to them when they noticed how I thrived during the monsoon season, whose cold temperatures left them shivering under layers of sweaters. Even compared to those who live in temperate zones, my body is unusually warm in sickness and in health: my family closes windows I have thrown open in the winter, and my doctor no longer panics when my fever rises to 104 degrees. In the case of humorally hot foods, I found my sensitivity only extended to those considered extremely hot. Eating large quantities of *durian* fruit produced a feverish sensation, a feeling of great satiety, and a tendency toward diarrhea (which Malays attribute to heat softening feces). *Durian* had the same effects on my neighbors, but during its season we all stuffed ourselves on its delicious flesh, ignoring any attempt at a balanced diet and oblivious of the consequences. Not being pregnant during my time in Malaysia, I was not considered vulnerable to the effects of most *bisa* fish. As a lifelong hater of fish, eating only small amounts out of necessity, I avoided exposure to the risks of eating large quantities of scombroid fish.

The most striking examples of my acculturation came from my experience of the embodiment of components of the self as understood by Malays. As part of a shaman's entourage, and later his "daughter," I spent much of my time observing shamanic rituals and interviewing healers and their patients. I was assured that the ceremonies I observed were just the tip of the iceberg: many of its dramas occurred unseen by observers but felt by participants. When I asked people how it felt to be in trance, they couldn't, or wouldn't, answer. They told me that the only way I could know was to experience it. I avoided the issue, feeling uncomfortable with the lack of control that trance implied. Well into the second year of my research, while attending a *Main Peteri* as part of the shaman's entourage, he motioned to me to sit down on the mat recently vacated by his patient. I thought he wanted to do a short ritual to release me from the dangers inherent in witnessing women give birth, which he had often performed for my benefit. Instead, he proceeded to recite the story of *Dewa Muda* (which he had deduced was my primary Inner Wind), accompanied by the band and his own rhythmic pounding on the floor. My trust in him was strong enough to allay my fears, and I allowed my consciousness to shift into an altered state. At the height of my trance, I felt the Wind blowing inside me with the force of a hurricane. When I later described my feelings in trance, people assured me it was a common experience. They also wondered at my surprise. One woman remarked, "Well, why did you think we call them Winds?"

My experience of *semangat* as a component of my self came as a result of its loss. My second period of research on Malaysia's east coast coincided with an epidemic of dengue hemorrhagic fever, carried by day-flying *Aedes* mosquitoes. I must have been incubating it during the last days of my research. Shortly after my arrival in New York City, my temperature rose to 107 degrees. I was admitted to the hospital, placed on an ice mattress, and covered with ice cubes. My doctor ordered several tests, including a bone marrow tap. Since this was a teaching hospital, it proved to be a great opportunity for a novice to practice his technique, removing a marrow sample from my pelvis. It took him four tries before success. The pain was exquisite. As waves of agony coursed through my body, part of me seemed to flee from its normal dwelling place. I had never responded to pain in quite those terms, although I certainly had experienced more intense and longer-lasting suffering several years before, when I was hospitalized with a case of severe pelvic inflammatory disease.

After the doctor had obtained his marrow sample, I felt as though some essential component had left its fleshy confines and was hovering high above my head. I felt depleted, lacking in energy and a prey to emotions. My nerves literally seemed to be on the surface of my body; my skin appeared to offer no protection. I left the hospital two weeks later, but feelings of depletion and vulnerability remained with me months later. I seemed to have lost part of my self, the part that Malays call *semangat,* the spirit of life.

A friend, then the editor of a popular health magazine, had recently written an article about her experiences in a sensory deprivation flotation tank. She hoped the relaxation it usually produces would be good for me, and arranged for me to have a session.

Before entering the tank, one must wash away the oil that normally covers the skin, thus removing any barrier between the body and the water of the tank. The tank is approximately seven feet long, four feet wide, and four feet high, half-filled with water that has been super-saturated with epsom salts until, like the Dead Sea, it can support a barely submerged body. After one enters the tank the hood is closed, leaving one in total darkness and silence. All one can hear are the whispers of one's breath, the beating of one's heart and the sound of blood coursing through the veins. There is no sense of time, no sense of space. I had lain there for an unknown length of time when I felt my body begin to undulate up and down, then slowly spin in a complete circle, a physical impossibility since my body is much too long for the width of the tank. Finally the spinning stopped, and it was then I saw the birds. First, there were flocks of swifts which flitted about, gathered together and coalesced into one brilliantly colored cockatoo. The cockatoo soon changed to a giant Garuda bird, the mount of Vishnu, but instead of the god, it was I who was riding on its back at the same time that my body was still resting on the water. The bird and its mount flew from a great distance closer and closer to my body until we merged and became one.

A feeling of wholeness and joy infused me; I knew my *semangat* had returned. After leaving the tank and showering once again to remove the salt, I experienced another change: my nerves were no longer exposed; they felt as though they had been covered by protective velvet.

That night I mused over my experience. I had hoped to benefit from the relaxing time my friend had described as usual for a float in a sensory deprivation tank, but I was completely surprised by the arrival of the birds. What did it mean? Why had I envisioned birds, and why those particular birds?

Semangat is often represented in Malay thought by a bird. Swifts, as common in Malaysia as sparrows in New York City, seem to be forever busy, always darting here and there. I was seen by my Malay neighbors as someone who rarely rested, never hesitating to stay awake all night to help deliver a baby or attend a healing ceremony, always willing to stop what I was doing to drive those in need to the hospital. The swifts seemed to me to represent that very visible part of my personality. The cockatoo symbolized another facet of my self, the *Dewa Muda* that loves beautiful clothes and jewelry, and revels in the admiration of others. The Garuda bird and its rider, Vishnu, belong to the Malays' religious past. For a thousand years before their conversion to Islam, Malays were Hindus. The high gods of Hinduism still exist in Malay mythology, often appearing in healing ceremonies as beneficent entities who speak through the voice of the shaman. Vishnu the Preserver was a highly appropriate symbol for the return of the spirit of life to an anthropologist who had so recently been absorbed in the study of Malay healing performances.

The Symbol and The Flesh

Noting the physical effects of eating, feeling the Inner Winds blowing in their bosoms during trance, and experiencing the loss and return of *semangat* would be incontrovertible proof to most east coast Malays of the validity of humoral reasoning and the existence of *angin* and *semangat* as essential parts of the self. I do not argue that Malays have discovered the truth about humanity and the workings of the universe. Experiences similar to mine and those of my Malay informants, had they been felt by people acculturated to other symbolic systems, would have been interpreted differently or assumed a different shape. Biomedical science, for instance, would offer a non-humoral explanation for the heat I felt after gorging on *durian,* pointing to the physiological effects of ingesting large quantities of fat. Explanation of my feelings in trance might be attributed to suggestion, catharsis, excitation of the nervous system, or production of endogenous chemicals.

The content of visions varies with the content of waking thoughts and assumptions about reality. South American Indians under the influence of Datura see jaguars and serpents, while medieval European believers in witchcraft, after taking the same drug, experienced flight to a witches' Sabbath and met Satan himself (Harner 1973).

In contemporary Euro-American society, patients in psychoanalysis soon find that the content, as well as the interpretation, of their dreams changes. Dreams of Freudian analysands are different from those of patients in Jungian analysis. Had I not been so deeply immersed in Malay thought when I suffered from dengue hermorrhagic fever and its aftermath, I would not have experienced my pain and its cessation as the loss and return of *semangat*. Were I a believing Christian, I might have interpreted my vision of the birds as a visitation from the Holy Spirit of the Annunciation that appeared to the Virgin Mary in the form of a dove. The content of the vision itself might have been different: perhaps, instead of a series of birds, I might have seen Christ and the Virgin clasping me to their bosoms as they restored my health.

The dialectic between symbolic reality and bodily experience supports rather than questions paradigms. Humoral reasoning reigned supreme in Europe for at least two thousand years, and no amount of contrary evidence could have been sufficient to cast doubt on its truth since any evidence was evaluated in the light of this powerful paradigm. It took a change of paradigm to eliminate humoral pathology from the canons of Western medical thought.

We all experience empirical reality, the reality of our own senses. Sensory input is vital to the maintenance of a symbolic system; moorings to an experiential world keep the symbolic structure from detaching itself from human existence. But the "proof" that they carry is only meaningful because of the symbolic structure which allows us to interpret experience in a way that helps us believe that the cosmos itself is meaningful, that things connect, that life has an aim, and that human beings, at least to some extent, can acquire knowledge to deal with the workings of an orderly universe.

References

Burton, B. T. (1965), *The Heinz Handbook of Nutrition*, New York: Macmillan.

Firth, R. (1974), "Faith and Skepticism in Kelantan Village Magic," in William R. Roff (ed.), *Kelantan: Religion, Society and Politics in a Malay State*, Kuala Lumpur: Oxford University Press.

Gordon, B. L. (1977), "Fish and Food Poisoning," *Sea Frontiers*, 23(4): 218–27.

Hairul, A. S. and Khan, Y. (1977), *Kamus Lenkap*, Petaling Jaya: Pustaka Jaman.

Halstead, B. W. (1959), *Dangerous Marine Animals*, Cambridge, MA: Cornell Maritime Press.

Halstead, B. W. (1967), *Poisonous and Venomous Marine Animals of the World*, Washington, DC: US Government Printing Office.

Harner, M. (ed.), (1973), *Hallucinogens and Shamanism*, London: Oxford University Press.

Iskandar, T. (1970), *Kamus Dewan*, Kuala Lumpur: Dewan Pustaka dan Bahasa.

Kapferer, B. (1983), *A Celebration of Demons: Exorcism and the Aesthetics of Healing in Sri Lanka*, Bloomington, IN: Indiana University Press.

Laderman, C. (1983), *Wives and Midwives: Childbirth and Nutrition in Rural Malaysia,* Berkeley: University of California Press.

Laderman, C. (1991), *Taming the Wind of Desire: Psychology, Medicine, and Aesthetics in Malay Shamanistic Performance,* Berkeley: University of California Press.

Mills, J. (1958), "Modifications in Food Selections Observed by Malay Women during Pregnancy and after Confinement," *Medical Journal of Malaya,* 13(2): 139–44.

Osman, M. T. (1976), "The Bomoh and the Practice of Malay Medicine," *The South East Asian Review,* 1(1): 16–26.

Provencher, R. (1971), *Two Malay Worlds,* Research Monograph No. 4, Center for South and Southeast Asia Studies, University of California, Berkeley.

Ramanamurthy, P. S. V. (1969), "Physiological Effects of 'Hot' and 'Cold' Foods in Human Subjects," *Journal of Nutrition and Diet,* 1: 187–91.

Wilkinson, R. J. (1959), *A Malay-English Dictionary,* London: Macmillan.

Wilson, C. S. (1970), "Food Beliefs and Practices of Malay Fishermen: An Ethnographic Study of Diet on the East Coast of Malaya," Ph.D. dissertation, University of California, Berkeley.

Wilson, C. S. (1971), "Food Beliefs Affect Nutritional Status of Malay Fisherfolk," *Journal of Nutrition Education,* 2(3): 96–8.

Zainal-Abidin, A. (1947), "The Various Significations of the Malay Word *Sejok,*" *Journal of the Royal Asiatic Society, Malay Branch,* 20(2): 41–4.

–16–

Sensing Divinity, Death, and Resurrection
Theorizing Experience through Miracles
Bilinda Straight

Let me catch you unaware like a clairvoyant dream that appears in quiet languages. The gazelles shake their heads, shake them this way and again—and you know something. The cows shuffle in the rose-gray light of dawn—and you know something. Even the birds have ways you recognize. And the beetles chirrup a signifying rhythm as you lie sleeping, just preparing to dream. This is the way of Nkai (divinity). This is one way of sensing the life of the universe.

The Language of Nkai

November 9, 2001. I am with Rereita Lemeteki, a prominent Samburu loiboni.[1] I am awed by him, by his ability to read Nkai's words everywhere, in everything around him. It was only recently that I have learned that some Samburu can understand the language of particular animals. I know that some understand birds, others cows, and some even understand hyenas. One Lkileku man I know recalled a man of the Lterito generation who knew the language of hyenas.[2] "And the hyena is saying, it is saying I am going to eat that one [person]" (Lentiwas interview 2001). The hyena's is a dreadful language, announcing impending death. The words of other animals, though, like birds, cows, and crickets, can predict good things as well as terrible ones. It is quite common for Samburu to understand the language of animals. Yet no one before Rereita Lemeteki has been able to understand the language of every animal. His *naibon* ("loibon ability") is great—and increasing—because his ancestors used their naibon to help but never to harm. This is Lemeteki's own explanation, but it is one also corroborated by everyone with whom I have discussed the subject.

Lemeteki lies awake at night, listening to the crickets chirping in the house, and he knows what Nkai is saying to him. On a path as he walks, he meets gazelles and jokes with them.

> So I even ask a Thompson's Gazelle, can you let me come closer? And it tells me I cannot "because you are a nuisance." Finally, it does agree, so it just talks to me while it is there. And it doesn't agree for me to come closer to it, because I say, "Do you agree if

I come and touch you?" "No, no, you will bother me. It is a mistake if you come near me." Finally, I just love and leave it, because it is true that if I come near it like that, it is a mistake. So as such, it is just the truth. It is Nkai who is in all those things, it is Nkai who talks. (Lemeteki interview, November 9, 2001)

When people come to ask for his professional advice, Lemeteki sometimes asks his own goats for the diagnosis and solution to the problem before him. He does not use an *nkidoŋ,* a gourd calabash with stones and other divination tools inside, like many loibonok. He is a *loibon le nkwe,* a loibon of the head. Nkai speaks to him through the particular turning of a goat's head, the way it scratches its leg, through the sounds of the crickets, and so many other things. He does not need to divine by throwing objects. He simply knows what Nkai is expressing through Nkai's own creation.

Divine Representations

While Lemeteki's reading of goats and crickets might typically, in Euro-American terms, be relegated to the "mystical," Samburu do not divide experience in this way. Rather, Lemeteki's ability to read the turning of a goat's head belongs to practical experience, in this case an inherited skill and also one given by Nkai in a world in which everything both proceeds from Nkai and simultaneously operates according to "obvious" (for Samburu) principles. These communications between humans and Nkai via the natural world are, for Samburu, an everyday part of what I am calling expansive experience.

In explaining what I mean by expansive experience, I will borrow a term from the philosopher/logician Charles Sanders Peirce. Peirce referred to "prescissing" (and related term prescind) as the "cutting off" that occurs in the act of experiencing a sign. I extend Peirce's arguments to suggest that prescissing occurs all over experience, beginning with the cutting off that necessarily occurs by virtue of our very physiology. Experience is never simply reducible to physiology, and yet the prescissing that occurs by way of our physiology is crucial to experience and the imagination—and these are simultaneous and multidirectional processes. For example, when we see, processes occur within our own retinas that eliminate "noise" in the visual field. This is one way we presciss by way of our physiology, one way we cut off elements of seemingly infinite information. At the same time, our prior experiences (including evolutionary ones) shape the retina itself and the cutting off, delimiting the choices it makes. Vision as an experiential process is already cultural. The prescissive cuttings of experience happen all over us and through us, from our cutting reality by way of our physiology to our "choice" to focus on one aspect of a dialogue, to interpret a text or a moment in one way or set of ways rather than another. At the level of conscious focused awareness, prescissive cuttings also allow us to consider our own bodies after the fact, as if they were texts to be interpreted, separate from the simultaneous dynamism of expansive experience.

This is a technical explanation for the enculturating aspects of experience we anthropologists take for granted, but it has more radical implications. I argue that in prescissing we reduce a seemingly infinite world—meeting world by way of an *acculturated physiology*—before exploding it in a potentially infinite world of signs of our own making. In that process, our expansive experiences of the world may not even be laid down in verbalizable memory, and yet in them we touch world and it touches us in ways that do not utterly disappear. Instead, those experiences become like phantasms, haunting our brain's architecture with the molecular tracks of a smell that merges with a feeling, moving literally through us, reincarnating from the infinitude of world to the imaginary of signs. Those signs, I suggest, whether verbal or mere hints of feeling, bear tangible signatures of their experiential processes of becoming. To remember a face is to conjure a shape that can be "seen" in the firings of neurons lighting up an MRI—we cannot see what another person sees, but we can witness a vision of a spectral presence that contains some aspect of the very form of that face. This is radical intersubjectivity. These are strange hauntings within the mundane. And moreover, these are invitations to consider that the imagination is *real* in crucial ways.

Summing up my core points here, prescissing is a conceptual tool for considering expansive experience simultaneously within and beyond the limits of signs and textuality. *Prescissing is the process by way of which we reduce the potentially infinite we are in contact with in world to the cognizably finite, the ground of those potentially infinite experiences in brute and thoughtful being in the world.* This is not a Kantian constitutive process whereby we use our a priori categories (or neuronal structures) to form associations, imposing form on an inchoate world. Rather, the process of prescissing is a reduction by way of our human physiology in combination with a lifetime of previous, culturally inflected experiences. That the world is unmanageably vast or so far incomprehensibly mysterious does not make it inchoate—we do not impose logos on chaos. Our signifying understandings are based—at some point in their biography—in the real world of which we are a part, with its own dynamism.

This experiential process implicates my own thoughts as well, and thus, even as I theorize expansive experience using Euro-American scholarly metaphors, I likewise slip in and out of the theories by which Samburu organize experience.[3] If some of us limit the world by way of our physiological, neuronal, and symbolic forgettings, in structuring their own experience Samburu nod to the reality of cuttings, creating their social and symbolic worlds through division. Samburu "cuts" are crucial to health and life itself—as in cutting girls apart from women (a "cut" made through clitoridectomy but also through beads, clothing, and behavior) (see Straight 2005a, 2005b); cutting every age, gender, and generation class apart from every other; and above all, cutting death apart from life. In an incisive discussion of Maasai beadwork, Corinne Kratz and Donna Pido have eloquently summed up the crucial importance of cutting (referring to it as a "cultural attitude") in ways that largely pertain to the Samburu as well:

> Maasai associate cuts in an ornament with natural and cultural phenomena like slashes in a piece of roasting meat, breaks in a line of cattle or people, or the short interruption when a Maasai woman fills a cup by pouring a little milk, stopping, and then pouring again to fill it up. A general cultural attitude unites these different "cuts": nothing should be continuous and unbroken. Maasai deliberately "cut" beadwork patterns and activities such as pouring, because to create pure color fields or a continuous milk flow would seem to claim the purity and power attributed only to God. (Kratz and Pido 2000: 53)

In their own references to cutting (*aduŋthe*) Samburu emphasis is not on the act of cutting itself but on the vital divisions (separations) and shared categories of persons or things it creates. Samburu *aduŋ* can be a radical creative act—creating men out of boys, women out of girls, and the dead out of and apart from the living. In the midst of this enactment of subjectivity, however, crossings between both things and persons can occur—including terrifying or wondrous crossings between the dead and the living.

A Theory of Miracles

Following a seven-year absence from the field after my Ph.D., I returned to northern Kenya for a year in 2001, attempting to learn as much about Samburu ethnophiloso-phy as I could, including engaging in extended discussions about what, if anything, Samburu believe happens after death.[4] In one of those unexpected moments of eth-nographic epiphany, one woman abruptly asserted that she had died once and come back to life. My attention was, of course, immediately captured. As she related her fantastic story, she made it pointedly clear that Nkai was responsible for her *apiu*—revival, resurrection, return from death. Was this a near-death experience? Spontaneous resuscitation? As far as she was concerned—and this proved to be a Samburu trope—this was an amazing/astonishing occurrence (*nkiŋasia*), possible because Nkai enacted it.

Academics in the twenty-first century are out of the habit of reporting on res-urrections.[5] Zombies, witchcraft, charismatic healings, even reincarnation, yes, but resurrection from the dead? That term lost its currency in the transition to the modern period (see Straight 2007, Chapter 7). Yet the claim that Nkai raises people from death is a common one, and even if the occurrence itself is relatively rare, I have managed to fill several notebooks about it narrated by those who experienced or witnessed it as well as by those who got the story second- or third-hand. I could have written an entire monograph on this phenomenon, but I have chosen instead to include it as one of many aspects of experience that Samburu themselves perceive as both extraordinary and possible. For the Samburu, the movement between the mundane and the extraordinary is continuous and seamless, because the majority of Samburu continue to experience the world as one enacted by and through Nkai.[6]

As Jean and John Comaroff have clarified with precision and intriguing detail (1991, 1997), the Christian message European missionaries brought to Africa was inseparable from a suite of insidious cultural assumptions. Those cultural assumptions included an acceptance of science as true in ways that impinged on indigenous explanations of experience, and in this Samburu were no exception, as both Catholic and Anglican missionaries frequently challenged Samburu explanations of Nkai's presence on empirical grounds while offering an equally fantastic alternative. Nevertheless, Samburu have continually and actively engaged in repartee with Catholic, Anglican, and various secular European forms of knowledge, sometimes in ways that, ironically, would make sense to one theologian in particular whose influence on European Christian thought has endured: namely, Saint Augustine (354–430 C.E.). In an intriguing book on medieval miracles, Benedicta Ward argues that "For Augustine, the mechanics of miracles were clear. They were wonderful acts of God shown as events in this world, not in opposition to nature but as drawing out of the hidden workings of God within a nature that was all potentially miraculous" (Ward 1987: 3). In a footnote, Ward offers this direct quote from Augustine: "For how can an event be contrary to nature when it happens by the will of God, since the will of the great creator assuredly is the nature of every created thing? A portent therefore does not occur contrary to nature but contrary to what is known of nature" (Augustine *de Civitate Dei* 21.8 quoted in Ward 1987: 222, n 5).

For Augustine apparently, miracles challenged our notion of the possible while also reminding us that there is more to know. (Should we explain, or explain away?) For Samburu as well, Nkai's appearance is always strange, disorienting, and worthy of comment. Samburu share a common cross-cultural position that the appearance of divinity is a wonder, a miracle, and yet for many (though not all), an acceptable mystery. Most commonly, Nkai appears in the sky (as rain clouds) in the shape of an elephant's trunk or in the shape of extraordinarily large snakes in caves and on hills. Less commonly and more amazingly, Nkai also sometimes appears in human form, allowing children and young people to wander freely between earth and heaven.

Resurrection

As I sat on a stool with friends and neighbors near my home in the Samburu highlands, two old men engaged in a spirited dialogue, each trying to outdo the other in his knowledge of Samburu recent and historical events. One was my neighbor, Leyielo, while the other was a friend of his visiting from the lowlands. By this time, I had talked formally and informally to dozens of people claiming first- or second-hand knowledge of *apiu*—resurrection from death.[7] Thus, I was amused that Leyielo was confused when queried about incidences of *apiu,* while his friend triumphantly took the high ground in this turn of the discussion.[8] He knew of several cases, including one in which a man's cattle nudged him back to existence from where his corpse lay, awaiting the hyenas.

> And he was left there laying in mortuary leaves, when the cattle came back in the evening. Some of his cattle went there and started to bellow at him and they [his cattle] took away those leaves. When people went to chase the cattle away from there they found him alive. And he was brought home ... And he came back to life and he recovered completely, that is, he was completely well. Now he will stay, performing all of his duties. (Friend of Leyielo's, Leyielo interview, 2003)

Leyielo's friend related another, more recent case—again naming precisely who the person was and whom he eventually married—that must have been even more startling to people, particularly to his mother. "He was taken to *soro* [the 'bush', wilderness] and he revived [*nepiu*], and came back home, straight to his mother's house in the evening. And he was carrying the animal hide used for his mortuary rites." At this point in the story, my neighbor Leyielo exclaimed "Unheard of!" to which his friend replied with laughter, "It is not just one person that this happened to!" (Leyielo interview, 2003).

Like most people relating cases of *apiu* ("resurrection"), Leyielo's friend asserted emphatically that these people are "completely dead"—"They stay there for some time, in death, because they die completely, they don't even breathe. ... They're not breathing, because people make sure that a person is not breathing ... they are taken from home when they have died, they're not half-dead" (Leyielo interview, 2003).

Through this emphatic assertion that people really are dead, Samburu affirm that what they are talking about is a miracle. Samburu *apiu*—"resurrection"—forces itself on the families who experience it, demanding that they accept the amazing. The utter astonishment that *apiu* provokes is readily apparent in the narration of the *apiu* of a young girl (warrior's girlfriend) who died during the Lkileku period (c. 1922–1936). The narrator in this case was one of my neighbors, a woman in her nineties who had been one of the young girl's own age-mates and a witness to the events as they occurred:

> Wasn't she taken away to be disposed of? [Mm.] She was laid. Isn't it that a person is usually laid? [Yes.] She lay there. The hyenas didn't eat her. [Mm.] Her father was not at home—that chief—he was not at home. [Yes.] Her brother, a Lkileku lmurran, got up. [Mm.] Is it not that people are usually checked to see whether hyenas have eaten them? [Yes.] He went, and as he went [mm] he found her just sitting like this, blinking her eyes. [Blinking her eyes?] Blinking her eyes. She just kept her eyes open like mine now. [Mm.] Don't the eyes get dry when a person dies? [Mm.] So she was just blinking her eyes like this. [Mmm.] The lmurrani was shocked. [Mmm.] He went back and called another lmurrani, coming. They came and found her just sitting, staring at people. They went, went to call others. (Nolpesi interview, 2001)

Samburu *apiu* remains a robust miracle—not only in lowland rural areas where Samburu insist on following "tradition," but also in hospitals, where Samburu demonstrate that they have yet to unreflectingly acquiesce in biomedicine's arrogantly definitive ontology. The persistent miracle of resurrection makes biomedical intervention and universal burial enigmatic transformations, leading Samburu to continually reconsider their understandings of life's edges, the contours of personhood, and the cutting practices that preserve them.

Keeping the implications of these miraculous Samburu experiences in view, I will conclude my relating of *apiu* where I ethnographically began—with the first narrative of *apiu* I ever heard, the one that stunned me in 2001 as I sat in the lowland house of a friend, calmly sipping my tea. "I saw one who *natipiuwa* ("resurrected/came back to life")[9] just recently—[he is] a Lmooli now. He died in Wamba Hospital. He died completely, completely, completely, completely, to the point that the doctors had chased me away" (Nompoi interview, 2001).

When Nompoi went in to see her son, the Italian doctor had already declared the child dead, and he was covered—including his face—with the green cloth that pronounced the biomedical death with more clarity than words (see also Sharp 2001). The nurses tried to send her away when they saw her, but she lingered in the ward anyway.

> I was told to go away—and I was carrying the other [my other child] on my back. I said, I waited until they [hospital employees] had gone away for a moment [when they weren't looking]. And I went close to touch [him]. I said, "*Akita!*" [exclamation of disgust/uneasiness]. Let me hold/touch him. [She had to touch despite the hazards associated with handling the dead.] While I was touching him I touched a vein that was doing like this—*tau, tau, tau.*[10] It continued for awhile until a person from there, from that settlement of Lemasagari—Do you know that family? [What? Yes.] This settlement on the lower side. [Yes.] And the heart stopped. This one looked at me while I was judging, opening [the cloth], and touching—looked at me and kept quiet. (Nompoi interview, 2001)

Nompoi continued touching her son, watching again for signs of a beating heart, while the nurses persevered in trying to get her to leave the room. Finally, she managed to get them to look at just the right moment, and they exclaimed, "Hae! hae! hae! He is alive!" They called for the doctor, who came to see and then left again to get something to inject the boy with. According to Nompoi, he made several attempts to revive the child after that, then covered the little boy again and told Nompoi to leave. She said, "M-m-m, not until I see you throw him in those pits that you people [use].[11] I kept sitting. We sat until the enemies were impatient."[12] Having told her that it would take hours before they would know whether or not the injections had worked, the doctor allowed her to keep vigil near her son, and eventually he completely revived. Indeed, he was a young lmurran when his mother told me of the miracle.

What precisely transpired here? How should we treat this mother's claims? While it is possible to debate the terms of resurrection and resuscitation, to suggest that this or another mother's child was never "really" dead or to assert that brain death constitutes the death of the person—by whatever criteria it should be defined—is to acquiesce in the hegemony of a single biocultural model whose ontological assumptions remain insidiously submerged. Yet empirical science has not only failed so far to offer satisfying answers to crucially important questions concerning the boundaries of life and personhood and the nature of experience;[13] it has continually succeeded in troubling these issues more—the "miracles of modern science" continue to astonish us. Thus, resurrection is an abiding reality, trope, and metaphor in the twenty-first century in the United States and Europe as among the Samburu—testament to a human desire and a recurring dilemma: *We have yet to account for experience,* even as we enduringly look at the shadowy notion of consciousness, at the elusive soul.

Crossing the Boundary

Have you ever stood outside in a place so distant from roads and cities that the countryside surrounded you in a circle whose edges met the horizon at the place where the world falls into space? At dusk the colors curl down, sneaking slowly behind the curtain of the universe and letting the stars escape to fill the dome that holds us in. We can't touch the edges, but we can see them out there where the colors merge and the night comes up—the black membrane that Leropili once told me we cannot pass beyond. We cannot leave our universe. Even the dead are contained here.

When a little girl named Turaso visited Nkai's home while a healthy child who then returned to prophesy, her family ritually cleansed the site she disappeared from. They were not entirely certain of what had transpired there, but they had an uneasy feeling that Turaso had successfully traversed a boundary they must struggle to maintain. In Samburu prescissive experience, *lkiye* ("death") already contains the exception, even if the majority of dead persons *do not return.* That is, while *apiu* ("resurrection") is the strangest, rarest, and most marvelous exception, there are other exceptions that happen more frequently, making the living and the dead both nomadic wanderers trespassing on one another's terrain. Even as Samburu continually strive to seal that transgressive wound, the form of this abjection itself is an *aleph,* an overdetermined point refracting a Samburu universe that is about both movement back and forth and, paradoxically, the cutting that would suspend that movement.

When they cross the path of the living, the *loip* ("shade," "ghosts") of the dead startle the persons who experience them—a jolt of the uncanny somewhat akin to the way lizards or snakes darting at the boundary of vision jar the senses with a movement that only slowly takes a definable shape. Sometimes the meaning of a strange experience shapes and reshapes itself very slowly, as in the case of child prophets like Turaso, as well as Remeta, and Ɖoto Malapen (see Straight 2007: Chapter 3 and pp. 170–72). Will this child return from wherever she has gone? Will Nkai want her so much so as to permanently claim her? When Turaso disappeared, her father and his neighbors searched everywhere for her, but she had utterly vanished without a trace and was drinking milk and honey at the beautiful home of Nkai. As it turned out, her father was right to offer sacrifices to "change the color" of that hill because his little girl was in some amount of danger. She was not sick or dying but had wandered into "Heaven," as it were, into the space that is somewhere else, the space of Nkai but also of death. While she sat there completely unafraid and enjoying the attention of a woman with plenty to feed her, two Nkai women argued back and forth about whether they would "take" little Turaso from her mother as punishment for her mother having taken a wooden post from the house of a dead woman. Because Turaso's mother did not realize her error, the Nkai woman who wanted to punish her relented, and Turaso was sent home.

Did Turaso care whether or not she was sent home? It is not possible to know, since this was not a question anyone remembers asking her. What those who knew her do claim is that she did not wish Nkai to take her father—when Nkai snatched him away Turaso refused to speak to Nkai for a very long time. In the most famous case currently remembered, however, the child in question—the famous Samburu prophetess, Ɖoto Malapen—crossed into Nkai's home throughout her life and sometimes fervently wished she could remain there.[14] Indeed, Ɖoto Malapen once told her daughter, "I want this child [her daughter, the narrator] of mine to die, then we would go there" (Malapen interview, 2002). That is, Nkai's home was so beautiful that Ɖoto Malapen wished she could take her daughter with her, but while Nkai allowed Ɖoto Malapen to travel there and back while yet alive, she knew that her daughter would have to die to go there. Indeed, the only other Samburu to experience that beautiful place, and those who most commonly see the dead, are those who are very close to death themselves—an understanding that probably contributes to parents' uneasiness when their children visit Nkai. Here, the back-and-forth movement that prophets experience between Nkai's home and their own settlements parallels the reciprocal visits between the dead and the dying, visits that Samburu perceive to be neither dreams nor visions in any simple sense but, rather, literal crossings between twin sides of the same universe.

My Samburu acquaintance Nompoi—whose son's *apiu* I earlier related—offered a vivid example of this crossing experience. Thus, once when she was so close to death that her relatives had already begun to prepare her mortuary hide, Nompoi ventured to that beautiful place on "that side," which Ɖoto Malapen, Remeta, and other prophets have described. As she explained, "Even a dead person's ears are pierced [can hear]. I could hear all that was spoken. I could hear people chewing *miraa* [khat, a stimulant]: 'Man! Give me sticks, man! Give me *chaŋaa* [liquor]. Buy us some more *chaŋaa*, do you hear?'" After this conversation about *miraa* and *chaŋaa*, she ventured farther away, finding herself in a pasture full of cows with giant udders. She tried to run after them but was turned back by an unspecified person.

Some cows came with bells, "porou," "porou," "porou," "mbuu"! Bulls. And if I see these cows, the breast of one is this big [demonstrates with her hands]. And this one [another udder] was the size of that [twenty-liter] jug. When I tried to run, the cows came closer to me. It was like I was going, I was reviving. I thought the dead/corpses/ghosts [*lmeneŋa*] were talking to me. They said, "Hey! Mother, don't go and meet those cows because they are not yours. Do you see that dust that is coming from there—on that gap? It's those cows that are coming up [those are your cows]. It's your boys who are driving those cows—wait for your boys' cows to come because these aren't yours." I sat back down and I was dead, do you hear? I came back and sat, and these cows were white. And those cows were black and their udders white, and the cows' breasts were the size of my leg. When I saw them [cows] standing and the young calves lowing, "mpaaa," mpaaa," "odurr," "odurr," "mpooo," and the bulls scratching the ground fighting, "otutututu," I was laying and just dead. (Nompoi interview, 2001).

What I have described here are the ways in which Samburu prescissively experience a reality that is always more than imaginary—the multitudinous, roaming manifestations of *loip* ("shade," "ghost," "spirit") are at once seen, felt, heard, and imagined. They are witness and witnessed; they are the thoughtful experiences that move in and out of life, as children wander into "Heaven," as grandparents take milk, take fat, take their own children before the eyes of many, as the dead wake up—blinking away a line that is uncanny *because* so strangely fluid. Ethnographically, I have examined *loip* as integrative of many kinds of experience—not merely ghostly echo or possessive spirit but divine occurrence, living projection, and ancestor with enduring carnal attributes. Theoretically, I have been persisting in telling stories with experiential trails, as experience happens within and through the imagination, merging the undeniable with the fantastic, the ordinary with the inexplicable, and forcing us to respect, re-see, revisit memory as not only elusive, illusory, and fictional but as a tangible, *effective* trace of a reality that haunts us because it is within, across, as well as beyond us.

Expansive experience is a way of theorizing this movement between the thoughtfully, imaginatively experienced and the experientially imagined, a movement that can be both wondrously and dangerously productive and that is not about the rupture and the gap but rather about a continuous sliding from one to the next incarnation. Indeed, to imagine the gap is to reimagine the facile logic of the imagination opposed to experience. The dream, the vision, and the nightmare are productive imaginings unfolding and folding into reality. Yet, even as the slide is inscrutable, the experiential witness must be heeded—we must relentlessly persevere in distinguishing between truth and lies. In the slide that is not a gap, in the movement that is not merely between one thing and another, immediacy must be granted its conceptual space even amid its own paradoxical impossibility. And so we come back again, recognizing the hazards of (particularly state-sponsored) imaginaries that monstrously deform experiences that do not belong to their authors—while simultaneously and crucially affirming the reality of the experiences of so many others, whose sufferings as well as joys undermine the claims of Official Memories, point toward alternative priorities, and open up a space for possibilities that some of us have not yet imagined how to imagine.

Notes

1. Loibonok (masculine plural) and nkoibonok (feminine plural) are healers, prophets, dreamers—men and women known to communicate with Nkai.
2. Lkileku were young men circa the 1930s, while Lterito were young men circa the late nineteenth and early twentieth centuries.
3. In discussing Samburu aduŋ, besides the neuronal arguments I invoke, I am also aware that I come very near to retracing Geertz's webs of signification (Geertz 1968) or, even more aptly, Ortner's key symbols (Ortner 1978). In its intentional aspect, mine is a gesture of appreciation for a fertile history of anthropological approaches and an attempt to push them in new directions—wedding them to Peirce, cognitive theories, and historical approaches, as well as a version of structuralism (and poststructuralism).
4. I also returned to the field during the summers of 2003, 2004, and 2005 as I was revising my book for publication.
5. See Shanafelt 2004 on how anthropologists have historically maintained "a gap between magic and miracle" (Shanafelt 2004: 319), as well as Favret-Saada 1980 and Stoller and Olkes 1987 for anthropologists' personal accounts of engaging with the extraordinary. Shanafelt supports a distinction between miracle as wonder to our interlocutors and occurrences strange to (particularly Euro-American) outsiders but not to our interlocutors. In this way, she is subverting traditional anthropological assumptions by which anything inexplicable to anthropologists is examined as "magic." For anthropological accounts of the miraculous and marvelous, see Geertz 1968; Grindal 1983. See Shanafelt 2004 for a fairly exhaustive critical summary. Grindal (1983) writes reflexively about seeing a resurrection; however, it is more accurately the witnessing of a corpse's temporary reanimation.
6. See Godfrey Lienhardt's (1961) classic work on divinity and experience among the Dinka where he also describes the ways in which Dinka experience through divinity's actions in the world (e.g., Lienhardt 1961: 280–81), although in different terms and to somewhat different ends than I do here. Lienhardt describes Dinka philosophical understandings as being inseparably connected to mundane and extraordinary experience. He also notes the sharedness of Dinka experience, and in doing so importantly opens up the possibility of considering the grounds of human experience as always already cultural and yet partaking of a sharedness that crosses cultural boundaries in ways I alluded to in Chapter 1 of *Miracles and Extraordinary Experience in Northern Kenya* and will describe in bits and pieces here.

7. *Apiu* is the root form of a verb meaning to come back to life after being dead—in other words, to revive, resurrect, spontaneously resuscitate.

8. Since Samburu in the highlands have been burying people for some time rather than placing them in the bush for the hyenas, it is not surprising that some people in the highlands have not heard of it happening. Nevertheless, I seldom came across a Samburu family either in the highlands or the lowlands in which at least one person had not heard of *apiu*.

9. This is the past tense of the verb *apiu* conjugated.

10. The Samburu term for heart is *ltau. Tau* would appear to be onomatopoeia.

11. See Stoller 1989 concerning Songhay ambivalence about hospitals: "When they arrived at the hospital, Mariama trembled. She knew that the hospital village housed the dying and the dead. People went to the hospital village and did not return to their homes" (Stoller 1989: 53).

12. Nompoi referred to the doctor and nurses here as elephants. Elephants can and do kill people, and thus the term is metaphorically associated with war enemies or implicit enemies. Foreigners to Samburu society, and Europeans particularly, are frequently put into this category.

13. See, for example, Carter 2002; Damasio 1999; Dennett 1984; LeDoux 2002; Pinker 1997.

14. She was alive as of 2002 when I last visited her, although she was becoming confused. It is important to note that Samburu like Doto Malapen often do not come from loibonok families. Thus, Doto Malapen had no legitimate connection to loibonok lineages, yet Nkai chose her, communicating with her throughout her life.

References

Carter, R. (2002), *Exploring Consciousness,* Berkeley, CA: University of California Press.

Comaroff, J. and Comaroff, J. (1991), *Of Revelation and Revolution, Volume 1: Christianity, Colonialism, and Consciousness in South Africa,* Chicago, IL: University of Chicago Press.

Comaroff, J. and Comaroff, J. (1997), *Of Revelation and Revolution, Volume 2: The Dialectics of Modernity on a South African Frontier,* Chicago, IL: University of Chicago Press.

Damasio, A. R. (1999), *The Feeling of What Happens,* San Diego, CA: Harvest Books.

Dennett, D. C. (1984), *Elbow Room: The Varieties of Free Will Worth Wanting,* Cambridge, MA: MIT Press.

Favret-Saada, J. (1980), *Deadly Words: Witchcraft in Bocage,* Cambridge: Cambridge University Press.

Geertz, C. (1968), *Islam Observed: Religious Development in Morocco and Indonesia,* New Haven, CT: Yale University Press.

Grindal, B. (1983), "Into the Heart of Sisala Experience: Witnessing Death Divination," *Journal of Anthropological Research,* 39(1): 60–80.

Kratz, C. and (Klumpp) Pido, D. (2000), "Gender, Ethnicity, and Social Aesthetics in Maasai and Okiek Beadwork," in D. Hodgson (ed.), *Rethinking Pastoralism in Africa,* Oxford: James Currey, pp. 43–71.

LeDoux, J. (2002), *Synaptic Self: How Our Brains Become Who We Are,* New York: Viking.

Lienhardt, G. (1961), *Divinity and Experience: The Religion of the Dinka,* Oxford: Clarendon Press.

Ortner, S. (1978), *Sherpas through Their Rituals,* Cambridge: Cambridge University Press.

Pinker, S. (1997), *How the Mind Works,* New York: W. W. Norton and Company.

Shanafelt, R. (2004), "Magic, Miracle, and Marvels in Anthropology," *Ethnos,* 69(3): 317–40.

Sharp, L. A. (2001), "Commodified Kin: Death, Mourning, and Competing Claims on Organ Donors in the United States," *American Anthropologist,* 103(1): 112–33.

Stoller, P. (1989), *Fusion of the Worlds: An Ethnography of Possession among the Songhay of Niger,* Chicago, IL: University of Chicago Press.

Stoller, P. and Olkes, C. (1987), *In Sorcery's Shadow: A Memoir of Apprenticeship among the Songhay of Niger,* Chicago, IL: University of Chicago Press.

Straight, B. (2005a), "Cutting Time: Beads, Sex, and Songs in the Making of Samburu Memory," in W. James and D. Mills (eds), *The Qualities of Time: Temporal Dimensions of Social Form and Human Experience,* ASA Monograph Series, Oxford: Berg, pp. 267–83.

Straight, B. (2005b), "In the Belly of History: Memory, Forgetting, and the Hazards of Reproduction," *Africa,* 75(1): 83–104.

Straight, B. (2007), *Miracles and Extraordinary Experience in Northern Kenya,* Philadelphia: University of Pennsylvania Press.

Ward, B. (1987), *Miracles and the Medieval Mind: Theory, Record and Event 1000–1215,* Philadelphia: University of Pennsylvania Press.

–17–

Zulu Dreamscapes
Senses, Media, and Authentication
in Contemporary Neo-Shamanism
David Chidester

Dreams must seem the most insubstantial of media, nothing more than "subjective apparitions," as the Anglican missionary and ethnographer Henry Callaway described Zulu dreams in 1871, a medium of sensory experience, "brain-sight" and "brain-hearing," without any material referents (Callaway 1872). But the Zulu interpretation of dreams documented by Callaway showed that dreams were often understood as calls to action. Through the medium of dreams, ancestors called for sacrificial offerings (Callaway 1868–70: 6), which would affirm ongoing relations of material exchange between the living and the dead, or an ancestor might call for the performance of homecoming rituals that would bring him "back from the open country to his home" (Callaway 1868–70: 142). Dreams, therefore, were not merely sensory media to be interpreted. Although they were rendered meaningful through a hermeneutics of dreams, they were also given force through an energetics of dreams that demanded practical responses with material consequences. As a result, dreams were thoroughly integrated into the material relations of exchange and orientation in Zulu ancestral religion.

Now, under globalizing conditions, Zulu dreaming is undergoing transformation. Global claims are being made on Zulu dreams. For example, Afrika Bambaataa, the African American godfather of Hip Hop, whose musical group, Zulu Nation, which was not African, Zulu, or a nation, nevertheless moved symbolically into South African space to identify two kinds of religion: On the one side, Afrika Bambaataa identified the "go to sleep slavery type of religion," the religion of the dream, the religion of the oppressed that sealed their oppression. On the other side, there was the "spiritual wake up, revolutionary," religion of conscious, positive action, "like the prophets," in which "knowledge, wisdom, [and] understanding of self and others" inform a "do for self and others type of religion" (Chidester 2005: 230–1). At the same time, indigenous Zulu dreams are going global, as in the case of the Zulu witchdoctor, sangoma, sanusi, and now shaman Credo Mutwa, the master of Zulu "dreams, prophecies, and mysteries" (Mutwa 2003), who has emerged in the global circuit of neo-shamanism (see Townsend 2004) as the bedrock of African indigenous authenticity to underwrite a variety of projects, including New

Age spirituality, alternative healing, and encounters with aliens from outer space (Chidester 2002).

In this new globalizing terrain, electronic media have dramatically expanded the Zulu dreamscape. Zulu dreaming, along with religious or spiritual interpretations of Zulu dreams, visions, and mysteries, has been proliferating through film and video, musical CDs and DVDs, and the expanding global dreamscape of neo-shamanism on the Internet. Nevertheless, in all of these media, we can find echoes of the nineteenth-century Zulu energetics of dreams that was based on sacrificial exchange and ancestral orientation.

First, we find echoes of sacrificial exchange, but now situated in the dilemmas posed by a global economy. Not only defined by the increased pace and scope of the flows of money, technology, and people, the global economy is also an arena for new mediated images and ideals of human possibility (Appadurai 1996), including the possibility that occult forces are both shadow and substance of global economic exchange (Comaroff and Comaroff 1999). In his own way, as we will see, Credo Mutwa has dealt with these dilemmas of the global economy by identifying aliens from outer space as the nexus of a sacrificial exchange into which he personally has entered by eating extraterrestrial beings in a sacramental meal and by being their sacrificial victim.

Second, addressing the demand for bringing ancestors home and reinforcing the sacred orientation revolving around the ancestral homestead, Credo Mutwa has tried for many years to establish a "Credo Mutwa village" in South Africa—in the township of Soweto during the 1970s, in the apartheid Bantustan of Bophuthatswana in the 1980s, in the game reserve of Shamwari during the 1990s—but none of these homes turned out to be sustainable. On the Internet, however, Credo Mutwa found a home. Mediated by the global network of neo-shamanism, he gained new credibility. While Credo Mutwa was going global, North American enthusiasts for New Age spirituality, including some white South African expatriates, found in this new global media an avenue for coming home to Africa by entering the "house of dreams" as a Zulu shaman.

In 1994 the American author, James Hall, described his initiation as a Zulu sangoma as "a journey to become the house of dreams" (Hall 1994: 202). In 2004 the South African expatriate, David M. Cumes, who had established a medical practice in California, underwent his initiation as a Zulu sangoma, observing, "I had heard the term 'a house of dreams' applied to aspects of the thwasa [initiation] experience" (Cumes 2004: 84). How should we understand this new "house of dreams" that is emerging in a new, globalizing arena?

As an entry into this new Zulu dreamscape, I want to examine the role of the human sensorium and electronic media. Exploring Zulu neo-shamanism as material religion, I situate my analysis at the nexus of religious dreaming, sensory repertoires, and electronic mediation. Religion, as Jeremy Stolow has observed, is "materialized in and through the most primary media of all, the human senses" (Stolow 2005: 129). If embodied senses are media, then electronic media can also be understood as both extensions and limitations of the human sensorium. Dreams, our most intimate, embodied media, are also sensory, whether ordinary or extraordinary. Although dreaming has often been regarded as imaginary and immaterial, as nothing more than "subjective apparitions," dreams are material productions, not merely because they are generated by the neurobiology of the brain (see Lieberman 2000), but also because they have the capacity to elicit practical responses with material consequences. In the case of Zulu neo-shamanism, dreams entail material investments in sacrificial exchange and ancestral orientation that echo an earlier Zulu hermeneutics and energetics of dreams but now under rapidly changing global conditions. Within this new Zulu dreamscape, indigenous sensory repertoires for arranging (and deranging) the human sensorium merge with the limits (and potential) of electronic media.

By examining the work of a variety of contemporary Zulu shamans, including Credo Mutwa and P. H. Mtshali, but also including James Hall, David Cumes, Ann Mortifee, and other so-called white sangomas, we can discern basic strategies for engaging senses and media. In this new Zulu dreamscape, dreams are a sensory medium, involving "brain-sight" and "brain-hearing," as Henry Callaway suggested, but they also incorporate all of the senses, simultaneously, synaesthetically, and expansively, perhaps even expanding to the twelve senses that Credo Mutwa will claim as the natural sensorium of human beings. All of this sensory experience, however, is thoroughly mediated through new electronic media. As I hope to show, Zulu neo-shamans have developed an ambivalent relationship to the very media that have made it possible for them to be shamans. Media, like sensory experience, is engaged in three ways—as limit, as potential, and as validation of the reality of this new Zulu shamanism. Within the dreamscapes of contemporary Zulu neo-shamanism, the human senses and electronic media are at play, and the question of authenticity is at stake, in the imaginative terrain that has opened between global exchanges and local homecomings.

Extraterrestrial Encounters

Vusamazulu Credo Mutwa has been described, internationally, as a Zulu shaman, the keeper of Zulu tradition, although he has often been characterized in South Africa as a fake, fraud, and a charlatan (Friedman 1997; Johnson 1997). An extremely creative and imaginative author (Mutwa 1964, 1966), artist, and sculptor, Credo Mutwa has been celebrated within the global network of contemporary neo-shamanism as the High Sanusi of the Zulu nation, the highest grade of African shaman and the official historian of the Zulu people of South Africa.

Over his long career, Credo Mutwa has been adept at reinventing himself in relation to various alien appropriations of his authenticity. During the 1950s Credo Mutwa was used to authenticate African artifacts for a curio shop in Johannesburg. Through his writings in the 1960s, his tourist attraction in Soweto in the 1970s, and his cultural village in Bophuthatswana in the 1980s, he was used to authenticate the racial, cultural, and religious separations of apartheid. During the 1990s, as he acquired the label "shaman" through the interventions of Bradford Keeney (2001), Stephen Larsen (Mutwa 1996, 2003), and other exponents of New Age spirituality, Credo Mutwa's authority was invoked to authenticate a diverse array of enterprises in saving the world from human exploitation, environmental degradation, epidemic illness, endemic ignorance, organized crime, or extraterrestrial conspiracy. In all of these projects, the indigenous authenticity of Credo Mutwa added value, credibility, and force because he represented the "pure voice," untainted by modernity, of an unmediated access to primordial truth (Chidester 2005: 172–89).

One of Credo Mutwa's supporters, the New Age conspiracy theorist David Icke, produced a five-hour video, *The Reptilian Agenda,* based on interviews with the Zulu shaman. In this video, Icke explains, we are introduced to "a unique human being, the most incredible man it has been my honour to meet." Mutwa is "keeper of the ancient knowledge," the truth of history, as opposed to the "nonsensical version of history we get from universities." The true history confirmed by both Icke's recent research and Mutwa's ancient knowledge centered on a global conspiracy of aliens from outer space.

A former sports broadcaster in Britain, David Icke developed a distinctive blend of personal spirituality and political paranoia that he promoted through books, public lectures, and an elaborate Web site (Icke 1999, 2002, 2005). Although he seemed to embrace every conspiracy theory, David Icke identified the central, secret conspiracy ruling the world as the work of shape-shifting reptilians from outer space. According-ing to Icke, these extraterrestrial reptiles interbred with human beings, establishing a lineage that could be traced through the pharaohs of ancient Egypt, the Merovingian dynasty of medieval Europe, the British royal family, and every president of the United States. Although they plotted behind the scenes in the secret society of the Illuminati, the aliens of these hybrid bloodlines were in prominent positions of royal, political, and economic power all over the world. Occasionally shifting into their lizard-like form, these aliens maintained a human appearance by regularly drinking human blood, which they acquired by performing rituals of human sacrifice.

David Icke invoked the indigenous African authority of Credo Mutwa to confirm this conspiracy theory about blood-drinking, shape-shifting reptiles from outer space. As Mutwa declared, "To know the Illuminati, Mr. David, you must study the reptile" (Icke 2002). In *The Reptilian Agenda,* Credo Mutwa confirms that extraterrestrials, the Chitauri, were a shape-shifting reptilian race that has controlled humanity for thousands of years. Subsequent to making this video, Icke and Mutwa appeared together on a popular American radio program, "Sightings," to explain the alien reptile conspiracy. They also reportedly joined forces on the eve of the new millennium to prevent an Illuminati ritual of human sacrifice at the Great Pyramid of Cheops. In his lectures, Icke insisted that Credo Mutwa provided proof for his conspiracy theory, as one observer noted, in the "pure voice of a primitive belief system" (Molloy 1999). In Credo Mutwa, therefore, David Icke found indigenous authentication for an alien conspiracy (see Icke 1999).

Authentication of the "truth" took different forms: First, this truth is a dangerous truth. Credo Mutwa is constantly subjected to death threats, including an attempt on his life just prior to filming, by those who want to prevent him from speaking the truth. The danger inherent in this truth is inherently validating. The conspiracy is not a "theory," Icke warns, because "theory does not kill people. The conspiracy is real."

Second, this truth is a "bizarre story," Icke admits, but it is confirmed by Credo Mutwa's "unique knowledge," which is drawn from secret traditions of "Africa, this enormous and astonishing continent." Icke advises: "as bizarre ... and as seemingly ridiculous as this story might seem" it is authenticated by the fact that Credo Mutwa "tells exactly the same story."

Third, this truth, in its African authentication, is a precarious tradition, since Credo Mutwa is one of only two Zulu Sanusi left alive, but this truth, at risk of vanishing, will be preserved on video "for as long as the electronic medium exists." So, while Credo Mutwa provides indigenous confirmation for Icke's "bizarre story," Icke, in return, promises permanence for Zulu tradition through modern electronic media.

In his video interviews for *The Reptilian Agenda,* Credo Mutwa describes his encounters with extraterrestrials with meticulous attention to the senses, creating a vivid impression of seeing, hearing, smelling, tasting, and touching aliens in two contexts—eating them and being violated by them.

According to Mutwa, African tradition provides wisdom on how to prepare, cook, and eat aliens from outer space. In 1958, he recalls, a UFO crashed in a mountainous area of Lesotho. A friend invited Mutwa over for a meal, promising him that they would be dining on "something holy," which turned out to be the meat of an extraterrestrial known as a Grey. Following African tradition, they had to eat this meal in a deep hole in the ground. As Mutwa reports, the meat of the alien was tough and dry, requiring much chewing, and it had the "same taste as a copper coin." After eating this "flesh of a god," Mutwa and his companion became deathly ill, suffering intense pain for a week, which seemed like a hundred years, blinded, deaf, and unable to breathe. After a week, they went "stark, raving, laughing mad." Then, suddenly, Mutwa recalls, he was "a person reborn." All of his senses were expanded. "I could see colours beyond colours," he recalls. "I could hear a voice in my head." His taste buds were "souped up," so that ordinary water tasted extraordinary. In the ecstasy of this extraordinary sensory experience, Mutwa recalls, "We were one with the entire universe." By eating the alien, Mutwa had acquired an extraterrestrial sensorium. "Do you think those senses you experienced are the senses of the Chitauri?" Icke asks. "Yes," Mutwa responds. "Senses like no human being has."

By contrast to this extraterrestrial ecstasy, in 1959 Mutwa underwent the alien agony of abduction. While looking for medicinal herbs in what is now Zimbabwe, Mutwa was taken into a space ship of the Chitauri, disappearing for a period of four days. Again, his account of alien abduction pays meticulous attention to the senses, the "strange humming sound," the images of destroyed cities as "pictures flooded my mind," and the horrible metallic, chemical smell of the Chitauri, the Greys, and other extraterrestrials. "I have seen the Chitauri," Mutwa assures us. "I have smelled them. I have personal experience with them." But that personal experience was entirely terrifying, an "eternity of pain" inflicted upon him by aliens who tortured him, experimented upon him, and forced him to have sexual intercourse with a female extraterrestrial. Throughout all of these ordeals, Mutwa recounted, he felt like the victim at a sacrifice. Returning to earth saturated with a "horrible non-human smell," and missing his trousers, Mutwa was attacked by dogs but was saved by villagers who recognized by his odor that he had been abducted by aliens. Although eating them had heightened his senses, being abducted by aliens had confused his senses. "Since that time I have become a very confused creature," he confides. "Since that time my mind does not seem to be my own."

Transatlantic Exchanges

In a blurb on the back of the recent book by David M. Cumes, *Africa in My Bones: A Surgeon's Odyssey into the Spirit World of African Healing* (2004), Credo Mutwa praises the author, "who walks along two roads" as both Western medical specialist and African ritual specialist, as both surgeon and sangoma, but also as someone who has developed a kind of double vision. "The world needs such people," Mutwa advises, "who see Africa through two eyes, the African eye and the Western eye." Born in South Africa, Cumes relocated to the United States to study medicine at Stanford and establish a successful practice as a urologist in Santa Barbara, California. Although he often visited the place of his birth, Cumes reported that he felt like an alien in Africa, which he described as a problem of vision, noting that in Africa he "felt like an onlooker rather than a participant." This problem of alienated vision, this subjectivity of the spectator, was resolved for Cumes through dreams that led him to undergo initiation as a sangoma. "The fact that my dreams were often quite prophetic," he recounted, "gave me reason to believe that I might be able to master this ancient discipline." In dreams, he was "called" by the ancestors to enter into the ancient discipline of "seeing" (Cumes 2004: ix). Now, as a Zulu sangoma, he practices divination as a kind of dreamwork. As Cumes explains, "reading the bones is a little like unraveling the metaphor of a dream. ... Divining is like interpreting someone's dream" (Cumes 2004: 7, 18).

On his Web site, Cumes features a video of his life story, his initiation, and his plans for a healing village in South Africa (Cumes 2006). To the sounds of rhythmic African music, the video begins with an image of an African woman, traditionally attired, her eyes and mouth wide open. Moving through rural and urban scenes, Cumes, in voice-over, proceeds to use tactile metaphors to describe his early life in South Africa, weighted down under the "heaviness of the apartheid system," alienated from "connection with the native" and "connection with Africa." Following his dreams and the advice of author Susan Shuster Campbell (2000, 2002), he was led to an "old Zulu teacher in Swaziland," P. H. Mtshali. Undergoing a rigorous, although abbreviated, initiation, Cumes graduated as a Zulu sangoma. Now, running his life based on messages "from the dreamworld," Cumes reports, "I just head wherever the dreams and bones tell me." One place the dreams told him to head was the South African province of Limpopo, where he is establishing a healing center, Tshisimane, in which visitors can benefit from massage, yoga, Reiki, and consultations with sangomas. "I saw the place in a dream," Cumes reveals.

As a white sangoma, David Cumes represents a recently emerging trend in contemporary neo-shamanism in which aspiring Euro-American shamans are turning to African traditions as a source of authentic dreams, visions, and connections. The West African, Malidoma Patrice Somé, has played an important role in this recent development (Somé 1993). John Hall, the American biographer of the great South African singer, Miriam Makeba, was a pioneer in taking initiation as a Zulu sangoma (Hall 1994). But South Africans have also played a part. While Credo Mutwa has some white initiates, such as the "white Zulu" C. J. Hood, who has represented him at events in the United States, calling upon everyone to return to their ancestral traditions (Heart Healing Center 2001; Wellness eJournal 2001), P. H. Mtshali has shown a particular interest in training white sangomas who are currently practicing in South Africa, like Claudia Rauber in Cape Town (Anonymous 2000; Viall 2004), or in North America, like Gretchen McKay in Orange County, California (Mtshali 2004: 58–64).

In some cases, however, white sangomas in the United States have not required formal initiation to claim indigenous African authenticity. For example, Kenneth "Bear Hawk" Cohen, who claims to have been adopted by the Cree, studied with the Zulu shaman, Ingwe, who was born in 1914 as M. Norman Powell in South Africa, but moved to the United States to establish his Wilderness Awareness School. On his Web site, "Bear Hawk" announces that this association with Ingwe places him "in the lineage of the Holy Man, Vusamazulu Credo Mutwa" (Cohen 2006). Similarly, Tom "Blue Wolf" Goodman, who claims to be a Native American shaman, the "Faith Keeper of the Star Clan, Y'falla Band of the Lower Creek People," also claims to be heir to the spiritual lineage of Vusamazulu Credo Mutwa. "I am keeper of my Grandfather's dream," he reveals. "My grandfather's medicine songs have been dreamed in South Africa by Sangoma spiritual leaders," spiritual leaders who are all led by "Vusamazulu Credo Mutwa, High Sanusi (High Priest) of the Zulu Nation" (Goodman 2004).

In North America, defenders of the integrity of indigenous traditions have labeled these white shamans as "plastic shamans" (Aldred 2000; Kehoe 1990). Web sites identify them and scorn them (Anonymous 2003). Although these innovations in neo-shamanism might very well be "plastic," in the sense of invented or even fake, they nevertheless suggest real religious issues of location, dislocation, and relocation in the Atlantic world. Just as the South African David Cumes, who became a medical doctor in California, underwent initiation as a Zulu sangoma to establish "connection with the native" or "connection with Africa," other expatriates have entered the dreamscape of Zulu neo-shamanism as a way of coming home. In Canada, two South Africans, one black, one white, but both having established careers in the creative and performing arts, followed their dreams into Zulu shamanism.

Sibongile Nene describes herself as a singer, actor, and consultant for individuals, businesses, and community building. She also describes herself as a sangoma. As an actress, she appeared in the feature film, *Jit* (1993). The plot of this film anticipated her later vocation as a ritual specialist in African ancestral religion: "Jokwa, a pesky ancestral spirit," wants the main character "to look after his aging parents, and keep her supplied with beer." Moving to Canada, Sibongile Nene continued acting and singing, but also moved into business consultancy. Returning regularly to South Africa, she took initiation as a Zulu sangoma, a process she conveys through music on her musical CD, *Sangoma*. On her Web site, Sibongile Nene offers her services as an "African Spirituality Consultant in the Sangoma tradition of the Bantu people of southern Africa" (Nene 2006).

Ann Mortifee, described in the press as "one of Canada's most extraordinary vocalists, composers, and playwrights," but also as a "musical shaman," guided and inspired by Credo Mutwa, was born and raised on a sugarcane farm in Zululand. In 2005 she released a CD, *Into the Heart of the Sangoma,* dedicated to Credo Mutwa, which musically conveyed her journey from her experience of inauthenticity in exile to the authenticity of home. In her successful creative and performing career in Canada, as Mortifee revealed in an interview, "I had created a persona, but felt I had nothing authentic to give to the world." Here, once again, dreams intervened. "For two years," she recalled, "I had recurring dreams about a black woman and stars." Then she read Credo Mutwa's *Song of the Stars* (1996). "I discovered the Zulu 'Song of the Stars' and learned about the sangoma, shamen [*sic*] of the Zulu nation." She flew to South Africa and her dreams eventually led her to Credo Mutwa (Weyler 2005).

Although she has told her story in interviews, Ann Mortifee's journey into Zulu shamanism is best conveyed by the music and commentary of her recording, *Into the Heart of the Sangoma*. Opening with the song, "Africa," she begins with her birth-place but also with her dreams. "Voices from my childhood linger in me still, voices that come from the dreamtime," she says. "It is the old Sangoma, Sikhowe, leading me deeper into the mystery." The next song, "I Dream," also evokes both Africa and the dreamtime. "One of my earliest recollections is of lying in my bed listening to the sounds of the African night," she says. "Something was out there beckoning to me, weaving a spell, which had the power, in some essential way, to mark my soul forever."

The next song, "The Stars Are Holes," finds her looking up into the night sky, but this song also directs her vision back home to South Africa. "Two years after writing this song," she says, "I found the very same story I had written in a book by Vusamazulu Credo Mutwa, the head Sangoma of the Zulu Nation. This strange occurrence caused me to go to South Africa and find him." Returning to South Africa, staying at a game reserve, she saw a herd of elephants that inspired the song, "Indlovu" (the elephant), and that night, she recalls, "I dreamed ... there walked a man whom I later knew to be Credo Mutwa. In the dream he said to me, 'Go to Shamwari tomorrow.'" Proceeding to this private game reserve in the Eastern Cape, where Credo Mutwa was employed for a while as a cultural advisor, she participated in "an ancient healing ceremony" at which she sang a song that she had just composed. "Who taught you this song?" the sangomas asked. When Mortifee replied that she had just made it up, the sangomas objected. "You did not make this up," they insisted. "This is the song we Sangomas sing when we go in search of spirit." Having established this connection in song and spirit, Mortifee's dreams were fulfilled by meeting Credo Mutwa. As musically represented in the song, "For There Are Loved Ones," Mortifee learned from Mutwa that her dreams revealed that she was connected to his ancestral lineage. Ann Mortifee explains:

> When I finally met Credo Mutwa, he said: "Tell me about the Sangoma of your dreams. What is her name?" "Sikhowe," I answered. "And tell me, what do her eyes look like?" "Well, one is black and the other is completely white." "And which one is white?" "The right one," I said. "And tell me what do her legs look like?" "They look like the trunks of a tree," I replied. "That woman is my grandmother," Mutwa said. "She had a cataract in her right eye, which turned it completely white. And she had elephantitis, which made her legs look like the trunk of a tree. So you see, it is my grandmother that has brought you to me."

In this affirmation and connection, driven by dreams, Ann Mortifee could finally feel as if she were at home in Africa. She had been called by the maternal ancestor, herself a sangoma, of the highest shaman of the Zulu nation. But she could also return home to North America unburdened by any guilt. "I want you to listen to me," Credo Mutwa reportedly said to her. "Never again be ashamed of the privilege into which you have been born. And never, never be ashamed of the great gifts that the gods have given you."

Ann Mortifee's greatest gift, by her own account, is music that opens to the sacred, which provides both a zone of protection and a vehicle for entering the numinous. "Sacred music has been a way of my stopping the world and entering into a place of deep protection," she explains. "Music is a vehicle through which we've always been able to contact the numinous" (Frymire 2003).

Senses and Media

In his classic treatment of "the holy," Rudolf Otto disagreed with this proposition that music, or any artistic medium, could be a vehicle for direct contact with the numinous. Pointing to the mistake of "confounding in any way the non-rational of music and the non-rational of the numinous itself" (1923: 49), Otto insisted that music and other arts could only suggest the numinous indirectly, coming most closely to representing the numinous through two methods that "are in a noteworthy way negative, viz. darkness and silence" (1923: 68). According to Otto, therefore, not seeing and not hearing—or better: seeing nothing, hearing nothing—were sensory experiences within the productions of artistic media that most closely approximated the numinous. Arguably, Otto's Protestant sensibility led him to engage aesthetic media through this negative theology of the senses.

By contrast, indigenous Zulu sensibility was actively engaged with sensory media of dreams and visions, exploring their potential as avenues for communicating with ancestors and responding to the energetics of exchange and orientation. In contemporary Zulu neo-shamanism, however, we find an ambivalent relationship to both the senses and electronic media, as vehicles for the numinous, which mirrors an understanding of the senses as limitation, as potential, and as validation for the extraordinary experiences of a shaman.

These three ways of dealing with senses and media are all registers of authenticity. By representing limits, senses and media stand as obstacles to authentic spiritual experience. But they also represent the boundary that is necessary to mark the transition from ordinary, everyday awareness to the extraordinary capacities of a shaman. In marking out limits, therefore, senses and media incorporate the classic ambivalence of liminality, as both wall and threshold, defining a boundary that simultaneously constrains and contains possibilities. Accordingly, senses and media also register as transcendent potential, serving as means for achieving, modes for expanding, or metaphors for signaling shamanic awareness. Authenticity, in this respect, is marked by realizing the potential of the human sensorium and electronic media as meaning-making resources. Extraordinary sensory experience, including the intensification, rearrangement, and merger of the senses, is directly related to the capacity of electronic media to capture meaning like a camera and transmit meaning like film. In the process, shamanic authenticity is reinforced by activating the latent potential in senses and media for the production and reception of extraordinary meaning. Finally, human senses and electronic media provide validation, obviously, since "seeing is believing," in cognitive terms, but also in forensic terms when the testimony of intense sensory experiences or popular media representations provide confirmation for shamanic claims. By engaging senses and media in these three ways, as limit, potential, and validation, Zulu neo-shamans have sought to authenticate new Zulu dreamscapes.

Senses and Media as Limits

The five conventionally recognized human senses, according to Credo Mutwa, are limits, blocking awareness of spiritual realities. Seeing, hearing, smelling, tasting, and touching are inadequate for engaging this higher awareness. Fortunately,

Mutwa assures us, these five senses are only part of a more expansive sensorium that extends to a total of twelve senses. As Mutwa insists, without explaining, "We in Africa know—and please don't ask me to explain further—that the human being possesses twelve senses—not five senses as Western people believe. One day this will be accepted scientifically—twelve." These additional seven senses, whatever they might be, are part of the natural sensory capacity of human beings. Although they transcend the five senses, these additional senses are simply human nature. Accordingly, Mutwa maintains that "we must not call those as yet unknown senses, supernatural" (Mutwa 1996: 30).

Neo-shaman John Hall also finds that the five senses are limits. They cannot account for his intense encounters with the lidloti, the ancestors, which he experienced in dreams and visions during his initiation as a sangoma. Reflecting on ordinary sensory limits, Hall cites the authority of Augustine of Hippo, who observed, "I can run through all the organs of sense, which are the body's gateway to the mind, but I cannot find any by which some facts could have entered" (Hall 1994: 61). Although Augustine used this argument to posit an interior sense, or seminal reason, as a capacity for knowledge that was independent of ordinary perception, Hall concludes that this acknowledgment of the limits of the senses opens the possibility of extrasensory perception. Augustine, Hall found, "might have been describing my puzzlement following a lidloti experience" (Hall 1994: 61).

Like the five senses, electronic media can be regarded as placing limits on awareness. At one point, Credo Mutwa advises anyone who wants to be a sangoma, with prophetic vision, to stay away from electronic media. As Mutwa warns, "People who are aspiring to develop their gifts of prophesy should avoid exposing themselves over much to electronic devices such as television sets, radio sets, and other electronic gadgets of this day and age because, for some reason, these electronic devices emit an inaudible sound that blankets all psychic power." This unheard sound, as an undercurrent of electronic media, supposedly blocks the extrasensory perceptions of a sangoma. Accordingly, a sangoma should develop his or her psychic powers in a rural area, not merely to be closer to an ancestral home, but also to be free of the limits to awareness generated by the modern network of electronic transmission and reception of media. "I have noticed over many years of close observation," Mutwa reports, "how difficult it becomes for a witch doctor from Soweto, for example, to foretell events in the future. This is unlike a witch doctor who has lived in an environment where these electronic devices do not exist. So there must be something in our electronic world that is destroying our God-given talents ... " (Mutwa 1996: 29).

John Hall also finds limits to electronic media. In a kind of allegory marking his independence from electronic media, he recalls that during his initiation he felt cut off from any news about the world outside. He acquired a radio, but it stopped working when its wiring was eaten by dozens of cockroaches. "They scrambled over my hands and arms and I dropped the radio in surprise and disgust," Hall recounts.

"It smashed to pieces on the floor" (Hall 1994: 112). Television, as well, was an unnecessary medium, as Hall reflects, "Not that I had seen a television image in over a year and a half. Nor had I needed to. Lidloti-vision had kept me enthralled" (Hall 1994: 196). The limits of television, therefore, had been transcended by a spiritual medium, ancestor-vision, which provided Hall with all of the information (and entertainment) he could desire.

Senses and Media as Potential

Although senses are limits, they also represent the potential for extraordinary experience. Eyes might be limited, but in distinguishing an authentic shaman, as P.H. Mtshali reveals, "the important thing is that they can 'see'" (Mtshali 2004: 22). Here the senses, as metaphors, represent the possibility of transcending the limits of ordinary perception. Credo Mutwa might have regarded the five conventional senses as limitations, but he also claimed to have entered an extraordinary trans-sensory ecstasy, an intense expansion of all the senses, after eating the meat of an extraterrestrial. Acquiring the sensory capacity of the reptilian extraterrestrials—"Senses like no human being has"—Mutwa saw, heard, smelled, tasted, and touched beyond ordinary perception.

This intensification and expansion of all the senses recalls the role of synaesthesia, the convergence, merger, or trans-modal transfer of the senses, in religious discourse and practice. In religious discourse, synaesthesia can evoke perception that is intense, unifying, and extraordinary (Chidester 1992). In ritual synaesthesia, ordinary perception is transcended in and through the senses, as when the persistent sound and visceral percussion of drumming induces shamanic "seeing" (Sullivan 1986).

During his initiation as a sangoma, John Hall experienced this synaesthetic merger of visceral percussion, sound, and sight. "The loud drums had once more beaten my mind into myself," he recalls. But he immediately turns to media as metaphor, noting, "I had no more self-consciousness viewing these images than a person does watching an involving movie." The next day, when he related his experience to an elder sangoma, she observed, "Sometimes, it is like you are watching television. It's that way with me. Things come at you, like the *bhayiskhobho*." As Hall realized, this SiSwati term, *bhayiskhobho*, was derived from the antiquated term, "bioscope," which had been widely used in South Africa for the "motion picture process" (Hall 1994: 54).

Similarly, David M. Cumes represented the potential of shamanic perception as electronic media. Sangomas are connected to a communication network like the Western communication network of "satellite phones, fax machines and the Internet." Since this sangoma communication network is based on a "sophisticated psychospiritual technology," Cumes advises, the "ancient African wisdom has a lot to teach us about communication" (Cumes 2004: 6). Although Cumes contrasts modern Western and traditional African communication networks, sometimes it seems as if both share the same "cosmic field," since Cumes observes that "light, sound, radio, TV, electromagnetic pulses ... are some of the knowable signals that travel through the cosmic field" (Cumes 2004: 105).

During his initiation, Cumes also had dreams and visions that drew upon modern media technology as metaphors for ancient spiritual wisdom. "One night," he reports, "I dreamt that I was given a new shiny black Mamiya camera. I was told the lens I needed was 150 to 16—more powerful on the wide angle than on the telephoto side." Relating this dream to his teacher, P. H. Mtshali, Cumes asked if the ancestors were instructing him to buy this type of camera to keep a photographic record of his initiation. But Mtshali interpreted this dream not as request but as gift from the ancestors, revealing to Cumes that the camera was a sign that "you are being given tools to give you a broader vision" (Cumes 2004: 44).

Senses and Media as Validation

In his tales of encounters with aliens from outer space, Credo Mutwa pays meticulous attention to sensory perception, with particular emphasis on the sense of smell, as if "smelling is knowing," especially in knowing the foul odor of the Chitauri, Greys, and other extraterrestrials. As Mutwa claims, "they are tangible, they are smellable." By his own account, Mutwa was close enough to smell them; he was close enough to be infused by their odor; and he continued to bear that alien odor when he returned to earth and villagers recognized the extraterrestrial stench. Such sensory details, we might assume, are cited to lend an aura of credibility to an unbelievable story. They provide a kind of visceral validation of the narrative.

Similarly, Hall, Cumes, and other white sangomas validate their accounts through vivid sensory detail, suggesting that their initiations revolve around a recovery of the senses. In their accounts, they see and hear extraordinary things, but they also smell fragrant herbs and foul concoctions, taste sour beer and disgusting medicines, and convulse in excruciating pain and induced vomiting in validating their initiations.

Electronic media also provide validation, not only as metaphors for spiritual perception, but also as enduring forms for transmitting indigenous spiritual wisdom. The relative permanence of video, as David Icke declared, promises to preserve the authentic Zulu wisdom of Credo Mutwa for "as long as this electronic medium lasts." Traditionally, according to Mutwa, this wisdom was kept secret, reserved for a small circle of initiates, and transmitted orally within a lineage of initiates from generation to generation. But now, as Mutwa declares, "Africa is dying," facing destruction from epidemic disease, endemic poverty, and global conspiracy. In this crisis, traditional ways of transmitting ancient wisdom are no longer viable. Urgently, everyone must know things that were previously known only by a few. Mass media, such as video, film, and the Internet, are now necessary for broadcasting the truth and surviving this crisis. Accordingly, modern media become valid modes of disseminating ancient wisdom.

At the same time, mass media content can be invoked to validate ancient Zulu tradition. According to Credo Mutwa, the extraterrestrial reptilians, the Chitauri, will soon be returning to earth to exercise their oppressive domination and exploitation of humanity directly. The Chitauri have been content to exercise their power in disguise, operating through devious, shape-shifting reptilians such as George W. Bush, Tony Blair, and other Illuminati who maintain their human-like appearance through regular rituals of human sacrifice and blood drinking. Very soon, however, the alien Chitauri will appear on earth in their true, hideous forms. According to Credo Mutwa, an important feature of this global conspiracy of extraterrestrial domination of humanity can be found in Hollywood films.

Recent movies, beginning with *ET: The Extraterrestrial,* have been preparing humanity to accept the Chitauri and willingly submit to their authority. According to Mutwa, one Star Wars character, Darth Maul, "is exactly what the Chitauri look like," while Stargate depicts "a slimy, cream-colored creature" that Mutwa finds is the "speaking likeness of Mobaba, emperor of the Chitauri." Discovering the Chitauri and their evil emperor appearing in Hollywood films, Mutwa demands: "Where do filmmakers get their information?"

On the one hand, Hollywood filmmakers appropriate ancient African traditions. For example, *Men in Black,* according to Mutwa, has appropriated indigenous African traditions about how to deal with aliens and how to dispose of extraterrestrial rubbish. Through these popular films, Mutwa complains, the authentic traditions of African "Men in Black" have been stolen and Westernized by Hollywood.

On the other hand, filmmakers draw their information directly from the Chitauri, or indirectly through the hybrid Illuminati, because Hollywood is working on behalf of their global conspiracy by familiarizing audiences with the strange appearance of the aliens. By suspending disbelief, Hollywood films are preparing audiences all over the world to accept their imminent subjugation to reptilian extraterrestrials.

Going Global, Coming Home

Although Credo Mutwa is an acknowledged expert on aliens from outer space, acknowledged not only by New Age conspiracy theorist David Icke but also by Harvard researcher John E. Mack (1999), this feature of his indigenous Zulu wisdom is not mentioned by white Zulu sangomas, such as John Hall and David M. Cumes, nor by the "musical shaman," Ann Mortifee, who has been guided and inspired by Credo Mutwa. As we have seen, while Credo Mutwa is going global, they are interested in coming home.

In developing a cultural and political analysis of Zulu popular music, Louise Meintjes has tracked mediations between the local and the global in which artists work in the studio on "performing Zuluness" while "imagining overseas" (Meintjes 2003). Similarly, Credo Mutwa has been situated in mediations between the local and the global by performing an indigenous Zulu vision of the world while looking overseas for a global audience. In the process, even if he displays a remarkable capacity for imaginative invention, Mutwa nevertheless suggests important features of a changing Zulu dreamscape.

During the nineteenth century, to tell a dream meant "to fetch" the dream, to go back to the place where the dream was originally experienced, its originating location, and carry it to the new place of telling. A dream, therefore, was portable, but it was situated in a specific landscape. It could be located and relocated, horizontally, within a terrain of human habitation. However, under colonial conditions of dispossession and dislocation, it became increasingly difficult "to fetch" dreams within an embattled terrain. As it became harder "to fetch" dreams, techniques for blocking dreams, including conversion to Christianity, were increasingly deployed. Credo Mutwa, I would like to suggest, has attempted to resolve this longstanding dilemma within the Zulu dreamscape by moving dreams, vertically, into the sky. The Zulu word for sleep, *butongo,* which means "to sleep," according to Credo Mutwa, means "the state of being one with the star gods." The Zulu word for dreaming, *ipupo,* which means "to dream," according to Credo Mutwa, means "to fly." As Mutwa explains, "The verb 'pupa' refers to flight, therefore to say 'I dreamt' means 'I flew'" (Mutwa 1996: 173). These imaginative etymologies, whatever their validity, effectively shift the hermeneutics and energetics of Zulu dreaming from the land to the sky.

"We need to develop a relationship with the dream reality," urges Zulu sangoma David Cumes (Cumes 2004: 92). As a white South African expatriate, Cumes dreamed of coming home to South Africa. His initiation as a sangoma enabled him to establish "connection with the native" and "connection with Africa." In his dream reality, these connections entailed a fundamental reorientation in South African space. Although black South Africans had suffered under a long history of colonialism and apartheid, Cumes now saw that whites in South Africa had also suffered. "Without our knowing it," he observes, "the apartheid system had discriminated against us too. As whites we had been forbidden access to another realm—we were not worthy and had been justifiably deprived. There were no signs to tell us, 'Whites not allowed,' but we were excluded all the same. We skirted around the authenticity of a magical continent thinking we were part of it when in fact we were not." Called by the ancestors to become a sangoma, Cumes was able to overcome the discrimination and alienation under which whites had suffered in South Africa. "Now the spirits had mandated and things had changed," he declared. "I was no longer underprivileged and would never be again" (Cumes 2004: 30).

Clearly, this testimony evokes a reorientation that is not of the sky but of the land. Locally, within South Africa, Cumes advances the argument that apartheid had disadvantaged white people by separating them from access to indigenous African spiritual traditions. Now, coming home, not as an observer but as a participant, he embraces the people and the land. Accordingly, Cumes represents his reorientation not as flying in the sky, expanding his global vision, but as a tactile connection, as being "blessed and touched by an unseen hand through a channel I did not even know" (Cumes 2004: 30). Here also, media, as a "channel," is evoked as metaphor, but the metaphor evokes the embodied reorientation established by a tactile connection with home.

In tracking Zulu dreamscapes, I have tried to show that dreams are not merely "subjective apparitions" or "brain-sensation." Nor are dreams only "texts" to be interpreted. Involved in an energetics of sacrificial exchange and spatial orientation, dreaming can be a religious practice, a practice that can be dramatically altered by the shifting social fields in which dreams are situated. In response to economic dispossession and social dislocation during the nineteenth century, Zulu dreamers increasingly turned to ritual techniques, which arguably included conversion to Christianity, for blocking ancestral dreams, seeking to turn off this sensory media. By contrast, contemporary neo-shamanism cultivates a sensory extravagance, an overabundance of sensory engagements with things that are not there, from alien reptilians to ancestral spirits, which demand ritual response. Any apparitions that might appear, therefore, must be regarded as real and engaged accordingly.

Global in scope, this new Zulu dreamscape is saturated by media. Despite expressing occasional concerns that electronic media might block dreams and visions, neo-shamans dwell in a mediated world, a world shaped by media technology, possibility, and authentication. As both dreamscape and mediascape, Zulu neo-shamanism is emerging within a new energetics of global exchange and global orientation.

References

Aldred, L. (2000), "Plastic Shamans and Astroturf Sundances: New Age Commercialization of Native American Spirituality," *American Indian Quarterly,* 24(3): 329–52.

Anonymous (2000), "Whites Embrace Traditional Healing in Swaziland," *Panafrican News Agency* (August 9), http://www.ancestralwisdom.com/whitethwasas. html (accessed February 14, 2007).

Anonymous (2003), "Native Religions and Plastic Medicine Men," http://www.wil liams.edu/go/native/natreligion.htm (accessed February 14, 2007).

Appadurai, A. (1996), "Disjuncture and Difference in the Global Cultural Economy," in *Modernity at Large: Cultural Dimensions of Globalization,* Minneapolis: University of Minnesota Press, pp. 27–47.

Callaway, H. (1868–70), *The Religious System of the Amazulu,* Springvale: Springvale Mission; reprinted Cape Town: Struik, 1970.

Callaway, H. (1872), "On Divination and Analogous Phenomena among the Natives of Natal," *Proceedings of the Anthropological Institute,* 1: 163–83.

Campbell, S. S. (2000), *Called to Heal: African Shamanic Healers,* Twin Lakes, WI: Lotus Press.

Campbell, S. S. (2002), *Spirit of the Ancestors,* Twin Lakes, WI: Lotus Press.

Chidester, D. (1992), *Word and Light: Seeing, Hearing, and Religious Discourse,* Urbana: University of Illinois Press.

Chidester, D. (2002), "Credo Mutwa, Zulu Shaman: The Invention and Appropriation of Indigenous Authenticity in African Folk Religion," *Journal for the Study of Religion,* 15(2): 65–85.

Chidester, D. (2005), *Authentic Fakes: Religion and American Popular Culture,* Berkeley: University of California Press.

Cohen, K. (2006), "About Kenneth 'Bear Hawk' Cohen," http://www.kennethcohen.com/sacred_earth/about.html (accessed February 14, 2007).

Comaroff, J. and Comaroff, J. L. (1999), "Occult Economies and the Violence of Abstraction: Notes from the South African Postcolony," *American Ethnologist,* 26(2): 279–303.

Cumes, D. M. (2004), *Africa in My Bones: A Surgeon's Odyssey into the Spirit World of African Healing,* Claremont, South Africa: Spearhead.

Cumes, D. M. (2006), "Holistic Urology and Surgery, Psycho-Spiritual Healing," http://www.davidcumes.com/ (accessed December 18, 2006).

Friedman, H. (1997), "Of Culture and Visions," *Mail and Guardian* (March 27).

Frymire, A. (2003), "What's Sacred Got to Do with It?" *Common Ground* (November), http://commonground.ca/iss/0311148/music_festival.shtml (accessed December 18, 2006).

Goodman, T. "Blue Wolf" (2004), "Rekindling the Ancient Fires: Sacred Journey to South Africa. Aquarius: A Sign of the Times," http://www.aquarius-atlanta.com/aug04/balance.shtml (accessed December 18, 2006).

Hall, J. (1994), *Sangoma: My Odyssey into the Spirit World of Africa,* New York: G. P. Putnam's Sons.

Heart Healing Center (2001), "Heart Healing," http://www.hearthealingcenter.com/earth-healers.htm (accessed September 27, 2002).

Icke, D. (1999), *The Biggest Secret,* London: Bridge of Love Publications.

Icke, D. (2002), "The Reptilian Brain," http://www.davidicke.com/icke/articles2/reptbrain.html (accessed December 18, 2006).

Icke, D. (2005), *The Reptilian Agenda,* Venice, CA: UFO TV.

Johnson, A. (1997), "The Angela Johnson Interview," *Mail and Guardian* (July 18).

Keeney, B. (ed.) (2001), *Vusamazulu Credo Mutwa: Zulu High Sanusi,* Stony Creek, CT: Leete's Island Books.

Kehoe, A. (1990), "Primal Gaia: Primitivists and Plastic Medicine Men," in James Clifton (ed.), *The Invented Indian: Cultural Fictions and Government Policies,* New Brunswick, NJ: Transaction, pp. 193–209.

Lieberman, P. (2000), *Human Language and Our Reptilian Brain: The Subcortical Bases of Speech, Syntax, and Thought,* Cambridge, MA: Harvard University Press.

Mack, J. E. (1999), *Passport to the Cosmos: Human Transformation and Alien Encounters,* New York: Three Rivers Press.

Meintjes, L. (2003), *Sound of Africa! Making Music Zulu in a South African Studio,* Durham, NC: Duke University Press.

Molloy, N. (1999), "David Icke's Lecture: The Biggest Secret," *Ufonet* (December 2), http://groups.yahoo.com/group/ufonet/message/3019 (accessed April 14, 2004).

Mortifee, A. (2005), *Into the Heart of the Sangoma,* Vancouver: Jabula Music.

Mtshali, P. H. (2004), *The Power of the Ancestors: The Life of a Zulu Traditional Healer,* Mbabane, Swaziland: Kamhlaba Publications.

Mutwa, C. (1964), *Indaba, My Children,* Johannesburg: Blue Crane Books.

Mutwa, C. (1966), *Africa Is My Witness,* Johannesburg: Blue Crane Books.

Mutwa, C. (1996), *Song of the Stars: The Lore of a Zulu Shaman,* ed. Stephen Larsen, Barrytown, NY: Station Hill Openings.

Mutwa, C. (2003), *Zulu Shaman: Dreams, Prophecies, and Mysteries,* ed. Stephen Larsen, Merrimac, MA: Destiny.

Nene, S. (2006), "Sibongile Nene, Sangoma: African Traditional Healer," http://www.sangoma.ca/ (accessed February 14, 2007).

Otto, R. (1923), *The Idea of the Holy,* trans. J.W. Harvey, Oxford: Oxford University Press.

Somé, M. P. (1993), *Ritual: Power, Healing, and Community,* Portland, OR: Swan Raven & Co.

Stolow, J. (2005), "Religion and/as Media," *Theory, Culture & Society,* 22(4): 119–45.

Sullivan, L. (1986), "Sound and Senses: Towards a Hermeneutics of Performance," *History of Religions,* 26: 1–33.

Townsend, J. B. (2004), "Core Shamanism and Neo-shamanism," in M. Namba Walter and E. J. Neumann Fridman (eds), *Shamanism: An Encyclopedia of World Beliefs, Practices and Culture,* 2 vols, Santa Barbara, CA: ABC-Clio, vol. 1, pp. 49–57.

Viall, J. (2004), "Claudia Uses Old Ways to Help with the New," *Cape Argus* (November 22): 13.

Wellness eJournal (2001), http://www.compwellness.com/eJournal/2001/0131.htm (accessed April 14, 2004).

Weyler, R. (2005), "Singer Interrupted by Life: Journeys with Ann Mortifee," Shared Vision, http://www.shared-vision.com/2005/sv1807/viewpoint1807.html (accessed December 24, 2005).

ABCDERIUM of Extra/
Sensory Powers
David Howes

In its full form the ABCDERIUM can be found on the homepage of the Concordia Sensoria Research Team (CONSERT). The CONSERT homepage is accessible via http://alcor.concordia.ca/~senses or www.david-howes.com/senses/. There the reader will find definitions of each of the terms listed below along with brief contextualizations, such as the source and date of the proposition that the faculty or form of percipience in question be reckoned as the—or, a—sixth sense, or seventh sense, and so forth.

One of the advantages of making the ABCDERIUM available on-line is that it can expand, interactively. Readers may submit documented suggestions for additional entries by sending them to senses@alcor.concordia.ca. Proposed new entries will be reviewed and may be incorporated into subsequent versions of the ABCDERIUM. More cross-cultural examples would be especially welcome.

Most all of the entries below have been mentioned in the body of this book, and are based on explicit characterizations of the faculty or form of percipience in question as the—or, a—sixth sense, and so forth. For example, as noted in the Introduction, speech was explicitly identified as the sixth sense in Raymond Lull's *Liber sexti sensus,* which dates from the fourteenth century; Franz Anton Mesmer appropriated the term and used it in the eighteenth century to designate animal magnetism; Sherrington extended this label to the newly discovered power of proprioception in the 1890s; since the 1930s, the sixth sense has come to be synonymous with extrasensory perception (ESP), and so forth.[1] More recently, Lyall Watson refers to the *vomeronasal organ* as the sixth sense in *Jacobson's Organ and the Remarkable Nature of Smell,*[2] and Michael Taussig (following Walter Benjamin) alludes to the *mimetic faculty* as a sixth sense in *Mimesis and Alterity.*[3]

In some cases liberties have been taken, such as listing a "film sense," which comes from the book of the same name by Sergei Eisentstein (1942). Though he never refers to the *film sense* as a sixth sense, Eisenstein is clearly describing a new, synaesthetic modality of perception produced by cinematic experience. Marshall McLuhan would have approved of this inclusion, for he saw all media as "extensions of the senses" and, therefore, generative of new forms of experience. Hence the inclusion of *media* in our list, and also *hallucinogens*—another source of excess sensation.

Alongside the relatively novel characterization of common sense as the sixth sense, the sense of beauty as the seventh sense, and so forth (see page 21), even the seemingly familiar senses of sight, hearing, smell, taste and touch merit a place in our index, for the understanding of their capacities varies widely across cultures and in different historical periods. In premodernity, for example, the sense of smell was believed to be able to sniff out sanctity and sin, while in our own time the Desana of Colombia hold that it is possible to smell emotions. The fluidity of the bounds of sense in any given cultural context is the reason for the slash in the term *extra/ sensory* as used in the title of this section: it is important not to prejudge what falls within and what lies "beyond the five senses" (the slash, being moveable, makes the suspension of judgment possible). The use of the term *power,* rather than *organ* or *faculty* is motivated by similar considerations. Powers can be acquired, though they may appear to be innate, and they can be developed, so their exercise always signals the role of technique in human perception.

Here, then, is a possible index of extra/sensory powers:

Animal Magnetism (Mesmer); Anomalous Cognition; Anpsi; Balance; Beauty; Being stared at (Sheldrake); Blink (Gladwell); Body (Cashinahua and other); Bones (Andean and other); Clairalience; Clairaudience; Clairgustance; Clairsentience; Clairvoyance; Coenesthesia; Common Sense; Common Sense, The (or *sensus communis*); Cosmic Consciousness; Déjà vu; Direction; Dowsing; Dreaming; Echolocation; Electroreception; ESP; Film Sense (Eisenstein); Genital; Gut Feeling; Hallucinogens; Hearing; Heart; Honor; Humor; Imagination; Inner Senses (Medieval); Instinct; Internal Senses (Eighteenth Century); Interoceptive Senses (Nineteenth and Twentieth Century); Intuition; Jacobson's Organ; Kinaesthesis; Liver; Magnetic; Mass Media; Memory; Mimetic Faculty; Mind (Buddhism); Moral Sense; Navigation; Occult; Pain; Paroptic Vision; Pineal Gland; Plant Psi; Precognition; Premonition; Pressure; Proprioception; Psychokinesis; Psychometry; Public Sense; Quintessence; Remote-viewing; Second Brain (Gershon); Second Sight (Scottish); Sight; Smell; Speech; Spiritual Senses (Origen, Swedenborg); Synaesthesia; Taste; Telepathy; Temperature; Third Ear; Third Eye; Touch; Trance; Unconscious (Freud); Vibration; Visionary; Whiskers; Wind (Navajo and other); X-ray; Yogic; Zen Meditation

Notes

1. The *Oxford English Dictionary* defines *sixth sense* as: "A supposed intuitive faculty by which a person or animal perceives facts and regulates action without the direct use of any of the five senses." This definition hardly does justice to the rich history of this concept. It is also problematic for the way it treats *the five senses* as self-evident while characterizing the sixth sense as

a "supposed" faculty, as suspect. The notion that human beings possess five senses is far less settled historically, cross-culturally or scientifically than this definition presumes. *The five senses* are no less putative, or more real, than the sixth. If anything, they are more symbolic for numbering five, "symbol of harmony and equilibrium, and symbol of man (who possesses five extremities: head, arms, legs)" (Bagot et al. 1998: 101). The numeral *six* does not carry the same symbolic weight (in the Western tradition). It lacks the connotation of completeness. These symbolic considerations go considerably further than any physiological considerations (e.g., Davis 1979; Rivlin and Gravelle 1984; Keeley 2002) toward explaining why the sixth sense seems supernumerary, and is forever condemned to play the role of supplement.

2. In animals, Jacobson's organ—or, the vomeronasal system—is a parallel olfactory sense responsible for detecting chemical signals (pheromones) emitted by members of the same species. It is uncertain whether this system is operative in humans, but Watson (1999: 191–215) nevertheless engages in much fascinating speculation concerning what such an organ might mean for the regulation of human action as part of a general campaign to rescue olfaction from its (unnatural) cultural oblivion in the West.

3. In *Mimesis and Alterity,* Taussig treats mimesis as "both the faculty of imitation and the deployment of that faculty in sensuous knowing, sensuous Othering" as in the way the magician seeks "to get hold of something by means of its likeness" and use "the power of the copy to influence what it is a copy of"—that is, to alter alterity (Taussig 1993: 68, 21, 250). Taussig's complex theory of magic, which is spelled out over many pages in *Mimesis and Alterity,* is contained in embryo in "Tactility and Distraction" (chapter 12).

References

Bagot, J.-D., Ehm, C., Casati, R., Dokic, J., and Pacherie, E. (1998), *L'ABCdaire des Cinq Sens,* Paris: Flammarion.

Davis, T. N. (1979), "A Sixth Sense?" *Alaska Science Forum,* 352, http://www.gi.alaska.edu/ScienceForum/ASF3/352.html.

Eisenstein, S. (1942), *The Film Sense,* New York: Harcourt, Brace and World.

Keeley, B. (2002), "Making Sense of the Senses: Individuating Modalities in Humans and Other Animals," *Journal of Philosophy,* 99(1): 5–28.

Rivlin, R. and Gravelle, K. (1984), *Deciphering the Senses: The Expanding World of Human Perception,* New York: Simon and Schuster, Inc.

Taussig, M. (1993), *Mimesis and Alterity: A Particular History of the Senses,* New York: Routledge.

Watson, L. (1999), *Jacobson's Organ and the Remarkable Nature of Smell,* London: Penguin Books.

Notes on Contributors

Ruth Barcan teaches in the Department of Gender and Cultural Studies at the University of Sydney. She is the author of *Nudity: A Cultural Anatomy* (2004) and is currently writing a book on alternative therapies and the senses.

Wilhelm H. I. Bleek (1827–1875) and **Lucy C. Lloyd** (1834–1914), who stood as brother- and sister-in-law to each other, were inspired by their passion for philology and fascination with the indigenous peoples of South Africa to create an archive of |Xam San texts, whence *Specimens of Bushmen Folklore* (1875). That archive is now known as the Lloyd Bleek Collection (www.lloydbleekcol lection. uct.ac.za), and contains the only remaining traces of the |Xam.

David Chidester is Professor of Religious Studies and Director of the Institute for Comparative Religion in Southern Africa (ICRSA) at the University of Cape Town. His publications include *Authentic Fakes* (2005), *Salvation and Suicide* (2003), *Christianity: A Global History* (2000), and *Savage Systems* (1996).

Mircea Eliade (1907–1986), the acclaimed historian of religion (and novelist), taught at universities in Calcutta and his native Romania as well as the Sorbonne before joining the University of Chicago in 1956. A prolific author, his books include *The Myth of the Eternal Return* ([1949] 1954) and the three-volume *A History of Religious Ideas* (1978–1985).

Jess Byron Hollenback teaches in the Department of History at the University of Wisconsin-Lacrosse. He is the author of Mysticism: Experience, Response and Empowerment (1996) and is currently writing a book provisionally entitled "The Miracle of Civilization," which will integrate natural history and human history.

David Howes is the author of *Sensual Relations* (2004) and the editor of other works in sensory anthropology, economic anthropology, and the anthropology of law. He teaches in the Department of Sociology and Anthropology at Concordia University and in the Faculty of Law at McGill University.

W. H. Hudson (1841–1922) was the paragon adventurer naturalist. An accomplished ornithologist, and close observer of animal ways, he made a living by writing memoirs of his encounters with nature, such as *Birds and Man* (1924) and *Far Away and Long Ago* (1923).

Carol Laderman is Professor of Anthropology at City College of the City University of New York. She is the author of *Taming the Wind of Desire* (1991) and co-editor (with Marina Roseman) of *The Performance of Healing* (1996).

Barbara G. Myerhoff (1935–1985) taught in the Department of Anthropology at the University of Southern California. She wrote *Peyote Hunt* (1974) and also scripted the Academy Award–winning documentary film *Number Our Days* (1976).

Jessica Riskin teaches in the Department of History, Stanford University. She is the author of *Science in the Age of Sensibility* (2002). She is currently writing a book about the use of machines as models for understanding human life and mind from Descartes to Darwin, tentatively entitled "Mind Out of Matter."

Leigh Eric Schmidt is the Chair of the Department of Religion, Princeton University. He is the author of *Consumer Rites* (1997), *Hearing Things* (2003), and co-author with Edwin Gaustad of *The Religious History of America* (2002).

Rupert Sheldrake is an independent scholar based in London. He has been hailed as "one of the world's most innovative biologists." Sheldrake also stands out for his interactive approach to the production of scientific knowledge, as is apparent from his Web page http://www.sheldrake.org/home page.html

Bilinda Straight is the editor of *Women on the Verge of Home* (2005) and author of *Miracles and Extraordinary Experience in Northern Kenya* (2007) as well as numerous essays on gender, sexuality, religion, material culture, and interethnic violence in northern Kenya. She is an associate professor in anthropology at Western Michigan University.

Michael Taussig is Professor of Anthropology at Columbia University. His publications include *The Devil and Commodity Fetishism in South America* (1980), *Shamanism, Colonialism, and the Wild Man* (1987), *Mimesis and Alterity* (1993), and *My Cocaine Museum* (2004).

Pamela Thurschwell took up a position as Senior Lecturer in English at the University of Sussex in 2007, having previously taught at University College London. She is the author of *Sigmund Freud* (2000), co-editor of *The Victorian Supernatural* (2004), and is currently working on a book about representations of adolescence in twentieth century literature and culture.

Louise Vinge, Professor of Literature at Lund University, Sweden, is now retired. The grande dame of sensory studies, her books include *The Five Senses: Studies in a Literary Tradition* (1975) and *The Narcissus Theme in Western Literature* (1967).

Nicholas J. Wade is Professor of Visual Psychology in the Department of Psychology at the University of Dundee. A frequent contributor to the journal *Perception,* he is also the author of *A Natural History of Vision* (1998) and *Perception and Illusion: Historical Perspectives* (2005), among other books.

Copyright Acknowledgments

I. Bearings

1. "The Search for a Sixth Sense: The Cases for Vestibular, Muscle, and Temperature Senses" by Nicholas J. Wade. From the article by the same title in *Journal of the History of the Neurosciences* (2003), vol. 12(2), pp. 175–202. Copyright © 2003 by Swets & Zeitlinger. Reprinted by permission of Taylor & Francis. Abridged.
2. "Sense of Direction" by W. H. Hudson. From *A Hind in Richmond Park,* pp. 134–49. Copyright © 1923 by J. M. Dent and Sons, Ltd. Abridged.
3. "Bushman Presentiments" by Wilhelm H. I. Bleek and Lucy C. Lloyd. From *Specimens of Bushmen Folklore,* pp. 330–31, 333, 335, 337, 339. Copyright © 1911 by George Allen & Co., Ltd., London.
4. "Anatomy of Mysticism" by Jess Byron Hollenback. From *Mysticism: Experience, Response, and Empowerment,* pp. 33–41, 48–9. Copyright © 1996 by The Pennsylvania State University. Reprinted by permission of The Pennsylvania State University Press. Abridged and rearranged.

II. Historical Investigations

5. "The Five Senses in Classical Science and Ethics" by Louise Vinge. From *The Five Senses: Studies in a Literary Tradition,* pp. 7, 11, 15–28. Copyright © 1975 by Louise Vinge and Kungl. Humanistiska Vetenskapssamfundet i Lund. Reprinted by permission of the author and The Royal Society of the Humanities at Lund.
6. "The Mesmerism Investigation and the Crisis of Sensationist Science" by Jessica Riskin. From chapter 4 of *Science in the Age of Sensibility: The Sentimental Empiricists of the French Enlightenment,* pp. 189–225. Copyright © 2002 by The University of Chicago. Reprinted by permission of The University of Chicago Press. Abridged.
7. "Swedenborg's Celestial Sensorium: Angelic Authenticity, Religious Authority, and the American New Church Movement" by Leigh Eric Schmidt. From chapter 5 of *Hearing Things: Religion, Illusion, and the American Enlightenment,* pp. 199–243. Copyright © 2000 by the President

III. Uncanny Sensations

IV. Cross-Cultural Investigations

Index